A Tricentennial Anthology of
SOUTH CAROLINA LITERATURE

A Tricentennial Anthology of
SOUTH CAROLINA
LITERATURE
1670–1970

Selected
and with introduction and notes

by

Richard James Calhoun
Clemson University

and

John Caldwell Guilds
University of South Carolina

UNIVERSITY OF SOUTH CAROLINA PRESS
Columbia, South Carolina

FOREWORD

An anthology, by definition, is "a collection of choice passages of literature, epigrams, or the like." Today's anthologies, however, are more likely to be a selection of literary works representative of an age, a national or regional literature, or an author.

The South Carolina Tricentennial Commission and its Creative Writing Committee believe that an anthology hopefully fulfilling both definitions will best express their desire to recognize those distinguished men of letters whose contributions to South Carolina literature have recorded, reflected, and influenced the culture of their state in the past 300 years.

It was not an easy undertaking. The success of *A Tricentennial Anthology of South Carolina Literature* is due in large measure to the dedication of its knowledgeable and scholarly editors, Dr. John C. Guilds and Dr. Richard Calhoun.

JAMES M. BARNETT
Executive Director
South Carolina Tricentennial Commission

CONTENTS

A Tricentennial Anthology of
SOUTH CAROLINA LITERATURE

INTRODUCTION

South Carolina's Tricentennial is an appropriate occasion for publishing the first collection embracing three centuries of South Carolina literature since George Armstrong Wauchope's *The Writers of South Carolina* in 1910 and J. C. Hungerpiller's much slimmer volume, *South Carolina Literature,* in 1931. Many of her neighboring states have more recent and more comprehensive anthologies of their literature than any ever compiled of South Carolina writing, and the time seems propitious for a new assessment of the literary accomplishments of this state.

The motivation for this collection would have met with the approval of South Carolina's most famous writers, William Gilmore Simms, Henry Timrod, and Paul Hamilton Hayne. It was a motivation they themselves felt. In 1857 Hayne founded South Carolina's best literary periodical to that time, *Russell's Magazine,* with the avowed aim of promoting a greater interest in writing among South Carolinians while maintaining high critical standards in a magazine of national standing. Timrod later lent Hayne, and *Russell's Magazine,* his full support. Simms, the first South Carolinian to win national literary acclaim and, according to Professor Jay B. Hubbell, "the central figure in the literature of the Old South," had even stronger convictions that each state, each region, must develop its own literary resources if there ever was to be a distinctive national literature. In addition to establishing numerous journals aimed at encouraging local writing, Simms also took great interest in publishing the works of South Carolina writers in his *Charleston Book.*

Whatever inner doubts Simms, Hayne, and Timrod had a century ago about the relative merits of Southern and New England literature, they never doubted that South Carolina at that time was the leader in Southern literature. Certainly no other Southern state could match the triumvirate of Simms, Hayne, and Timrod, or the number of meritorious literary magazines, however shortlived, produced in Charleston. However, though we desire to acknowledge the achievement of those four remarkable decades, the purpose of this anthology is also to fill in the gaps before and after the period from 1830 to 1870. We hope to demonstrate that South Carolina literature is of merit throughout her three hundred years and that not all of her literary heritage lies buried in Magnolia Cemetery. For example, we hope to prove that the *South-Carolina Gazette* was an important colonial magazine; that Joseph Brown Ladd wrote a few poems which belong in standard anthologies as representative eighteenth-century poetry, comparing favorably with efforts of the more celebrated Connecticut "Wits"; that the current critical estimate of Timrod, Hayne, and Simms might rise if selections other than their usual anthology pieces were known and studied; and that the work now being done on a scholarly edition of Simms might well be extended to other worthy South Carolina writers.

The much discussed Southern renaissance beginning in the 1920s did not appreciably affect South Carolina, and we readily admit that the Poetry Society of South Carolina in that decade rates second billing critically to the Vanderbilt Fugitives. But we also feel that several members of that society wrote a number of stories and poems of merit and that at least one previously neglected member of that group, Beatrice Ravenel, deserves serious critical attention.

No extravagant claims may yet be made for the merits of twentieth-century South Carolina writing, but the full impact of National Book Award-winner James Dickey upon the literary milieu of the state has not yet been felt. It is to be hoped that Dickey's eminence as one of the outstanding poets writing in the English language today (a reputation which has crystallized since he joined the University of South Carolina English faculty in 1968) will usher in another South Carolina literary revival.

Regardless of what the selections in this anthology may do to improve the standing of contemporary South Carolina literature, it remains evident that the state, despite producing one Pulitzer Prize-winning novelist and several other writers who were at least prolific and widely read, was essentially bypassed by the major Southern literary movement during the period from 1920 to 1950. The question, why did South Carolina not produce a Faulkner, or Wolfe, or Tennessee Williams during this period, might be further explored as a consequence of this anthology.

A word needs to be said about the basis upon which the selections were made. Our main criterion has been literary merit, tempered by a desire to find representative selections from each century. Unfortunately, the extraneous literary criterion of length also had to be considered, with the result that some selections were excluded because they were too long. We have not established definitive tests for the pieces included in this collection. Our anthology is intended for general readers and in no way meets, or is intended to meet, the textual standards required of a scholarly edition. Some authors perhaps worthy of inclusion have been omitted (Hervey Allen, for example) because we were unable to secure reprinting permission before going to press.

To select works as objectively as we could under these limitations, we queried scholars in the field of Southern literature about their choices for inclusion. Accordingly, we should like to express our thanks for their recommendations to Professors Jay B. Hubbell, James B. Meriwether, Charles R. Anderson, C. Hugh Holman, Richard Beale Davis, Louis Rubin, Hennig Cohen, Claude Neuffer, Floyd Watkins, Rayburn Moore, Frank Durham, Alfred S. Reid, Calhoun Winton, C. B. Green, and Louis Henry. We should also like to express our appreciation to Mrs. Denham Sutcliffe, Mrs. Margaret Kwist, and Mr. Gordon Gourley of the Clemson University Library staff; to Mr. E. L. Inabinet and Mr. Kenneth Toombs of the University of South Carolina libraries; and to Miss Margaret J. Yonce and Mr. Hugh Cooper, graduate research assistants at the University of South Carolina.

Footnotes are those of the authors.

R.J.C.
J.C.G.

William Hilton (1617–75)

William Hilton, eldest son of William Hilton the Pilgrim, was born in England in 1617 and brought as a child to Plymouth aboard the *Anne* in 1623. Interested in the sea and in ships, young Hilton acquired the title William the Mariner. When in 1662 Charles II granted Carolina to the Lords Proprietors, Captain Hilton was commissioned to explore the coast and report its possibilities to a group of Barbados planters. His ship, *Adventure,* arrived off the Carolina coast in August 1663, and explored waterways in the Port Royal area. Encountering Spanish soldiers, he headed out to sea and on Monday, September 28, 1663, sighted the promontory since known as Hilton Head. His narrative, "Relation of A Discovery," was published in London in 1664. Hilton died in 1675 in Charlestown, Massachusetts.

A Relation of a Discovery, by
William Hilton, 1664

A Relation of a Discovery lately made on the Coast of Florida, (From Lat. 31. to 33 Deg. 45 Min. North-Lat.)

By William Hilton Commander, and Commissioner with Capt. Anthony Long, and Peter Fabian, in the Ship Adventure, which set Sayl from Spikes Bay, Aug. 10. 1663. and was set forth by several Gentlemen and Merchants of the Island of Barbadoes.

Giving an account of the nature and temperature of the Soyl, the manners and disposition of the Natives, and whatsoever else is remarkable therein, together with Proposals made by the Commissioners of the Lords Proprietors, to all such persons as shall become the first Setlers on the Rivers, Harbors, and Creeks there.

A true Relation of a Voyage, upon discovery of part of the Coast of Florida, from the Lat. of 31 Deg. to 33 Deg. 45 m. North Lat. in the Ship Adventure, William Hilton Commander, and Commissioner with Captain Anthony Long and Peter Fabian; set forth by several Gentlemen and Merchants of the Island of Barbadoes; sailed from Spikes Bay, Aug. 10. 1663.

After Sixteen days of fair weather, and prosperous winds, Wednesday the 26 instant, four of the clock in the Afternoon, God be thanked, we espied Land on the Coast of Florida, in the lat. of 32 deg. 30 min. being four Leagues or thereabouts to the Northwards of Saint Ellens, having run five hundred and fifty Leagues; and to the Westward of the Meridian of Barbadoes, three hundred thirty and one Leagues. This Evening and the Night following we lay off and on: Thursday the 27th instant, in the morning, we stood in with the Land, and coasted the Shoar to the Southward, Ankering at Nights, and sending our Boat out a Mornings, till we came into the lat. of 31 deg. but found no good harbour that way. On Sunday the 30th instant, we tacked, and stood Northward: and on Wednesday the second of September, we came to an Anchor in five fathoms at the mouth of a very large opening of three Leagues wide, or thereabouts, in the lat. of 32 deg. 30 min. and sent our Boat to sound the Channel. On Thursday the third, we entered the Harbour, and found that it was the River Jordan, and was but four Leagues or thereabouts

N. E. from Port Royal, which by the Spanyards is called St. Ellens:
within Land, both Rivers meet in one. We spent some time to sound
the Chanels both without and within, and to search the Rivers in several
branches, and to view the Land. On Saturday the fifth of September,
two Indians came on Board us from the N. E. shoar, whom we entertained courteously, and afterwards set them on shoar. On Sunday the
sixth, several Indians came on Board us, and said they were of St.
Ellens; being very bold and familiar; speaking many Spanish words,
as, *Cappitan, Commarado,* and *Adeus.* They know the use of Guns, and
are as little startled at the firing of a Peece of Ordnance, as he that hath
been used to them many years: they told us the nearest Spanyards were
at St. Augustins, and several of them had been there, which as they
said was but ten days journey; and that the Spanyards used to come to
them at Saint Ellens, sometimes in Canoa's within Land, at other times
in small Vessels by Sea, which the Indians describe to have but two
Masts. They invited us to come to St. Ellens with our Ship, which they
told us we might do within Land. Munday the 14 September, our Long-
Boat went with twelve hands within Land to St. Ellens. On Wednesday
the 16th, came five Indians on board us; one of them pointing to another, said, he was the Grandy Captain of Edistow: whereupon we took
especial notice of him, and entertained him accordingly, giving him
several Beads, and other trade that pleased him well: He invited us to
bring up our Ship into a branch on the N. E. side, and told us of one
Captain Francisco, and four more English that were in his custody on
shoar; whereupon we shewed him store of all Trade, as Beads, Hoes,
Hatchets and Bills, etc., and said, he should have all those things if he
would bring the English on board us; wch he promised should be done
the next day. Hereupon we wrote a few lines to the said English, fearing it to be a Spanish delusion to entrap us. In the dark of the same
Evening came a Canoa with nine or ten Indians in her with their Bowes
and Arrowes, and were close on board before we did discern them: We
haled them, but they made us no answer, which increased our jealousie:
So we commanded them on board, and disarmed them, detaining two
of them prisoners, and sending away the rest to fetch the English; which
if they brought, they should have theirs again. At length they delivered
us a Note written with a coal, which seemed the more to continue our

jealousie, because in all this time we had no news of our long-boat from St. Ellens, which we feared was surprized by the Indians and Spanyards. But to satisfie us that there were English on shoar, they sent us one man on board about twelve of the clock in the Night who related to us the truth of the matter, and told us they were cast away some four or five leagues to the Northward of the place we then rode, on the 24th of July past, being thirteen persons that came on shoar, whereof three of them were kill'd by the Indians. On Thursday the 17th of September the Long-boat returned from St. Ellens, which presently we sent on shoar to fetch the other English, the Indians delivering us three more; and coming aboard themselves, we delivered them their two men. Then we demanded of the chief Commander where the rest of our English were: he answered, Five were carried to St. Ellens, three were killed by the Stonohs, and the other man we should have within two dayes. We replyed to him again, That we would keep him and two more of his chief men, till we had our English that were yet living; and promised them their liberty, with satisfaction for bringing us the English. Now to return to the businesse of our Design; the entertainment we had at S. Ellens put us in great fear of the Indians treachery; for we observed their continual gathering together, and at last began with stern-look'd countenances to speak roughly to us, and came to search our mens Bandileers and pockets; yet inviting us to stay that night with them: but we made a sudden retreat to our Boat, which caused the Indian King to be in a great rage, speaking loud and angry to his men; the drift of which discourse we understood not. That which we noted there, was a fair house builded in the shape of a Dove-house, round, two hundred foot at least, compleatly covered with Palmeta-leaves, the wal-plate being twelve foot high, or thereabouts, and within lodging Rooms and forms; two pillars at the entrance of a high Seat above all the rest: Also another house like a Sentinel-house, floored ten foot high with planks, fastned with Spikes and Nayls, standing upon substantial Posts, with several other small houses round about. Also we saw many planks, to the quantity of three thousand foot or thereabouts, with other Timber squared, and a Cross before the great house. Likewise we saw the Ruines of an old Fort, compassing more than half an acre of land within the Trenches, which we supposed to

be Charls's Fort, built, and so called by the French in 1562, etc. On
Monday, September 21. one English youth was brought from St. Ellens
aboard us by an Indian, who informed us that there were four more of
their company at St. Ellens, but he could not tell whether the Indians
would let them come to us: For saith he, Our Men told me, that they
had lately seen a Frier and two Spanyards more at St. Ellens, who told
them they would send Soldiers suddenly to fetch them away. This day
we sayled up the River with our Ship to go through to St. Ellens. On
Tuesday the 22 instant, three Indians came on board; one of them we
sent with a Letter to the English Prisoners there. On Wednesday the
23d, we sent out Boat and Men to sound the Chanel, and finde out the
most likely way to St. Ellens with our Ship by Combeheh. In the mean
time came many Canoa's aboard us with Corn, Pumpions, and Venison,
Deer-skins, and a sort of sweet-wood. One of our men looking into an
Indian basket, found a piece of Spanish Rusk: it being new, we demanded of the Indian where he had it; who said, of the Spaniards. In
the interim, while we were talking, came a Canoa with four Indians
from St. Ellens, one standing up, and holding a paper in a cleft stick;
they told us they had brought it from the Spanish Captain at St. Ellens.
We demanded how many Spaniards were come thither; who said, Seven,
and one English-man: We received their Letter writ in Spanish, but
none of us could read it: We detained two of the chiefest Indians, one
of them being the Kings Son of S. Ellens, and that kept one of the
English prisoners; the other two we sent away with a Letter to the
Spaniard, wherein we gave him to understand, that we understood not
his letter; and told the Indians, when they brought the English, they
should have their men again, with satisfaction for their pains. On Thursday, 24 instant, we sayling further up the River to go through, at last
came to a place of fresh water, and Anchored there, sending our Boat
ashoar with a Guard to get water. Towards night came the first Indian
that we sent to St. Ellens with a letter to the English, who brought us
another letter from the Spaniards, and an Answer of ours from the
English, writ in the Spaniards letter. The Spaniard sent us a quarter of
Venison, and a quarter of Pork, with a Complement, That he was
sorry he had no more for us at that time. We returned him thanks, and
sent him a Jug of Brandy; and withal, that we were sorry we understood

not his letter. This night about twelve of the Clock we had a most violent gust of winde, but of no long continuance. On Friday 25 September, we weighed, and returned down the River six leagues, or thereabouts, because we perceived the Indians had gathered themselves in a Body from all parts thereabouts, and moved as the Ship did: and being informed by an Indian that the Spaniards would be there the next day; we took in Fire-wood, and continued there that night, at which time one of our Indian Prisoners made his escape by leaping over-board in the dark. On Saturday the 26. we weighed, and stood down to the Harbours mouth, and stayed there till Monday the 28. In all which time came no one to us, though we stay'd in expectation of their coming continually; therefore put out to Sea, concluding their intentions not to be good. Being out of the River Jordan, we directed our course S. W. four leagues or thereabouts for Port-Royal, to sound the Chanel without from the poynts of the Harbour outwards; for we had sounded the Harbour within from the points inward when our Boat was at St. Ellens: And now being athwart the Harbours mouth, we sent our Boat with the Mate and others, who found the N. E. and E. N. E. side of the opening of Port-Royal to be Sholes and Breakers to the middle of the opening; and three leagues or thereabouts into the Sea, from the side aforesaid, is unsafe to meddle with: but the S.W. and W. side we found all bold steering in N. N. W. two or three miles from the S. W. shoar, sayling directly with the S.W. head-land of the entrance of Port-Royal: the said head-land is bluft, and seems steep, as though the trees hung over the water: But you must note, that if you keep so far from the S.W. side, that you stand in N. N. W. with the bluft head aforesaid, you shall go over the Outskirt of the E. N. E. sholing, and shall have but three or four fathom for the space of one league or thereabouts, and then you shall have six and seven fathoms all the way in: But if you borrow more on the S.W. side, till you have brought the S. W. head of the Entry to bear N.N.E. you shall have a fair large Chanel of six, seven, and eight fathoms all the way in, and then five, six, seven and eight fathoms within the Harbour, keeping the Chanel, and standing over to the Northward: we supposed that it flows here as at the River Jordan, because they are but four leagues asunder, and flows S. E. and N.W. seven foot and half, and sometimes eight foot perpendicular:

the Mouth of Port-Royal lyes in 32 deg. 20 min. lat. Now as concerning
the entrance of the River Jordan, lat. 32 deg. 30 min. or thereabouts,
you shall see a range of Breakers right against the opening, two or three
leagues off the S. W. Point; which you must leave to the Northward,
and steer in with the said S. W. Point, giving a range of Breakers that
runs from the said Point a small birth, and you shall have two, three,
and four fathoms at low water; and when you come one mile from
the Point aforesaid, steer over directly to the N. E. Point, and you shall
have six or seven fathom all the way. Within the N. W. Point is good
Anchoring: you shall have five fathoms fair aboard the shoar: and you
shall have five, six, seven, and eight fathoms, sayling all along upon
the River, ten leagues, and a large turning Chanel: It flows here S. E.
and N. W. seven foot and a half, and eight foot at common Tydes. The
River Grandy, or as the Indians call it Edistow, lyes six leagues or
thereabouts from the River Jordan, and seems to be a very fair opening:
but because the chief Indian of that Place was on board us, and the
Countrey all in Arms, we not knowing how the winde might crosse us,
it was not thought fit to stay there: But some of those English that had
lived there, being Prisoners, say, that it is a very fair and goodly River,
branching into several branches, and deep, and is fresh water at low
Tide within two leagues of the Mouth; it seeming to us as we passed by,
a good entrance large and wide, lat. 32 deg. 40 min. in or thereabouts.
Now our understanding of the Land of Port-Royal, River Jordan, River
Grandie, or Edistow, is as followeth: The Lands are laden with large
tall Oaks, Walnut and Bayes, except facing on the Sea, it is most Pines
tall and good: The Land generally, except where the Pines grow, is a
good Soyl, covered with black Mold, in some places a foot, in some
places half a foot, and in other places lesse, with Clay underneath mixed
with Sand; and we think may produce any thing as well as most part
of the Indies that we have seen. The Indians plant in the worst Land,
because they cannot cut down the Timber in the best, and yet have
plenty of Corn, Pumpions, Water-Mellons, Musk-mellons: although
the Land be overgrown with weeds through their lazinesse, yet they
have two or three crops of Corn a year, as the Indians themselves inform us. The Country abounds with Grapes, large Figs, and Peaches;
the Woods with Deer, Conies, Turkeys, Quails, Curlues, Plovers, Teile,

Herons; and as the Indians say, in Winter, with Swans, Geese, Cranes, Duck and Mallard, and innumerable of other water-Fowls, whose names we know not, which lie in the Rivers, Marshes, and on the Sands: Oysters in abundance, with great store of Muscles; A sort of fair Crabs, and a round Shel-fish called Horse-feet; The Rivers stored plentifully with Fish that we saw play and leap. There are great Marshes, but most as far as we saw little worth, except for a Root that grows in them the Indians make good Bread of. The Land we suppose is healthful; for the English that were cast away on that Coast in July last, were there most part of that time of year that is sickly in Virginia; and notwith-standing hard usage, and lying on the ground naked, yet had their perfect healths all the time. The Natives are very healthful; we saw many very Aged amongst them. The Ayr is clear and sweet, the Coun-trey very pleasant and delightful: And we could wish, that all they that want a happy settlement, of our English Nation, were well trans-ported thither, etc.

From Tuesday the 29th of September, to Friday the second of Octo-ber, we ranged along the shoar from the lat. 32 deg. 20 min. to the lat. 33 deg. 11 min. but could discern no Entrance for our Ship, after we had passed to the Northwards of 32 deg. 40 min. On Saturday the third instant, a violent storm came up, the winde between the North and the East; which Easterly windes and fowl weather continued till Monday the 12th. By reason of which storms and fowl weather, we were forced to get off to Sea to secure our selves and ship, and were horsed by reason of a strong Current, almost to Cape Hatterasse in lat. 35 deg. 30 min. On Monday the 12th aforesaid we came to an Anchor in seven fathom at Cape Fair-Road, and took the Meridian-Altitude of the Sun, and were in the lat. 33 deg. 43 min. the winde continuing still Easterly, and fowl weather till Thursday the 15th instant; and on Friday the 16th, the winde being at N. W. we weighed, and sailed up Cape Fair-River, some four or five leagues, and came to an Anchor in six or seven fathom; at which time several Indians came on Board, and brought us great store of Fresh-fish, large Mullets, young Bass, Shads, and several other sorts of very good well-tasted Fish. On Saturday the 17th, we went down to the Cape to see the English Cattle, but could not finde them, though we rounded the Cape: And having an Indian Guide with us, here we rode till the 24th instant; the winde being against us, we could not go up the River with our Ship; in which time we went on shoar, and viewed the land of those quarters. On Saturday we weighed, and sayled up the River some four leagues or thereabouts. Sunday the 25th, we weighed again, and towed up the River, it being calm, and got up some fourteen leagues from the Harbours mouth, where we mored our Ship. On Monday the 26 October, we went down with the Yoal to Necoes, an Indian Plantation, and viewed the Land there. On Tuesday the 27th, we rowed up the main River with our long-Boat and twelve men, some ten leagues or thereabouts. On Wednesday the 28th, we rowed up about eight or nine leagues more. Thursday the 29th was foul weather, of much rain and winde, which forced us to make Huts, and lye still. Friday the 30th, we proceeded up the main River, seven or eight leagues. Saturday the 31, we got up three or four leagues more, and came to a Tree that lay athwart the River: but because our Provisions were neer spent, we proceeded no further, but returned downward the remainder of that day; and on Monday the second of November, we came aboard our Ship. Tuesday the third, we lay still to refresh ourselves. On Wednesday the 4th, we went five or six leagues up the River to search a branch that ran out of the main River towards the N. W. In which branch we went up five or six leagues: not liking the Land, we returned on board that night about midnight, and called that place Swampy-branch. Thursday the fifth instant, we staid aboard; on Friday the 6th we went up Greens River, the mouth of it being against the place we rode with our Ship. On Saturday the 7th, we proceeded up the said River some fourteen or fifteen leagues in all, and found that it ended in several small branches; the Land for the most part being marshy and swamps, we returned towards our ship, and got aboard in the night: Sunday the 8th instant we lay still, and on Monday the 9th we went again up the main River, being well provided with Provisions and all things necessary, and proceeded upwards till Thursday noon 12th instant, at which time we came to a place where two Islands were in the middle of the River, and by reason of the crookednesse of the River at that place, several Trees lay athwart both branches, which stopped up the passage of each branch, that we could proceed no further with our

Boat; but we went up the River side by land some three or four miles, and found the River to enlarge it self: So we returned, leaving it as far as we could see up a long reach running N. E. we judging our selves from the Rivers mouth North near fifty leagues; we returned, viewing the Land on both sides the River, and found as good tracts of land, dry, well wooded, pleasant and delightful as we have seen any where in the world, with great burthen of Grasse on it, the land being very level, with steep banks on both sides the River, and in some places very high, the woods stor'd with abundance of Deer and Turkies every where; we never going on shoar, but saw of each also Partridges great store, Cranes abundance, Conies, which we saw in several places; we heard several Wolves howling in the woods, and saw where they had torn a Deer in pieces. Also in the River we saw great store of Ducks, Teile, Widgeon, and in the woods great flocks of Parrakeeto's; the Timber that the woods afford for the most part consisting of Oaks of four or five sorts, all differing in leaves, but all bearing Akorns very good: we measured many of the Oaks in several places, which we found to be in bignesse some two, some three, and others almost four fathoms; in height, before you come to boughs or limbs, forty, fifty, sixty foot, and some more, and those Oaks very common in the upper parts of both Rivers; Also a very tall large Tree of great bignesse, which some do call Cyprus, the right name we know not, growing in Swamps. Likewise Walnut, Birch, Beech, Maple, Ash, Bay, Willough, Alder and Holly; and in the lowermost parts innumerable of Pines, tall and good for boards or masts, growing for the most part in barren sandy ground, but in some places up the River in good ground, being mixed amongst Oaks and other Timber. We saw several Mulberry-trees, multitudes of Grape-Vines, and some Grapes which we did eat of. We found a very large and good tract of Land on the N. W. side of the River, thin of Timber, except here and there a very great Oak, and full of Grasse, commonly as high as a mans middle, and in many places to his shoulders, where we saw many Deer and Turkies; also one Deer with very large horns, and great in body, therefore called it Stag-Park: it being a very pleasant and delightful place, we travelled in it several miles, but saw no end thereof. So we returned to our Boat, and proceeded down the River, and came to another place some twenty five leagues from the Rivers mouth on the same side, where we found a place no lesse delightful than the former; and as far as we could judge, both Tracts came into one. This lower place we called Rocky-point, because we found many Rocks and Stones of several bignesse upon the Land, which is not common. We sent our Boat down the River before us; our selves travelling by Land many miles, were so much taken with the pleasantnesse of the Land, that travelling into the woods so far, we could not recover our Boat and company that night. On Sunday the morrow following we got to our Boat, and on Monday the 16th of November, we proceeded down to a place on the East-side of the River some twenty three leagues from the Harbours mouth, which we call'd Turkie-Quarters, because we killed several Turkies thereabouts. We viewed the Land there, and found some tracts of good Land, and high, facing upon the River about one mile inward, but backwards some two miles all Pine-land, but good pasture-ground: we returned to our Boat, and proceeded down some two or three leagues, where we had formerly viewed, and found it a tract of as good Land as any we have seen, with as good Timber on it. The banks of the River being high, therefore we called it High-Land Point. Having viewed that, we proceeded down the River, going on shoar in several places on both sides, it being generally large Marshes, and many of them dry, that they may more fitly be called Medows: the wood-land against them is for the most part Pine, and in some places as barren as ever we saw Land, but in other places good Pasture-ground: And on Tuesday the 17th instant, we got aboard our Ship, riding against the mouth of Green's River, where our men are providing wood, and fitting the Ship for the Sea: In the interim, we took some view of the Land on both sides of the River there, finding some good Land, but more bad, and the best not comparable to that above. Friday the 20th instant was foul weather, yet in the Afternoon we weighed, and went down the River some two leagues, and came to Anchor against the mouth of Hilton's River, and took some view of the Land there on both sides, which appeared to us much like unto that at Green's River. Monday 23. we went with our Long-boat well victualled and manned up Hilton's River; and when we came three leagues or thereabouts up the said River, we found this and Green's River to come into one, and so continued for four or five leagues, which causeth a great Island betwixt them. We proceeded still up the River, till they parted again, keeping up Hilton's River on the Larboard side, and followed the said River five or six leagues further, where we found another large branch of Green's River to come into Hilton's, which maketh another great Island. On the Star-board side going up, we proceeded stil up the River some four leagues, and returned, taking a view of the Land on both sides, and now judge our selves to be from our ship some eighteen leagues W. and by W. One league below this place came four Indians in a Canoa to us, and sold us several baskets of Akorns, which we satisfied for, and so left them; but one of them followed us on the shoar some two or three miles, till he came on the top of a high bank, facing on the River, we rowing underneath it, the said Indian shot an Arrow at us, which missed one of our men very narrowly, and stuck in the upper edge of the Boat, which broke in pieces, leaving the head behind. Hereupon we presently made for the shoar, and went all up the bank except four to guide the Boat; we searched for the Indian, but could not finde him: At last we heard some sing further in the Woods, which we thought had been as a Chalenge to us to come and fight them. We went towards them with all speed, but before we came in sight of them, we heard two Guns go off from our Boat, whereupon we retreated with all speed to secure our Boat and Men: when we came to them, we found all well, and demanded the reason of their firing the Guns: they told us that an Indian came creeping on the Bank as they thought to shoot at them, therefore shot at him a great distance with Swan-shot, but thought they did him no hurt, for they saw him run away. Presently after our return to the Boat, while we were thus talking, came two Indians to us with their Bows and Arrows, crying *Bonny, Bonny:* we took their Bows and Arrows from them, and gave them Beads, to their content. Then we led them by the hand to the Boat, and shewed them the Arrow-head sticking in her side, and related to them the businesse; which when they understood, both of them manifested much sorrow, and made us understand by signes, that they knew nothing of it: so we let them go, and marked a Tree on the top of the bank, calling the place Mount-Skerry. We looked up the River as far as we could discern, and saw that it widened it self, and came running directly down the Countrey: So we returned, and viewed the Land on both sides the River, finding the banks steep in some places, but very high in others. The banks sides are generally Clay, and as some of our company doth affirm, some Marle. The Land and Timber up this River is no way inferiour to the best in the other, which we call the main River: So far as we discovered, this seems as fair, if not fairer than the former, and we think runs further into the Countrey, because there is a strong Current comes down, and a great deal more drift-wood. But to return to the business of the Land and Timber: We saw several plats of Ground cleared by the Indians after their weak manner, compassed round with great Timber-Trees; which they are no ways able to fall, and so keep the Sun from their Corn-fields very much; yet nevertheless we saw as large Corn-stalks or bigger, than we have seen any where else: So we proceeded down the River, till we found the Canoa the Indian was in who shot at us. In the morning we went on shoar, and cut the same in pieces: the Indians perceiving us coming towards them, run away. We went to his Hut, and pulled it down, brake his pots, platters, and spoons, tore his Deer-skins and mats in pieces, and took away a basket of Akorns: So we proceeded down the River two leagues, or thereabouts, and came to another place of Indians, bought Akorns and some Corn of them, and went downwards two leagues more: at last we espied an Indian peeping over a high bank: we held up a Gun at him; and calling to him, said, *Skerry:* presently several Indians appeared to us, making great signes of friendship, saying, *Bonny, Bonny,* and running before us, endeavouring to perswade us to come on shoar; but we answered them with stern countenances, and said, *Skerry,* taking up our guns, and threatening to shoot at them; but they cryed still *Bonny, Bonny:* And when they saw they could not prevail, nor perswade us to come on shoar, two of them came off to us in a Canoa, one padling with a great Cane, the other with his hand; they came to us, and laid hold of our Boat, sweating and blowing, and told us it was *Bonny* on shoar, and at last perswaded us to go ashoar with them. As soon as we landed, several Indians, to the number of near forty lusty men, came to us, all in a great sweat, and told us *Bonny:* we shewed them the Arrow-head in the Boats-side, and a piece of the Canoa which we had cut in pieces: the chief man of them made a large

Speech, and threw Beads into our Boat, which is a signe of great love and friendship; and made us to understand, when he heard of the Affront which we had received, it caused him to cry: and now he and his men were come to make peace with us, making signes to us that they would tye his Arms, and cut off his head that had done us that abuse; and for a further testimony of their love and good will towards us, they presented to us two very handsom proper young Indian women, the tallest that we have seen in this Countrey; which we supposed to be the Kings Daughters, or persons of some great account amongst them. These young women were ready to come into our Boat; one of them crouding in, was hardly perswaded to go out again. We presented to the King a Hatchet and several Beads, also Beads to the young women and to the chief men, and to the rest of the Indians, as far as our Beads would go: they promised us in four days to come on board our Ship, and so departed from us. When we left the place, which was presently, we called it Mount-Bonny, because we had there concluded a firm Peace. Proceeding down the River two or three leagues further, we came to a place where were nine or ten Canoa's all together; we went ashoar there, and found several Indians, but most of them were the same which had made Peace with us before: We made little stay there, but went directly down the River, and came to our Ship before day. Thursday the 26th of November, the winde being at South, we could not go down to the Rivers mouth: but on Friday the 27th, we weighed at the mouth of Hilton's River, and got down one league towards the Harbours mouth. On Sunday the 29th, we got down to Crane-Island, which is four leagues or thereabouts above the Entrance of the Harbours mouth. Now on Tuesday the first of December, we made a purchase of the River and land of Cape-Fair, of Wattcoosa, and such other Indians as appeared to us to be the chief of those parts: they brought us store of Fresh-fish aboard, as Mullets, Shads, and other very good Fish: this River is all Fresh-water fit to drink. Some eight leagues within the mouth, the Tide runs up about thirty-five leagues, but stops and riseth a great deal farther up; it flowes at the Harbours mouth S. E. and N. W. six foot at Neap-Tides, and eight foot at Spring-Tides: the Chanel on the Easter-side by the Cape-shoar is the best, and lyes close aboard the Cape-land, being three fathoms

at High-water, in the shallowest place in the Chanel just at the Entrance; but as soon as you are past that place half a Cables length
inward, you shall have six or seven fathoms, a fair turning Chanel into
the River, and so continuing four or five leagues upwards; afterwards
the Chanel is more difficult in some places six or seven fathoms, four
or five, and in other places but nine or ten foot, especially where the
River is broad. When the River comes to part, and grows narrow,
there is all Chanel from side to side in most places; in some places
you shall have five, six, or seven fathoms, but generally two or three,
Sand and Oaze. We viewed the Cape-land, and judged it to be little
worth, the Woods of it shrubby and low, the Land sandy and barren;
in some places Grass and Rushes, and in other places nothing but clear
sand: a place fitter to starve Cattel in our judgement, then to keep
them alive; yet the Indians, as we understand, keep the English Cattle
down there, and suffer them not to go off the said Cape, as we suppose, because the Countrey-Indians shall have no part with them, and
as we think, are fallen out about them, who shall have the greatest
share. They brought aboard our Ship very good and fat Beef several
times, which they could afford very reasonable; also fat and very large
Swine, good cheap penny-worths: but they may thank their friends of
New-England, who brought their Hogs to so fair a Market. Some of
the Indians brought very good Salt aboard us, and made signes, pointing to both sides of the Rivers mouth, that there was great store thereabouts. We saw up the River several good places for the setting up of
Corn or Saw-mills. In that time as our businesse called us up and
down the River and Branches, we kill'd of wild-fowl, four Swans, ten
Geese, twenty nine Cranes, ten Turkies, forty Duck and Mallard, three
dozen of Parrakeeto's, and six or seven dozen of other small Fowls,
as Curlues and Plovers, etc.

Whereas there was a Writing left in a Post at the Point of Cape
Fair River, by those New-England-men that left Cattel with the Indians there, the Contents whereof tended not only to the disparagement of the Land about the said River, but also to the great discourage-
ment of all those that should hereafter come into those parts to settle:
In Answer to that scandalous writing, We whose names are under-

written do affirm, That we have seen facing on both sides of the River, and branches of Cape-Fair aforesaid, as good Land, and as well Timbered, as any we have seen in any other part of the world, sufficient to accommodate thousands of our English Nation, lying commodiously by the said River.

On Friday the 4th of December, the winde being fair, we put out to Sea, bound for Barbadoes; and on the 6th day of January, 1663/4, we came to Anchor in Carlisle-Bay; and after several known apparent dangers both by Sea and Land, have now brought us all in safety to our long-wish'd-for and much desired Port, to render an Accompt of our Discovery, the verity of which we aver.

ANTHONY LONG

WILLIAM HILTON

PETER FABIAN

A Copy of the Spanyard's first Letter

I am come to this Town of Infidel-Indians, to seek some English, which my Governour and Captain-General, Don Alonso de Arangows, de Colis, Cavallier, and Knight of the Order of St. James, for his Majesty, had notice that there was a Ship lost in that Port in which you are, that the men might not run any hazard of their lives, as those with me here have. Don Adeleyers, with the Governor of the Garison of S. Augustine, are gone to ransome and free the Subjects of the King your Master, Charles the Second: Wherefore I advise you, that if these Indians (although Infidels and Barbarians) have not killed any of the Christians, and do require as a gift or courtesie for those four men, four Spades, and four Axes, some Knives, and some Beads, and the four Indians which you have there, you deliver them, and that for their sakes that shall sayl on this Coast: you may send a Boat, who when she comes athwart the Port of St. Ellens, may hoist an Ancient twice or thrice, and I will do the same. The shortnesse of the dispatch I desire, for I want provision for my Soldiers, and the way is large. Your Servant desires you would give me a speedy Answer; and what may be done in your service, I shall do very willingly: And if you have none that can interpret the Spanish Tongue, you may write in your own, for here are your Countrey-men that can understand it: but if you can, let it be in Spanish.

From the Capt. ALANSO ARGUELES

From St. Ellens the 22 of Septemb. 1663

The Copies of our Letters sent to the English and Spaniards at St. Ellens, with the Answer of Mr. William Davis, and the Spaniards also, here inclosed.

Loving Friends and Country-men,

Wee are come up the River with our Ship, and are resolved to come through by Combiheh, to St. Ellens, and to get you away by fair means, or otherways. If that will not do, we have five of your company already: and the Captain of Edistow, and one more are Prisoners with us, whom we intend to keep till we have rescued all the English Prisoners out of the hands of the Indians. Send us word by this Bearer what you know concerning the Spanyards; for the youth Morgan tells us that the Spanyards are come with Soldiers to fetch you away. Fail not to inform us how things are. Nothing else at present, but remain

Your friend and Servant
WILL. HILTON

From on Board the *Adventure,* Septemb. 21, 1663

An Answer to the Spanyards Letter not understood

Honoured Sir,

Whereas wee received a Letter from you, the Contents whereof we understand not, because none of us could read Spanish: Our businesse is to demand and receive the English Prisoners from the hands of the Indians, and then they shall have their Indians which we have detained on Board, with satisfaction for their pains. We understand not at present that we have any businesse with you. Not else at present, but remain

Your Friend and Servant in what I may,
WILL. HILTON

From on Board the *Adventure,* Septemb. 23. 1663
To his honoured Friend the Spanish Captain at St. Ellens

An Answer to Mr. William Davis his Lines written to us in the Spanyard's Letter, Viz.

Mr. William Davis,

Wee received your Lines in the Spanish Letter, but hear nothing of your coming to us. Let your Keepers send you, and that without delay; for you may assure them, That we will be gone, and carry the Indians away with us, except they send the English suddenly on Board, and then they shall have their Indians upon our receipt of the English. Not else at present, but thank the Spanish Captain for the Pork and Venison he sent us. Remain

Your loving Friend
WILL. HILTON

From on Board the *Adventure,* September 24. 1663
To Mr. William Davis at St. Ellens

Sir,

Wee have received your second Letter, and give you no Answer, for the Reason mentioned in our former Letter to you. Please to inform the Indians, That if they bring not the English Prisoners on Board us without further delay, we are resolved to carry their Indians we have on Board away: But if they will bring the English, they shall have theirs, with satisfaction. Also we thank you for your Venison and Pork. Not else at present, but remain

Sir,
Your Friend and Servant in what I may
WILL. HILTON

From on Board the *Adventure,* Septemb. 24, 1663
To his Honoured Friend, the Spanish Captain at St. Ellens

A Copy of the Spanyard's second Letter

My Governour and Capt. General, as soon as he had News that a Ship, by Nation English, was lost in that Port in which you now are, sent me with Soldiers of the Garison of St. Augustine in Florida, as they have at other times done, to free them from death; for which cause I came to this Port of St. Ellens, where I found all these Indians in a fright, fearing that you will do them some mischief: So having found four men of those that were lost, I thought good to advise you, that you might carry them in your company, giving some gifts to those Indians which they desire; which is, four Spades, four Axes, some Knives, and some Beads. This they desire, not as payment, but onely as an acknowledgment of a kindness for having saved their lives; which they have always done as Naturals who have given their obedience to the King our Master. And they do also desire you to let go those four Indians which are there: You may send a Boat when you discover the Points of St. Ellens; may hoist an Ancient two or three times, and I will do the same. I desire your Answer may be sodain; for I am scarce of Provisions, and the way is somewhat long: and if you have no body who understands Spanish, you may write in English, for here are your Countrey-men who will interpret it.

By the Captain ALANSO ARGUILES.

From St. Ellens, Septemb. 23. 1663.

Proposals made to all such Persons as shall undertake to become the first Setlers on Rivers, Harbours, or Creeks, whose Mouth or Entrance is Southwards or Westwards of Cape St. Romana in the Province of Carolina, and execute the same at their own hazard and charge of Transportation, Ammunition, and Provisions, as is hereafter expressed, etc.

I

Imprimis, It is agreed and consented to by us Thomas Mudyford, and Peter Colleton, Esquires, who are impowered by the Lords Proprietors to treat in their behalf; That in consideration of the good service which Captain Anthony Long, Captain William Hilton, and Mr. Peter Fabian have done in making so clear a Discovery on that Coast, They shall each of them enjoy to them and their Heirs for ever one thousand Acres of Land apiece upon the said River, Harbour, or Creeks, on such places as they shall desire, not taken up before.

II

Item, To Master Pyam Blowers, and Master John Hancock, five hundred Acres apiece, in manner as aforesaid.

III

Item, To all the Sea-men and Adventurers in the said Ship, one hundred Acres apiece in manner as aforesaid.

IV

Item, To every person that hath subscribed and paid, or hath subscribed and shall pay within two moneths next after the Date hereof, unto the Treasurer appointed by the Committee for defraying the Charge of the late Discovery, and towards the publique Stock, five hundred Acres of Land, besides what they are otherwayes to receive and enjoy each for every thousand pounds of Sugar, and so for greater or lesser quantity proportionably, to possesse and enjoy the same in manner as aforesaid; the said Adventurers having promised, That the severall and respective Persons above-intended, shall within five years next ensuing, have one Person white or black, young or old, transported at their Charge as aforesaid, on that or some other parcel of Land in the Province, for every hundred of Acres of Land that is or shall be due to them for their adventures as aforesaid: But when once taken up, to settle the same within one year after it is once taken up, or lose the Land.

V

Item, To every Person that goes, or sends an Agent at his or their own cost with the first Ship or Fleet, or within six weeks next after the first Ship or Fleet that shall be set out from this Island (none to be accompted as first Setlers but such as do send in the first Fleet) Armed with a good Firelock, ten pounds of Powder, and twenty pounds of Bullet, or Lead, and Victualled for six moneths, shall have one hundred Acres of Land, and the like quantity of Acres for every Manservant that he carrieth so armed and provided, to the person at whose charge they shall be transported as aforesaid.

VI

Item, To every person that shall second the first Undertakers, that is to say, shall go within two months next after those that are accompted as first Setlers, armed and provided as aforesaid, seventy Acres of Land,

and seventy Acres for every Man-servant that he or they shall carry or send Armed and provided as aforesaid.

VII

Item, To every person provided as aforesaid, that shall go within two years after the first undertakers, fifty Acres of Land, and as much to him or them for every Man-servant he or they shall carry or send, armed and provided as aforesaid.

VIII

Item, To every Free-woman above the age of twelve years, that shall go, or be carried thither within the first five years, forty Acres of Land.

IX

Item, To all Male-Children above the age of fourteen years, the same quantity that is allowed to Free-men, and on the same Conditions.

X

Item, The Lords Proprietors will grant unto every Parish one hundred Acres of Land for the Church and other publique uses.

XI

Item, To every person that hath subscribed, and shall pay to the above-mentioned Discovery, who shall go or send an Agent within the first five years next after the first Setlers, forty Acres of Land; and as much to them for every Man-servant they shall carry or send within that time armed and provided as aforesaid, and the like quantity for all others so transporting themselves or servants within the first three years, who are not Subscribers.

XII

Item, To every Man-servant that shall go with the first Undertakers, fifty Acres of Land; and to such as go with the second Adventurers thirty Acres, and for all other servants that shall go within the first five years, twenty Acres, and for every Woman-servant ten Acres, to become due at the Expiration of the first Term of their servitude in that Countrey.

XIII

Item, To the Owner of every Negro-Man or Slave, brought thither to settle within the first year, twenty acres; and for every Woman-Negro or Slave, ten acres of Land; and all Men-Negro's, or slaves after that time, and within the first five years, ten acres, and for every Woman-Negro or slave, five acres.

XIV

Item, That all the before-mentioned parcels of Land given, or to be given, allotted or granted to any person or persons whatsoever, shall be held and enjoyed to them, their Heirs and Assigns for ever, in free and common Soccage, according to the Tenure of East-Greenwich within the County of Kent, within the Kingdom of England (and not *in Capite,* or by Knights-service) paying as a fine once for all to the Lords Proprietors, or their Agents impowered to receive the same, one half-peny per acre for every Acre of Land that is or shall be taken up as aforesaid, or the value of the said half-peny per Acre, when the person who is to receive it shall receive his Deed or Copy of Record for his Land so taken up; and in lieu of all, and all manner of Rents, Services, Fines, Taxes and Impositions whatsoever, one ear of Indian Corn for every hundred acres of Land so taken up, at a certain time and place prescribed, if lawfully demanded.

XV

Item, It is further agreed, That every person shall or may take up their Land, or any part thereof, where they please, in any place not before taken up: Provided they do therein submit to such Method as the Governor and Council for the time being shall judge most safe and convenient.

XVI

Item, That the Lords Proprietors shall grant to the Free-Holders the Priviledge of choosing an annual Assembly, wherein by the consent of the said Lords, or their Delegates, they shall be impowered to make Lawes, and them confirm, publish, and abrogate, as in the great Charter is expressed; and that the Assembly may lawfully, without the consent of the Governour, complain to the said Lords of such Grievances as lye upon the People.

XVII

Item, That forasmuch as the Lords Proprietors or their Delegates may not be at all times there present, to consent to such Lawes as are or shall be thought necessary; In such Case all Lawes and Orders made by the Governour, Council and Assembly, shall be in force untill the Denyal thereof by the Lords Proprietors shall be to them signified under their Hands in Writing.

XVIII

Item, That the said Free-Holders shall have the freedome of Trade, Immunity of Customes, and Liberty of Conscience, and all other Priviledges made good unto them as amply and as fully as is at large expressed in the great Charter granted to the said Lords Proprietors from His Majesty.

Francis Le Jau (1665–1717)

Born in Angers, France, in 1665, Francis Le Jau received his M.A. and B.D. degrees at Trinity College, Dublin, being ordained a priest in the Church of England in 1696, and serving as canon of St. Paul's Cathedral in London, 1696–1700. Le Jau came to the New World as Anglican missionary to the West Indies in 1700. In 1706 he was appointed pastor at Goose Creek in South Carolina, where he served as a missionary to the Indians. In 1717 he became rector at St. Philip's Church in Charleston, dying in that city on September 15, 1717.

From the *Carolina Chronicle*

[Le Jau to the Secretary, December 2, 1706]
St James Goose creek in South Carolina
Decembr. 2d 1706
Sr

I left Virginia the 12th of Octr. last, and the Divine Providence brought me safe here the 18th of the same Month. I was mightily afflicted when the first News I heard was that of the unexpected Death of our Revd. Brother Mr. Samuel Thomas departed this Life ten days before my Coming he is universally Lamented by all good Men for his Great Zeal and Edifying Life, It is thought he Contracted the pestiltial feaver by lying in Charles Town, he was not sick for above a week, and having Implored the Divine Assistance to the last Moment, God in his mercy I hope took him to his holy Heaven Octr. 10th. I flatter'd my self wth the hopes of his Dear Company, help and Advices, But I must submit, and the Lord I adore who has hitherto preserved me, I firmly trust to his Great Goodness that he will take Care of me and direct me in my Mission. We are also deprived of the Presence of our Brother Mr. Auchinleck who has thought fit to stay in Bermudas where I suppose a Minister was wanting. Mr. Dunn has been afflicted with the Feaver and Ague, and as he was on the recovery is fall'n sick again, and Continues so still; I hope there is no danger. His Parishioners on the Southward of this Colony are willing he shou'd come among them and leave the Neighbourhood of Charles Town that has been so sickly these 7 or 8 Months; I saw him 5 days agoe disposed to comply with their desire. He Charged me to give his Duty to his Grace the President and the Honble. the Members of the Society; Upon my first Landing I saw the Inhabitants rejoycing: they had kept the day before holy for a thanksgiving to Almighty God for being safely delivered from an Invasion from the French and Spaniards, who came with 5 Vessels the 27th. of August last Landed in three places and hav-

Francis Le Jau, *The Carolina Chronicle of Dr. Francis Le Jau, 1706–1717,* ed. Frank J. Klingberg (Berkeley and Los Angeles: University of California Press, 1956), pp. 16–21. Reprinted by permission of The Regents of the University of California. Professor Klingberg used the records of the Society for the Propagation of the Gospel in Foreign Parts.

ing had 40 Men killed and left 230 Prisoners were forced back to Sea
the 31st. of the same Month; We took one of their Ships and lost but
one Man. We hope they wont attempt the like any more, and in case
of any such Accident, we are well secured by Fortifications and all
things in great Order, but our barr 5 Miles from the Town is a good
defence, it has but 14 foot water in: The reception I met with was
extraordinarily kind, and far more respectfull than I deserve, and I
dayly receive great tokens of goodness from his Excy. Sr. Nathaniel
Johnson our Govr. and Mr. Chief Justice Nich: Trott a very learned
person, and who is about a Work the best of the kind I ever knew,
it is a New sort of Hebrew Lexicon. There are several other worthy
Persons who delight in shewing how much they value the Dignity of
our Character, and Generally I have met with all the Civility I cou'd
wish, even from the Dissenters I have seen. The Sickness wch was still
raging in Town obliged me to make no stay at all there, but I presently was Carryed to the Country in the parish the Society was pleased
to give me the care of. There I continue among very good and Obliging persons of whom I must declare that by their diligence and attention they shew a true desire to become good Servants of the Lord Jesus.
The Change of Climate and the Fatigue of my Voyage had somewhat
disordered my health. Thro' God's blessing I am pretty well for the
present; and when I am seasoned to the Country I hope I'le do well.
Our Church and parsonage house will be fitted up in a short time,
Materials are getting ready very fast. In the mean time Great and
Charitable Care is taken of me at Mr. Moore's, son to Col Moore who
dyed a week before Mr Thomas and in him the Clergy has lost a true
friend and the Country a very great Support, But it is not possible for
me to forbear declaring the kind usage I receive of the Lady the Coll
Widow and all the Family: I am the more particular on this Accot.
because I think it an Act of Justice to undeceive the world; and let
such Clergymen as the Society please to send come freely they will find
matters as I say, and much better; for I must own that for Gentility
politeness and a handsome way of Living this Colony exceeds what I
have seen. Poor families may come here and live very well; I don't
talk of geting easily great Estates which desire shou'd never be in the
heart of a Christian, but I mean they shall have a plenty of things neces-

sary for life if they be industrious. For this is the finest Climate I ever saw, the Soil produces every thing without much trouble, and at this time the weather is finer than in Aprill with you in England. The Sickness is I bless God over we are told it is now got into Virginia and New York. Virginia indeed was very sickly when I came way.

Upon the Alarm the Inhitants made above 1400 good Men in the Town and a great many in the Country besides; There is 100 Families in my parish few Dissenters, several Negroes come to Church, but I will tell the particulars with the help of God according to the form prescribed in the Instructions; in a little time, for I am in a manner unsettled yet. However I must give the Society this Opinion of mine concerning the Spiritual Good of the Indians our Neighbours; I dayly see several of them who seem very quiet, sweet humour'd and patient, content with little which are great Dispositions to be true Christians. They speak divers Languages in their several Nations but I am certainly informed by a Considerable Indian trader, who is now always in the house with me called Mr. Pike a kinsman to Mr. Moore that there is a Language called the Savannas which is fine smoth and easy to be got, and may be called the transcendent Language of America, spoke every where thro' the Continent as Latin was formerly in Europe and Arabick is still in Affrica; and there is an Indian town an 100 Miles of S. Carolina, about S.W. where some English Traders live and that Language may be learn'd. I propose that some young Men not yet in holy Orders, tho' with a tincture of good Learning, shou'd be encouraged to come upon that Account and humbly submit my Judgment to that of the Society. Our Assembly which is the Parliament of the Colony is now sitting. The two Acts that made so much Noise are repealed. The Ecclial Court of Comss. is dissolved. A New Act is passed to erect Eight parishes and to allow to Ministers 50 £ a year for the present and 3 years hence the Salary will be 100 £ of this Country money which by what I perceive when I buy necessarys will answer to about 60 £ Sterling. So now I have about 30 £ here to depend upon besides what Gratuity the Society is pleased to allow to me, and which I humbly request to be Continued for the necessary Maintenance of my numerous family the passage of whom will prove very Chargeable and I am afraid must come but indifferently provided where Cloathing and

Necessary Stuff is sold at 2 or 300 p Cent. We want 4 Ministers more and some School Masters who can be Clarks. If some french Minister wou'd come here there is the same Maintenance from the Country for two of them, and if they cou'd serve an English parish 'twou'd do better. As for me I design under the Direction of the Holy Spirit to do all the Service and good I can among all men here; according to the promise I made to My Lord of London I will now and then as I am able visit the French plantations; but will chiefly behave my self according to the Commands I receive from His Grace the President and the Honble. Society.

If there was any papers directed for me from the Society and deliver'd to Mr. Thomas, I suppose they must be lost, his goods have been viewed and appraised of late and nothing was found for me but the 2 Boxes of Books and Sheets: but no Letters nor Directions, so that I have proceeded according to the Intimation given to me by Mr. Dunn and seeing the Acts repealed have made no Difficulty to resolve to stay here, and send an Invitation to my Wife and family to undertake the Voyage and come to me: There has been and still is a misunderstanding between The Minister of the Town and the people of the Country I have meddled no further in the business than by endeavouring to promote peace and am very sorry had not the good fortune to succeed. I pray for Grace to all and that the Spirit of Union and love may reign here; that's all I do for the present with the Particular Care of my parish, tho' I never deny coming to Town when I am invited 'tis 10 Miles of this place where I live and indeed I am received in Charles Town with true Christian love by all, God be blessed. I am desired by the Gentlemen of my Parish to return their humble thanks to the Society for the Great Bible and Common prayer book, and Book of Homilies they have received, and all our poor people and Negroes who had a Share in the Distribution of the Small Tracts pray earnestly for the prosperity of the Society; I joyn with all my heart with them, praying to Almighty God for the preservation of His Grace The President, Their Lords the Bishops and the rest of the Members my Charitable Benefactors of that Honble. Society. And begging the Continuacon of their favour with the Assistance of their prayers with my Lords Blessing I conclude this Letter wishing it may safely come to your hands, & assuring you that

I will write by all Convenient Opportunites. Honour me Good Sr. with the Continuance of your friendship which I value very much. I pray for your spiritual and temporal Welfare and do remain with due respect.

Sr.

Your most humble & Obedient Servant

Francis Le Jau

I did not see yet Mr Hasel the Deacon he keeps at the Govrs. 30 miles of me. One Mr. Kelson who succeeded me in St. Christophers is here and willing to settle wth. us.

Directions are To Jno. Chamberlayne Esqr.

Charles Woodmason (1720?–77?)

Although little is known about his early life, Charles Woodmason was probably born in London about 1720. He emigrated to South Carolina in or about 1752, leaving behind a son and a wife, whose plans to join him failed to materialize. Woodmason quickly became a large landholder in the Peedee River region and a respected "Planter and Merchant," prominent in affairs of church and state in Charleston. In 1765–66 he returned to England briefly to become an ordained Anglican minister. Woodmason's experiences during his ministry in the South Carolina backcountry were the basis for his *Journal* (not published until 1953), an invaluable document for social historians of colonial South Carolina. Both as poet and journalist Woodmason made significant contributions to the literature of the colony. Returning to his native England in 1774, he died there at an unknown date, but probably in 1777.

C. W. *in* Carolina *to* E. J. *at* Gosport

While you, my friend, indulg'd in each desire,
Your blooming bride with rapt'rous love admire;
From grave to gay with various authors change,
Or blithe from concert to assembly range,
Me harder fate to foreign lands conveys;
In foreign lands the muse my call obeys.
The land, tho' foreign, softest seasons bless,
To the pleas'd native bounteous in excess.
Ev'n I, who pine for less indulgent skies,
Am charm'd where'er I turn my wond'ring eyes.
Almost I seem to tread enchanted ground,
And endless beauty fills the circuit round.
    Thy pleasing name I echo thro' the woods,
Then wish thee with me near these chrystal floods,
To view *Santee* tumultuous in its course,
And trace the great *Port Royal* to its source:
To see *Savanna* draw his watry store,
Thro' the long windings of a swampy shore,
And rapid *Ashley* with impetuous tide,
Thro' the long chain of num'rous islands glide.
    With transport fir'd, attentive I survey,
The two *Podees* to *Winyaw's* bason stray,
Parents of floods! who rolling thro' the plain,
The *Cherokees* of half their moisture drain,
And swol'n with rains, or swift dissolving snow,
Distribute wealth and plenty where they flow.
    Their names, enfranchiz'd by the tuneful throng,
Were never yet immortaliz'd in song:
They, lost in silence and oblivion, lye,
Till time ordains to flow in poetry.
Ah! were I blest with tuneful *Gaselee's* skill,
Thy streams, *Black-River,* shou'd my numbers fill,
Where *Cleland, Powel* and *Trapier* reside,
And learning's toil rude savages deride,
Sometimes to *Pon-pon's* banks I calm retire,

Or shallow *Stono's* fertile shores admire.
Stono, a languid stream, derives its course,
From various urns, and from a doubtful source,
When wilt thou, *Wando,* in poetic lays,
Acquire, like *Helicon,* immortal praise?
When shall some deathless muse exalt thy fame,
Fair *Edistow,* and dignify thy stream?
Broad *Waccamow,* which now obscurely strays,
May gain distinction while it yields the bays,
And farther than her *rice* can find its way,
Ashpoo may be convey'd some future day.

    Here could my humble muse, a train run o'er
Of gen'rous names, that honor *Cooper's* shore:
The *Cordes's Harlstons, Beresfords,* and *Beard,*
(By ties of virtuous friendship long endear'd)
With *Broughton, Simmons, Austen,* and *Durand,*
The pride and grace of *Carolina's* land!
Did not the tilting bark unwilling stay,
And southern breezes chide the short delay:
The pleasing talk, at present, I suspend,
And bid a *Langhorn's* pen their worth commend.

    Oh! would a spark of empyreal fire,
With *Parker's* warmth my ravish'd breast inspire,
Unnumber'd beauties in my verse should shine,
And *Carolina* grace each flowing line.
See how her fragrant groves around me smile,
That shun the coast of *Britain's* stormy isle,
Or when transplanted and preserv'd with care,
Curse the cold clime, and starve in northern air.
Here, kindly warmth, their mounting juice ferments,
To taller growth and more exalted scents:
Ev'n loosen'd sands with tender myrtles bloom,
And trodden weeds exhale a rich perfume.

    Bear me, some god, to worthy *Michi's* seat,
Or give me shade in *Taylor's* calm retreat,
Where western gales eternally reside,

And bounteous seasons lavish all their pride;
Blossoms, and fruits, and flow'rs, together rise,
And the whole year in gay confusion lyes.
    What! tho' a second *Carthage* here we raise,
A late attempt, the work of modern days,
Here *Drayton's* seat and *Middleton's* is found,
Delightful villa's! be they long renown'd.
Swift fly the years when sciences retire,
From frigid climes to equinoctial fire:
When *Raphael's* tints, and *Titian's* strokes shall faint,
As fair *America* shall deign to paint.
Here from the mingled strength of shade and light,
A new creation shall arise to sight,
And sculpture here in full perfection shine,
Dug, for her hand, our *Apalachian* mine.
Methinks I see, in solemn order stand,
The first advent'rers to this blooming land:
Ashley and *Archdale, Colleton,* and *Boon,*
Bull, Johnson, Izzard, heroes worthy *Rome,*
See Indian chiefs whom cruelties renown,
Submit their country to the *British* crown,
Domes, temples, bridges, rise in distant views,
And sumtuous palaces the sight amuse.
    How has kind heav'n adorn'd this happy land,
And scatter'd blessings with a lib'ral hand!
But what avail her unexhausted stores,
Her woody mountains, and her sunny shores,
With all the gifts that heav'n and earth impart,
The smiles of nature, and the charms of art?
While noxious reptiles in her vallies reign,
And stinging insects fill the watry plain,
While droughts and hurricanes at once impair,
The smiling prospects of the plenteous year.
The red'ning orange, and the bearded grain
Are scarce enjoy'd, or snatch'd with fear and pain:
The planter joyless views luxuriant vines,

And in the myrtle's fragrant shade repines;
Scorch'd in his boasted aromatick grove,
From heat no shelter, no recess for love.
    O *Britain!* queen of isles, serenely bright,
Profuse of bliss, and pregnant with delight,
Eternal pleasures in thy borders reign,
And smiling plenty leads thy wanton train.
On foreign mountains may the sun refine
The grapes of soft juice, and mellow it to wine.
With citron groves adorn a distant soil,
And the fat olive swell with floods of oil,
Thy sons ne'er envy warmer climes that lye
Stretch'd in bright tracts beneath a cloudless sky,
Nor yet at heav'n with impious frowns repine,
Tho' o'er their heads, the frozen *Pleiades* shine.
    Struck with thy name, my country, which resounds
From many a voice, to ocean's utmost bounds;
Dear, conscious mem'ry wounds my breast with pain,
I long to tread paternal fields again:
To hear my lisping boy's delight exprest,
And snatch my *Stella* to my panting breast.

The Need for Education:

"Speak O Ye Charlestown Gentry, who go in Scarlet and fine Linen and fare sumptuously ev'ry day."

N.B.

The Back Parts of S. C. not being laid out into Parishes, and no provision made for the Poor, The Country in General was cover'd with Swarms of Orphans, and other Pauper vagrant vagabond Children to the Great Increase of all Manner of Vice and Wickedness. I therefore excited the People to petition the Legislature for the Establishment of some Public Schools, where these Children might be taught the Principles of Religion, and fitted to become useful Members of Society. The Commons House of Assembly adopted the Petition, and made Provision for Six Schools of fifty Children each, at six different Places, to be on foot for 14 Years. But when the Bill was sent up to the Council, The Honorable Othneil Beale (President, and a New England Independent) made several Alterations—At which the House took such Offence, that the Bill was never reconsidered, and thereby miscarried. The Bill directed That all the Children should be Educated in your Proffession of the Church of England. Mr. Beale in his Bigotted Zeal for Independency would have left Matters at Large: and Grammar and the Languages taught in them. Such a Latitude, would rather have encreas'd, than rem[ed]ied the Evil it was intended to Cure: For as the Children were Orphans, and destitute of Friends, they had no Connections, and were Children of the Public, Who doubtless had the best Right to frame both their Civil and religious Principles.

A Rumour having prevail'd that the Bill had pass'd into a Law, The People met to draw up an Address of Thanks And sent for me to officiate at that and some other Public Meetings, when this Sermon was propos'd being deliver'd but postpon'd till the Act took Place, and now, will never be revived. . . .

Charles Woodmason, "The Need for Education" from *The Journal*, in *Carolina Backcountry*, ed. Richard J. Hooker. Chapel Hill, published for the Institute of Early American History and Culture at Williamsburg, Virginia, by The University of North Carolina Press, 1953, pp. 118–22. Copyright 1953 by The University of North Carolina Press. Reprinted by permission of the publisher.

Not many Years past [this beautiful country was] A Desert, and Forrest, overrun with Wild Beasts, and Men more Savage than they, but now Peopled and Planted to a degree incredible for the Short Space of Time—And which I never could make them [in Charleston] believe, nor could I my Self have believ'd without Ocular Demonstration. . . . And next to the Almighty, We are in a dutiful and respectful Manner to thank the Legislature for this their Patriotic favour and investing us with this Blessing of our Birth Right, *Liberty* and the *Laws.* So that now We may call our Selves Free Men.

But the Legislature wisely considering That Evils are much easier prevented than Eradicated—And convinc'd, That the Num'rous Troops of Banditti and Freebooters and Unsettled, Profligate Persons of both Sexes, originally sprung from the Great Number of Orphan and Neglected Children scatter'd over these Back Countries, who live expos'd in a State of Nature, and were oblig'd almost to associate with Villains and Vagabonds for Subsistence They (very judiciously) have ordered Six Schools to be founded among You for training up 50 Poor Children in each, in the fundamental Principles of the Christian Religion, and first Elements of Learning to qualify them for Business, and train them up to become useful and Valuable Members of Society. So that hereby, the Ax is laid to the Root of Licentiousness, and We have a Prospect before us of seeing some Stop put to that deluge of Vice and Impiety which now overflows this Land. Let me congratulate You my Dear fellow Christians hereon—Let me say, this is the Happiest, the most blessed Day I have seen since in these Parts! Long have I labour'd to bring these Public Blessings to Good Effect. My Zeal has been Great tho' my Interest and Applications Weak. And I care not who takes the Honour so You but enjoy the Profit of the Good Intentions of the Public in Your favour. And my enlarg'd Hopes are, that the Name of God will in due Time spread from hence across this Great Continent to the Bounds of the Western Ocean, or South Sea—And that from the rising of the Sun even unto the going down of the Same *the Gospel of Christ will be great among the Gentiles, and in every Place Incense be offer'd unto His Name and a Pure Offering* (Mal 1.)

This Satisfaction I can carry with me at my Return to England, That I am the first Episcopal Minister ever seen or heard in these Parts; and that I have carried the Holy Bible, and read the Liturgy of our Church, in Places, and to Persons, who never before heard a Chapter, or had heard the Name of God or of Christ, save in Oaths and Curses. I am oblig'd to severals among You (and especially to the Good People of this House) for their Pilotage and Assistance in these my Travels, and for carrying of me over Indian Creek, Reedy River, and other Waters, quite over the Line to the Stragglers in the Cherokee Country—And I take this Public Opportunity of returning You my thanks As You have been Witnesses that my Text has been verified in this Wild Region and that as far as the *Cherokee* Hills and to the *Catawba* Nation, the Poor have had the Gospel preached unto them. . . .

The Benefits [of the proposed schools] may not only result to the present Age but likewise extend to future Generations—As it may prove a Means of lessening the Number of Negroes that are now employ'd as family Servants and therefrom by Degrees freeing this Land from an Internal Enemy that may one day be the total Ruin of it. At least it may put an End to some Species of Vice that too much prevails from the Slavery of these Poor *Africans*. . . .

Only look into the Indian Settlements near us—See there the Poor Wretches! And where for want of due Instruction, the most Savage Dispositions and detestable Practises contrary to the Principles of Humanity as well as of Religion, are transmitted down from one Wretched Generation of Creatures to another—And who for want of Knowledge are, in many Respects but one degree removed from the Brute Creation! Would we wish to see any of our own Complexion, Descendants of Freeborn Britons in such a State of Barbarism and Degeneracy?—And yet We began to be almost on the borders of it. Behold on ev'ry one of these Rivers, What Number of Idle, profligate, audacious Vagabonds! Lewd, impudent, abandon'd Prostitutes Gamblers Gamesters of all Sorts—Horse Theives Cattle Stealers, Hog Stealers—Branders and Markers Hunters going Naked as Indians. Women hardly more so. All in-a-manner useless to Society, but very pernicious in propagating Vice, Beggary, and Theft—Still more pernicious as We have frequently found, when United in Gangs and Combinations—Such bold and dangerous Offenders as contemn all Order and Decency —broke ev'ry Prison almost in America Whipp'd in ev'ry Province—

and now set down here as Birds of Prey to live on the Industrious and Painstaking, Wretches, who have defy'd all Authority, and defeated the Laws of ev'ry Country. . . . Speak O Ye Charlestown Gentry, who go in Scarlet and fine Linen and fare sumptuously ev'ry day. Speak O Ye overgrown Planters who wallow in Luxury, Ease, and Plenty. Would You, Could You Can You see or suffer Poor helpless, pretty Boys— Beautiful, unguarded, promising Young Girls, for want of Timely Care and Instructions to be united with a Crew of Profligate Wretches *Whose Mouth is full of Cun[n]ing Deceit and Lyes,* from whom they must unavoidably learn Idleness, Lewdness, Theft, Rapine Violence and it may be, Murder. . . .

And I hope too, that some Attention will be paid as to learning them to sing after the Parochial Manner that so they may be useful at Church on Sundays—to carry on that Noble Part of Divine Worship quite neglected in our Congregations—and which Neglect carries many to Separate Assemblies, solely to join in Singing Hymns.

South-Carolina Gazette (1732–75)

Founded in 1732 by Thomas Whitmarsh, the *South-Carolina Gazette* was the most important newspaper in the pre-Revolutionary South. Following Whitmarsh, its successive editors were Lewis Timothy, Elizabeth Timothy, Peter Timothy, and Thomas Powell. More than a news medium, the *Gazette* served as an outlet for Charleston literary effort. Among its best writings are "Extract of 'a POEM intitled INDICO'," which, according to the *South-Carolina Gazette* of August 25, 1757, was taken from "A Collection of POEMS, on *various* SUBJECTS: By a Resident of SOUTH-CAROLINA," and the poem "On Liberty-Tree," by "Philo Patriae," which appeared in the issue for September 21, 1769. Professor Jay B. Hubbell (*The South in American Literature, 1607–1900*, p. 160) calls "On Liberty-Tree" one of the "best pieces of Revolutionary writings to come out of the colony."

Extract of "a POEM, intitled INDICO"

The Means and Arts that to Perfection bring,
The richer Dye of INDICO, I sing.
Kind Heav'n! whose wise and providential Care
Has granted us another World to share,
These happy Climes to Antients quite unknown,
And fields more fruitful than *Britannia's* own;
Who for Man's Use has blest with Herbs the Soil,
Who crowns with Joy the wary Planter's Toil,
Do thou propitious grant the Help I need,
Success shall follow and my Labours speed.

   IF Time permits, the Shady Forest clear,
And turn the Fallow for the following Year;
Beneath the noxious Pine the Soil is sour,
And spreading Oaks prevent the genial Pow'r
Of mellowing Suns; but yet, Experience shews,
In these hot climes that rich Herbage grows,
The following Summer, where in Winter past
The hungry Swine had found a Winter Mast.

   Begin when first bleak Winter strips the Trees,
When Herds first shudder at the Northern Breeze,
'Tis time the Walnut and the Cypress tall
And tow'ring Pride of Verdant Pines to fall.
Arm'd with destructive Steel thy Negroes bring,
With Blows repeated let the Woodlands ring;
With winged Speed, the tim'rous Deer from far
Shall fly the Tumult of the Sylvan War,
When rattling Oaks and Pines promisc'ous bound,
And distant Groves re-eccho to the Sound.
Whilst the bright Flames shall seize the useless Log
For brush and trunks thy fertile Acres clog
Then peaceful sleep—secure thy Herds shall be,

Anonymous, "Extract of 'a POEM, intitled INDICO'," *South-Carolina Gazette,*
Aug. 25, 1757. (See *Agricultural History,* XXX [Jan. 1956], pp. 42–43.)
Reprinted by permission of the Agricultural Society and Hennig Cohen.

And live to feast thy Country Friends and thee.
When midnight Wolves, impell'd by Hunger's Pow'r,
With fiercest Rage the darken'd Forest scow'r,
Scar'd by the dreaded Flames, they'll turn away,
And hideous howl when baulk'd of whist for Prey.
Most skilful Planters in the Judgment rest,
That rotten Soil for INDICO's the best:
But let not that thy Hopes of Crops impair,
Some stiffer Soils great Droughts may better bear.
I've seen a Crop of Weed, like Thicket grown,
From stubborn Clay, on some Plantations mown.
Such Lands with double Exercise prepare,
And double Harvest shall reward thy Care.
Laborious Toil!—But all is Toil below,
Since Heav'n pronounc'd to mortal Man this Woe.
Immediate Want, or Dread of Future, can
With pow'rful Influence sway the Mind of Man.
Hence urging Poverty is justly stild
Mother of Arts, Invention's call'd her Child.
All hail, great Source of Industry! of Yore
A Goddess deem'd, when fam'd *Fabricius* bore
The Sway in *Rome,* and yet content to share
But one small Field, to plant his rural Fare.
Here from a State's tempestuous Troubles free,
Amidst the Sweets of honest Poverty,
In Freedom, Privacy, and calm Content,
He reap'd those Bounties Providence has sent:
She first inspir'd the *Mantuan* Bard, who sung
The Care of Flocks, and of their tender Young;
Who taught the lab'ring Hind to plough and sow,
The various Seasons of the Year to know,
To prune his Vines, to plant, to graft his Trees,
And reap the Labour of sagacious Bees.
Nor Rage of Seas, nor distant Worlds affright,
Nor native Soil, or Nature's Ties, our Flight

From them retard; if she her dire Commands
Impose on Man: She calls unnumber'd Bands
Of valiant Youth to War, she fires the Cold,
Spurs on the Drone, and makes the Coward bold.
All-conquering *Rome* to thee first owes her Birth,
How universal is thy Pow'r on Earth!
She peopled this new World, she still explores
Angola's Coast, and savage *Gambia's* Shores,
In Search of Slaves, a Race in Numbers great,
Whose Constitutions, temper'd to the Heat
By situation of their native Soil,
Best bear the scorching Suns, and rustic Toil:

But joyful Spring returns, the Winter's past,
The trees bud forth nor dread the Northern Blast,
Break off Delays, and thus prepare the Plain,
Let Two Feet void 'twixt every Trench remain.
Tho' some, imprudently, their Room confine,
Allowing half that Space to every Line.
Give Room, one Stem as much shall yield,
And richer far the Weed: So shall thy Field
With greater Ease from noxious Herbs be freed,
And knotty Grass that choaks the tender Weed.
So shall the Root by larger Banks be fed,
Nor fear the Rays from piercing Phæbus shed.
Cautious of this, in Lines direct and true
(For Order's best, and pleases best the View)
Extend thy long-stretch'd Furrows o'er the Plain
Then invocating Heav'n for speedy Rain
Sprinkle the Seed, &c.

On Liberty-Tree

Honos erit huic quoque Arbori
Quereus Libertati Sacra.

As Druid Bards, in Times of old,
E'er Temples were enshrin'd with Gold,
Beneath the Umbrage of a Wood,
Perform'd their Homage to their God;
So let the Muse expatiate free,
Under thy Shade, delightful Tree!
Its humble Tribute while it pays
To LIBERTY in votive Lays.

Some on the *Laurel* fix their Love,
Some on the *Myrtle* do approve
While others on the *Olive's* Bough,
With lavish Song their Praise bestow;
But me, nor *Laurel* does delight,
Nor *Cytherea's Grove* invite,
Nor shall *Minerva's Tree* proclaim
As the LIVE-OAK so high a Fame.

No Region boasts so firm a Wood,
So fit to cut the Crystal Flood
And Trade's wide blessings to convey,
From Land to Land, from Sea to Sea.
No Soil e'er grew a Tree so fair,
Whose Beauty can with thine compare.
Unmatch'd thy awful Trunk appears,
The Product of an Hundred Years.
Thy graceful Head's bent gently down,
Which ever-verdant Branches crown.

"Philo Patriae" [pseudonym], "On Liberty-Tree," *South-Carolina Gazette*, Sept. 21, 1769. (See *South Carolina Historical and Genealogical Magazine*, XLI [1940], pp. 119–22.) Reprinted by permission of The South Carolina Historical Society.

Thro' thy twinn'd Foliage Zephyrs play,
And feather'd Warblers tune their Lay.

Here LIBERTY divinely bright,
Beneath thy Shade, enthron'd in Light,
Her beaming Glory does impart
Around, and gladdens ev'ry Heart.

Hail! O Heav'n-born Goddess hail!
Each Bosom warm, each Breast assail,
With Flame, like that which *Greece* inspir'd,
When with thy living Lyre fir'd:
Or, such, as late by thee imprest
Glow'd in a *Pym's* and *Hambden's* Breast,
Those fav'rite Sons, whose gen'rous Soul,
No Threat cou'd awe, no Bribe controul,
Who nobly brave, did dare arraign
A worthless Stuart's tyrant Reign.
Propitious still, thy Vot'ries aid,
Beneath this TREE, Celestial Maid!

Hither to Thee thy SONS repair,
On thee, repose each anxious Care;
Bravely resolv'd to live or die,
As thou shalt guide their Destiny.

No secret Schemes, no sly Intrigues,
No Measures dark, no private Leagues
(Such as in Courts are daily found)
Do e'er approach thy sacred Ground:
But hither in the Face of Day
Thy gentle SONS their Duty pay.

Hither resort the Friends of Man
His common Rights and Claims to scan;
United, firmly to maintain
Those RIGHTS, which God and Nature mean.
RIGHTS! which when truly understood,

Are Cause of universal Good.
Rights! which declare, "That all are free,
"In Person and in Property.
"That Pow'r supreme, when giv'n in Trust,
"Belongs but to the Wise and Just
"That Kings are Kings for this sole Cause,
"To be the Guardians of the Laws.
"That Subjects only should obey,
"Only submit to sov'reign Sway,
"When Sov'reigns make those Laws their Choice
"To which the People give their Voice.
"That in free States, 'tis ever meant
"No Laws should bind, without *Consent;*
"And that, when other Laws take Place,
"Not to *resist,* wou'd be Disgrace;
"Not to *resist,* wou'd treach'rous be,
"Treach'rous to Society."

These, these are Rights, most just and true
Which FREEDOM'S SONS proclaim their Due.
SONS! not unworthy of their Sires,
Whom ev'ry Spark of Glory fires;
Whom Violence shall ne'er controul,
Nor check the Vigour of their Soul:
Determin'd, to their latest Hour,
T' oppose and check despotic Power.
Sworn Foes to Tyrants lawless Sway,
They'll to Posterity convey
That gen'rous *Plan,* so dearly bought
For which their fam'd Forefathers fought:
That *Plan!* which formed in NASSAU'S Days,
Will ever gain a Briton's Praise.

Be these your Arts, be these your Laws,
Ye SONS, engaged in FREEDOM'S Cause;
With zealous Heart, undaunted Breast,
It's sacred Guardians stand confest.

Wide and more wide, may thy Domain,
O LIBERTY! its Power maintain,
Parent of Life! true Bond of Law!
From whence alone our Bliss we draw
Thou! who dids't once in antient *Rome,*
E'er fell Corruption caus'd its Doom,
Reign in a *Cato's* godlike Soul,
And *Brutus* in each Thought controul;
Here, here prolong thy wish'd for Stay,
To bless and cheer each passing Day,
Tho' with no pompous Piles erect,
Nor sculptur'd Stones, thy shrine is deckt;
Yet here, beneath thy fav'rite Oak,
Thy Aid will all thy SONS invoke.
Oh! if thou deign to bless this Land,
And guide it by thy gentle Hand,
Then shall AMERICA become
Rival, to once high-favour'd *Rome.*

PHILO PATRIAE

Sept 18, 1769

Eliza Lucas Pinckney (1723–93)

Famous as the woman who introduced indigo to the South Carolina economy, Eliza Lucas Pinckney also presented posterity with a spirited and intelligent account of life in eighteenth-century South Carolina by means of her letters and journals. Born on the West Indies island of Antigua in 1723, she was sixteen when her parents moved to Carolina, where her father owned estates. When Lieutenant Colonel Lucas returned to Antigua, Eliza took charge of the three Carolina plantations, experimenting with various plants, including indigo. In 1744 she married Charles Pinckney, who, during their fourteen-year marriage, served as speaker of the House of Commons Assembly, member of the Royal Council, Chief Justice of the Province, and colonial agent to the Crown. Two of her sons, General Charles Cotesworth Pinckney and General Thomas Pinckney, distinguished themselves as officers in the Revolutionary War, helping to shape the destiny of South Carolina and the nation.

From the *Journal and Letters*

Dear Madam

I flatter myself it will be a satisfaction to hear I like this part of the world as my lott has fallen here which I really do. I prefer England to it tis true but think Carolina greatly preferable to the West Indies and was my Papa here I should be very happy. We have a very good acquaintance from whom we have received much friendship and Civility. Charles Town the principal one in this province is a polite agreeable place the people live very Gentilie and very much in the English Taste. The Country is in General fertile and abounds with Venison and wild fowl; the Venison is much higher flavour'd than in England but tis seldom fatt. My papa and Mamas great indulgence to me leaves it to me to chuse our place of residence either in town or in Country but I think it more prudent as well as most agreeable to my Mama and self to be in the Country during my father's absence we are 17 mile by land and 6 by water from Charles Town where we have about 6 agreeable families around us with whom we live in great harmony I have a little library well furnishd for my papa has left me most of his books in wch I spend part of my time. My Musick and the Garden wch I am very fond of take up the rest of my time that is not imployd in business of wch my father has left me a pretty good share and indeed 'twas unavoidable as my Mama's bad state of health prevents her going through any fatigue. I have the business of 3 plantations to transact wch requires much writing and more business and fatigue of other sorts than you can imagine   but least you should imagine it too burthensome to a girl at my early time of life give me leave to assure you I think myself happy that I can be useful to so good a father. and by rising very early I find I can go through much business but least you should think I shall be quite moapd with this way of life I am to inform you there are two worthy Ladies in Crs Town Mrs Pinckney and Mrs Cleland who are partial enough to me to be always pleased to have me with them and insist upon my making their houses my home when in town and press me to relax a little much oftener than tis in my power to accept of their obliging intreaties but I sometimes am with one or the other for 3 weeks or a month at a time and then enjoy all the pleasures Crs Town affords but nothing gives me more than subscribing myself

Dr Madam

yr most affectionate and

Most obliged humble Servt

ELIZA LUCAS

To my good friend Mrs Boddicott

Memdm *March* 11th 1741

Wrote a long letter to my father about the Indigo and all the plantation affairs and that Mr H B—— had been very much deluded by his own fancys and imagined he was assistied by the divine spirrit to prophesey Chrs town and the country as farr as Pon Pon bridge should be destroyd by fire and sword to be executed by the negroes before the first day of next month   he came to town 60 mile twice besides sending twice to acquaint the Govr with it   people in genl were very uneasy tho' convinced he was no prophet but they dreaded the consiquence of such a thing being put in to the head of the slaves and the advantage they might take of us   from thence he went on (as it was natural to expect when he gave himself up intirely to his own whims) from one step to another till he came to working mirracles and lived for several days in the woods barefooted and alone and with his pen and ink to write down his prophecies till at length he went with a wand to devide the waters and predicted he should die that night but upon finding both fail, the water continued as it was and himself a living Instance of the falicy of his own predictions was convinced he was not guided by the infallible spirrit but that of delusion and sent a letter to the speaker upon it wch I now enclose you, shall send by Capt Gregory if it can be got ready in time for him the Turpintine & neats foot oil.

Dear Miss Bartlett

By yr enquiry after the Comett I find yr curiosity has not been strong enough to raise you out of your bed so much before your usual time as mine has been. but to answer your queries—The Comett had the appearance of a very large Starr with a tail to my sight about 5 or 6 foot long it's real magnitude must really be prodigious. the tail was much paler than the comett itself. not unlike the milky way—twas a fortnight ago that I saw it The light of the comett to my unphilosophical eyes seems to be natural and all it's own how much it may really borrow from the sun I am not astronomer enough to tell—

. . .

I assure you the sight of a comett is not the only pleasure you lose by lying late in the morning—but I am in doubt if you will like any more of a sermon on that matter—

Wappo April 16

Dr Miss Bartlett

. . .

I promised to tell you when the mocking bird began to sing the little warbler has done wonders the first time he opend his soft pipe this spring he inspired me with the spirit of rhyming and produced the 3 following lines while I was lacing my stays

> Sing on thou mimick of the feathred kind
> And let the rational a lesson learn from thee
> to mimick (not defects) but harmony

If you let any mortal besides yourself see this exquisite piece of poetry you shall never have a line more than this specimen and how great will be your loss you who have seen the above may judge as well as

yr m o St

E LUCAS

June ye 4th 1741

Hon'd Sir

. . .

The Cotton Guinea corn. and most of the Ginger planted there was cutt off by a frost. I wrote you in a former letter we had a good crop

of Indigo upon the ground. I make no doubt this will prove a very
valuable Commodity in time if we could have the seed early enough to
plant the end of March that the seed might be dry enough to gather
before our frost

. . .

My Dr Papa
    yr m obed and ever D D
        Eliza Lucas.

May 22d 1742

    I am now set down my dear Brother to obey your Commands and
give you a short description of the part of the World I now inhabit—
So Carolina then is an Extensive Country near the Sea. Most of the
settled part of it is upon a flatt. the Soil near Charles Town sandy but
further distant, clay and swamp lands. It abounds with fine navigable
rivers and great quanties of fine timber—The Country at a great distance that is to say about a hundred and fifty mile from Crs Town very
hilly The soil in general very fertile and there are few European or
American fruits or grain but what grow here the Country abounds
with wild fowl Venison and fish Beef Veal and Mutton are here in
much greater perfection than in the Islands tho' not equal to that of
England—Fruit extreamly good and in profusion, and the oranges ex-
ceed any I ever tasted in the West Indies or from Spain or Portugal.
The people in general hospitable and honest and the better sort add to
these a polite gentile behaviour. The poorer sort are the most indolent
people in the world, or they would never be wretched in so plentiful a
country as this. The winters here are fine and pleasant but 4 months
in the year are extreamly disagreeable excessive hott much thunder and
lightening and musketoes and sand flies in abundance Crs Town the
Metropolis, is a neat pretty place the inhabitants polite and live a very
gentile manner the streets and houses regularly built. the ladies and
gentlemen gay in their dress. upon the whole you will find as many
agreeable people of both sexes for the size of the place as almost any

where St Phillip's Church in Crs Town is a very Elegant one and much frequented. there are severl more places of publick Worship in the town and the generality of people of a religious turn of mind.

I began in haste and have observed no method or I should have told you before I came to Summer, that we have a most charming Spring in this Country especially for those who travel through the Country for the Scent of the young Myrtle and yellow Jessamine with which the woods abound is delightful. The staple commodity here is rice and the only thing they export to Europe. Beef, Pork and Lumber they send to the West Indies.

Pray Inform me how my good friend Mrs Boddicott my cousin Bartholomew and all my old acquaintance doe Mama and Polly joyn in love

with Dr Brother

your's affectely

E LUCAS

To George Lucas Esqr

Wappo. May 2d

Dear Miss Bartlett

I send by the bearer my compts to Mrs Pinckney and the last volume of Pamela, she is a good girl and as such I love her dearly but I must think her very defective and even blush for her while she allows herself that disgusting liberty of praising herself, or what is very like it, repeating all the fine speeches made to her by others when a person distinguished for modesty in every other respect should have chose rather to conceal them or at least let them come from some other hand especially as she might have considered those high compts might have proceeded from the partiallity of her friends or with a view to encourage her and make her aspire after those qualifications wch are ascribed to her whch I know experimently to be often the case but then you answer she was a young Country Girl had seen nothing of life and it was natural for her to be pleased with praise and she had not art enough to conceal it true before she was Mrs B—— it be excusable when only wrote to her father and mother but after she had the advantage of Mr B's conversation and others of sense and distinction I must be of a nother oppinion. but here arises a difficulty, we are to be made acquainted by the Authour of all particulars how then is it to be done. I think by Miss Darnford or some other lady very intimate with Mrs B. How you smile at my presumption for instructing one so farr above my own level as ye Authour of Pamela (whom I esteem much for the regard he pays to virtue and religion throughout his whole piece) but my dr Miss Bartlett contract your smile into a mortified look for I acquit the Authour, he designed to paint no more than a woman and he certainly designed it as a reflection upon the vanity of our sex that a character so compleat in every other instance should be so greatly defective in this, defective indeed for when she mentions that poor creature Mr H's applauses it puts me in mind of the observation in don Quixott how grateful is praise even from a madman.

I have run thus far before I was aware for I have nither capacity or inclination for chritisism tho' Pamela sets me the example by critisizing Mr Lock and has taken the liberty to disent from that admirable Author. one word more and I have done and that is I think the Author has kept up to nature (one of the greatest beauties in the whole ps) for had his Heroin no defect the character must be unnatural as it would be in me to forget my respects to your worthy Uncle and Aunt Pinckney and that I am

yrs &c.

E Lucas

Septr 8th 1742.

Wrote to Miss Mary Fayweather in Boston. The same time wrote my Father a full and long acct of 5 thousand Spainyards landing at St Symons. We were greatly alarmed in Carolina; 80 prisoners now in Crs Town, they had a large fleet, but were scattered by bad weather. Our little fleet from Carolina, commanded by Capt Hardy could not get to ye Genls assistance, the Enemy were sailed to St Marks. 'Tis said Capt. Hardy instead of cruising off St Augustine barr where it was probable he would find them returned with all the men to Crs Town, wch has greatly disgusted the Govr and Council as well as the rest of the Inhabitance. There is sent now 3 Men of Warr and 4 provincial vessels under the command of Capt. Frankland.

.

Nov 3rd 1759—

Dr Sir

As I wrote to you ye 19th of Septr 'tis not necessary to trouble you again so soon but I can't resist the temptation of writing to you by a man of warr wch is to sail immediately unless there are merchants enough that will be ready soon to sail under her Convoy and then she will make a long stay.

The papers will inform you of our publick transactions and that the Govr with a body of men set out on fryday ye 10th of Octr for the Cherokee nation in order to obtain satisfaction for the murders committed by them and make a good peace at the head of the army or take satisfaction by carrying the warr into their own country they have been very insolent and t'is high time they were chastised. be so good as to assure my dear boys we think ourselves very safe in Crs town or they may be frightened at the rumour of an Indian warr my blessings attend them they are continually in my thoughts and the constant subject of my prayers I can't give them a greater proof of my affection than suffering this painful separation.

Feby 17—1760

To Honble Mrs King Ocham Court Surrey
My dr Madam.

. . .

There is so little chance of letters by single ships getting safe I am obliged to trouble one friend to tell another I have wrote to them which is the case at present I must beg the favor of you when you see Mrs Onslow to make my best compts to her and inform her I wrote to her in Novr last by ye Brigantine Spy Capt Lyford to Bristol—Govr Lyttleton, with our army is safely returned from the Cherokee Expedition where they went to demand satisfaction for the murders committed on our people—the first army yt ever attempted to go into that wild Country. they had been very insolent and committed many outrages in our back settlements   nor ever expected White men would have resolution enough to march up their Mountains. Govr Lyttleton has acted with much spirit and conduct and gained much honour in the affair— and obtained from them what Indians never before granted   such of the murderers as they could then take and Hostages for the rest till they could be taken   if you have any curiosity to know more particulars, Mr Morley, to whom I inclose it can furnish you with the Carolina Gazett

March 15th 1760.

. . .

A great cloud seems at present to hang over this province   we are continually insulted by the Indians in our back settlements and a violent kind of small pox rages in Chrs Town that almost puts a stop to all business   sevl of those I have to transact business with are fled into the country   but by the Divine Grace I hope a month or two will change the prospect, we expect shortly troops from Gen'l Amherst wch I trust will be able to manage these savage enemies and ye small pox as it does not spread in ye Country must soon be over for want of subjects   I am now at Belmont to keep my people out of the way of ye violent distemper   for the poor blacks have died very fast even by inoculation   but ye people in Chrs Town were inoculation mad I think I may well call it and rushed into it with such precipitation yt I think it impossible they could have had either a proper preparation or attendance had there been 10 Doctrs in town to 1—the Doctrs could not help it the people would not be said nay. We lose with this fleet our good Govr Lyttleton   he goes home in the Trent man of warr before he goes to his Govt at Jamaica. My sincere thanks to Mr & Mrs Watson
    Poor John Motte who was inocculated in England is now very bad with ye small pox   it could never never have taken then to be sure.

April 23. 1760.   The small pox is, I thank God, much abated. those that now have it, have it favorably. indeed few have it now but by inocculation. Our Indian affairs are much in the same situation as 4 weeks ago when the Trent sailed.

To the Honble Mrs King at Ocham Court.

July 19th 1760.

Dr Madm

. . .

I hope the good people of England wont give all their superfluous money to French prisoners and to build foreign Churches, but reserve some for their poor fellow subjects in America for if they go on to make new conquests in America and neglect the protection of their old colonies they may have importations of distressed people from the Southernmost part of North America to exercise their charity upon. My most respectful Compts wait on Mr King, he will oblige me very much in employing me to get him some seeds, if there is any in particular that may escape me I hope he will be so good to mention it. Our talest trees are Oaks—wch we have of various sorts—Pines—& Magnolias wch in low moist land such as Ocham Court, grow to a very great height, and is a most beautiful tree. as well as the tall Bay wch grow to a prodigious height. Neither the Acorns or cones are got ripe enough to gather or I would send them in this ship but will certainly do so by the first good opportunity after they are ripe. Harriott joins in affectionate Compts and My most respectful compts wait on my Ld & Lady King and I am

Dr Madm

With great gratitude

yr most obliged and

Most obedt Servt

ELIZA PINCKNEY.

To the honable Mrs King.

April 13. 1761.

Dr Madam

. . .

Our hopes and expectations are a good deal raised by the great fleet we are told is bound for America from England this spring we flatter ourselves they will take the Missisippi in their way wch if they succeed in must put an end to all our Indian warrs as they could never molest us if ye French from thence did not supply them with arms and ammunition Our army has marched for ye Cherokee nation they consist of regular troops and provincials 'tis a disagreable service but they have this to comfort them whether they are successful or other ways they may be pretty sure of gathering laurels from the bounty of the English news writers for after the incomiums upon ye last Cherokee expedition there surely can nothing be done there that don't merit praise If the 50 Mohocks arrive safe that we expect from Genl Amherst I hope we shall be able to quel those barbarians for the Mohocks are very fine men, five of them are now here and they are looked upon by the rest of the Indians with both dread and respect for they think them the greatest warriors in the world. Many thanks to good Mr King for my beer which is extreamly good though it had a long voyage and went first to Lisbon. My most respectful compliments wait on my Lady and Lord King and the young Ladies. Harriott is out of town with Lady Mary Drayton and don't know when the fleet sails or would do herself the honour to write to Miss Wilhelmina by it

     I am with great gratitude & affection

Dr Madam

Your most obliged & most obedt Servant

E Pinckney

Feby 27. 1762

To Honble Mrs King Ocham Court Surrey

. . .

When my dear Madam shall we have peace till then I have very little prospect of seeing my children and friends in England and a Spanish Warr we are told, is unavoidable. We are pretty quiet here just now but tis much to be feared 'twill continue no longer than the winter—we never were so taxed in our lives but what are our Taxes to your's—however we are a young Colony and our Sea does not throw up sands of gold as surely the British does—to enable you to bear such prodigious Expenses.

Henry Laurens (1724–92)

Born in Charleston, March 6, 1724, Henry Laurens was a leading colonial figure in the South and in the nation. Owner of the city's largest export business and plantations in South Carolina and Georgia, he served in the South Carolina Provincial House of Commons from 1757 until 1776. Traveling extensively in England and on the Continent from 1771 to 1774, he met many of the illustrious men of the time. He was elected as a delegate to the Continental Congress and served as its president from 1777 to 1778. Sent as Minister to Holland in 1779, en route he was captured by the British, who imprisoned him in the Tower of London until 1781. However, Laurens shortly reversed his situation, serving as unofficial minister to England during the period 1782–83. Returning home, he served as a member of the Continental Congress during 1787, dying in Charleston on December 8, 1792.

A
Narrative of the Capture of Henry Laurens,
OF HIS
CONFINEMENT IN THE TOWER OF LONDON, &C.
1780, 1781, 1782

I was commissioned by Congress to proceed to Holland, and endeavor to borrow money, anywhere in Europe, on account of the United States of America.

Before my embarkation, I applied to a member of the committee for foreign affairs, for a copy of a sketch of a treaty, projected by Mynheer Vanberkel, of Amsterdam, and Mr. William Lee, in the service of Congress, as a foundation for what might be a proper treaty, between the United Provinces and the United States, when the independence of the latter should be established. The gentleman replied: "You may take the original, it has never been read in Congress, and is a paper of no authority." He gave me the original; I threw it into a trunk of papers, chiefly waste, intending to garble the whole at sea, and preserve the few which I should think worth saving. This unauthentic paper—the project-eventual of two gentlemen, in their private capacities,—was made by Great Britain the foundation of a war with the United Provinces.

There being none of the frigates of the United States in port, I embarked at Philadelphia, the 13th August, 1780, on board the brigantine Mercury, a packet belonging to Congress, commanded by Capt. William Pickles; a vessel with good accommodations, and esteemed an excellent sea boat, and as fast a sailer as any in America; the sloop-of-war Saratoga, of 16 guns, commanded by Capt. Young, being ordered to convoy the Mercury to the banks of Newfoundland; and, moreover, I had orders from the Marine office to Capt. Nicholson, of the Deane frigate, of —— guns, and to Capt. Nicholson, of the —— frigate, of —— guns, who were every moment expected to arrive from a cruize, to join the sloop-of-war, and to convoy the Mercury as above mentioned. These two frigates we met within the capes of Delaware. I sent the order to the first in command, and required his attention. In return, he informed me both ships were in want of fresh water; that they would run up the bay, take in water, and come down again immediately. The

Mercury anchored in Penni port, where we waited four or five days for the frigates; but having no account of them, nor, indeed, did I much expect them, for at that time, little regard was paid to orders, inconsistent with the captain's own convenience. The wind being favorable, and the equinox advancing, I ordered the sloop-of-war and the Mercury to prepare for sailing. We proceeded and went to sea the same day. The sloop continued with the Mercury to the sixth day; when finding that the latter far outsailed the former, and that we were obliged to shorten sail every night, in order to keep with the convoy, by which much time was lost; and considering the sloop as a very slender defence, I recommended to Capt. Young to make a short cruise and return to the Delaware.

On the 3d September, at the first dawn of day, a sail in sight was announced, far to leeward. Capt. Pickles put the Mercury close upon a wind; and had he continued her so, the strange sail would not have come up with us; but he altered his opinion, and put her before the wind,—her worst sailing, especially as she was badly ballasted with sand. The vessel in sight altered her course also; and about nine o'clock, began to fire her bow guns. At eleven o'clock, her shot went over the Mercury, and two between her masts. Capt. Pickles then hauled down the American flag. The pursuer came up, and proved to be the Vestal, British frigate, of 28 guns, commanded by Capt. George Keppel. Such papers as were thought to be of importance, on board the Mercury, were thrown overboard or burned; but the trunk of useless papers above mentioned, remained. My Secretary, Major Moses Young, asked me what he should do with them. I replied, "they may remain where they are; they are of no consequence." But recollecting there were private letters among them, and being urged, I consented they should also be thrown overboard. This was done in some confusion; the papers were put into a long bag, and 20 or 25 lbs. weight of shot upon them. The air in the long bag buoyed up just the mouth of it. The people on board the frigate instantly perceived and hooked it up. These were Mr. Laurens' papers, so much talked of throughout Europe, for arranging of which the British Ministry gave Mr. Galloway, according to report, £500 sterling, and were at a farther expense to bind in rough calf, gild and letter them in 18 folio volumes, and afterwards returned the whole to Mr. Laurens again.

Capt. Keppel had not thought them of such value. After great labor, in drying and perusing, he said to me; "Mr. Laurens, you must certainly have destroyed your mail. I find nothing of any importance among these papers." I acknowledged the destruction of papers, which I thought ought not to appear, and then related every circumstance of the bag which he had taken.

About one o'clock, Capt. Keppel sent an officer in his barge to conduct me to the Vestal. He received me very cordially, on the quarter-deck; conducted me into his cabin, where he paid me this compliment: "I am glad to see you, Mr. Laurens, in my cabin. At the same time as a gentleman, I am sorry for your misfortune." I offered Capt. Keppel my sword and my purse, containing about fifty guineas' value in gold; he refused both. "Put up your money, sir, I never plunder." I could be lavish in praises of Capt. Keppel, for his polite and kind conduct towards me, in all respects.

Among other questions, Capt. Keppel asked why I had exposed myself in so small a vessel unarmed. I informed him of the convoy I had, and that of which I had been disappointed. He replied, "It is fortunate for me the Nicholsons did not obey their orders; if they had," said he, "I should have lost the Vestal. I have only 108 men on board, and not above twenty of them seamen. They might have taken the Fairy, too, she is just at hand."

Soon after the Mercury's colors had been struck, I observed my Secretary, Mr. Young, appeared in a gloomy countenance. I encouraged him to keep up his spirits. "I feel a satisfaction," said I, "in being captured by a British ship-of-war. I shall now be sent to England, where I shall be of more real service to my country than I could possibly be in any other part of Europe."

The 14th or 15th September, the Vestal and Fairy, which had joined her, entered the Basin of St. Johns, Newfoundland. Soon after we had anchored, Admiral Edwards sent his compliments, desiring I would dine with him that and every day while I should remain in the land.

The Admiral received me politely at dinner; seated me at his right hand; after dinner he toasted the King; I joined. Immediately after he asked a toast from me. I gave "General Washington," which was repeated by the whole company, and created a little mirth at the lower end of the table. The Admiral, in course of conversation, observed I had been pretty active among my countrymen. I replied that I had once been a good British subject, but after Great Britain had refused to hear our petitions, and had thrown us out of her protection, I had endeavored to do my duty. The Americans, I added, had not set up an independence. Great Britain had made them independent, by throwing them out of her protection, and committing hostilities upon them by sea and land. Nothing remained for Congress but to declare to the world that the United Colonies were independent. The Admiral said he believed Great Britain would be glad to have peace with the Colonies upon any terms, except adhering to the treaty of alliance with France. I answered that was a *sine qua non;* it was impossible the United States could violate that treaty. They cannot lay down their arms but in conjunction with France. The Admiral regretted.

While I was in Newfoundland, I never heard the term rebel; and as occasions required, I spoke as freely of the United States, of Congress, and of independence, as ever I had done in Philadelphia. Nine Captains of British men-of-war, honored me by a visit on board the Vestal; every one spoke favorably of America, but lamented her connection with France. One of these gentlemen advised me, upon my arrival in London, to take apartments at the New Hotel; "Then," said he, "we shall know where to find you." I smiled and asked, "If there was not a hotel in London, called Newgate." "Newgate!" exclaimed two or three; "they dare not send you there." "Well, gentlemen, wait a few weeks and you will hear of the hotel where I shall be lodged."

Capt. Lloyd, the Admiral's Captain, made me a present of a sensible pamphlet, written and published by himself, under the signature of "Valens," in which the war carried on by Great Britain against America is condemned, and Lord Mansfield treated with just severity for the part he had acted in the British House of Lords.

Capt. Keppel left the Vestal under the command of his friend, the Honorable Capt. Barclay, of the Fairy, and entered this vessel himself, taking me on board with him; and about the 18th September, sailed for England. We had not lost sight of the Island of Newfoundland, when a cry of fire was made on board the Fairy, said to be near the powder room door, and that unguarded in the usual way. Officers and men, except Capt. Keppel, at first were in confusion; but his presence of mind, example and activity calmed them, and the fire, though very alarming, was soon suppressed. The Fairy made a rough, wet and short passage.

In ten days we landed at Dartmouth. I was put under the charge of Lieut. Norris, who in a post chaise with four horses, drove rapidly towards London. Mr. Norris having friends in and near Exeter, stopped in that city two days and three nights. He was absent from me almost the whole time. In that interval, a gentleman whom I had never seen nor heard of before, called upon, and in strong terms invited me to make my escape. Said, nothing was more easy; I might go to his house, which was very private and retired, and there stay till the bustle of enquiry and pursuit should be over, and then I might go very safely out of the kingdom to Holland or Flanders. I thanked the friendly gentleman, but absolutely declined the proposition. He asked, "If I was under any parol promise to Mr. Norris?"—"No, sir; but the confidence that young gentleman has reposed in me, I think, implies a parol." "Why, sir, kings and princes in your circumstances have made escapes." "True, sir, but I feel no inclination or desire to escape." The gentleman was amazed, I thought I saw a prospect before me, and was perfectly tranquil.

Lieut. Norris appeared, and proceeded to London. We arrived at the admiralty office late in the evening of the 5th October. Some hours were taken up to collect two or three of the ministers, and a justice of the peace. About 11 o'clock at night, I was sent under a strong guard, up three pair of stairs, in Scotland-Yard, into a very small chamber. Two king's messengers were placed for the whole night at one door, and a subaltern's guard of soldiers at the other. As I was, and had been for some days, so ill as to be incapable of getting into or out of a carriage, or up or down stairs, without help, I looked upon all this parade to be calculated for intimidation. My spirits were good, and I smiled inwardly.

The next morning, 6th October, from Scotland-Yard I was conducted again, under guard, to the secretary's office, White Hall, where were present, Lord Hillsborough, Lord Stormont, Lord George Germain, Mr. Chamberlain, solicitor of the treasury, Mr. Knox, under secretary, Mr. Justice Addington, and others.

I was first asked, by Lord Stormont, "If my name was Henry Laurens." "Certainly, my Lord, that is my name." Capt. Keppel was asked, "If that was Mr. Laurens?" He answered in the affirmative.

His Lordship then said: "Mr. Laurens, we have a paper here," holding the paper up, "purporting to be a commission from Congress to you, to borrow money in Europe for the use of Congress. It is signed Samuel Huntingdon, President, and attested by Charles Thomson, Secretary. We have already proved the handwriting of Charles Thomson." I replied: "My Lords, your Lordships are in possession of the paper, and will make such use of it as your Lordships shall judge proper." I had not destroyed this paper, as it would serve to establish the rank and character in which I was employed by the United States.

Another question was asked me, which I did not rightly understand. I replied: "My Lords, I am determined to answer no questions but with the strictest truth; wherefore, I trust, your Lordships will ask me no questions which might ensnare me, and which I cannot with safety and propriety answer."

No farther questions were demanded. I was told by Lord Stormont, I was to be committed to the Tower of London on "suspicion of high treason." I asked, "If I had not a right to a copy of the commitment?" Lord Stormont after a pause, said: "He hesitated on the word right," and the copy was not granted.

Mr. Chamberlain then very kindly said to me: "Mr. Laurens, you are to be sent to the Tower of London, not to a prison; you must have no idea of a prison." I bowed thanks to the gentlemen, and thought of the new hotel, which had been recommended by my friends in Newfoundland.

A commitment was made out by Mr. Justice Addington, and a warrant by their Lordships to the Lieutenant of the Tower, to receive and confine me.

From White Hall, I was conducted in a close hackney coach, under the charge of Col. Williamson, a polite, genteel officer, and two of the

illest-looking fellows I had ever seen. The coach was ordered to proceed by the most private ways to the Tower. It had been rumored that
a rescue would be attempted. At the Tower the Colonel delivered me
to Maj. Gore, the residing Governor, who, as I was afterwards well informed, had previously concerted a plan for mortifying me. He ordered rooms for me in the most conspicuous part of the Tower, (the
parade). The people of the house, particularly the mistress, entreated
the Governor not to burthen them with a prisoner. He replied, "It is
necessary. I am determined to expose him." This, was, however, a
lucky determination for me. The people were respectful and kindly
attentive to me, from the beginning of my confinement to the end;
and I contrived after being told of the Governor's humane declaration,
so to garnish my windows by honeysuckles, and a grape vine running
under them, as to conceal myself entirely from the sight of starers, and
at the same time to have myself a full view of them.

Governor Gore conducted me to my apartments at a warder's house.
As I was entering the house, I heard some of the people say: "Poor
old gentleman, bowed down with infirmities. He is come to lay his
bones here." My reflection was, "I shall not leave a bone with you."
I was very sick, but my spirits were good, and my mind forboding
good, from the event of being a prisoner in London.

Their Lordships' orders were, "To confine me a close prisoner; to
be locked up every night; to be in the custody of two wardens, who
were not to suffer me to be out of their sight *one moment* day or night;
to allow me no liberty of speaking to any person, nor to permit any
person to speak to me; to deprive me of the use of pen and ink; to
suffer no letter to be brought to me, nor any to go from me," &c. As
an apology, I presume, for their first rigor, the warders gave me their
orders to peruse. A sentinel, with fixed bayonet, was placed at the door
of the barrack, in which I was confined, part of whose duty it was to
keep off all strangers from approaching within thirty feet of the door.
And now I found myself a close prisoner, indeed; shut up in two small
rooms, which together made about twenty feet square; a warder my
constant companion; and a fixed bayonet under my window; not a
friend to converse with, and no prospect of a correspondence.

Next morning, 7th October, Gov. Gore came into my room, with a workman, and fixed iron bars to my windows; altogether unnecessary. The various guards were sufficient to secure my person. It was done, as I was informed, either to shake my mind or to mortify me. It had neither effect. I only thought of Mr. Chamberlain's consolation.

I asked Mr. Gore, "What provision was to be made for my support?" He replied, "He had no directions." I said, "I can very well provide for myself, but I must be allowed means for obtaining money." He gave no answer. In a word, I discovered I was to pay rent for my little rooms, find my own meat and drink, bedding, coals, candles, &c. This drew from me an observation to the gentleman jailer, (the officer who locks up a prisoner every night,) who would immediately report it to the Governor: "Whenever I caught a bird in America I found a cage and victuals for it."

What surprised me most was, although the Secretaries of State had seen the ill state of my health, and must also have heard of my continuing ill by reports, daily made to them, they never ordered or caused to be provided for me, any medical assistance. The people around me thought, for a considerable time, my life in imminent danger. I was of a different opinion.

When the Governor had retired from his iron bars, neither my servant nor baggage being yet arrived, I asked the warder, "If he could lend me a book for amusement." He gravely asked: "Will your honor be pleased to have 'Drilincourt upon death?' " I quickly turned to his wife, who was passing from making up my bed: "Pray, Madam, can you recommend an honest goldsmith, who will put a new head to my cane; you see this old head is much worn?" "Yes, sir, I can." The people understood me, and nothing more was said of 'Drilincourt.'

The 14th October, Mr. William Manning, and my son Henry, through the intercession of the Bishop of Worcester, obtained from the Secretaries of State a warrant to visit me. They were restricted to half an hour, and to converse only in presence and hearing of two extra officers, besides the warder.

The 17th I was informed an unsealed letter had been sent for me by Capt. Lloyd, Admiral Edward's Captain. The Governor was pleased to arrest, and never deliver it to me.

Joseph Brown Ladd (1764–86)

A romantic and tragic figure in South Carolina history, Joseph Brown Ladd was born in Newport, Rhode Island, July 7, 1764, and began writing ballads and satires at the age of fourteen, though he was licensed to practice medicine in 1783. On the recommendation of General Nathanael Greene, Ladd moved to Charleston in the spring of 1784, quickly establishing himself both as a physician and a man of letters, and, in 1786, publishing *The Poems of Arouet*. On October 20, 1786, he fought a duel with Ralph Isaacs, the culmination of an exchange of insults printed in the Charleston *Morning Post*. Mortally wounded, Ladd refused to shoot his opponent. He lingered for a few days, dying on November 2, 1786, at a time when he was apparently becoming one of the most popular poets in America. Professor Jay B. Hubbell says, "His poems are easy, facile, and timely. They are a good index to what American readers liked in the closing years of the eighteenth century" (*The South in American Literature, 1607–1900*, p. 164).

Ode to Retirement

Hail, sweet retirement! hail!
  Best state of man below;
To smooth the tide of passions frail,
  And bear the soul away from scenery of wo.
When retired from busy noise,
Vexing cares, and troubled joys,
To a mild, serener air,
In the country, we repair;
Calm enjoy the rural scene,
Sportive o'er the meadows green,
When the sun's enlivening ray,
Speaks the genial month of May;
Lo! his amorous, wanton beams,
Dance on yonder crystal streams;
In soft dalliance pass the hours,
Kissing dew-drops from the flowers;
While soft music through the grove,
Sweetly tunes the soul to love;
And the hills, harmonious round,
Echo with responsive sound.
There the *turtle dove* alone,
Makes his soft melodious moan;
While from yonder bough 'tis heard,
Sweetly chirps the *yellow bird:*
There the *linnet's* downy throat,
Warbles the responsive note;
And to all the neighboring groves,
Robin redbreast tells his loves.

  There, AMANDA, we might walk,
And of soft endearments talk;
Or, anon, we'd listen, love,
To the gently cooing dove.
In some sweet embowering shade,
Some fair seat by nature made,
I my love would gently place,

On the tender-woven grass;
Seated by thy lovely side,
Oh! how great would be my pride;
While my soul should fix on thine—
Oh! the joy to call thee mine.

For why should doves have more delight,
Than we, my sweet AMANDA, might?
And why should larks and linnets be
More happy, lovely maid, than we?

There the pride of genius blooms,
There sweet contemplation comes;
There is science, heavenly fair;
Sweet philosophy is there.
With each author valued most,
Ancient glory, modern boast:
There the mind may revel o'er
Doughty deeds of days of yore;
How the mighty warriors stood—
How the field was dyed in blood—
How the shores were heaped with dead—
And the rivers streamed with red—
While the heroes' souls on flame,
Urged them on to deathless fame:
Or we view a different age,
Pictured in the historic page;
Kings descending from a throne—
Tyrants making kingdoms groan—
With each care on state allied,
With all the scenery of pride:
Or perhaps we'll study o'er
Books of philosophic lore;
Read what Socrates has thought,
And how god-like Plato wrote;
View the earth with Bacon's eyes,
Or with Newton read the skies;
See each planetary ball,

One great sun attracting all;
All by gravitation held,
Self-attracted, self-repelled:
We shall cheat away old time,
Passing moments so sublime.
   Hail, sweet retirement! hail!
     Best state of man below;
  To smooth the tide of passions frail,
    And bear the soul away from scenery of wo.

What Is Happiness?

'Tis an empty, fleeting shade,
By imagination made;
'Tis a bubble, straw, or worse;
'Tis a baby's hobby horse;
'Tis a little living, clear;
'Tis ten thousand pounds a year;
'Tis a title; 'tis a name;
'Tis a puff of empty fame,
Fickle as the breezes blow;
'Tis a lady's YES or NO:
And when the description's crowned,
'Tis just *no where* to be found.

John Drayton (1767–1822)

John Drayton was born in Charleston, June 22, 1767. After attending the College of New Jersey (Princeton), he was admitted to the bar and practiced law in South Carolina from 1788 until 1794. He had a distinguished record of public service, as a member of the South Carolina House of Representatives (1792–98), as lieutenant governor (1798–1800), and as Governor of South Carolina (1800–04 and 1808–10), as a member of the South Carolina Senate (1812–22), and as United States District Judge for South Carolina from 1812 until his death in Charleston on November 27, 1822. It was on his recommendation that South Carolina College was established. Drayton was the author of *Letters Written during a Tour Through the Northern and Eastern States of America* (1794) and *A View of South Carolina* (1802). He was also editor of his father's papers, *Memoirs of the American Revolution from its Commencement to Year 1776, Inclusive* (2 volumes, 1822).

From *Memoirs of the Revolution in South Carolina*

On the morning of Friday the 28th day of June, Col. Moultrie rode to the north-eastern point of Sullivan's Island, to visit the troops stationed there, under Col. Thomson. When he arrived, he saw the enemy's boats in motion at the back of Long-Island; as if, they intended a descent upon that advanced post: and at the same time, he perceived the men of war, loose their top-sails. This, having been the signal of their getting under way the day before, he hurried back to the fort; and on his arrival, immediately ordered the long roll to beat, and the officers and men to their posts. The guns were scarcely manned, and powder issued from the magazine, when the British squadron was perceived with their courses drawn up, bearing down upon Fort Sullivan; and at the same time, between ten and eleven o'clock, the Thunder bomb-ship, covered by the Friendship armed vessel of twenty-six guns, anchored at the distance of a mile and a half, bringing the salient angle of the eastern bastion to near north by west, and began to throw shells upon the fort; one of which, fell upon the magazine—but, did no considerable damage. The flood tide being strong, and the wind fair from the southward and west, the Active, 28 guns—the Bristol, 50 guns—the Experiment, 50 guns—and Solebay, 28 guns, soon came within striking distance of the fort: when, a fire of cannon commenced upon them from the south-western bastion. But the Active, which was the leading ship, continued her course, until she arrived within four hundred yards of the fort: when, she anchored with springs on her cable, and poured in her broadside of cannon-balls. The Bristol, Experiment, and Solebay, ranging up in the rear of the Active, anchored in like manner, leaving intervals between each other; and the Syren and Acteon of 28 guns, and Sphinx, of 20 guns, formed a line parallel with them, opposite the intervals. The example of the Active was followed by the ships, as they took their stations; and a heavy and incessant cannonade issued from their batteries: while from the fort a return was made, slow, but sure. When this severe trial of metal and skill, was going on between the veteran ships of the British navy, and the newly raised troops of an infant republic, from a low fort of palmetto logs; the Thunder, bomb-ship, was throwing thirteen inch shells in quick succession—several of which, fell into the fort: they were however, immediately buried in the loose sand, so that very few of them burst upon the garrison.

No prospect, of silencing the fort, appearing; about 12 o'clock, the Acteon, Sphinx and Syren, were ordered to pass the fort, and take a position in Rebellion Road towards the cove of Sullivan's Island; for the purpose of enfilading the front platforms of the south-east curtain and its two bastions—whose fire, was dreadfully destructive to the British ships and crews. This manœuvre, was what General Lee had foreseen; but, Almighty Providence confounded the plan; and, frustrated the attempt. For, while the detached frigates, were standing well over towards the Lower Middle-Ground opposite the fort, so as to make a tack and pass clear of the front line of ships, then closely engaged; they got entangled on the shoal—when the Sphinx and Acteon ran foul of each other. The Syren got off, as did the Sphinx, with the loss of her bowsprit: but the Acteon, was left immoveably fixed on the sand. The Sphinx and Syren, now retrograded; and bearing away under cover of the ships engaged, they retired awhile, to prepare themselves for farther action. About this time of the day, the Thunder bomb-ship, having thrown fifty or sixty shells, with little effect, ceased firing. This, was occasioned by her having anchored at too great a distance; and the Engineer, (Col. James of the Royal regiment of artillery) was therefore compelled to overcharge the mortars: whose recoil shattered the beds, and so damaged the ship, as to render her unfit for farther service. The combat, was now only kept up, by the four ships first engaged: and in the afternoon, the enemy's fire was increased, by a reinforcement of the Syren and Friendship. During this severe cannonade, barges passed from one ship to the other, and to and from the transports; for the purpose of removing the wounded, and obtaining fresh men, as occasion required; and the firing from the ships continued animated, and incessant, until near seven o'clock in the evening. From this time, it slackened with the setting sun; and they only returned the fire from the fort, which was opened upon them now and then; but, in doing so, they returned it twenty fold. At half past nine, the firing on both sides ceased; and at 11 o'clock, the ships slipped their cables, without any noise or piping; and returned with the last of the ebb tide to their station near Five-Fathom-Hole.*

The engagement had scarcely begun, when General Clinton made dispositions for attacking the north-east end of Sullivan's Island, defended by Colonel Thomson. For this purpose, the armed schooner Lady William and a sloop, which had been lying in the Creek between Long-Island and the main, came nearer that advanced post for the purpose of covering the landing of the British troops—a number of shells were thrown from the mortar battery upon the entrenchments on Sullivan's Island—and the soldiers and some light field-pieces, were embarked in boats; but Thomson returned their fire from his 18-pounder; which evincing, their passage across the breach would be disputed with heavy cannon, discouraged the enemy from making the attempt; and they remained quiet spectators of the action during the rest of the day. About five o'clock in the afternoon, Col. Thomson was reinforced by Col. Muhlenburg, with seven hundred continentals from Haddrell's Point; which, rendered his situation more safe, against any attempts from Long-Island; and effectually put to rest, any desire, which General Clinton might still have entertained, for visiting Colonel Thomson's quarters.

At the commencement of the action, Colonel Moultrie, was only provided with 4,600 pounds weight of powder; equal to about twenty-six rounds for the cannon, and twenty rounds of musketry each man. Soon after the action began, a farther supply of powder of 500 pounds weight, was obtained from Charlestown; and 300 pounds weight from the South-Carolina schooner Defence commanded by Captain Tufts, then lying in the cove at the rear of the fort. So, that the whole amount of powder with which Colonel Moultrie was supplied, for maintaining that important fortress, was only 5,400 pounds weight.

---

*Through the enterprize of our citizens, some of their anchors have been recovered; and on this 28th June 1821, a public notice was fixed up at the Exchange in Charleston, that one of these anchors, weighing upward of 4,400 pounds weight, (and which probably belonged to one of the 50 gun ships,) was to be seen on a wharf in the city.

While the British men of war, were pouring their broadsides, in one continued storm of balls and grape shot; the cannon from the fort were slowly discharged, after being pointed with precision by the officers commanding: hence, almost every shot from the fort, took effect; which in a great degree made up for the scarcity of powder. On this occasion, the fort expended, during the action, about 4,766 pounds weight of powder: while the Bristol alone, carrying the Commodore's flag, expended 150 barrels of powder; equal to about 15,000 pounds weight.* The Experiment carried 12-pounders, on both decks: therefore, calculating at one third the weight of powder to the ball, she probably expended in the same time, about 70 barrels of powder. On this calculation, allowing 36 barrels to the Active and Solebay, constantly engaged, 20 to the Syren and Friendship, partially engaged, and 10 to the Acteon—an amount of 340 barrels of powder is produced, (besides, what the Thunder bomb-ship used;)—equal to about 34,000 pounds weight of powder; and at three for one, to 102,000 pounds weight of shot. Many, of these balls; were buried in the spungy logs of the fort; many, passed over the island, into the marsh, towards the main; and it was computed not less than 12,000 shot, were discharged against the fort; of which, 1,200 shot of different calibers, and some thirteen inch shells, were collected in the fort and its vicinity, a few days after the action; which more than reimbursed the number of shot, which had been discharged from the fort.†

Soon after the action commenced, the three 12-pounders which were in the cavalier, to the left of the fort, were abandoned; the works not being sufficiently high, to protect the men who manned them. And some time after, the flag-staff of the fort, was shot away; and fell with the flag outside of the fort. Serjeant Jasper of the grenadiers of the second regiment, no sooner perceived this misfortune, than he leaped down from one of the embrasures, and disengaging the flag from the staff, he returned with it through a heavy fire from the shipping; and fixing it on a spunge-staff, he planted it once more on the summit of

---

*She carried 32-pounders, on her main deck.
†See the London Remembrancer for 1776, Part III, page 71.

the merlon, amidst a shower of balls. Then giving three cheers, he re-tired to his gun; where, he fought throughout the engagement. The loss of this flag, was observed at the different posts, and at Charlestown; when some thought the fort had surrendered: but with its restoration, the drooping spirits of the people were restored—and, while they gloried in the gallantry of the garrison of Fort Sullivan; they offered up their prayers to heaven, for victory.

The fire from the fort, was principally directed at the Bristol and Experiment ships, carrying each, fifty guns. The first, was the flag-ship, on board of which Sir Peter Parker was stationed: and Lord William Campbell, the late Governor of the Province, having volunteered his services on board, he was complimented by Sir Peter, with a command on her lower deck. Twice was Sir Peter's quarter-deck cleared of every man but himself, by the deadly fire from the fort; and, even Sir Peter himself, received two wounds: the gallant Commodore, however, re-mained at his post, encouraging his crew, and reinforcing his ship with men, from the other vessels, not so hotly engaged. At one time, the spring-rope of his ship was shot away; when the Bristol swang round by the wind, and rode with her stern to the fort. All the fort guns, were therefore pointed at her; and for some time, she was raked fore and aft—the word passing along the platforms of the fort, *"to mind the Commodore—mind, the two fifty gun ships."* The day, being very sultry with a burning sun; the wind was extremely light, and the water consequently smooth. Had it been otherwise, it is probable the Bristol could not have been kept from filling; as she was shot through in many places, betwixt wind and water; and was otherwise so dam-aged in her large knees and timbers, that the carpenters of the squad-ron, were called to her assistance, while the battle raged in all its fury. The Experiment, was also exceedingly damaged in her hull; several of her ports, being beaten in.

On the part of the fort, at one time, three or four of the enemy's broadsides struck the merlons, at the same moment; which gave them such a tremor—that it was apprehended, a few more, equally well de-livered, would have tumbled them down—and during the whole engagement, the south-western curtain of the fort was so enfiladed by the line of fire from the ships—and the cannon mounted there, were so often struck and indented by balls and grape-shot—that had the frigates taken their station at the cove as was intended, they could not have been opposed from the guns on this side; as the men on the platform would have been exposed to the raking fire of the shipping in front of the fort; which unless the frigates could have been beaten off by the batteries at Haddrell's Point, at long shot, would have made it a slaughter stage indeed, as General Lee had said.

While the battle was raging, Gen. Lee dispatched a letter to Col. Moultrie, by Major Byrd, one of his aids; ordering him if he should expend his ammunition, without beating off the enemy, or driving them on ground; to spike up his guns, and retreat with all the order possible: he however intimated to him, that he knew the Colonel would be careful, not to throw away his ammunition. Thus situated, Col. Moultrie was placed in a most delicate situation. If he exhausted his ammunition, he was to desert the fort; and thereby subject Col. Thomson at the extreme end of the island, to be cut off, with the whole of his command. If he could retain a part of the ammunition, he was not required by the order to abandon the fort. He prudently pursued the latter mode of conduct; and by ordering the discharges of the cannon to be slackened to intervals of about ten minutes each gun; he was enabled so to protract the defence—as to save himself the dishonour, and his country the loss, which would have resulted had the fort been so hastily abandoned. The powder, however, getting much reduced, and a rumour spreading, that the British troops had effected a landing between Col. Thomson and the fort; Colonel Moultrie ordered the cannon to cease firing; or if they did, to fire extremely slow upon the shipping.† And hence, it was supposed by the British, that at this period, the fort was silenced.‡ This, was between the hours of three and

---

†At this time, the powder was almost expended; only a few cartridges being left for grape-shot, in case the enemy should attempt to land, from the shipping or from Long-Island.
‡At this time, Lieutenant Spencer of the artillery, came on the platform, ready to spike the cannon when ordered; but Col. Moultrie ordered him to carry off the spikes.

five, in the afternoon. However, a supply of powder being received; the firing from the fort was delivered at shorter intervals, through the remainder of the day. About five o'clock in the afternoon, when the supply of powder arrived, General Lee with his aids passed in a boat from Haddrell's Point to Fort Sullivan, through the British line of fire: and ascending the platform of the fort, he pointed two or three of the cannon, which were discharged at the enemy. He remained there, about a quarter of an hour; then saying to Col. Moultrie, "I see you are doing very well here, you have no occasion for me—I will go up to town again;" he left the fort in the care of those, who had so well defended it; and returned to Haddrell's Point through the same line of fire, in which he had proceeded.*

From every information, respecting the situation of the enemy, there is reason for believing, that had the fort been better supplied with powder, so that a cessation of firing for two hours, with trifling exceptions, had not taken place, the two fifty gun ships, would have been obliged to strike their colours, or they would have been sunk. As during a good part of the day, the tide was against their retreating; and if they had proceeded towards Fort Johnson or Charlestown, they would have had greater force and difficulties to contend with. And such was the slaughter on board of these two ships, before the fire of the fort slackened; that a remonstrance was made to Sir Peter Parker, that if the fire from the fort continued equally severe, these two ships and their crews, would be destroyed. It was then contemplated, to abandon them; and to tow off the frigates: but, by this time, the fort, through the want of ammunition, was in a manner placed *hors de combat;* by which, his Britannic Majesty's ships were saved, from total ruin.

This heavy and continued cannonade from the British ships of war, damaged the fort in a very small degree; as most of the shot passed over it towards the main land, cutting off the branches of trees in their way. Many shot however struck the fort, and penetrated the palmetto logs; but their spungy texture received them without any splinters be-

---

*See an extract of a letter from General Lee, dated Charlestown, July 2d, 1776, to the President of Congress: giving an account of this engagement—in the London Remembrancer for 1776, Part III, page 70. Also, as issued in General Orders, by General Washington at New-York—Part III, page 71.

ing detached; and hence, less injury was done to the garrison, than might otherwise have taken place. Ten men of the second regiment, one matross of the fourth regiment of artillery, and a mulatto boy, belonging to Lieutenant Dunbar were killed; and twenty-three of the second regiment including two officers, Lieutenants Henry Gray and Thomas Hall, and two matrosses of the fourth regiment of artillery, were wounded: the total number of killed being twelve, and the wounded twenty-five.* The eighteen-pounder next but one to the flag-staff, in the south-eastern bastion, had a large piece of its muzzle shot off: and the next eighteen-pounder westward of it, which was commanded by Captain Ashby, was at one time divested of half the men who manned it. For, as six men (three of a side) were in the act of hand-spiking the piece up to the embrazure, after its being loaded; a cannon-ball entered the embrazure, and cut down at once, all three of the men who were on one side. Their names were, Luke Flood, Richard Rodgers, and Isaac Edwards, belonging to Captain Ashby's company; and so deadly was the effect of the ball which struck them, that they fell down on the platform immediately, torn to pieces; and without saying a word, gasped away their lives. Not quite so sudden a death had the noble-minded Serjeant M'Daniel* of Captain Huger's company; for, although he had his stomach and bowels shot away by a cannon-ball, yet life and vigour remained in him long enough, to enable him to address his comrades in these words: *"Fight on my brave boys; don't let liberty expire with me to-day."* So noble a sentiment, passed with rapidity along the platforms; animating the officers and men with an increased desire of performing their duties; and of revenging the death of a man, so honorably transferred, in the service of his country!

In this action, the Bristol and Experiment were greatly damaged, in their hulls, spars, and rigging: and they were shot through by many of the 26-pound shot; it is said not less than seventy balls went through the Bristol. She had upwards of one hundred men killed and wounded,

---

*Five of these wounded, died soon after.
*In accounts given of this battle, he has heretofore been erroneously called M'Donald.

and the Experiment not much less: and each of their Captains lost an arm, and died in a few days after.‡ Twice, the quarter-deck of the Bristol, was cleared of every person, except Sir Peter; and he received two splinter wounds, one on his thigh, and the other on his knee. The Bristol had nine 26-pound shot in her mainmast; which obliged them to cut it away fifteen feet below the hounds—her mizen-mast was stricken by seven 26-pound shot, and was so shattered, as to render it necessary for its entire removal. The Experiment, had her mizen-gaff shot away; the other vessels sustained but little damage, as the fire from the fort was principally directed upon the Bristol and Experiment. The Solebay, had eight men killed, and four wounded. The Active, one lieutenant killed, and six men wounded. And Lord William Campbell, who during part of the action had commanded and fought some of the lower-deck 32-pounders of the Bristol, received a wound in his left side, which, it is said, ultimately caused his death.

‡Captain *Morris* of the Bristol, and Captain *Scott* of the Experiment.

David Ramsay (1749–1815)

David Ramsay proved to be South Carolina's most noted early historian, publishing the influential *History of the American Revolution* (1789), a *History of South Carolina* (1809), and a *History of the United States* (1816–17). Born in Lancaster County, Pennsylvania, on April 2, 1749, he graduated from Princeton in 1765, receiving his M.D. from the College of Pennsylvania in 1772. A member of the South Carolina legislature (1776–80, 1781–82, and 1784–90), he was a delegate to the Continental Congress (1782–85), and a member of the South Carolina Senate for three terms (1792, 1794, 1796). Ramsay died in Charleston, May 8, 1815.

Marion's Brigade

Marion and his brigade were so distinguished, and at the same time so detached in their operations, as to merit and require particular notice.

General Francis Marion was born at Winyaw, in 1733. His grandfather was a native of Languedoc, and one of the many Protestants who fled from France to Carolina to avoid persecution on the account of religion. He left thirteen children, the eldest of whom was the father of the general. Francis Marion, when only sixteen years of age, made choice of a seafaring life. On his first voyage to the West Indies he was shipwrecked. The crew, consisting of six persons, took to the open boat, without water or provisions, except a dog who jumped into the boat from the sinking vessel. They were six days in the boat before they made land, having nothing to eat in that time but the dog, whom they devoured raw. Two of the crew perished. Francis Marion, with three others, reached land. This disaster, and the entreaties of his mother, induced him to quit the sea. In Littleton's expedition against the Indians in 1759, he went as a volunteer in his brother's militia troop of horse. In Grant's expedition to the Indian country in 1761, he served as a lieutenant under Captain William Moultrie. On the formation of a regular army in 1775, to defend his native province against Great Britain, he was appointed a captain in the Second South Carolina regiment, and had gradually risen to the rank of colonel before Charlestown fell. Fortunately for his country, he had fractured his leg and retired from the garrison, which prevented his being made a prisoner of war. After the surrender, he retreated to North Carolina. On the approach of General Gates he advanced with a small party through the country towards the Santee. On his arrival there he found a number of his countrymen ready and willing to put themselves under his command, to which he had been appointed by General Gates. This corps afterwards acquired the name of Marion's Brigade. Its origin was as singular as its exploits were honorable.

In the month of June, 1780, a British captain named Ardesoif, arrived at Georgetown and published a proclamation, inviting the people to come in, swear allegiance to King George, and take protection. Many of the inhabitants of Georgetown submitted. But there remained a portion of that district stretching from the Santee to the Peedee, containing the whole of the present Williamsburg and part of Marion district, to which the British arms had not penetrated. The inhabitants of it were generally of Irish extraction, and very little disposed to submission. At this crisis there was a meeting of this people to deliberate on their situation. Major John James, who had heretofore commanded them in the field and represented them in the State Legislature, was selected as the person who should go down to Captain Ardesoif and know from him upon what terms they would be allowed to submit. Accordingly he proceeded to Georgetown in the plain garb of a country planter, and was introduced to the Captain at his lodgings.

After narrating the nature of his mission, the Captain surprised that such an embassy should be sent to him, answered "that their submission must be unconditional." To an inquiry, "whether they would be allowed to stay at home upon their plantations in peace and quiet," he replied, "though you have rebelled against his majesty he offers you a free pardon, of which you were undeserving, for you ought all to have been hanged. As he offers you a free pardon you must take up arms in support of his cause." To Major James suggesting "that the people he came to represent would not submit on such terms," the Captain, irritated at his republican language, particularly at the word "represent," replied, "you damned rebel! if you speak in such language, I will immediately order you to be hanged up to the yard arm." Major James perceiving what turn matters were likely to take, and not brooking this harsh language, suddenly seized the chair on which he was seated, brandished it in the face of the Captain, made his way good through the back door of the house, mounted his horse and made his escape into the country. This circumstance which appears now so trivial, gave rise to Marion's brigade. When the whole adventure was related at a meeting of the inhabitants of Williamsburg, it was unanimously determined that they would again take up arms in defence of their country and not against it. Major James was desired to command them as heretofore, and they arranged themselves under their revolutionary Captains, William M'Cottry, Henry Mowzon and John James, junior.

The small band thus resolved on further resistance was about two hundred men. Shortly after, Colonel Hugh Giles joined them with two companies, Thornly's and Witherspoon's. On this accession of force a consultation was held, and it was agreed to dispatch a messenger to General Gates, who about this time had arrived on the confines of the State, requesting him to send them a Commander. Shortly after these events, Colonel Tarleton crossed the Santee at Lenud's ferry, and hearing of the late proceedings in Williamsburg, approached at the head of some cavalry to surprise the party of Major James; but Captain M'Cottry, as soon as he received notice of his movements, marched his company of fifty men to give him battle. Tarleton was posted at King's Tree bridge, on Black river, and M'Cottry approached him at midnight; but by means of the wife of the only loyalist in that part of the country, Tarleton gained intelligence of M'Cottry's movements, and marched away a few hours before the latter arrived. M'Cottry pursued him, but without effect.

In this route Tarleton burnt the house of Captain Mowzon and took Mr. James Bradley* prisoner.

In the meantime Lieutenant-Colonel Hugh Horry arrived from Georgetown with a small party and took command of the force already raised by Major James, and on all occasions very much animated the men by his gallantry and persevering patriotism. The messenger,

---

*This gentleman was taken prisoner by stratagem. Colonel Tarleton came to his house and passed himself for Colonel Washington of the American army. Bradley made much of his guest, and without suspicion freely communicated to him the plans and views of himself and other Carolinians for co-operating with their countrymen against the British. When the interview and its hospitalities were ended, Tarleton requested Bradley to accompany him as a guide to a neighboring place. This service was cheerfully performed. On their arrival, Tarleton's party appeared in full view and took charge of Bradley as a prisoner. The host thus taken by order of his late guest was sent to Camden jail, and there confined in irons. He was frequently carted to the gallows to witness the execution of his countrymen as rebels, and was told to prepare for a similar fate as his time was next. On such occasions, and when interrogated at courts-martial, he made no other reply than that "I am ready and willing to die in the cause of my country; but remember, if I am hanged, I have many friends in General Marion's brigade, and my death will occasion a severe retaliation." Either awed by his virtues or apprehensive of the consequences, his captors did not execute their threats. His life was spared, but he was kept in irons as long as the British had possession of the upper country. He bore the marks of these rugged instruments of confinement till the day of his death, and would occasionally show them to his young friends, with a request "that if the good of their country required the sacrifice, they would suffer imprisonment and death in its cause."

however, had been dispatched to Gates, and on the first or second of August, General Francis Marion arrived to the great joy of all the friends of America. He was accompanied by Colonel Peter Horry, Major John Vanderhorst, Captains Lewis Ogier and James Thems, and Captain John Milton, of Georgia. In a few days after taking the command, General Marion led his men across the Peedee at Post's ferry to disperse a large party of tories commanded by Major Gainey, collected between great and little Peedee. He surprised them in their camp; killed one of their captains and several privates. Two of his own party were wounded. Major James was detached at the head of a volunteer troop of horse to attack their horse. He came up with them, charged and drove them into little Peedee swamp. Marion returned to Posts's ferry and threw up a redoubt on the east bank of Peedee to awe the tories, still numerous in that neighborhood. While thus employed he heard of the defeat of Gates, at Camden, August 16th, 1780. Without communicating the intelligence, he immediately marched for Nelson's ferry on the Santee, in the hope of intercepting some of the prisoners on their way to Charlestown. Near Nelson's he was informed of a party on their way down, and found by his scouts that the British had stopped at the house on the main road on the east side of Santee. The General waited till near daylight next morning and then divided his men into two divisions. A small party under Colonel Hugh Horry* was directed to obtain possession of the road at the entrance of the swamp, and the main body led by himself was by a circuitous route to attack the British in the rear. Colonel Horry in taking his position, had advanced in the dark too near to a sentinel who fired upon him. In a moment he with his little party rushed up to the house, found the British arms piled before the door and seized upon them. Thus by a party of sixteen American militia was a British guard of thirty-two men taken, and one hundred and fifty prisoners released. Colonel Horry had one man wounded. However, the news of the defeat of Gates, which now became public, damped all joy for the complete success of this well conducted attack. On the same day General Marion marched back for his old position on the Peedee. On the way many of his militia,

---

*This gallant officer was the bosom friend of General Marion. Wherever the latter was personally engaged in action, the former was to be seen at his side.

and, with the exception of two, the whole of the regulars released from the enemy, deserted. But by the exertions of the General and his officers, the spirits of the drooping began to revive. About the 14th of September, 1780, when Marion had under his command only 150 men, he heard of the approach of Major Weyms, from the King's Tree, at the head of a British regiment and Harrison's regiment of tories. Major James was instantly dispatched at the head of a party of volunteers to reconnoitre, and with orders to count the enemy. On his return a council of war was called. The British force was reported to be double that of Marion's. Gainey's party of tories in the rear had always been estimated at 500 men. Under these discouraging circumstances the line of march was directed back towards Lynch's creek. This was a most trying occasion. Men were called upon to leave their property and their families at the discretion of an irritated relentless enemy. About half of Marion's party left him; Colonels Peter and Hugh Horry, Colonels John Erwin and John Baxter, Major John Vanderhorst, Major John James, Major Benson, and about sixty others continued with their General. Captain James, with ten chosen men, was left to succor the distressed and to convey intelligence.* The next morning Marion arrived at his redoubt; and at sunset the same evening turned towards North Carolina, and soon reached the eastern bank of Drowning creek in that State. Major James obtained leave to return at the head of a few volunteers; and General Marion continued on to the White marsh, near the source of the Waccamaw. In a little time the Major returned with intelligence of the depredations and house burnings committed by Weyms. Many of Marion's party were reduced from easy circumstances to poverty.

After a few days more of repose, the General returned by forced marches towards South Carolina. When near to Lynch's creek he was informed that a party of tories, much more numerous than his own, lay at Black Mingo, fifteen miles below. Every voice was for the General to lead on his men to an attack; and they were gratified.

The tories lay at Shepherd's ferry on the south side of that creek. To approach them Marion was obliged to cross the creek at a bridge one

---

*He continued in the vicinity of the British encampments and to fire upon stragglers from it as long as his powder and ball lasted.

mile above the ferry. As soon as the front files of his advance had struck the bridge, with their horses' feet, an alarm gun was fired by the enemy and they were advantageously posted to receive him. A sharp conflict ensued. In an interval of platoons Marion was heard to call out, "advance cavalry and charge on the left." Instantly the tories broke and ran for Black Mingo swamp. The parties had been engaged for a considerable time so near to each other that the wads of their guns struck on each side, and both fired balls and buckshot. Neither had bayonets, or they would have been used. Captain Logan, and one private of Marion's party were killed; but of those engaged, nearly one-half were wounded. Two gallant officers, Captain Mowzon and his Lieutenant Joseph Scott, were rendered unfit for further service.

The tories had five killed, and a considerable number wounded. Several of these had lately been companions in arms with Marion's party, but from mistaken views had changed sides. The General without delay marched into Williamsburg. In a short time his party was four hundred strong.

Thus re-inforced the General proceeded up Lynch's creek, to chastise the tories who had assisted Weyms. On his march he obtained information that Colonel Tynes was collecting a large body of tories in the fork of Black river, distant about thirty miles. The General instantly proceeded towards them; crossing the north branch of Black river, he came up with Tynes—surprised and completely defeated him without the loss of a man. When Marion approached, the first party of tories was playing cards; and Captain Gaskens one of the plundering companions of Weyms, was killed with a card in his hand. Several other tories were killed and wounded. In all these marches Marion and his men lay in the open air with little covering, and with little other food than sweet potatoes and meat mostly without salt. Though it was in the unhealthy season of autumn, yet sickness seldom occurred. The General fared worse than his men; for his baggage having caught fire by accident, he had literally but half a blanket to cover him from the dews of the night, and but half a hat to shelter him from the rays of the sun. Soon after the defeat of Tynes, General Marion took a position on Snow's Island. This is situated at the conflux of the Peedee and Lynch's creek, is of a triangular form, and is bounded by Peedee on the northeast—

by Lynch's creek on the north—and by Clark's creek, a branch of the latter, on the west and south. Here, by having command of the rivers, he could be abundantly supplied with provisions, and his post was inaccessible except by water. Major John Postell was stationed to guard the lower part of the river Peedee. While there, Captain James De-Peyster of the royal army, with twenty-nine grenadiers, having taken post in the house of the major's father, the major posted his small command of twenty-eight militia-men in such positions as commanded its doors and demanded their surrender. This being refused, he set fire to an out-house and was proceeding to burn that in which they were posted; and nothing but the immediate submission of the whole party restrained him from sacrificing his father's valuable property to gain an advantage for his country.

From Snow's Island during the winter next after the fall of Charlestown, General Marion sent out his scouts in all directions. In January 1781, he sent two small detachments of militia dragoons, under the command of Major Postell and Captain Postell, to cross the Santee. The former destroyed a great quantity of valuable stores at Manigault's ferry; the latter did the same at another place in the vicinity. Thence he marched to Keithfield near Monk's Corner, where he destroyed fourteen wagons loaded with soldiers' clothing and baggage; besides several other valuable stores, and took forty prisoners chiefly British regulars, and effected the whole without any loss. In the course of these desultory operations, Marion killed and captured a number of the British and their tory friends more than double of his own force.

In the course of the contest, a new race of young warriors had sprung up. The General was desirous of employing them, and to give some repose to those who had served from the beginning. Among these the brothers, the Postells, were all active and enterprising. Major Benson commanded the cavalry; under him was John Thompson Green; under them were Daniel Conyers and James M'Cauley; who on every occasion signalized themselves. Captain M'Cottry commanded a company of riflemen.* Wherever his name was repeated it struck terror into the hearts of the enemy. The warfare was various and bloody.

*No man was more beloved by his men than M'Cottry; his active services brought upon him a complication of disorders which shortened his life.

Lieutenant Roger Gordon, of Marion's party being upon a scout upon Lynch's creek, stopped at a house of refreshments. While there, the house was beset and fired by a Captain Butler and a party of tories greatly superior in number. Gordon's party surrendered upon a promise of quarters, but after laying down their arms, Butler fell upon them and butchered them in cold blood.

In consequence of this massacre "no quarters for tories" was the cry with Marion's men when going into action. Still however the regular British forces were treated with lenity, and agreeably to the generally received rules of war, when they laid down their arms. The pruning hook was converted into a spear; and the saw, under the hands of a common blacksmith, became a terrible sabre. Powder and ball were much wanted. On account of the small stock of both, the orders often were to give the British one or two fires and to retreat. Those fires were always well directed and did great execution.

Marion so effectually thwarted the schemes of the British against South Carolina, that to drive him out of the country was with them a favorite object. The house burnings and devastations perpetrated by Weyms and the tories under his direction, had not produced that intimidation and disposition to submit which had been vainly expected from men who disregarded property when put in competition with liberty. A new and well concerted attempt to destroy, or disperse, the brigade which had given so much trouble to the late conquerors was made early in 1781.

Colonel Watson moved down from Camden along the Santee, and Colonel Doyle crossing Lynch's creek marched down on the east side of it. The point of their intended junction was supposed to be at Snow's Island. General Marion heard first of the approach of Watson, and marched from Snow's Island with almost the whole of his force to meet him. At Tawcaw swamp, nearly opposite to the mouth of the present Santee canal on the east side of the river, he laid the first ambuscade for Watson. General Marion had then but very little ammunition, not more than twenty rounds to each man. His orders were to give two fires and retreat; and they were executed by Colonel Peter Horry with great effect. Watson made good the passage of the swamp, and sent Major Harrison with a corps of tory cavalry and some British in pursuit of Horry. This had been foreseen by the cautious Marion; and Captain Daniel Conyers, at the head of a party of cavalry, was placed in a second ambuscade. As soon as the tories and British came up, Conyers, in a spirited and well-directed charge, killed with his own hands the officer who led on the opposite charge. Conyer's men followed his gallant example. Many of Harrison's party were killed, and the remainder made their escape to the main body of the British. Such work required little powder and ball. General Marion continued to harass Watson on his march, by pulling up bridges and opposing him in like manner at every difficult pass until they had reached near the lower bridge on Black river, seven miles below King's Tree. Here Watson made a feint of marching down the road to Georgetown. Marion being too weak to detach a party to the bridge, had taken an advantageous post on that road; when Watson wheeling suddenly about gained possession of the bridge on the west side. This was an important pass on the road leading into the heart of Williamsburg and to Snow's Island. The river on the west runs under a high bluff; the grounds on the opposite side are low and the river, though generally fordable, was then raised by a swell nearly up to the summit of the opposite shore. Watson still hesitated about passing.

General Marion, informed of Watson's movement, without delay approached the river, plunged into it on horseback and called to his men to follow. They did so. The whole party reached the opposite shore in safety, and marched forward to occupy the east end of the bridge. Marion detached Major James with forty musqueteers, and thirty riflemen under M'Cottry to burn the bridge. The riflemen were posted to advantage on the river bank, but as soon as their friends had gained possession of the east end of the bridge, and had applied fascines to it, Watson opened the fire of his artillery upon them, but it was unavailing. The west bank of the river was so much elevated above the east that before his field pieces could be brought to bear upon the Americans, his artillerists were exposed to the fire of the riflemen, who deliberately picked them off as they advanced to the summit of the hill. In the meantime Major James' party had fired the bridge. Thus were Marion's friends saved from similar plunderings and conflagrations with those they had suffered under Weyms. The practice of Watson was to burn all the houses of Marion's men that were in the line of his march.

Watson was so much intimidated by this affair, that he immediately quitted the lower bridge and proceeded by forced marches to Georgetown. General Marion repassed Black river, and hung alternately on the rear, the flanks, or the front of the enemy until they had reached Sampit bridge, nine miles from Georgetown. There M'Cottry gave them a parting fire from his riflemen. During these transactions, Watson commanded five hundred men, and Marion not half that number. The loss of the British is unknown, that of Marion but one man.

The three officers, and all the men employed by the General at the lower bridge, were inhabitants, whose plantations and families would have been exposed to the enemy had they made good their passage. From Sampit bridge Marion marched directly for Snow's Island. There he heard of the approach of Doyle, who had driven Colonel Erwin from the Island and taken possession of the pass of Lynch's creek, at Witherspoon's ferry. When M'Cottry, advancing in front, arrived at Witherspoon's, on the south bank of the creek, the British on the north were scuttling the ferry boat. He approached softly to the edge of the water and gave them an unexpected fire. A short conflict took place between ill-directed musketry, whose balls hit the tops of the trees on the opposite side, and riflemen, whose well directed aim seldom failed of doing execution at every fire. Doyle fell back to Camden.

In addition to these skirmishes, Marion made two descents on Georgetown. In the first, he came unexpectedly on a body of tories, whom he charged and dispersed after their Captain and several of their men were killed. In this affair Captain Marion, brother of the present member of Congress from Charlestown District, was killed and, it was believed, after he had been taken prisoner.

Marion's second descent was more successful. With a party of militia he marched to Georgetown, and began regular approaches against the British post in that place. On the first night after his men had broken ground, their adversaries evacuated their works and retreated to Charlestown. Shortly after, one Manson, an inhabitant of South Carolina, who had joined the British, appeared in an armed vessel and demanded permission to land his men in the town. This being refused, he sent a few of them ashore and set fire to it. Upwards of forty houses were speedily reduced to ashes.

After the return of General Greene to Carolina, in 1781, Marion acted under his orders, and the exploits of his brigade, no longer acting by itself, made a part of the general history of the revolutionary war.

Washington Allston (1779–1843)

A distinguished painter and poet, though currently underrated, Washington Allston was born at Brook Green Domain on November 5, 1779. He graduated from Harvard College in 1800 and, in 1801, sailed to London to study art with Benjamin West. Allston returned to the United States in 1809, painting in both Boston and Charleston until his death in 1843. Two of his most famous paintings are *Rosalie* and his *Portrait of Coleridge.* He wrote *The Sylphs of the Seasons* (1813) and *Monaldi* (1841), and his *Lectures on Arts and Poems* was published posthumously in 1850.

America to Great Britain

All hail! thou noble land,
    Our Fathers' native soil!
O, stretch thy mighty hand,
    Gigantic grown by toil,
O'er the vast Atlantic wave to our shore!
    For thou with magic might
    Canst reach to where the light
    Of Phœbus travels bright
        The world o'er!

The Genius of our clime,
    From his pine-embattled steep,
Shall hail the guest sublime;
    While the Tritons of the deep
With their conchs the kindred league shall proclaim.
    Then let the world combine,—
    O'er the main our naval line
    Like the milky-way shall shine
        Bright in fame!

Though ages long have past
    Since our Fathers left their home,
Their pilot in the blast,
    O'er untravelled seas to roam,
Yet lives the blood of England in our veins!
    And shall we not proclaim
    That blood of honest fame
    Which no tyranny can tame
        By its chains?

While the language free and bold
    Which the Bard of Avon sung,
In which our Milton told
    How the vault of heaven rung
When Satan, blasted, fell with his host;—
    While this, with reverence meet,

Ten thousand echoes greet,
From rock to rock repeat
    Round our coast;—

While the manners, while the arts,
    That mould a nation's soul,
Still cling around our hearts,—
    Between let Ocean roll,
Our joint communion breaking with the Sun:
    Yet still from either beach
    The voice of blood shall reach,
    More audible than speech,
        "We are One."

Rosalie

"O, pour upon my soul again
That sad, unearthly strain,
That seems from other worlds to plain;
Thus falling, falling from afar,
As if some melancholy star
Had mingled with her light her sighs,
And dropped them from the skies!

"No,—never came from aught below
This melody of woe,
That makes my heart to overflow,
As from a thousand gushing springs,
Unknown before; that with it brings
This nameless light,—if light it be,—
That veils the world I see.

"For all I see around me wears
The hue of other spheres;
And something blent of smiles and tears
Comes from the very air I breathe.
O, nothing, sure, the stars beneath
Can mould a sadness like to this,—
So like angelic bliss."

So, at that dreamy hour of day
When the last lingering ray
Stops on the highest cloud to play,—
So thought the gentle Rosalie,
As on her maiden reverie
First fell the strain of him who stole
In music to her soul.

The French Revolution

The Earth has had her visitation. Like to this
She hath not known, save when the mounting waters
Made of her orb one universal ocean.
For now the Tree that grew in Paradise,
The deadly Tree that first gave Evil motion,
And sent its poison through Earth's sons and daughters,
Had struck again its root in every land;
And now its fruit was ripe,—about to fall,—
And now a mighty Kingdom raised the hand,
To pluck and eat. Then from his throne stepped forth
The King of Hell, and stood upon the Earth:
But not, as once, upon the Earth to crawl.
A Nation's congregated form he took,
Till, drunk with sin and blood, Earth to her centre shook.

Art

O Art, high gift of Heaven! how oft defamed
When seeming praised! To most a craft that fits,
By dead, prescriptive Rule, the scattered bits
Of gathered knowledge; even so misnamed
By some who would invoke thee; but not so
By him—the noble Tuscan—who gave birth
To forms unseen of man, unknown to earth,
Now living habitants; he felt the glow
Of thy revealing touch, that brought to view
The invisible Idea; and he knew,
E'en by his inward sense, its form was true:
'T was life to life responding—highest truth!
So, through Elisha's faith, the Hebrew Youth
Beheld the thin blue air to fiery chariots grow.

On the Late S. T. Coleridge

And thou art gone, most loved, most honored friend!
No, never more thy gentle voice shall blend
With air of Earth its pure ideal tones,
Binding in one, as with harmonious zones,
The heart and intellect. And I no more
Shall with thee gaze on that unfathomed deep,
The Human Soul—as when, pushed off the shore,
Thy mystic bark would through the darkness sweep,
Itself the while so bright! For oft we seemed
As on some starless sea—all dark above,
All dark below—yet, onward as we drove,
To plough up light that ever round us streamed.
But he who mourns is not as one bereft
Of all he loved: thy living Truths are left.

William Crafts (1787–1826)

Born in Charleston on January 24, 1787, William Crafts graduated from Harvard in 1805 and received the M.A. degree there in 1807. Law was his profession, but literature became his avocation. Admitted to the South Carolina bar in 1809, he practiced law in Charleston from 1809 until 1826, serving as a member of the South Carolina House of Representatives, 1810–13, and of the South Carolina Senate, 1820–26. While in Charleston he frequently contributed essays to the Charleston *Courier,* and he published in the *Courier* two slim volumes of poetry, *The Raciad, and Other Poems* in 1820 as well as *The Sea Serpent: A Dramatic Jeu d'Espirit* (1819). He seemed little aware of what English Romantic poets were writing, except for Byron and Thomas Moore, writing instead imitations of neoclassical poetry, with Pope as his prime model. Crafts died in Lebanon Springs, New York, September 23, 1826. Hugh Swinton Legaré lamented his early death and his unfulfilled poetic career, attributing it in part to Crafts' unhappy division of his talents between law and poetry.

Love's Benediction

Be as thou art for ever young,
   Still on thy cheek the vernal bloom,
The honey's essence on thy tongue,
   And on thy lips the rose perfume.

Be as thou art, for ever fair,
   Still beam with love, those eyes of thine;
For ever wave thy yellow hair,
   And round thy graceful bosom twine.

Those coral lips, those teeth of pearl,
   Those smiles, those glances, and those sighs;
Heaven save them long, my charming girl,
   To bless this heart, to bless these eyes.

For all of thee, thank heaven, is mine;
   And I am happier made by thee;
As when the oak supports the vine,
   'Tis glad and looketh cheerfully.

Love a Prisoner

The snow-drop is in bloom,
  And the young earth's perfume,
    Scents anew the floating air;
  It is the breath of love—
  Beneath, around, above,
    Young love is there.
Come, let us strive to snare him—see,
Love smiling waits for you and me.

  Bind him with the jas'mine flower,
  Hide him in a myrtle bower,
    On thornless roses let him rest;
  See his gracious eyelids move,
  Hope and joy are eyes of love,
    Kiss them and be blest.
Love gives his own dear heart to be
One half for you, one half for me.

  The tongue may lose its power,
  As Babel's noisy tower,
    Confounded it of yore;
  But the language of the eye,
  Survives, (though others die,)
    Delicious as before.
Love gives his darling eyes, to be,
One eye for you, and one for me.

The Mermaid

Child of neither land nor sea,
   Yet to both of them allied;
Offspring of a fair ladye,
   Who in depths of ocean died.

Wretched on her coral bed,
   Far beneath the purple sea,
Ere the vital spark had fled,
   Thus my mother pray'd for me.

"Gracious Heaven! let one atone,
   Seal my aching eyes in night;
Save my little unborn one,
   Let my orphan see the light."

Cradled in the stormy wave,
   Sea-nymphs watch'd my infant sleep;
Nurs'd upon my mother's grave,
   God preserv'd me in the deep.

Human head, and hands, and heart,
   Heaven in mercy gave to me,
Still that I might seem a part
   Of the human family.

Yet to fit me for the cave,
   Where the ocean fountains flow,
Safely to o'ercome the wave,
   Made me like a fish below.

Many such as me there are,
   Vestals of the virgin billow;
Neither envy nor despair,
   Mars us on our sedgy pillow.

Sing we in the soothing strain,
   When the bark securely flies;
Mourn we in the howling main,
   When the gallant vessel dies.

The Infidel Girl

I love a little infidel,
  Of snow-white cheek, and coal-black eye,
Within whose angel form doth dwell
  A soul of stainless purity.

She cannot boast a Christian name,
  Nor sparkling crucifix doth wear
But oft a title covers shame,
  And signs are insincere.

Let monkish priests, with bigot frown,
  Condemn her to the shades of woe;
Her lot I'll dare to make mine own,
  Whate'er their pride presumes to know.

It cannot be that God on high,
  Should give so fair a form to earth,
And close the portals of the sky,
  Against such loveliness and worth.

The streams of heavenly kindness flow
  In channels deep and wide,
Mortals in vain their shores would know,
  In vain their waters guide.

The maid by prejudice opprest,
  May fairest blush and sweetest smile—
As pearl, that grows for beauty's breast,
  'Neath mountain torrents lives the while.

The sweetest flower is lowliest,
  And latest sees the sun,
And evening hour is holiest,
  For gaudy day is done.

Like star of eve, serenely bright,
  Like ocean coral fair;
Like flower concealed from mortal sight,
  Whose fragrance chides the air.

Secluded thus—thus formed to bless,
   The little infidel retires,
To bloom in lonely loveliness,
   And veil her glowing fires.

William John Grayson (1788–1863)

William Grayson, born at Beaufort on November 2, 1788, graduated from South Carolina College in 1809, studied law, and was admitted to the bar in 1822. He served in the South Carolina legislature, 1822–31, was sent to Congress from 1833 to 1837, and served as Collector of Customs at Charleston from 1841 until 1853, retiring to his plantation in the latter year. A strong defender of slavery, he also wanted to preserve the Union. He was a frequent contributor to the *Southern Quarterly Review* and to *Russell's Magazine,* and the author of *Chicora, an Indian Legend* (1856) and *The Country* (1858). Grayson's best-written work was probably his *Biographical Sketch of James Louis Petigru,* published in 1856, but his most popular work was his pro-slavery poem, *The Hireling and the Slave* (1854). He died in Newberry on October 4, 1863, and lies in Magnolia Cemetery in Charleston.

From *The Hireling and the Slave*

> See yonder poor o'erlaboured wight,
> So abject, mean and vile,
> Who begs a brother of the Earth
> To give him leave to toil,
> And see his lordly fellow-worm
> The poor petition spurn,
> Unmindful tho' a weeping wife
> And helpless offspring mourn.
>
> BURNS

Where Hireling millions toil, in doubt and fear,
For food and clothing, all the weary year,
Content and grateful, if their Masters give
The boon they humbly beg—to work and live;
While dreamers task their idle wits to find,
A short hand method to enrich mankind,
And Fourier's scheme and Owen's deep device,
The drooping hearts of list'ning crowds entice
With rising wages, and decreasing toil,
With bounteous crops from ill-attended soil:
If, while the anxious multitudes appear,
Now glad with hope, now yielding to despair,
A Seraph form, descending from the skies,
In mercy sent, should meet their wond'ring eyes,
And smiling, promise all the good they crave,
The homes, the food, the clothing of the Slave,
Restraint from vice, exemption from the cares
The pauper Hireling ever feels or fears;
And, at their death, these blessings to renew,
That wives and children may enjoy them too,
That, when disease or age their strength impairs,
Subsistence and a home should still be their's;
What wonder would the promised boon impart,
What grateful rapture swell the Peasant's heart;
How freely would the hungry list'ners give
A life-long labour, thus secure to live!
  And yet the life, so unassailed by care,

So blest with moderate work, with ample fare,
With all the good the pauper Hireling needs,
The happier Slave on each plantation leads;
Safe from harassing doubts and annual fears,
He dreads no famine, in unfruitful years;
If harvests fail from inauspicious skies,
The Master's providence his food supplies;
No paupers perish here for want of bread,
Or lingering live, by foreign bounty fed;
No exiled trains of homeless peasants go,
In distant climes, to tell their tales of woe;
Far other fortune, free from care and strife,
For work, or bread, attends the Negro's life,
And Christian Slaves may challenge as their own,
The blessings claimed in fabled states alone—
The cabin home, not comfortless, though rude,
Light daily labour, and abundant food,
The sturdy health, that temperate habits yield,
The cheerful song, that rings in every field,
The long, loud laugh, that freemen seldom share,
Heaven's boon to bosoms unapproached by care,
And boisterous jest and humour unrefined,
That leave, though rough, no painful sting behind;
While, nestling near, to bless their humble lot,
Warm social joys surround the Negro's cot,
The evening dance its merriment imparts,
Love, with his rapture, fills their youthful hearts,
And placid age, the task of labour done,
Enjoys the summer shade, the winter's sun,
And, as through life no pauper want he knows,
Laments no poorhouse penance at its close.
　　His too the Christian privilege to share
The weekly festival of praise and prayer;
For him the Sabbath shines with holier light,
The air is balmier, and the sky more bright;
Winter's brief suns with warmer radiance glow,

With softer breath the gales of autumn blow,
Spring with new flowers more richly strews the ground,
And summer spreads a fresher verdure round;
The early shower is past; the joyous breeze
Shakes patt'ring rain drops from the rustling trees,
And with the sun, the fragrant offerings rise,
From Nature's censers to the bounteous skies;
With cheerful aspect, in his best array,
To the far forest church he takes his way;
With kind salute the passing neighbour meets,
With awkward grace the morning traveller greets,
And joined by crowds, that gather as he goes,
Seeks the calm joy the Sabbath morn bestows.
   There no proud temples to devotion rise,
With marble domes that emulate the skies;
But bosomed in primeval trees that spread
Their limbs o'er mouldering mansions of the dead,
Moss cinctured oaks and solemn pines between,
Of modest wood, the house of God is seen,
By shaded springs, that from the sloping land
Bubble and sparkle through the silver sand,
Where high o'er arching laurel blossoms blow,
Where fragrant bays breathe kindred sweets below,
And elm and ash their blended arms entwine
With the bright foliage of the mantling vine:
In quiet chat, before the hour of prayer,
Masters and Slaves in scattered groups appear;
Loosed from the carriage, in the shades around,
Impatient horses neigh and paw the ground;
No city discords break the silence here,
No sounds unmeet offend the listener's ear;
But rural melodies of flocks and birds,
The lowing, far and faint, of distant herds,
The mocking-bird, with minstrel pride elate,
The partridge whistling for its absent mate,
The thrush's soft solitary notes prolong,

Bold, merry blackbirds swell the general song,
And cautious crows their harsher voices join,
In concert cawing, from the loftiest pine.
　　When now the Pastor lifts his earnest eyes,
And hands outstretched, a suppliant to the skies;
No rites of pomp or pride beguile the soul,
No organs peal, no clouds of incense roll,
But, line by line, untutored voices raise,
Like the wild birds, their simple notes of praise,
And hearts of love, with true devotion bring,
Incense more pure to Heaven's eternal King,
On glorious themes their humble thoughts employ,
And rise transported with no earthly joy;
The blessing said, the service o'er, again
Their swelling voices raise the sacred strain;
Lingering, they love to sing of Jordan's shore,
Where sorrows cease, and toil is known no more.

Hugh Swinton Legaré (1797–1843)

Hugh Swinton Legaré, born in Charleston on January 2, 1797, came of Scotch and Huguenot ancestry. As a boy he studied under Moses Waddel at Willington Academy before entering South Carolina College (later the University), where, as a student of ancient and modern languages, he graduated first in his class. He later studied law in Charleston, served in the state legislature, managed a plantation on John's Island, and became attorney-general of the state. Elected to Congress in 1836, he was appointed U.S. Attorney-General in 1841 and, in 1843, became Secretary of State *ad interim* upon Webster's resignation. With Stephen Elliott, Legaré founded the *Southern Review* (1828–32), the most distinguished Southern journal of its time. His scholarly, political, and literary writings were published posthumously in two volumes in 1845, two years after his death.

Classical Learning

It is impossible to contemplate the annals of Greek literature and art, without being struck with them, as by far the most extraordinary and brilliant phenomenon in the history of the human mind. The very language—even in its primitive simplicity, as it came down from the rhapsodists who celebrated the exploits of Hercules and Theseus, was as great a wonder as any it records. All the other tongues that civilized man have spoken, are poor and feeble, and barbarous, in comparison of it. Its compass and flexibility, its riches and its powers, are altogether unlimited. It not only expresses with precision, all that is thought or known at any given period, but it enlarges itself naturally, with the progress of science, and affords, as if without an effort, a new phrase, or a systematic nomenclature whenever one is called for. It is equally adapted to every variety of style and subject—to the most shadowy subtlety of distinction, and the utmost exactness of definition, as well as to the energy and the pathos of popular eloquence—to the majesty, the elevation, the variety of the epic, and the boldest license of the dithyrambic, no less than to the sweetness of the elegy, the simplicity of the pastoral, or the heedless gaiety and delicate characterization of comedy. Above all, what is an unspeakable charm—a sort of *naiveté* is peculiar to it, which appears in all those various styles, and is quite as becoming and agreeable in a historian or a philosopher—Xenophon for instance —as in the light and jocund numbers of Anacreon. Indeed, were there no other object in learning Greek but to see to what perfection language is capable of being carried, not only as a medium of communication, but as an instrument of thought, we see not why the time of a young man would not be just as well bestowed in acquiring a knowledge of it—for all the purposes, at least, of a liberal or elementary education—as in learning algebra, another specimen of a language or arrangement of signs perfect in its kind. But this wonderful idiom happens to have been spoken, as was hinted in the preceding paragraph, by a race as wonderful. The very first monument of their genius—the most ancient relic of letters in the Western world—stands to this day altogether unrivalled in the exalted class to which it belongs.* What

---

*Milton is, perhaps, more sublime than Homer, and, indeed, than all other poets, with the exception, as we incline to think, of Dante. But if we adopt his

was the history of this immortal poem and of its great fellow? Was it a single individual, and who was he, that composed them? Had he any master or model? What had been his education, and what was the state of society in which he lived? These questions are full of interest to a philosophical inquirer into the intellectual history of the species, but they are especially important with a view to the subject of the present discussion. Whatever causes account for the matchless excellence of these primitive poems, and for that of the language in which they are written, will go far to explain the extraordinary circumstance, that the same favoured people left nothing unattempted in philosophy, in letters and in arts, and attempted nothing without signal, and in some cases, unrivalled success. Winkelman† undertakes to assign some reasons for this astonishing superiority of the Greeks, and talks very learnedly about a fine climate, delicate organs, exquisite susceptibility, the full developement of the human form by gymnastic exercises, &c. For our own part, we are content to explain the phenomenon after the manner of the Scottish school of metaphysicians, in which we learned the little that we profess to know of that department of philosophy, by resolving it at once in an original law of nature: in other words, by substantially, but decently, confessing it to be inexplicable. But whether it was idiosyncrasy or discipline, or whatever was the cause, it is enough for the purposes of the present discussion, that the *fact* is unquestionable.

In one of Mr. Grimké's notes, we have the following remarks upon

---

own division of poetry into three great classes, viz. the epic, the dramatic, and the lyrical—the Paradise Lost, like the Divina Commedia, is more remarkable for Lyrical, (and sometimes for dramatic) than for epic beauties—for splendid details, than an interesting whole—for prophetic raptures bursting forth at intervals, than for the animation, the fire, the engrossing and rapid narrative of a metrical Romance. Who cares anything about the story or the plot, or feels any sympathy with the dramatis personæ—not even excepting Adam and Eve, whose insipid faultlessness reminds one of the Italian proverb—tanto buon che val niente. Besides, are not the preposterous vauntings and menaces of the devil against the Omnipotent, like the swaggering insolence of a slave behind his master's back—or his conspiracy like that of Caliban with Trinculo and Stephano, against the magic powers of Prospero? Devoted, as we are proud to avow ourselves, to Milton, we have always felt there was something even savouring of the comic in his Rabbinical plot.
†Historie de l'Art, &c.—*Liv.* 4.

the story of Demosthenes' having repeatedly copied the great work of Thucydides with his own hand.

"Were instructors in *our* day to recommend an imitation of this example of the Athenian orator, it would be considered as *downright folly.* If the student of Divinity were told to copy Butler's Analogy, the student of Law, Blackstone's Commentaries, the student of Belles Lettres, *Kames* or *Alison,* and the student of Philosophy, Paley or Locke, it would be pronounced an unpardonable waste of time, and a very unintelligible mode of improvement."

Undoubtedly it would, and by no man sooner than Demosthenes himself, if he had the good fortune to live again "in *our* day." But what earthly analogy is there between the two cases? In that of the Greek orator, we see a young man preparing himself for the very hazardous career of a public speaker, in such an assembly as we have already described—the shrewd, sagacious, cavilling, hypercritical, but most polished and *musical* Athenian Demus—by endeavouring to acquire a perfect command of his language—the great instrument by which he was to accomplish every thing. In order to effect this, he not only attended the schools of Isæus and Plato, but he did what was still better; he selected the *model* which he thought most perfect, and traced its lineaments over and over again, until he acquired, or rather surpassed, if possible, the excellencies of his great master. Besides, Mr. Grimké does not seem to be aware that the Greek language, admirable as it was in itself—vast and various as its powers had appeared in the older poets —and much as had been done for its prose by Plato, Isocrates, and others, had not yet attained to its utmost perfection—at least, for the purposes of popular declamation; and that it was actually reserved for Demosthenes, by these very studies which would, it seems, be looked upon as "downright folly" in *our* day, to give it its last finishing—to impart to it,

> ————the full resounding line,
> The long majestic march and energy divine:*

*So says Philostratus. βιος Ισοχρατους. In Cicero's time, the Pseudo or soidisant Attics, who pestered him with their affectations and impertinences, held up Thucydides as the most perfect model of Attic purity and elegance. The orator himself, however, declares for Demosthenes—Quo ne Athenas quidem ipsas magis credo fuisse Atticas.—*Orat. ad Brut.* c. 7.

but whoever heard Butler's Analogy or Kames' Elements commended for style, and who could not master their sense and argument without copying them at all?

But our main purpose in quoting these remarks of Mr. Grimké, was to advert to the conclusion he draws from them, which we shall endeavour to turn against his own argument. It is as follows:

"Does not this act of Demosthenes very remarkably illustrate the fundamental difference between the ancients and moderns, that the former regarded *style* as an *end;* the latter as a means: that the former excel CHIEFLY in *style,* the latter PRE-EMINENTLY in *thought.*"

We will treat this sentence (which we print just as it stood in the original) as Jupiter, among the poets, so often treats the prayers of unhappy mortals—half of it shall be granted, the other half dispersed in air. We think it undoubtedly true, as a general proposition, that the ancients, especially the Greeks, were more fastidious in regard to style than the moderns, and this is the very reason why they have been, and ought to be, universally preferred as models to form the taste of youth upon. But it is as undoubtedly wrong to affirm, that they were less scrupulous about sense or thought. Of their extreme delicacy and correctness of taste, innumerable proofs might be cited from all the writings of antiquity, but especially from that rich mine of philosophical criticism, both theoretical and practical, the rhetorical writings of Cicero. His manner of expressing himself upon this subject is quite remarkable. He speaks of the niceness and scrupulosity of the Attic ear*—which was so great that a single false quantity or misplaced accent would excite the clamours of a whole theatre,† besides many other instances which our limits forbid us to adduce. An example of the same thing that has always struck us very forcibly, is to be found in the gibes which Æschines, even upon an occasion of such extraordinary interest and importance as the famous accusation of Ctesiphon, so confidently indulges in, with regard to certain expressions that had escaped

---

*Teretes et religiosas aures Atticorum.—(We quote this and the following from memory.) Brutus c. 9.
†At in his (numeris et modis,) &c. tota theatra reclamant:—*Brutus.* Something like this may be seen in the parterre of the Theatre Français; but Paris is not Athens.

his great rival in former debates; as if, said Demosthenes, it concerned the well-being of the commonwealth, whether I used this word or that or stretched forth my arm thus or thus. Yet we are willing that the whole cause of Greek literature should depend upon that single controversy, and upon the opinion of any liberal and enlightened critic, as to the merits of those very orations so laboriously prepared, and so unsparingly censured. Indeed, (as has already been remarked with respect to the comedies of Aristophanes) what better proof can be given of the wonderful refinement of an Athenian audience than that this peerless orator felt it *necessary* to take so much pains in preparing his harangues, and met with such triumphant success in delivering them? It is impossible to imagine a work of genius, executed in a more simple and severe taste; and Hume does not, we think, exaggerate their merit when he affirms, that of all human productions, the orations of Demosthenes present us with the models which approach nearest to perfection.* But wherein, principally, did that wonderful excellence consist? In this—that his style, elaborate and admirable as it was, seemed to make no part of his concern, and that he was wrapped up with his whole heart and soul, in the subject—in the occasion—in the measure proposed—in the glory of Athens, and the welfare and liberties of all Greece. So it is with the other Greek classics. This naked simplicity of style, united with the highest degree of refinement, is what strikes a modern reader most, especially before he is become familiar with it. Yet this peculiar people, who would tolerate no expressions but the most chaste and natural†—who would have spurned from the βημ a public speaker that did not know how to sink the rhetorician in the statesman and the man of business‡—to whom any thing like the ambitious ornaments so much admired in this philosophic age, would have been an abomination§—this people it is, that are represented as

---

*Essay xiii of Eloquence.
†See Longinus, c. 3.
‡Isocrates Παναθηναικὸς in exordio.
§Cicero characterizes the Asiatic style—as opimum quoddam et tanquam adipatæ dictionis genus, (Brutus, c. 8,)—(a felicitous and *untranslateable* phrase) which the Rhodians did not relish much, and the Attics could not tolerate at all. We fear the style so much in vogue nowadays—in Scotland especially—is in this category.

considering *style* as an *end,* instead of a *means,* and as sacrificing sense to sound!

The conclusion which we draw from Mr. Grimké's premises is, as we have already intimated, that this proposed *defect* of the classical authors, would be alone sufficient to keep them where they are in our schools. We shall now add the last consideration which our limits will permit us to suggest, on this part of the subject.

In discussing the very important question whether boys ought to be made to study the Classics, as a regular part of education—the innovators put the case in the strongest possible manner against the present system, by arguing as if the young pupil, under this discipline, was to learn nothing else but language itself. We admit that this notion has received some sort of countenance from the excessive attention paid in the English schools to prosody, and the fact that their great scholars have been, perhaps, (with many exceptions to be sure) more distinguished by the refinement of their scholarship, than the extent and profoundness of their erudition. But the grand advantage of a classical education consists far less in acquiring a language or two, which, as languages, are to serve for use or for ornament in future life, than in the things that are learned in making that acquisition, and yet more in the *manner* of learning those things. It is a wild conceit to suppose, that the branches of knowledge, which are most rich and extensive, and most deserve to engage the researches of a mature mind, are, therefore, the best for training a young one. Metaphysics, for instance, as we have already intimated, though in the last degree unprofitable as a science, is a suitable and excellent, perhaps, a necessary part of the intellectual discipline of youth. On the contrary, international law is extremely important to be known by publicists and statesmen, but it would be absurd to put Vattel (as we have ourselves seen it done, in a once celebrated academy, in a certain part of the United States,) into the hands of a lad of fifteen or sixteen. We will admit, therefore, what has been roundly asserted at hazard, and without rhyme or reason, that classical scholars discontinue these studies after they are grown wise enough to know their futility, and only read as much Greek and Latin as is necessary to keep up their knowledge of them, or rather to save appearances, and gull credulous people; yet we maintain that the concession does not affect the result of this controversy in the least. We regard the whole period of childhood and of youth—up to the age of sixteen or seventeen, and perhaps longer—as one allotted by nature to growth and improvement in the strictest sense of those words.* The flexible powers are to be trained rather than tasked—to be carefully and continually practised in the preparatory exercises, but not to be loaded with burthens that may crush them, or be broken down by over-strained efforts of the race. It is in youth, that Montaigne's maxim, al-ways excellent—is especially applicable—that the important question is, not who is most learned, but who has learned the best. Now, we confess we have no faith at all in young prodigies—in your philosophers in teens. We have generally found these precocious smatterers sink in a few years into barrenness and imbecility, and that as they begin by being men when they ought to be boys, so they end in being boys when they ought to be men. If we would have good fruit we must wait until it is in season. Nature herself has pointed out, too clearly to be mis-understood, the proper studies of childhood and youth. The senses are first developed—observation and memory follow—then imagination begins to dream and to create—afterwards ratiocination, or the dia-lectical propensity and faculty, shoots up with great rankness†—and last of all, the crowning perfection of intellect, sound judgment and solid reason, which, by much experience in life, at length ripen into wisdom.‡ The vicissitudes of the seasons, and the consequent changes in the face of nature, and the cares and occupations of the husbandman, are not more clearly distinguished or more unalterably ordained. To break in upon this harmonious order—to attempt to anticipate these pre-established periods, what is it, as Cicero had it, but, after the manner of the Giants, to war against the laws of the Universe, and the wisdom that created it? And why do so? Is not the space in human life, between the eighth and twentieth year, quite large enough for acquiring *every* branch of liberal knowledge, as well as is needed, or, indeed, can be

[*See Plato, Rep. 1. vi. 498.]
[†Plato, Rep. 1. 7. 53. 9 b.]
[‡Quid est autem non dicam in homine sed in omni cœlo atque terra, ratione divinius? (Quæ, quum adolevit, atque perfecta est, nominatur rite sapientia. Cic. de Leg. Lib. 1. c. 7.]

acquired in youth? For instance, we cite the opinion of Condorcet, repeatedly quoted, with approbation, by Dugald Stewart, and if we mistake not, by Professor Playfair too, (each of them the highest authority on such a subject,) that any one may, under competent teachers, acquire all that Newton or La Place knew, in *two* years. The same observation, of course, applies *a fortiori* to any other branch of science. As for the modern languages, the study of French ought to be begun early for the sake of the pronunciation, and continued through the whole course, as it may be, without the smallest inconvenience. Of German, we say nothing, because we cannot speak of our own knowledge; but for Italian and Spanish, however difficult they may be, especially their poetry—to a mere English scholar, they are so easy of acquisition to any one who understands Latin, that it is not worth while even to notice them in our scheme. All that we ask then, is, that a boy should be thoroughly taught the ancient languages from his eighth to his sixteenth year, or thereabouts, in which time he will have his taste formed, his love of letters completely, perhaps enthusiastically awakened, his knowledge of the principles of universal grammar perfected, his memory stored with the history, the geography, and the chronology of all antiquity, and with a vast fund of miscellaneous literature besides, and his imagination kindled with the most beautiful and glowing passages of Greek and Roman poetry and eloquence: all the rules of criticism familiar to him—the sayings of sages, and the achievements of heroes, indelibly impressed upon his heart. He will have his curiosity fired for further acquisition, and find himself in possession of the golden keys, which open all the recesses where the stores of knowledge have ever been laid up by civilized man. The consciousness of strength will give him confidence, and he will go to the rich treasures themselves and take what he wants, instead of picking up eleemosynary scraps from those whom, in spite of himself, he will regard as his betters in literature. He will be let into that great communion of scholars throughout all ages and all nations—like that more awful communion of saints in the Holy Church Universal—and feel a sympathy with departed genius, and with the enlightened and the gifted minds of other countries, as they appear before him, in the transports of a sort of Vision Beatific, bowing down at the same shrines and glowing with the same holy love of whatever is most pure and fair, and exalted and divine in human nature. Above all, our American youth will learn, that liberty—which is sweet to all men, but which is the *passion* of proud minds that cannot stoop to less—has been the nurse of all that is sublime in character and genius. They will see her form and feel her influence in every thing that antiquity has left for our admiration—that bards consecrated their harps to her*—that she spoke from the lips of the mighty orators —that she fought and conquered, acted and suffered with the heroes whom she had formed and inspired; and, after ages of glory and virtue, fell with *Him*—her all-accomplished hope—*Him*, the LAST of ROMANS —the self-immolated martyr of Philippi.† Our young student will find his devotion to his country—his free country—become at once more fervid and more enlightened, and think scorn of the wretched creatures who have scoffed at the sublime simplicity of her institutions, and "esteem it," as one expresses it, who learned to be a republican in the schools of antiquity,‡ much better to imitate the old and elegant humanity of Greece, than the barbaric pride of a Norwegian or Hunnish stateliness; and, let us add, will come much more to despise that slavish and nauseating subserviency to rank and title, with which all European literature is steeped through and through. If Americans are to study any foreign literature at all, it ought, undoubtedly, to be the Classical, and especially the Greek.

The very difficulties of these studies, which make it necessary that so many years should be devoted to them—the novelty, the strangeness of the form, are a great recommendation. This topic is a most important one, and we would gladly follow it out; but we have already far exceeded our limits. We will just observe, that the reason, which Quinctilian gives for beginning with the Greek, is of universal application. The mother-tongue is acquired as of course—in the nursery—at the fire-side—at the parental board—in society—every where. It is familiar to us long before we are capable of remarking its peculiarities. This familiarity has its usual effects of diminishing curiosity and interest,

---

*See Lowth's first Lecture before referred to.
†Who can read Appian's account of this ever memorable battle without shedding tears? [Brutus quidem noster, excellens omni genere laudis, &c. Cic. 2. Acad. Post. 1. 3. Cf. Plutarch in Brut.]
‡Milton—Areopagitica.

and of making us regard, without emotion and even without attention, what, if it came recommended by novelty, would leave the deepest impression. It is so with every thing in nature and in art. "Difficulties increase passions of every kind, and by rousing our attention and exciting our active powers, they produce an emotion, which nourishes the prevailing affection."* Before his eighth year, a boy should be perfectly well grounded in the rudiments of English—and then if his master be a scholar that deserves the name, he could learn his own language better by having occasion to use it in translations, both prose and metrical, of the ancient languages, than by all the lessons and lectures of a mere English teacher from his birth to his majority. Indeed, it would be difficult, in the present state of our literature to imagine any thing more insipid, spiritless, imperfect, and unprofitable than such a course. But we must break off here.

We were going to appeal to experience, but we know the answer that will be made. It is not sufficient: but this too must be deferred. In the mean time, we earnestly exhort our readers to consider the state of the question as we have put it. Not to have the curiosity to study the learned languages is not to have any vocation at all for literature: it is to be destitute of liberal curiosity and of enthusiasm; to mistake a self-sufficient and superficial dogmatism for philosophy, and that complacent indolence which is the bane of all improvement for a proof of the highest degree of it. As somebody quoted by Horne Tooke says, *qui alios a literarum et linguarum studio absterrent, non antiquæ sapientiæ, sed novæ stultitiæ doctores sunt habendi.* Mr. Grimké's speculative opinions we think utterly erroneous—his excellent example cannot be too closely imitated—but it is unfortunately easy for all to repeat the one, while few have the industry and perseverance to follow the other.

*Hume's Essay XXII of Tragedy.

Crafts' Fugitive Writings

This is a brief but just account of the signal and melancholy failure of a man from whom so much was expected in his youth. It is a mistake to suppose, that devotion to literary pursuits had any thing to do with it, and that, for the best of all reasons, viz. that Mr. Crafts never was devoted to literary pursuits, at least, after he came to the bar. "His favorite intercourse with the Muses," if by that is meant inditing sonnets for the newspapers, and songs for "festive occasions," may, indeed, have contributed to bring him into disrepute with men of business—but these effusions did him quite as little honor in the opinion of men of letters. The truth is, that so far from suffering by his reputation as a scholar, he was very much, if not mainly indebted to it, for his extraordinary popularity and success at the outset of his career. A felicitous allusion, an apt quotation, the elegance of his diction, and the various other graces of a classical education that adorned his style, were quite peculiar to him among his contemporaries, and contributed very much to secure for him the character, which he ever afterwards enjoyed, of *the* man of genius *par excellence.* In this respect, as in many others, Mr. Crafts was eminently fortunate—for there can be no doubt but that, throughout the Southern States at least, and, perhaps, throughout the whole country, a taste for literary studies (much more any serious or continued application to them) stands very much in the way of a young man in the pursuits of active life. It raises a presumption among worldly people, that he can never become *practical,* and such a notion when it has once taken root in the public mind, is, beyond all comparison, the most formidable obstacle a man of talents can encounter in such a state of society as ours. Still farther is it from being correct that the "classic structure" of Mr. Crafts' mind, was what prevented him from becoming sufficiently conversant with special pleading. A "classic structure of mind," if there is any meaning in the phrase, is precisely the thing that is wanted in that most refined of all intellectual exercises—for we will take it upon us to assure the very respectable author of the "Memoir," that the notions of his correspondent upon this subject, are as far as possible from being just. "Pleading," or as it is vulgarly called, "special pleading," is neither more nor less than the art of stating a case upon paper, with the utmost brevity and precision that its circumstances will admit of. Instead of "exhausting," it teaches a lawyer to *exclude* every topic that is not necessarily connected with the issue to be submitted to the Court; and, instead of "hackneying every argument," however incidental or unimportant, to select and to set forth the strongest point of his case, and that alone. It has been said a thousand times, and deserves to be repeated a thousand more, that there is nothing out of the exact sciences, that can bear a moment's comparison with the subtle and rigorous logic of our Common Law Pleadings.* "Let none enter here without a knowledge of geometry," was what a Greek philosopher is said to have written over the door of his school. We say the same thing of pleading, in reference to the bar. If a young man finds that he cannot understand the principles, or relish the beauties of this admirable system of reasoning, let him be assured that law is not his vocation. His ignorance may escape detection in the haste and confusion of a Nisi Prius scramble, and he may even be pre-eminently successful in the management of his cases before juries; but his want of that exact and scientific knowledge of legal principles, of which good pleading is at once the fruit and the test, must make itself glaringly manifest in every argument before the higher tribunals. We have no manner of doubt, (be it recorded in passing) that much of the confusion and delay attendant upon our judicial proceedings, is owing to the increasing deficiency of the bar in this particular.

We have dwelt the longer upon this part of the subject, because we fear that the unfortunate error which led Mr. Crafts to neglect his professional studies, and proved ultimately fatal to his hopes, still prevails among our young barristers to a most pernicious extent. His example is an impressive one. We are confident, that, had he employed the first four or five years after his admission to the bar, in the assiduous study of law, he would have continued, to the end of his life, to hold the same elevated rank in society, which his talents had commanded for him at first. We are aware that a notion has generally prevailed, that

---

*As the Common Law is said to be the perfection of reason so its system of pleading is the perfection of reasoning. However, in England not unfrequently
Le raisonnement en bannit la raison:
and some improvements, though, perhaps, they might mar the science, would help justice.

his reasoning powers were irremediably feeble, and that he could never have done much in a mere didactic and practical style of speaking. We are not of this opinion ourselves. The frivolities and crudities with which all his later speeches, whether at the bar or in the legislature, were overrun, furnish no fair criterion of his intellectual character, which had been for a long time sadly on the wane. Nay, for the reasons already given, we do not think that he ever did full justice to his talents for public speaking. The specimen of forensic eloquence, preserved in the present collection, although, perhaps, creditable enough to a young man, is by no means a flattering representation of Mr. Crafts' talents as an orator. It was our good fortune to hear him, in the winter of that very year, deliver, at Columbia, an incomparably better speech— the only one, indeed, which ever gave us an idea of what his powers in debate would have been, had he cultivated them with care, and employed them, seriously and zealously, for the accomplishment of important practical ends, instead of wasting them upon occasions of mere parade and show, and directing them to no other object than the obtaining for himself a little ephemeral applause. The earnest and strenuous advocacy of some real interest—an effort in the orator to impart his own convictions to his audience, and to persuade them to act in conformity with his views—this is an essential element of "true eloquence," which, as Milton* admirably expresses it, "we find to be none but *the serious and hearty love of truth.*" Now, it was precisely this all-important ingredient of "true eloquence" that was wanting in Mr. Crafts' ordinary style of speaking. He sunk the orator in the rhetorician —he forgot the subject in the manner, and sacrificed the ends to the means. Instead of pushing his point with might and main, with powerful argument, and an honest, hearty zeal, like a man of business, a statesman, an advocate, a patriot intent upon the matter in hand—he thought of nothing but the appearance he was to make before his audience. There was always something in his manner that reminded one of an under-graduate at a college exhibition. His whole air, and demeanor, and diction, were expressive of artifice and study. His passion for producing effect, was perpetually breaking out, and his style was

---

*An apology for Smectymnuus.

depraved and deformed by every variety of *concetti*—we mean of course, his general style; for there were times when he spoke with more simplicity and singleness of purpose, and, consequently, with much greater eloquence. The occasion alluded to just now, was one of these. He was urging the impeachment of a man who had been guilty of many outrageous acts of injustice and oppression in the exercise of an inferior judicial office. All the leading lawyers of the house opposed him. We shall never forget his manner of delivering that speech, which was, for a young man, truly admirable, and has, in some respects, probably, never been surpassed on that floor. His shrill but musical voice, elevated to a thrilling pitch—his fine countenance animated with the ardor of debate—the perfect grace and *decorum* of his gesticulation, free from all constraint or artifice—the unaffected elegance and manly simplicity of his diction—the clearness of his statements—the closeness and cogency of his reasonings—the apparent disinterestedness of his zeal—his lofty indignation against injustice—the vigor and perseverance with which he maintained his ground in the debate, against a formidable array of talent and influence—all conspired to give earnest of a high degree of excellence at a more advanced period of life.

We do not mean to say, that, by any application to study or business, however serious and intense, Mr. Crafts could have made himself a *first-rate* debater or an orator after the manner of Demosthenes. Nature had not cast him in that mould. His character was more distinguished by the amiable, than by the sterner virtues, and his understanding was not one of the very largest capacity. Even his physical qualities, although all of them exceedingly prepossessing and attractive, were not of a commanding cast. He was more remarkable for the grace than the dignity, for the beauty than the strength of his person, and there was something effeminate in his exquisitely touching and melodious voice. In short, he was not what is called, in a phrase of the day, a man of great calibre, but he had, certainly, marked talent, and nothing but his suicidal indolence and perverse vanity prevented his becoming able in business and debate. He might have made himself a most brilliant and effective orator in any assembly in the world. Perhaps, no public speaker in this country, ever expressed himself with more uniform purity and elegance, and, occasionally, with more felicity and beauty. He had the great merit of never fatiguing his hearer, while he seldom spoke without delighting him with the point and brilliancy of his occasional sallies, and supplying him with excerpts for his common-place book or the next conversation. It was these shining passages, indeed—the *dulcia vitia* of his style —that attracted so much attention from bad judges, and, at last, as we have already observed, took the place, in almost all that he wrote and spoke, of the simple elegance and severe graces which he had emulated in his early studies.

Montesquieu defines talent "un don que le ciel nous á fait en secrèt et que nous revélons sans le savoir." We like this definition, although it is not the most precise that can be imagined, and were we called upon to exemplify it, we should cite the instance of Mr. Crafts. He was not a man of genius—for that is a word not to be profaned;—he never became an able man, as we have seen—yet it is impossible to read these imperfect remains, picked up here and there, out of a heap of ephemeral rubbish, without perceiving that he was highly gifted by nature. It is very remarkable, too, that (so far as our intercourse with him enabled us to judge) he seldom knew when he had done a good thing. His most hasty and careless compositions, often happened to be his best; while those which he took the most pains with, were sure to be written in his worst taste. He set most value upon such of his compositions as were overrun with metaphor and exaggeration, with antithesis and epigram —while there were simple effusions—spontaneous beauties—which flowed from his pen without his knowing it—which, to borrow a very pretty thought of Sir Walter Scott's, his fancy yielded him with as little effort as a tree resigns its leaves to the gale in autumn, and which he appreciated as men are apt to do, whatever costs them least. But, though their merits escaped him, they were at once perceived and felt by others —by the unlearned as well as the learned—by gentle and simple, by people of taste, and by people of no taste. We were very much struck with the effect which his editorial essays in the *Courier* immediately produced. We have heard him say with a good natured triumph, that, by the end of each month, he regularly got back what he had published, with interest, from all parts of the United States.

We shall, doubtless, be considered by his friends as greatly underrating his poetical talent, when we say that nothing of his that we have seen in verse, would deserve to be published in a separate volume. The author of the "Memoir" entertains a very exalted opinion of some of his minor poems, which he pronounces the best specimens of the Anacreontic style, that are to be found in our language. We think this altogether extravagant. We do not consider these verses as at all better than can be had, at any time, for the "poetical corner" of a fashionable newspaper, or monthly magazine. We have read over all that are collected in the volume before us, with great attention, but our previous opinion has only been confirmed by the attempt to correct it. The poem entitled the "Raciad," is lively and spirited, and may be read with interest. "Sullivan's Island" is equally commendable—but their merit is not high enough to challenge honor from gods, or men, or pillars.

William Elliott (1788–1863)

Born in Beaufort on April 27, 1788, William Elliott graduated from Harvard in 1809 and began a career as a gentleman farmer on his father's plantation. He served as a member of the South Carolina House of Representatives, resigning in 1832 rather than vote for nullification. His *Carolina Sports by Land and Water* (1846) was extremely popular for more than a decade, being reissued in 1859. In 1850 he published *Fiesco, A Tragedy,* and in 1852 *The Letters of Agricola.* Elliott died in Charleston on February 3, 1863.

The Sea-Serpent

Who has not heard of the sea-serpent? There was no educated man in the United States, at least, who had not read with wonder, not unmixed with awe, of the visits of this formidable animal to the coasts of New England. Nothing could be better authenticated than the existence of this undescribed marine monster—nothing more circumstantial and truth-like than the statements published in the Boston papers of the visits made by the nondescript, to the vicinity of Gloucester Point and Nahant! We were told how it appeared on a certain day off Gloucester and was seen by two skippers commanding separate vessels—how it approached one of the sail, as if for the purpose of attack—how its eyes were fierce and fiery—how its head, large as a flour barrel, was raised three feet above the water—how its length was from 90 to 120 feet—how its back while it moved along presented the appearance of bunches which projected above the surface, and how, after approaching within fifty yards of the vessel, it dived beneath it and disappeared, to the unspeakable relief of the crew! It seemed impossible, from the mass of corroborative testimony, to question two important facts—first, the existence of this strange and formidable animal, and secondly, that it took the form of a serpent! It was no myth, but an actual, living, formidable, unchronicled monster of the deep; and, in the excited state of the public mind, expeditions were planned with a view to capture it, and put to rest all future incredulity, by exhibiting it to the gaze of the people.

I remember dining, during this excited state of the public mind, with Dr. Robbins of Boston, at his cottage at Nahant. I well remember the sumptuous fare spread before us by our hospitable host—the delicacy of the viands, the lusciousness of the fruits, the richness of the wines; but what I recall with more especial pleasure, is that Prescott the historian was among the guests, and charmed every stranger present by his colloquial powers, and by a modesty of deportment which sat on him too naturally to have been assumed. By my side, too, sat my early friend and cherished classmate, Francis C. Gray of Boston—now, alas! no more—the refined gentleman, the accomplished scholar, the keen, discriminating writer, whose unnumbered kindnesses come crowding thickly on my memory, as I recall his name—and dim my eyes while I write, with tears!

The cottage of Dr. Robbins, was seated on the very cliff, and over-looked the sea. The cloth was hardly removed, when a murmuring noise from without induced us to look out, and we observed that the adjoining rocks, were being fast populated by an anxious crowd, who were looking intently toward the sea; our eyes took the same direction—and there on the smooth surface, lay the sea-serpent! There was the ripple, there were the bunches—just as they had been described in print, there was the long *wake,* leaving it uncertain what was the actual body, and what represented the displacement of the water caused by the rapid motion of the animal. An excitement seized upon us all, and obeying an impulse which my former training may well explain, I resolved to volunteer with any party that should attempt his capture. Meantime, the serpent disappeared, and when he next presented himself on the surface we brought a telescope to bear on him, and found to our infinite chagrin, that the object which magnified by the haze of the atmosphere, had seemed to us the veritable sea-serpent, had now shrunk to the dimensions of a despicable horse-mackerel!

"But surely sir, you have mistaken your latitude—you are adrift without a compass! What have you to do with the sea-serpent? He is the peculiar property of New England, he never condescends to show himself elsewhere, he is of the Pilgrim States, their very specialty; as much and as exclusively theirs, as the gift of witchcraft, the privilege of detecting, and the divine right of punishing it. With what propriety, therefore, can you pretend to introduce him in a book of "Carolina Sports?"

Have patience! most choleric reader! Patience is a piscatory as well as an Apostolic virtue; as needful (you may find,) to the reader of fish stories, as to the fisherman himself. Patience, and we shall see.

The March winds were whistling sharply, as is their wont, along the southern Atlantic sea-board, when the gallant steamer Wm. Seabrook loosed her hawser from the wharf at Savannah to which she had been moored, and pressed forward on her inland voyage to Charleston. At her wheel stood her stalwart commander, Blankinsop, long known and well reputed in all the region roundabout. And now the steamer glides

through the yellow waters of the Savannah River, between fields celebrated for their production of rice, and enriched by the deposit from
these same turbid yellow waters, until they rival Egypt in fertility. And
well they may—for while only one annual inundation enriches the
Egyptian soil, here, twice in the short life of every moon, are these fields
refreshed and renewed by fertilizing inundations; and now the steamer
approaches the sea, whose salt tides contend for mastery with the fresh
waters from the high lands, that having long held undisputed possession
of the channel, are now urging boisterously their exclusive and prescriptive right, against the encroachments of the ocean. And now she
winds along the corkscrew channel—worn by the contending tides in
the soft oozy bottom—and weathers the black-oyster rocks, and rounds
the tail of Grenadier bank with its flankers of snow-white breakers, and
then she bears up for Callibogue Sound, and passes the mouth of the
river of "May"—Laudonnières' river of that name, or else wrongfully
baptized in it, by some bungling geographer; and then with rapid
strokes, she dashes through Skull Creek—Hilton Head on the starboard,
Pinckney Island on the larboard bow—till all at once she emerges on
the broad, deep estuary of Port Royal, already familiar to the reader as
the sporting ground and the battle ground of the devil-fish! And now
the steamer was merrily dashing the foam from her prow—weathering
the tail of Paris bank, and pointing up Beaufort River toward the town
of that name, when lo and behold! what startling spectacle then met the
gaze of the astonished commander! What but the veritable sea serpent!
that tired, we may suppose, of the monotony of his eastern haunts, was
amusing himself with an excursion to the South, and had looked in
(*en passant*) on the pleasant harbor of Port Royal! Mars and Bellona!
what did the captain do? There lay alongside of him this leviathan of
sea monsters, "long as his steamboat, stout as his yawl." There he lay in
his interminable length, his bunches all visible (as may be seen on the
frontispiece of many a veracious pamphlet of the day), each several
bunch of the series set down by authority, and verified by a Gloucester
affidavit! What did the captain do? Why, like a prudent and considerate
commander, he did not do what you or I, in a dare-devil spirit might
have done—*he did not* attack the monster! He would not risk owner's
property, you see! If he attacked the strange craft, and came to damage

thereby, he might forfeit insurance, for this risk was not put down in the policy, you know! So, giving the monster a wide berth, he turned tail, blew off three terrific blasts at him from his steam whistle, and drove away for the town of Beaufort, as if the devil himself was in his rear!

The captain had no sooner reached the wharf, and disclosed his startling intelligence, than the whole town was aflame with excitement!

"What is this?" said a fine looking burly gentleman, who came bustling down with an air of official authority about him. "What hoax are you playing off on us? The sea-serpent in Broad River! Tell that to the marines!"

"As sure as you live," said the captain, "I saw him two hours ago."

"The hell you did! Why did you not hawser him, and bring him up to town?"

"He was as large round as my yawl boat, and as long as the steamer," said the captain, explanatorily.

"The old one of course," said the stout gentleman. "But what should the devil or any of his vicegerents find to do in these waters? I should be glad to know! Didn't the Saints make such a clean sweep of us some years back, that devil a subject can now be found among us, fit for his majesty's service?"

"I don't know that," said a keen looking, ascetic man, in a quiet tone, "he might get some, from what I hear, by voluntary enlistment!"

"The captain took an afternoon observation," hinted one.

"Twilight magnifies," said another. But in spite of jeers and doubts, the captain's testimony was positive, earnest and unvarying, and the conviction soon became general that the monster was really in Port Royal! Then came the unanimous determination to capture him at all hazards!

"We'll teach this Yankee craft to cruise in our waters," said one.

"Doubtless, he has his belly stuffed with abolition tracts," said a hungry looking secessionist, leading off on the grateful scent.

"Gentlemen," said a third, "the sea-serpent is here—that's a fact. We must capture him, that's another fact, or soon will be. Who'll volunteer? He shall not insult us by his presence in these waters—us, who have encountered and beaten the devil-fish, who are his betters for aught we know—us, who have trailed behind them all night in our undecked skiff, on the open sea, and mastered them with the rising sun. We'll kill him, gentlemen; we're the boys to do it." And it was resolved!

The steamer whose intelligence had caused such unwonted commotion in this ordinarily tranquil town, now steamed off for her destination, unconscious of, and indifferent to, the ferment she had excited. Oh, Beaufort! thou mother of beautiful women and illustrious men, who devotest thy daughters to Heaven, in this world and the next; but dismissest thy sons in an opposite direction! Thou unmatchable town, that, devouring the oyster, still delightest in the shell! Whose mansions, streets, and roads, are all of shell-work; that blindest the eyes of thy people with concrete dust, and with concrete walls defendest thyself against the approach of thy enemies! Thou mathematical paradox, whose angles become right lines by "order of council," and whose right lines are as tortuous as angles! Thou financial wonder! whose taxes increase as thy means diminish, and whose inhabitants grow rich by borrowing from each other! Oh, Beaufort! lovely always, but like a freckled beauty, loveliest at a distance! what a storm of excitement burst over you on this eventful night, and startled you from your accustomed somnolency! There was many a lovely eye that did not close a lid, for fear of the encroachment of the serpent! There was many a manly heart that waked as well, but throbbed with impatience to grapple with, and subdue him! They did not sleep; long before midnight the lieges of Beaufort were afloat, intent on mischief. Prominent among them was Capt. J. G. B., once the honored captain of the Beaufort Volunteer Guards—now the commander of the consolidated corps of artillery and guards. He was to command the artillery of the expedition. A man of honor and worth was he; a high-toned man, whose only quarrel with life was, that his military aspirations had never been gratified: that his misgoverned country had never indulged in the luxury of war, nor afforded him the opportunity for that distinction, for which his soul pined! "Here is a chance after all," said the captain, rubbing his hands. "It is not war, but something almost as good!" Then there was Captain G. P. E., whilom captain of this same artillery. He was to command the squadron. Confident was he of making minced-meat of the sea-monster! "Had he not driven bayonets and pikes and harpoons innumerable into devil-fish? Was he to be daunted now? No, not he! He would draw the serpent's teeth, and leave them in pawn with his friend who swore so terribly! He would give his flesh to the sharks—his skeleton to Dr. ———, in exchange for a unicorn, or to his friend the colonel, in exchange for his favorite mermaid! His skin he would present to the museum at Salem, to be exhibited gratis to the enterprising people of Gloucester, and in exchange, if they could find one, for the skin of a witch."

They launched a flat, which, in consideration, doubtless, of his known antipathy to serpents, they dubbed "Saint Patrick," and in it embarked Captain B. with his six-pounder, well supplied with ammunition, and with a select squad of artillerists to serve it. Next came Captain G. P. E. in his sail boat, "The Eagle," with a lighter armament, but indorsed by an apparatus fitted for devil-fishing, such as harpoons, ropes, and buoys. Lastly, came a skiff, to ply between the heavier boats, and pick up stragglers should any be tossed overboard in the expected fray. Here was good strategy—an anchor to windward, a loop-hole for retreat, were it necessary, and security for some at least of the assailants, for it would be difficult for his highness, with all his imputed fierceness and voracity, to take down three boats at a gulp!

Full of spirit, and of high hope and expectation, the party now embarked, and went merrily on their way with wind and tide in their favor, until at dawn of day they found themselves on the waters of Broad River, by the way of Archer's Creek. They cast their eyes wistfully east, south and west, over the wide expanse, but no serpent was to be seen. They agreed to divide, and signal each other should either party come in sight of the enemy. "St. Patrick," with the skiff in company, passed up the river with the tide (you are too fond of that, my dear St. Patrick!). The Eagle spreads her wings and sails away to seaward, against the tide. After sailing on that tack for some time without seeing anything unusual, she turns to rejoin her consort, who had now made an interval of several miles between the boats; when the look-out boy stationed in the bow of the Eagle calls out, "I see something ahead!" "Where?—where?" and all hands rush to the head of the boat to see, and beheld close aboard of them an object like a boat turned bottom up. "Gentlemen," said Captain George, "look out, the object is right ahead—but a hundred yards off—we shall be in the jaws of the serpent before we can stop! Helm down." The boat would not answer the helm, there was too much live weight at the bows. "To your places, gentlemen! Let go sheet ropes!" She fell off from the wind, and the boat passes, just without touching, the object which had called forth this sudden commotion. "Very like a whale," cried Captain George, as he gazed at the unknown. "Look there! another; we're in a shoal of whales! There's five of them, as I live; three full grown and two young ones! No sea-serpent, after all; but game, nevertheless, and royal game too; a perfect god send to us—let us signal our consort, and bring them to action."

"Ah, Saint Patrick! that habit of yours, of taking it aisy, and going with wind and tide, has brought you into trouble! These four miles of head wind and tide, and hard tugging at the oars, before you can face the enemy, all come of this obliging disposition of yours!" The whales, too, were going against the tide, so that the match after all was not so very unequal, and St. Patrick, after a hard tug, with a swaggering air, that seemed to say, "arrah now, won't I take the consait out of you?" ranged up alongside the enemy, and when he had got within a hundred yards, let go a six-pound ball at the first whale that showed himself above the water. "They take no notice of us!" said the baffled artillery-man. "Try another shot." They tried another and another, but the balls went dancing and ricocheting over the waves innocent of blood! No wonder! the wind blew high, the sea was rough, and Saint Patrick (shame on him) was a leetle unsteady! "Now, Slowman," said Captain B., "try your hand; your father was our crack shot, and *you* boast that you can bring down a sparrow on the wing with your six-pounder; show us your skill, now!" "Well, captain, but a sparrow on the wing is easier than a whale under water; but here goes!" And he rams down a canister of grape, and when the next whale rises, a shower of balls is flying about his head. "Ha, ha! he feels us now!" The whale flings his fluke aloft, and brings it down on the water with a report that rivalled our cannon, then plunges downward, and when he next shows himself on the surface, there are some keen-sighted sportsmen aboard who aver that they spy a hole in his jacket, and a piece of blubber fat sticking out of the orifice!

Meanwhile, the whales began to move at increased speed toward the sea, and it became doubtful whether St. Patrick could retain his position so as to continue the action.

"Come," said Captain George, "they must not escape us. I'll go in the skiff, and tackle them with my devil-fish harpoon. Who'll steer the skiff? I'll take two boys to row."

"But, maussa," said Pompey (who was one of the skiff hands), "I can't go close dat ting in maussa new boat anyhow. He tail strong as steam engine, and he knock the boat all to shivers."

"Don't want you, Pompey; another hand will do as well, or better."

So off they start; Captain George, staff in hand, at the bow, while two hands pulled vigorously at the oars. The ripple caused by the motion of the fish against the current, showed their direction, even while they were submerged. So, rowing parallel to the shoal, the whale had no sooner emerged, than the boatmen were ordered to pull right in for his head. The boat actually touched him, when Captain George struck the harpoon into his head, and as he seemed stunned or insensible, drove it in with both hands, till the skiff recoiled with the force of the blow. Thirty fathoms of rope, attached to the harpoon, had been wound round a cask, which was now thrown overboard, and the cask began to spin around in a marvellous manner, until the whole line was unwound, when it went bobbing under and reappearing, with the rapid or slower movement of the fish.

Three cheers went up from the assembled sportsmen at the execution of this daring feat; and high hopes were entertained that they would succeed in capturing the whale. The fish, meanwhile, floundered and plunged, and lashed the water with his powerful fluke, whirling over while on the surface, until the rope was observed to be twisted several times round his body, while the staff was seen sticking from his throat. The sportsmen, in their three boats, followed closely in his wake, waiting for him to exhaust himself, and in the interim, betook themselves to breakfast. Suddenly, the cask became motionless. They approach, pull upon the line, and, to their deep mortification, discover that the harpoon had drawn out.

"Now is *my* turn," said Captain John; and, taking his place in the skiff, he repeated the exploit of Captain George—struck a fish with great force, which, like his predecessor, contrived, after a short struggle, to rid himself of the harpoon.

"My turn is come again," said Captain George; and, planting himself a second time in the bow of the skiff, he struck his harpoon deeply, this time, in the body of the fish. Again were witnessed the furious plunges and contortions of the whale; again the harpoon tore out, and the baffled sportsmen, on the failure of this, their third cast, had to confess to themselves, that their tackle was inadequate to the capture of a whale. The wind now veered to the east, and a rain-storm set in, so that it was necessary to draw off from the enemy, and make a harbor for the security of the boats, and especially of that which was burdened with a piece of artillery, which was accordingly done.

The next day was Sunday, and our sportsmen did not follow the example of the commanders of modern Christian armies, who apparently select that day for an engagement. They staid at home, and retook their positions on Monday, with better knowledge, better equipments, and in every way better prepared for success. But all too late—the enemy had fled! The captain of a coaster met them on their retreat, as they left the harbor; and nothing more was heard of them, except that rumor reported one of them as having been stranded on the island of Kiawah!

When, during the pursuit of these whales, the fish occasionally threw themselves in line, following in each other's wakes near the surface, with their fins projecting above the water, the close resemblance to an immense serpent was brought strikingly to the minds of our sportsmen; and it was easy to perceive, how, in a hazy atmosphere, or during an agitated sea, the sporting of a shoal of whales might represent (to the mind of an excited mariner), and be honestly mistaken for the redoubtable sea-serpent!

When the expedition returned to Beaufort, there were some to taunt it with its want of success.

"Well, Captain George, where is your prize? You have not caught the whale, after all."

"No," says Captain George, "but we have done better; we have killed the sea-serpent!"

John C. Calhoun (1782–1850)

The "shining champion of the plantation regime" was born of Scotch-Irish parentage in Abbeville District, on March 18, 1782. John Caldwell Calhoun prepared for college under the tutelage of Dr. Moses Waddel, his brother-in-law, graduating from Yale in 1804, after which he studied law. His career was brilliant and controversial. Elected to Congress in 1811, he became Secretary of War (1817–25) under Monroe, and served as Vice-President (1825–32) under Presidents John Quincy Adams and Andrew Jackson. An advocate of state rights and nullification, he wrote the "South Carolina Exposition" (1828), his best statement of those views. Resigning the Vice-Presidency in 1832 to become U.S. Senator from South Carolina, Calhoun served continuously (with the exception of 1844, when he was Secretary of State) until his death in Washington in 1850. His important speeches and political treatises were collected in six volumes in 1853–55.

Speech on Henry Clay's Compromise Resolutions

Having now shown what cannot save the Union, I return to the question with which I commenced, How can the Union be saved? There is but one way by which it can with any certainty; and that is, by a full and final settlement, on the principle of justice, of all the questions at issue between the two sections. The South asks for justice, simple justice, and less she ought not to take. She has no compromise to offer but the Constitution, and no concession or surrender to make. She has already surrendered so much that she has little left to surrender. Such a settlement would go to the root of the evil, and remove all cause of discontent, by satisfying the South she could remain honorably and safely in the Union, and thereby restore the harmony and fraternal feelings between the sections which existed anterior to the Missouri agitation. Nothing else can, with any certainty, finally and forever settle the questions at issue, terminate agitation, and save the Union.

But can this be done? Yes, easily; not by the weaker party, for it can of itself do nothing—not even protect itself—but by the stronger. The North has only to will it to accomplish it—to do justice by conceding to the South an equal right in the acquired territory, and to do her duty by causing the stipulations relative to fugitive slaves to be faithfully fulfilled—to cease the agitation of the slave question, and to provide for the insertion of a provision in the Constitution, by an amendment, which will restore to the South in substance the power she possessed of protecting herself, before the equilibrium between the sections was destroyed by the action of this Government. There will be no difficulty in devising such a provision—one that will protect the South, and which at the same time will improve and strengthen the Government, instead of impairing and weakening it.

But will the North agree to do this? It is for her to answer this question. But, I will say, she cannot refuse, if she has half the love of the Union which she professes to have, or without justly exposing herself

John C. Calhoun, "Speech on Henry Clay's Compromise Resolutions" and "Disquisition on Government" in *Calhoun: Basic Documents,* ed. John M. Anderson (State College, Pa.: Bald Eagle Press, 1952), pp. 322–24, 86–97. Copyright 1952 by Bald Eagle Press. Reprinted by permission of the publisher.

to the charge that her love of power and aggrandizement is far greater than her love of the Union. At all events, the responsibility of saving the Union rests on the North, and not the South. The South cannot save it by any act of hers, and the North may save it without any sacrifice whatever, unless to do justice, and to perform her duties under the Constitution, should be regarded by her as a sacrifice.

It is time, Senators, that there should be an open and manly avowal on all sides, as to what is intended to be done. If the question is not now settled, it is uncertain whether it ever can hereafter be; and we, as the representatives of the States of this Union, regarded as governments, should come to a distinct understanding as to our respective views, in order to ascertain whether the great questions at issue can be settled or not. If you, who represent the stronger portion, cannot agree to settle them on the broad principle of justice and duty, say so; and let the States we both represent agree to separate and part in peace. If you are unwilling we should part in peace, tell us so, and we shall know what to do, when you reduce the question to submission or resistance. If you remain silent, you will compel us to infer by your acts what you intend. In that case, California will become the test question. If you admit her, under all the difficulties that oppose her admission, you compel us to infer that you intend to exclude us from the whole of the acquired territories, with the intention of destroying irretrievably the equilibrium between the two sections. We would be blind not to perceive, in that case, that your real objects are power and aggrandizement, and infatuated not to act accordingly.

I have now, Senators, done my duty in expressing my opinions fully, freely, and candidly, on this solemn occasion. In doing so, I have been governed by the motives which have governed me in all the stages of the agitation of the slavery question since its commencement. I have exerted myself, during the whole period, to arrest it, with the intention of saving the Union, if it could be done; and, if it could not, to save the section where it has pleased Providence to cast my lot, and which I sincerely believe has justice and the Constitution on its side. Having faithfully done my duty to the best of my ability, both to the Union and my section, throughout this agitation, I shall have the consolation, let what will come, that I am free from all responsibility.

From "Disquisition on Government"

I shall, in conclusion, proceed to exemplify the elementary principles, which have been established, by giving a brief account of the origin and character of the governments of Rome and Great Britain; the two most remarkable and perfect of their respective forms of constitutional governments. The object is to show how these principles were applied, in the more simple forms of such governments; preparatory to an exposition of the mode in which they have been applied in our own more complex system. It will appear that, in each, the principles are the same; and that the difference in their application resulted from the different situation and social condition of the respective communities. They were modified, in each, so as to conform to these; and, hence, their remarkable success. They were applied to communities in which hereditary rank had long prevailed. Their respective constitutions originated in concession to the people; and, through them, they acquired a participation in the powers of government. But with us, they were applied to communities where all political rank and distinction between citizens were excluded; and where government had its origin in the will of the people.

But, however different their origin and character, it will be found that the object in each was the same,—to blend and harmonize the conflicting interests of the community; and the means the same,—taking the sense of each class or portion through its appropriate organ, and considering the concurrent sense of all as the sense of the whole community. Such being the fact, an accurate and clear conception how this was effected, in their more simple forms, will enable us better to understand how it was accomplished in our far more refined, artificial, and complex form.

It is well known to all, the least conversant with their history, that the Roman people consisted of two distinct orders, or classes,—the Patricians and the Plebeians; and that the line of distinction was so strongly drawn, that, for a long time, the right of intermarriage between them was prohibited. After the overthrow of the monarchy and the expulsion of the Tarquins, the government fell exclusively under the control of the patricians, who, with their clients and dependents, formed, at the time, a very numerous and powerful body. At first, while there was danger of the return of the exiled family, they treated the plebeians with kindness; but, after it had passed away, with oppression and cruelty.

It is not necessary, with the object in view, to enter into a minute account of the various acts of oppression and cruelty to which they were subjected. It is sufficient to state, that, according to the usages of war at the time, the territory of a conquered people became the property of the conquerors; and that the plebeians were harassed and oppressed by incessant wars, in which the danger and toil were theirs, while all the fruits of victory, (the lands of the vanquished, and the spoils of war,) accrued to the benefit of their oppressors. The result was such as might be expected. They were impoverished, and forced, from necessity, to borrow from the patricians, at usurious and exorbitant interest, funds which they had been enriched through their blood and toil; and to pledge their all for repayment at stipulated periods. In case of default, the pledge became forfeited; and, under the provisions of law in such cases, the debtors were liable to be seized, and sold or imprisoned by their creditors in private jails prepared and kept for the purpose. These savage provisions were enforced with the utmost rigor against the indebted and impoverished plebeians. They constituted, indeed, an essential part of the system through which they were plundered and oppressed by the patricians.

A system so oppressive could not be endured. The natural consequences followed. Deep hatred was engendered between the orders, accompanied by factions, violence, and corruption, which distracted and weakened the government. At length, an incident occurred which roused the indignation of the plebeians to the utmost pitch, and which ended in an open rupture between the two orders.

An old soldier, who had long served the country, and had fought with bravery in twenty-eight battles, made his escape from the prison of his creditor,—squalid, pale, and famished. He implored the protection of the plebeians. A crowd surrounded him; and his tale of service to the country, and the cruelty with which he had been treated by his creditor, kindled a flame, which continued to rage until it extended to the army. It refused to continue any longer in service,—crossed the Anio, and took possession of the sacred mount. The patricians divided in opinion as to the course which should be pursued. The more violent insisted on an appeal to arms, but, fortunately, the counsel of the moderate, which recommended concession and compromise, prevailed. Commissioners were appointed to treat with the army; and a formal compact was entered into between the orders, and ratified by the oaths of each, which conceded to the plebeians the right to elect two tribunes, as the protectors of their order, and made their persons sacred. The number was afterwards increased to ten, and their election by centuries changed to election by tribes;—a mode by which the plebeians secured a decided preponderance.

Such was the origin of the tribunate;—which, in process of time, opened all the honors of the government to the plebeians. They acquired the right, not only of vetoing the passage of all laws, but also their execution; and thus obtained, through their tribunes, a negative on the entire action of the government, without divesting the patricians of their control over the Senate. By this arrangement, the government was placed under the concurrent and joint voice of the two orders, expressed through separate and appropriate organs; the one possessing the positive, and the other the negative powers of the government. This simple change converted it from an absolute, into a constitutional government,—from a government of the patricians only, to that of the whole Roman people,—and from an aristocracy into a republic. In doing this, it laid the solid foundation of Roman liberty and greatness.

A superficial observer would pronounce a government, so organized, as that one order should have the power of making and executing the laws, and another, or the representatives of another, the unlimited authority of preventing their enactment and execution,—if not wholly impracticable, at least, too feeble to stand the shocks to which all governments are subject; and would, therefore, predict its speedy dissolution, after a distracted and inglorious career.

How different from the result! Instead of distraction, it proved to be the bond of concord and harmony; instead of weakness, of unequalled strength;—and, instead of a short and inglorious career, one of great length and immortal glory. It moderated the conflicts between the orders; harmonized their interests, and blended them into one; substituted devotion to country in the place of devotion to particular orders; called forth the united strength and energy of the whole, in the hour of danger; raised to power, the wise and patriotic; elevated the Roman name above all others; extended her authority and dominion over the greater part of the then known world, and transmitted the influence of her laws and institutions to the present day. Had the opposite counsel prevailed at this critical juncture; had an appeal been made to arms instead of to concession and compromise, Rome, instead of being what she afterwards became, would, in all probability, have been as inglorious, and as little known to posterity as the insignificant states which surrounded her, whose names and existence would have been long since consigned to oblivion, had they not been preserved in the history of her conquests of them. But for the wise course then adopted, it is not improbable,—whichever order might have prevailed, —that she would have fallen under some cruel and petty tyrant;—and, finally, been conquered by some of the neighboring states,—or by the Carthaginians, or the Gauls. To the fortunate turn which events then took, she owed her unbounded sway and imperishable renown.

It is true, that the tribunate, after raising her to a height of power and prosperity never before equalled, finally became one of the instruments by which her liberty was overthrown:—but it was not until she became exposed to new dangers, growing out of increase of wealth and the great extent of her dominions, against which the tribunate furnished no guards. Its original object was the protection of the plebeians against oppression and abuse of power on the part of the patricians. This, it thoroughly accomplished; but it had no power to protect the people of the numerous and wealthy conquered countries from being plundered by consuls and proconsuls. Nor could it prevent the plunderers from using the enormous wealth, which they extorted from the impoverished and ruined provinces, to corrupt and debase the people; nor arrest the formation of parties, (irrespective of the old division of patricians and plebeians,) having no other object than to obtain the control of the government for the purpose of plunder. Against these formidable evils, her constitution furnished no adequate security. Under their baneful influence, the possession of the government became the object of the most violent conflicts not between patricians and plebeians,—but between profligate and corrupt factions. They continued with increasing violence, until, finally, Rome sunk, as must every community under similar circumstances, beneath the strong grasp, the despotic rule of the chieftain of the successful party;—the sad, but only alternative which remained to prevent universal violence, confusion and anarchy. The Republic had, in reality, ceased to exist long before the establishment of the Empire. The interval was filled by the rule of ferocious, corrupt and bloody factions. There was, indeed, a small but patriotic body of eminent individuals, who struggled, in vain, to correct abuses, and to restore the government to its primitive character and purity;—and who sacrificed their lives in their endeavors to accomplish an object so virtuous and noble. But it can be no disparagement to the tribunate, that the great powers conferred on it for wise purposes, and which it had so fully accomplished, should be seized upon, during this violent and corrupt interval, to overthrow the liberty it had established, and so long nourished and supported.

In assigning such consequence to the tribunate, I must not overlook other important provisions of the Constitution of the Roman government. The Senate, as far as we are informed, seems to have been admirably constituted to secure consistency and steadiness of action. The power,—when the Republic was exposed to imminent danger,—to appoint a dictator,—vested, for a limited period, with almost boundless authority; the two consuls, and the manner of electing them; the auguries; the sibylline books; the priesthood, and the censorship;—all of which appertained to the patricians,—were, perhaps, indispensable to withstand the vast and apparently irregular power of the tribunate; —while the possession of such great powers by the patricians, made it necessary to give proportionate strength to the only organ through which the plebeians could act on the government with effect. The government was, indeed, powerfully constituted; and, apparently, well proportioned both in its positive and negative organs. It was truly an iron government. Without the tribunate, it proved to be one of the most oppressive and cruel that ever existed; but with it, one of the strongest and best.

The origin and character of the British government are so well known, that a very brief sketch, with the object in view, will suffice. The causes which ultimately moulded it into its present form, commenced with the Norman Conquest. This introduced the feudal system, with its necessary appendages, a hereditary monarchy and nobility; the former in the line of the chief, who led the invading army; —and the latter in that of his distinguished followers. They became his feudatories. The country,—both land and people,—(the latter as serfs,) was divided between them. Conflicts soon followed between the monarch and the nobles,—as must ever be the case under such systems. They were followed, in the progress of events, by efforts, on the part both of monarchs and nobles, to conciliate the favor of the people. They, in consequence, gradually rose to power. At every step of their ascent, they became more important,—and were more and more courted,— until at length their influence was so sensibly felt, that they were summoned to attend the meeting of parliament by delegates; not, however, as an estate of the realm, or constituent member of the body politic. The first summons came from the nobles; and was designed to conciliate their good feelings and secure their co-operation in the war against the king. This was followed by one from him; but his object was simply to have them present at the meeting of parliament, in order to be *consulted* by the crown, on questions relating to taxes and supplies; not, indeed, to discuss the right to lay the one, and to raise the other,—for the King claimed the arbitrary authority to do both,—but with a view to facilitate their collection, and to reconcile them to their imposition.

From this humble beginning, they, after a long struggle, accompanied by many vicissitudes, raised themselves to be considered one of the estates of the realm; and, finally, in their efforts to enlarge and secure what they had gained, overpowered, for a time, the other two estates; and thus concentrated all power in a single estate or body. This, in effect, made the government absolute, and led to consequences which, as by a fixed law, must ever result in popular governments of this form;—namely:—to organized parties, or, rather, factions, contending violently to obtain or retain the control of the government; and this, again, by laws almost as uniform, to the concentration of all the powers of government in the hands of the military commander of the successful party.

His heir was too feeble to hold the sceptre he had grasped; and the general discontent with the result of the revolution, led to the restoration of the old dynasty; without defining the limits between the powers of the respective estates.

After a short interval, another revolution followed, in which the lords and commons united against the king. This terminated in his overthrow; and the transfer of the crown to a collateral branch of the family, accompanied by a declaration of rights, which defined the powers of the several estates of the realm; and, finally, perfected and established the constitution. Thus, a feudal monarchy was converted, through a slow but steady process of many centuries, into a highly refined constitutional monarchy, without changing the basis of the original government.

As it now stands, the realm consists of three estates; the king; the lords temporal and spiritual; and the commons. The parliament is the grand council. It possesses the supreme power. It enacts laws, by the concurring assent of the lords and commons,—subject to the approval of the king. The executive power is vested in the monarch, who is regarded as constituting the first estate. Although irresponsible himself, he can only act through responsible ministers and agents. They are responsible to the other estates; to the lords, as constituting the high court before whom all the servants of the crown may be tried for malpractices, and crimes against the realm, or official delinquencies;—and to the commons, as possessing the impeaching power, and constituting the grand inquest of the kingdom. These provisions, with their legislative powers,—especially that of withholding supplies,—give them a controlling influence on the executive department, and, virtually, a participation in its powers;—so that the acts of the government, throughout its entire range, may be fairly considered as the result of the concurrent and joint action of the three estates;—and, as these embrace all the orders,—of the concurrent and joint action of the estates of the realm.

He would take an imperfect and false view of the subject who should consider the king, in his mere individual character, or even as the head of the royal family,—as constituting an estate. Regarded in either light, so far from deserving to be considered as the First Estate, —and the head of the realm, as he is,—he would represent an interest too inconsiderable to be an object of special protection. Instead of this, he represents what in reality is, habitually and naturally, the most powerful interest, all things considered, under every form of government in all civilized communities,—*the tax-consuming interest;* or, more broadly, the great interest which necessarily grows out of the action of the government, be its form what it may;—the interest that *lives by the government.* It is composed of the recipients of its honors and emoluments; and may be properly called, the government interest, or party;—in contradistinction to the rest of the community,—or, (as they must be properly called,) the people or commons. The one comprehends all who are supported by the government;—and the other all who support the government:—and it is only because the former are strongest, all things being considered, that they are enabled to retain, for any considerable time, advantages so great and commanding.

This great and predominant interest is naturally represented by a single head. For it is impossible, without being so represented, to distribute the honors and emoluments of the government among those who compose it, without producing discord and conflict:—and it is only by preventing these, that advantages so tempting can be long retained. And, hence, the strong tendency of this great interest to the monarchical form;—that is, to be represented by a single individual. On the contrary, the antagonistic interest,—that which supports the government, has the opposite tendency;—a tendency to be represented by many; because a large assembly can better judge, than one individual or a few, what burdens the community can bear;—and how it can be most equally distributed, and easily collected.

In the British government, the king constitutes an Estate, because he is the head and representative of this great interest. He is the conduit through which, all the honors and emoluments of the government flow; —while the House of Commons, according to the theory of the government, is the head and representative of the opposite—the great taxpaying interest, by which the government is supported.

Between these great interests, there is necessarily a constant and strong tendency to conflict; which, if not counteracted, must end in violence and an appeal to force,—to be followed by revolution, as has been explained. To prevent this, the House of Lords, as one of the estates of the realm, is interposed; and constitutes the conservative power of the government. It consists, in fact, of that portion of the community who are the principal recipients of the honors, emoluments, and other advantages derived from the government; and whose condition cannot be improved, but must be made worse by the triumph of either of the conflicting estates over the other; and, hence, it is opposed to the ascendency of either,—and in favor of preserving the equilibrium between them.

This sketch, brief as it is, is sufficient to show, that these two constitutional governments,—by far the most illustrious of their respective kinds,—conform to the principles that have been established, alike in their origin and in their construction. The constitutions of both originated in a pressure, occasioned by conflicts of interests between hostile classes or orders, and were intended to meet the pressing exigencies of the occasion; neither party, it would seem, having any conception of the principles involved, or the consequences to follow, beyond the immediate objects in contemplation. It would, indeed, seem almost impossible for constitutional governments, founded on orders or classes, to originate in any other manner. It is difficult to conceive that any people, among whom they did not exist, would, or could voluntarily institute them, in order to establish such governments; while it is not at all wonderful, that they should grow out of conflicts between different orders or classes when aided by a favorable combination of circumstances.

The constitutions of both rest on the same principle;—an organism by which the voice of each order or class is taken through its appropriate organ; and which requires the concurring voice of all to constitute that of the whole community. The effects, too, were the same in both;—to unite and harmonize conflicting interests;—to strengthen attachments to the whole community, and to moderate that to the respective orders or classes; to rally all, in the hour of danger, around the standard of their country; to elevate the feeling of nationality, and to develop power, moral and physical, to an extraordinary extent. Yet each has its distinguishing features, resulting from the difference of their organisms, and the circumstances in which they respectively originated.

In the government of Great Britain, the three orders are blended in the legislative department; so that separate and concurring acts of each is necessary to make laws; while, on the contrary, in the Roman, one order had the power of making laws, and another of annulling them, or arresting their execution. Each had its peculiar advantages. The Roman developed more fully the love of country and the feelings of nationality. *"I am a Roman citizen,"*—was pronounced with a pride and elevation of sentiment, never, perhaps, felt before or since, by any citizen or subject of any community, in announcing the country to which he belonged.

It also developed more fully the power of the community. Taking into consideration their respective population, and the state of the arts at the different periods, Rome developed more power, comparatively, than Great Britain ever has,—vast as that is, and has been,—or, perhaps, than any other community ever did. Hence, the mighty control she acquired from a beginning so humble. But the British government is far superior to that of Rome, in its adaptation and capacity to embrace under its control extensive dominions, without subverting its constitution. In this respect, the Roman constitution was defective;—and, in consequence, soon began to exhibit marks of decay, after Rome had extended her dominions beyond Italy; while the British holds under its sway, without apparently impairing either, an empire equal to that, under the weight of which the constitution and liberty of Rome were crushed. This great advantage it derives from its different structure, especially that of the executive department; and the character of its conservative principle. The former is so constructed as to prevent, in consequence of its unity and hereditary character, the violent and factious struggles to obtain the control of the government,—and, with it, the vast patronage which distracted, corrupted, and finally subverted the Roman Republic. Against this fatal disease, the latter had no security whatever; while the British government,—besides the advantages it possesses, in this respect, from the structure of its executive department,—has, in the character of its conservative principle, another and powerful security against it. Its character is such, that patronage, instead of weakening, strengthens it:—For, the greater the patronage of the government, the greater will be the share which falls to the estate constituting the conservative department of the government; and the more eligible its condition, the greater its opposition to any radical change in its form. The two causes combined, give to the government a greater capacity of holding under subjection extensive dominions, without subverting the constitution or destroying liberty, than has ever been possessed by any other. It is difficult, indeed, to assign any limit to its capacity in this respect. The most probable which can be assigned is, its ability to bear increased burdens;—the taxation necessary to meet the expenses incident to the acquisition and government of such vast dominions, may prove, in the end, so heavy as to crush, under its weight, the laboring and productive portions of the population.

I have now finished the brief sketch I proposed, of the origin and character of these two renowned governments; and shall next proceed to consider the character, origin and structure of the Government of the United States. It differs from the Roman and British, more than they differ from each other; and, although an existing government of recent origin, its character and structure are perhaps less understood than those of either.

James Mathewes Legaré (1823–59)

Born in Charleston on November 26, 1823, James Mathewes Legaré, a kinsman of Hugh Swinton Legaré, studied law in Charleston and spent his life dividing his talents among his legal, artistic, literary, and mechanical interests. In addition to writing poems and articles for various Northern and Southern periodicals, Legaré published in 1847 *Orta-Undis, and Other Poems,* a collection containing his best work. He died in Aiken on March 30, 1859. Though J. M. Legaré has generally been neglected by critics and scholars, in the judgment of Professor Jay B. Hubbell he was "one of the best Southern poets of his time" (*The South in American Literature, 1607–1900,* p. 559).

The Reaper

How still Earth lies!—behind the pines
The summer clouds sink slowly down.
The sunset gilds the higher hills
And distant steeples of the town.

Refreshed and moist the meadow spreads,
Birds sing from out the dripping leaves,
And standing in the breast-high corn
I see the farmer bind his sheaves.

It was when on the fallow fields
The heavy frosts of winter lay,
A rustic with unsparing hand
Strewed seed along the furrowed way.

And I too, walking through the waste
And wintry hours of the past,
Have in the furrows made by griefs
The seeds of future harvests cast.

Rewarded well, if when the world
Grows dimmer in the ebbing light,
And all the valley lies in shade,
But sunset glimmers on the height.

Down in the meadows of the heart
The birds sing out a last refrain,
And ready garnered for the mart
I see the ripe and golden grain.

To a Lily

Go bow thy head in gentle spite,
Thou lily white.
[Fo]r she who spies thee waving here,
With thee in beauty can compare
As day with night.

Soft are thy leaves and white: Her arms
Boast whiter charms.
Thy stem prone bent with loveliness
Of maiden grace possesseth less:
Therein she charms.

Thou in thy lake dost see
Thyself: So she
Beholds her image in her eyes
Reflected. Thus did Venus rise
From out the sea.

Inconsolate, bloom not again
Thou rival vain
Of her whose charms have thine outdone:
Whose purity might spot the sun,
And make thy leaf a stain.

Haw-Blossoms

While yesterevening, through the vale
Descending from my cottage door
I strayed, how cool and fresh a look
All nature wore.

The calmïas and golden-rods,
And tender blossoms of the haw,
Like maidens seated in the wood,
Demure, I saw.

The recent drops upon their leaves
Shone brighter than the bluest eyes
And filled the little sheltered dell
Their fragrant sighs.

Their pliant arms they interlaced,
As pleasant canopies they were:
Their blossoms swung against my cheek
Like braids of hair.

And when I put their boughs aside
And stooped to pass, from overhead
The little agitated things
A shower shed

Of tears. Then thoughtfully I spoke;
Well represent ye maidenhood,
Sweet flowers. Life is to the young
A shady wood.

And therein some like golden-rods,
For grosser purposes designed,
A gay existence lead, but leave
No germ behind.

And others like the calmïas,
On cliff-sides inaccessible,
Bloom paramount, the vale with sweets
Yet never fill.

But underneath the glossy leaves,
When, working out the perfect law,
The blossoms white and fragrant still
Drop from the haw;

Like worthy deeds in silence wrought
And secret, through the lapse of years,
In clusters pale and delicate
The fruit appears.

In clusters pale and delicate
But waxing heavier each day,
Until the many-colored leaves
Drift from the spray.

Then pendulous, like amethysts
And rubies, purple ripe and red,
Wherewith God's feathered pensioners
In flocks are fed.

Therefore, sweet reader of this rhyme,
Be unto thee examples high
Not calmïas and golden-rods
That scentless die:

But the meek blossoms of the haw,
That fragrant are wherever wind
The forest paths, and perishing
Leave fruits behind.

On the Death of a Kinsman*

I see an Eagle winging to the sun—
Who sayeth him nay?
He glanceth down from where his wing hath won:
His heart is stout, his flight is scarce begun,—
Oh hopes of clay!

Saw he not how upon the cord was lain
A keen swift shaft;
How Death wrought out in every throbbing vein,
In every after agony of pain,
His bitter craft!

Like old Demetrius, the sun had he
Beheld so long,
Now things of earth no longer could he see,
And in his ear sang Immortality
A pleasant song.

Icarus like, he fell when warm and near
The sunshine smiled:
He rose strong-pinioned in his high career—
—*Thy dust remains, thy glorious spirit where,*
Minerva's child?

Therefore him Fame had written fair and high
Upon her scroll,
Who fell like sudden meteor from the sky,
Who strenuous to win at last did die
E'en at the goal.
               * Hon. Hugh S. Legaré

JUNE 21st, 1843

Augustus Baldwin Longstreet (1790–1870)

Born in Augusta and best known for his *Georgia Scenes* (1835), Augustus Baldwin Longstreet also had strong ties with South Carolina. Attending Dr. Waddel's famous academy at Willington, he later recorded his experiences there in *Master William Mitten* (1864). Longstreet was a graduate of Yale, studied law in Litchfield, Connecticut, and practiced successfully before converting to Methodism in 1837 and becoming a Methodist minister. During his later years, he served as president of Emory College, Centenary College, and the University of Mississippi, as well as the University of South Carolina (1857–65). He died in Oxford, Mississippi, on July 9, 1870. Though Longstreet never supported himself by his writing, he is now best remembered for his stories in the tradition of Southwestern frontier humor.

The Horse-Swap

During the session of the Supreme Court, in the village of ———,
about three weeks ago, when a number of people were collected in the
principal street of the village, I observed a young man riding up and
down the street, as I supposed, in a violent passion. He galloped this
way, then that, and then the other; spurred his horse to one group of
citizens, then to another; then dashed off at half speed, as if fleeing
from danger; and, suddenly checking his horse, returned first in a
pace, then in a trot, and then in a canter. While he was performing
these various evolutions, he cursed, swore, whooped, screamed, and
tossed himself in every attitude which man could assume on horseback.
In short, he *cavorted* most magnanimously (a term which, in our
tongue, expresses all that I have described, and a little more), and
seemed to be setting all creation at defiance. As I like to see all that is
passing, I determined to take a position a little nearer to him, and to
ascertain, if possible, what it was that affected him so sensibly. Accordingly, I approached a crowd before which he had stopped for a
moment, and examined it with the strictest scrutiny. But I could see
nothing in it that seemed to have anything to do with the cavorter.
Every man appeared to be in good humour, and all minding their own
business. Not one so much as noticed the principal figure. Still he
went on. After a semicolon pause, which my appearance seemed to produce (for he eyed me closely as I approached), he fetched a whoop,
and swore that "he could out-swap any live man, woman, or child that
ever walked these hills, or that ever straddled horseflesh since the days
of old daddy Adam. Stranger," said he to me, "did you over see the
Yallow Blossom from Jasper?"

"No," said I, "but I have often heard of him."

"I'm the boy," continued he; "perhaps a *leetle,* jist a *leetle,* of the best
man at a horse-swap that ever trod shoe-leather."

I began to feel my situation a little awkward, when I was relieved
by a man somewhat advanced in years, who stepped up and began to
survey the *"Yallow Blossom's"* horse with much apparent interest. This
drew the rider's attention, and he turned the conversation from me to
the stranger.

"Well, my old coon," said he, "do you want to swap *hosses?"*

"Why, I don't know," replied the stranger; "I believe I've got a beast I'd trade with you for that one, if you like him."

"Well, fetch up your nag, my old cock; you're jist the lark I wanted to get hold of. I am perhaps a *leetle,* jist a *leetle,* of the best man at a horse-swap that every stole *cracklins* out of his mammy's fat gourd. Where's your *hoss?"*

"I'll bring him presently; but I want to examine your horse a little."

"Oh! look at him," said the Blossom, alighting and hitting him a cut; "look at him. He's the best piece of *hoss*flesh in the thirteen united univarsal worlds. There's no sort o' mistake in little Bullet. He can pick up miles on his feet, and fling 'em behind him as fast as the next man's *hoss,* I don't care where he comes from. And he can keep at it as long as the sun can shine without resting."

During this harangue, little Bullet looked as if he understood it all, believed it, and was ready at any moment to verify it. He was a horse of goodly countenance, rather expressive of vigilance than fire; though an unnatural appearance of fierceness was thrown into it by the loss of his ears, which had been cropped pretty close to his head. Nature had done but little for Bullet's head and neck; but he managed, in a great measure, to hide their defects by bowing perpetually. He had obviously suffered severely for corn; but if his ribs and hip bones had not disclosed the fact, *he* never would have done it; for he was in all respects as cheerful and happy as if he commanded all the corn-cribs and fodder-stacks in Georgia. His height was about twelve hands; but as his shape partook somewhat of that of the giraffe, his haunches stood much lower. They were short, strait, peaked, and concave. Bullet's tail, however, made amends for all his defects. All that the artist could do to beautify it had been done; and all that horse could do to compliment the artist, Bullet did. His tail was nicked in superior style, and exhibited the line of beauty in so many directions, that it could not fail to hit the most fastidious taste in some of them. From the root it dropped into a graceful festoon; then rose in a handsome curve; then resumed its first direction; and then mounted suddenly upward like a cypress knee to a perpendicular of about two and a half inches. The whole had a careless and bewitching inclination to the right. Bullet obviously knew where his beauty lay, and took all occasions to display it to the best advantage. If a stick cracked, or if any one moved suddenly about him, or coughed, or hawked, or spoke a little louder than common, up went Bullet's tail like lightning; and if the *going up* did not please, the *coming down* must of necessity, for it was as different from the other movement as was its direction. The first was a bold and rapid flight upward, usually to an angle of forty-five degrees. In this position he kept his interesting appendage until he satisfied himself that nothing in particular was to be done; when he commenced dropping it by half inches, in second beats, then in triple time, then faster and shorter, and faster and shorter still, until it finally died away imperceptibly into its natural position. If I might compare sights to sounds, I should say its *settling* was more like the note of a locust than anything else in nature.

Either from native sprightliness of disposition, from uncontrollable activity, or from an unconquerable habit of removing flies by the stamping of the feet, Bullet never stood still; but always kept up a gentle fly-scaring movement of his limbs, which was peculiarly interesting.

"I tell you, man," proceeded the Yellow Blossom, "he's the best live hoss that ever trod the grit of Georgia. Bob Smart knows the hoss. Come here, Bob, and mount this hoss, and show Bullet's motions." Here Bullet bristled up, and looked as if he had been hunting for Bob all day long, and had just found him. Bob sprang on his back. "Boo-oo-oo!" said Bob, with a fluttering noise of the lips; and away went Bullet, as if in a quarter race, with all his beauties spread in handsome style.

"Now fetch him back," said Blossom. Bullet turned and came in pretty much as he went out.

"Now trot him by." Bullet reduced his tail to *"customary"*; sidled to the right and left airily, and exhibited at least three varieties of trot in the short space of fifty yards.

"Make him pace!" Bob commenced twitching the bridle and kicking at the same time. These inconsistent movements obviously (and most naturally) disconcerted Bullet; for it was impossible for him to learn, from them, whether he was to proceed or stand still. He started to trot, and was told that wouldn't do. He attempted a canter, and was checked again. He stopped, and was urged to go on. Bullet now rushed into the wide field of experiment, and struck out a gait of his own, that completely turned the tables upon his rider, and certainly deserved a patent. It seemed to have derived its elements from the jig, the minuet, and the cotillon. If it was not a pace, it certainly had *pace* in it, and no man would venture to call it anything else; so it passed off to the satisfaction of the owner.

"Walk him!" Bullet was now at home again; and he walked as if money was staked on him.

The stranger, whose name, I afterward learned, was Peter Ketch, having examined Bullet to his heart's content, ordered his son Neddy to go and bring up Kit. Neddy soon appeared upon Kit; a well-formed sorrel of the middle size, and in good order. His *tout ensemble* threw Bullet entirely in the shade, though a glance was sufficient to satisfy any one that Bullet had the decided advantage of him in point of intellect.

"Why, man," said Blossom, "do you bring such a hoss as that to trade for Bullet? Oh, I see you're no notion of trading."

"Ride him off, Neddy!" said Peter. Kit put off at a handsome lope.

"Trot him back!" Kit came in at a long, sweeping trot, and stopped suddenly at the crowd.

"Well," said Blossom, "let me look at him; maybe he'll do to plough."

"Examine him!" said Peter, taking hold of the bridle close to the mouth; "he's nothing but a tacky. He an't as *pretty* a horse as Bullet, I know; but he'll do. Start 'em together for a hundred and fifty *mile;* and if Kit an't twenty mile ahead of him at the coming out, any man may take Kit for nothing. But he's a monstrous mean horse, gentleman; any man may see that. He's the scariest horse, too, you ever saw. He won't do to hunt on, no how. Stranger, will you let Neddy have your rifle to shoot off him? Lay the rifle between his ears, Neddy, and shoot at the blaze in that stump. Tell me when his head is high enough."

Ned fired, and hit the blaze; and Kit did not move a hair's breadth.

"Neddy, take a couple of sticks, and beat on that hogshead at Kit's tail."

Ned made a tremendous rattling, at which Bullet took fright, broke his bridle, and dashed off in grand style; and would have stopped all farther negotiations by going home in disgust, had not a traveller arrested him and brought him back; but Kit did not move.

"I tell you, gentlemen," continued Peter, "he's the scariest horse you ever saw. He an't as gentle as Bullet, but he won't do any harm if you watch him. Shall I put him in a cart, gig, or wagon for you, stranger? He'll cut the same capers there he does here. He's a monstrous mean horse."

During all this time Blossom was examining him with the nicest scrutiny. Having examined his frame and limbs, he now looked at his eyes.

"He's got a curious look out of his eyes," said Blossom.

"Oh yes, sir," said Peter, "just as blind as a bat. Blind horses always have clear eyes. Make a motion at his eyes, if you please, sir."

Blossom did so, and Kit threw up his head rather as if something pricked him under the chin than as if fearing a blow. Blossom repeated the experiment, and Kit jerked back in considerable astonishment.

"Stone blind, you see, gentlemen," proceeded Peter; "but he's just as good to travel of a dark night as if he had eyes."

"Blame my buttons," said Blossom, "if I like them eyes."

"No," said Peter, "nor I neither. I'd rather have 'em made of diamonds; but they'll do, if they don't show as much white as Bullet's."

"Well," said Blossom, "make a pass at me."

"No," said Peter; "you made the banter, now make your pass."

"Well, I'm never afraid to price my hosses. You must give me twenty-five dollars boot."

"Oh, certainly; say fifty, and my saddle and bridle in. Here, Neddy, my son, take away daddy's horse."

"Well," said Blossom, "I've made my pass, now you make yours."

"I'm for short talk in a horse-swap, and therefore always tell a gentleman at once what I mean to do. You must give me ten dollars."

Blossom swore absolutely, roundly, and profanely, that he never would give boot.

"Well," said Peter, "I didn't care about trading; but you cut such high shines, that I thought I'd like to back you out, and I've done it. Gentlemen, you see I've brought him to a hack."

"Come, old man," said Blossom, "I've been joking with you. I begin to think you do want to trade; therefore, give me five dollars and take Bullet. I'd rather lose ten dollars any time than not make a trade, though I hate to fling away a good hoss."

"Well," said Peter, "I'll be as clever as you are. Just put the five dollars on Bullet's back, and hand him over; it's a trade."

Blossom swore again, as roundly as before, that he would not give boot; and, said he, "Bullet wouldn't hold five dollars on his back, no how. But, as I bantered you, if you say an even swap, here's at you."

"I told you," said Peter, "I'd be as clever as you, therefore, here goes two dollars more, just for trade sake. Give me three dollars, and it's a bargain."

Blossom repeated his former assertion; and here the parties stood for a long time, and the by-standers (for many were now collected) began to taunt both parties. After some time, however, it was pretty unanimously decided that the old man had backed Blossom out.

At length Blossom swore he "never would be backed out for three dollars after bantering a man"; and, accordingly, they closed the trade.

"Now," said Blossom, as he handed Peter the three dollars, "I'm a man that, when he makes a bad trade, makes the most of it until he can make a better. I'm for no rues and after-claps."

"That's just my way," said Peter; "I never goes to law to mend my bargains."

"Ah, you're the kind of boy I love to trade with. Here's your hoss, old man. Take the saddle and bridle off him, and I'll strip yours; but lift up the blanket easy from Bullet's back, for he's a mighty tender-backed hoss."

The old man removed the saddle, but the blanket stuck fast. He attempted to raise it, and Bullet bowed himself, switched his tail, danced a little, and gave signs of biting.

"Don't hurt him, old man," said Blossom, archly; "take it off easy. I am, perhaps, a leetle of the best man at a horse-swap that ever catched a coon."

Peter continued to pull at the blanket more and more roughly, and Bullet became more and more *cavortish:* insomuch that, when the blanket came off, he had reached the *kicking* point in good earnest.

The removal of the blanket disclosed a sore on Bullet's back-bone that seemed to have defied all medical skill. It measured six full inches in length and four in breadth, and had as many features as Bullet had motions. My heart sickened at the sight; and I felt that the brute who had been riding him in that situation deserved the halter.

The prevailing feeling, however, was that of mirth. The laugh became loud and general at the old man's expense, and rustic witticisms were liberally bestowed upon him and his late purchase. These Blossom continued to provoke by various remarks. He asked the old man "if he thought Bullet would let five dollars lie on his back." He declared most seriously that he had owned that horse three months, and had never discovered before that he had a sore back, "or he never should have thought of trading him," &c., &c.

The old man bore it all with the most philosophic composure. He evinced no astonishment at his late discovery, and made no replies. But his son Neddy had not disciplined his feelings quite so well. His eyes opened wider and wider from the first to the last pull of the blanket; and, when the whole sore burst upon his view, astonishment and fright seemed to contend for the mastery of his countenance. As the blanket disappeared, he stuck his hands in his breeches pockets, heaved a deep sigh, and lapsed into a profound revery, from which he was only roused by the cuts at his father. He bore them as long as he could; and, when he could contain himself no longer, he began, with a certain wildness of expression which gave a peculiar interest to what he uttered: "His back's mighty bad off; but dod drot my soul if he's put it to daddy as bad as he thinks he has, for old Kit's both blind and *deef,* I'll be dod drot if he eint."

"The devil he is," said Blossom.

"Yes, dod drot my soul if he *eint.* You walk him, and see if he *eint.* His eyes don't look like it; but he'd *jist as leve go agin* the house with you, or in a ditch, as any how. Now you go try him." The laugh was now turned on Blossom; and many rushed to test the fidelity of the little boy's report. A few experiments established its truth beyond controversy.

"Neddy," said the old man, "you oughtn't to try and make people discontented with their things. Stranger, don't mind what the little boy says. If you can only get Kit rid of them little failings, you'll find him all sorts of a horse. You are a *leetle* the best man at a horse-swap that ever I got hold of; but don't fool away Kit. Come, Neddy, my son, let's be moving; the stranger seems to be getting snappish."

From *Master William Mitten*

Four o'clock the next day (Saturday) found them at the public house, or rather boarding house, of Mr. Nelson Newby, Abbeville District, South Carolina. It was a rude log house, with two rooms, about fifteen feet square each, and an entry nearly as large, between them. In the rear of it was another building of the same material, somewhat shorter and narrower than the first. This was the dining room. Six or seven small edifices of the same kind scattered around, with little order, served as students' lodges. A rail fence (or rather the remains of one) three feet high, enclosed the whole. About twenty boys of various sizes, were busily engaged in cutting, splitting, and piling wood, at the doors of their respective tenements—the roughest looking set of students that ever repeated the notes of Homer and Virgil since the world began. The prospect looked gloomy, even to the Captain, and terrific to William.

"Uncle," whispered he, "these can't be big people's sons!"

"Well—don't know—they're pretty rough looking fellows—but —they seem to be very industrious boys." Poor comfort to William. The Captain and his landlord, of course, soon became acquainted; and the first expressing a wish to see Mr. Waddel, the last kindly offered to escort him to the teacher's residence.

"It is not far out of the way to go by the Academy; would you like to see it"; said Mr. Newby.

"Very much," replied the Captain.

They set forward, and at the distance of about two hundred and fifty yards from Mr. Newby's premises they entered a street, shaded by majestic oaks, and composed entirely of log huts, varying in size from six to sixteen feet square. The truth of history demands that we should say that there was but one of the smallest size just indicated, and that was the whimsical structure of a very whimsical fellow by the name of Dredzel Pace. It was endangered from fire once, and *four* stout students took it up by the corners and removed it to a place of safety.

The street was about forty yards wide, and its length was perhaps double its width; and yet the houses on either side did not number more than ten or twelve; of course, therefore, they stood generally in very open order. They were all built by the students themselves or by architects of their hiring. They served for study-houses in cold or rainy weather, though the students were allowed to study where they pleased within convenient reach of the monitors. The common price of a building, on *front row,* water proof, and easily chinked, was five dollars. The chinking was generally removed in Summer for ventilation. In the suburbs, were several other buildings of the same kind, erected by literary recluses, we suppose, who could not endure the din of the city at play-time—*at play-time,* we say, for there was no din in it in study hours. At the head of the street, eastward, stood the Academy, differing in nothing from the other buildings but in size and the number of its rooms. It had two; the smaller devoted to a primary school of a few boys and girls, over which Moses Waddel Dobbins, a nephew of the Rector, presided. These soon left, and Mr. Dobbins became assistant-general to his uncle. The larger was the recitation room of Mr. Waddel himself, the prayer room, court room, and general convocation room for all matters concerning the school. It was without seats, and just large enough to contain one hundred and fifty boys standing erect, close pressed, and leave a circle of six feet diameter at the door, for jigs and cotilions at the teacher's regular *soirees,* every Monday morning.

A delightful spring gushed from the foot of the hill on which the school-house stood, and, at the distance of but a few paces, poured its waters into a lovely brook which wound through a narrow plain covered with stately beeches. Venerable old chroniclers of revered names and happy days, where are ye! It was under the canopy of these beautiful ornaments of the forest, by the side of that whispering brook, that we felt the first gleam of pleasure that we ever derived from anything in Latin. And here are the words which awakened it:

> *"Tityre tu patulæ recubans sub tegmine fagi,*
> *Silvestrem tenui musam meditaris avena."*

Our party having taken a hasty survey of these things bent their way to *Castle Carberry.* As they journeyed on, Mr. Newby pointed out the ground over which Sam Shanklin and Mr. Waddel had a notable race. Sam had offended *"Old Moses"* (so he were called, even in his prime, which he had now hardly left,) and as the latter approached him whip in hand, Sam took to his heels, not dreaming that old Moses would follow him. But he was mistaken; he did follow him, and gained upon him at every step, a little. Sam, finding his pursuer too fleet for him, sought safety in lofty leaping; so he made for a brush-heap. Just as he reached it, old Moses fetched him a wipe upon the legs that energized his activity to unmatchable achievement, and he cleared the brush-heap at a bound. Here the race ended. The Captain laughed heartily at the story; but William saw no fun in it.

Castle Carberry stood on the highway leading from Augusta, Georgia, to Abbeville Court-house, South Carolina, and about equi-distant from Mr. Newby's and the Academy. By whom it was erected, we are not informed; probably by Samuel Shields, an assistant of Mr. Waddel, who had occupied it for two years previous to the time of which we are speaking, and who was just now gathering up his goods and chattels for his final departure from the place, and for a much more interesting engagement.* Its name was doubtless derived from Maria Roche's novel—*The Children of the Abbey,* which had a great run in that day; but to tell wherein the two Castle Carberry's were alike, would puzzle the greatest conundrum-solver that ever lived. Upon the retirement of Mr. Shields, Alexander B. Linton succeeded to his possessions, and James L. Petigru to his office (not as some have most erroneously supposed, the Mr. Pentigall, of the "Georgia Scenes,") though it was in this very castle that the great question was discussed: "Whether at public elections should the votes of faction predominate by internal suggestions or the bias of jurisprudence?" Mr. Petigru had been in Columbia College, a year or more before the discussion came off.

Some two or three students always boarded themselves at Castle Carberry. It served as a nucleus around which other edifices of like kind and for like purposes gathered, all built of the common material. We think its tenants were, in Mitten's day, Alex B. Linton, Henry Rassenel, Samuel Weir, and William D. Martin.

At Castle Carberry the promenaders re-entered the big road which they had left at Newby's, having now seen all of Willington *proper;* Willington *common* embraced every house within three miles of the Academy. As they entered the road, a messenger called for Mr. Newby

---

*He soon after married a young lady of Vienna.

to return home on some special business. He gave the Captain directions to Mr. Waddel's, and returned. The directions were simply to keep the road to the next house. A walk of a quarter of a mile, or a little over, brought the Captain and his charge to the residence of the renowned teacher. It was a comfortable, framed building, two stories high, neatly, but plainly paled in—very rare things in that vicinity.

Some six or eight more boys, like the Newbyites, were differently employed about the premises.

"Do you know, my son," said the Captain, addressing one of them, "whether Mr. Waddel is at home?"

"Yes sir," said the youth, springing to the door, and opening it, "walk in, take seats, and I will call him."

He disappeared, and in a moment returned with Mr. Waddel.

"Mr. Waddel, I presume," said the Captain.

"Yes, sir."

"Thompson, sir, is my name, and this is my nephew, William Mitten, whom I have brought to place under your instruction."

"It is rather chilly, here," said the teacher, shaking their hands cordially, "walk into my study, where I have a good fire. Won't you go in, David?" added he to the guide, who was about retiring.

"No, I thank you sir," said David.

"That's a sprightly youth," said the Captain, as he moved towards the study, "and he is a namesake of mine."

"Yes," said the teacher, "he is a clever boy—the son of the celebrated Doctor Ramsay."

"What! Doctor Ramsay, the patriot, statesman, and historian—who married the accomplished daughter of the renowned Henry Laurens, President of the first Congress of the United States, Minister to Holland, and father of the gallant John Laurens, the beloved of Washington?"

This was a clear *splurge** for William's benefit.

"The same," said Mr. Waddel.

"Well, I feel myself honored in bearing the boy's name."

Before this conversation ended, all were seated in the teacher's study. It was crowded with books—partly the teacher's private library

*A splurge is a moral *cavort.* Both are embraced in the generic term, *cutting shines. Ga. Vocab.*

—partly, books laid in for the students which he furnished at cost and charges on Philadelphia prices.

"Have you studied Latin, William?" inquired Mr. Waddel.

"Yes, sir."

"How far have you gone?"

"I was reading Virgil, when I quit school."

"Well, I have a large Virgil class, which will be divided on Monday. I have found that some of them are keeping others back; and I have ordered them to get as long a lesson as they can for Monday morning. Those who get the most and recite the best, will be put in one class and the rest in another. Now, you can take either division of this class that you may be found qualified for, or you may enter the *Selectœ* class, which will commence Virgil in two or three months. Meet me at the Academy on Monday morning, and we will see what will be best."

"How many pupils have you, Mr. Waddel?" inquired the Captain.

"About one hundred and fifty."

"Where do they board?"

"Just where they please, among the neighbors around. They all take boarders, and reside at different distances from the academy, varying from a few hundred yards to three miles."

"Have the students to cut and haul their own firewood, and make their own fires?"

"Not always. At some of the boarding houses the landlords have these things done for them, and at all, they may hire servants to perform them, if they will, or, rather, if they can; but, as at every house there is at least a *truck wagon* and horse at the service of the students, and wood is convenient and abundant, and to be had without stint or charge, they generally supply themselves, and make their own fires."

During this conversation, which from the beginning to end, was of the most alarming interest to William, his eyes wide open, were fixed on Mr. Waddel, who was an object of still more alarming interest to him. He had never seen—we have never seen—a man of sterner features than Mr. Waddel bore. From the time that William entered the house to the time that he left it, "shadows, clouds, and darkness" were gathering and deepening upon his mind; relieved only by one faint gleam of light from young Ramsay, whom he regarded as the concentrated extract of all that was august, and great, and gifted, and good in the United States, if not in the world; and an ample verification *per se* of all that his Uncle had told him about "big men's sons."

William was entered in due form a student of Mr. Waddel's school; and the Captain having enquired of the post office at which the students received their letters, and pressed Mr. Waddel to give him early information of William's conduct, standing and progress, he left with his charge for Mr. Newby's. A long silence ensued. At length it was broken by William.

"Mr. Waddel is the grummest looking man I ever saw."

"Pretty sour," said the Captain. "But I don't reckon he is as bad as he looks to be. The boys seem cheerful around him; and David Ramsay seemed perfectly easy in his presence."

The truth is, the Captain was sore pressed for encouragements himself, and it was the luckiest thing in the world for him that he happened to fall in with young Ramsay just when he did.

"I had an idea," continued the Captain, "of proposing to Mr. Waddel to take you to board with him; but it occurred to me that you might prefer to board somewhere else, and I am perfectly willing to accommodate you in this matter."

"Uncle, I wouldn't board with him for five hundred thousand dollars."

"Well, my son, I will not place you with him. I think the best way will be for you to board at Mr. Newby's for the present. After you become acquainted with the other boarding houses, you can take your choice among them."

Silence ensued, which we fill up with a more particular account of Mr. Waddel. As he was made a Doctor of Divinity soon after the time at which we are speaking of him, we will anticipate a little, and call him henceforth *Doctor* Waddel.

He was about five feet nine inches high; of stout muscular frame, and a little inclined to corpulency. In limb, nearly perfect. His head was uncommonly large, and covered with a thick coat of dark hair. His forehead was projecting, and in nothing else more remarkable. His eyes were grey, and overshadowed by thick, heavy eye-brows, always closely knit in his calmest hours, and almost over-lapping in his angry moods. His nose was bluntly acquiline. His lips were rather thick, and generally closely compressed. His complexion was slightly adust. His *tout ensemble* was, as we have said, extremely austere; but it was false to his heart; for he was benevolent, affectionate, charitable, hospitable, and kind. He was cheerful, and even playful, in his disposition. Good boys felt at perfect ease in his presence, and even bad ones could, and did, approach him with the utmost freedom. He never whipt in a passion—indeed, he seemed to be in his most pleasant moods when he administered correction, and hence, a stranger to him would naturally suppose that he took pleasure in flogging. It was not so, however. He hardly ever whipt, but upon the report of a monitor; and after a year or two from Master Mitten's introduction to him, very rarely, but upon a verdict of a jury of students. His government was one of *touching* "moral suasion"; but he administered it in a new way. Instead of infusing it gently into the head and heart, and letting it percolate through the system, and slowly neutralize the ill humors with which it came in contact, he applied it to the extremities, and drove it right up into the head and heart by percussion. He seemed to regard vices as consuming fires, and he adopted the engine process of extinguishing them. One would suppose that moral reforms, so hastily produced could not last; but we have living cases to prove that they have lasted for fifty-three years, and are still fresh and vigorous. It is a very remarkable fact that Doctor Waddel never flogged a boy for a deficient lesson. To be "turned off," as it was called—that is, to have to get a lesson over a second time, was considered such a disgrace by the students, that if this did not cure the fault, whipping, he well knew would not. He would often mount his horse at eight o'clock at night, and visit the students at their boarding houses. Sometimes he would visit them *incognito,* and recount his observations the next day to the whole school, commending such youths as he found well employed, and censuring such as he found ill employed. And what were the fruits of this rigid but equitable discipline? From under the teachings of this man have gone forth one Vice-President, and many Foreign and Cabinet Ministers; and Senators, Congressmen, Governors, Judges, Presidents, and Professors of Colleges, eminent Divines, Barristers, Jurists, Legislators, Physicians, Scholars, Military and Naval officers innumerable.

Captain Thompson returned to Mr. Newby's. His name had been

made known to the boys during his absence. One of them introduced himself to him as the son of Doctor Hay, a near and dear friend of the Captain, in times gone by. The youth was made acquainted with William—offered him a part of his bed and study, which were accepted. Before retiring to rest, the Captain paid a hasty visit to William's new dormitory. He found him at a table with three others, who were studying their lessons before a rousing fire. They seemed very cheerful and happy. After a few questions, he withdrew, and left them to their studies. An early hour the next morning found him on his way homeward.

John B. Irving (1800–81)

John Beaufain Irving was born in Jamaica on September 28, 1800, and was educated in England at Rugby and Cambridge, although he spent part of his childhood in Charleston with his grandfather. He studied medicine in Philadelphia and, after his marriage in 1823 to Anna Maria Cruger, settled in Charleston to practice and become a prosperous rice planter on the Cooper River. For over thirty years the secretary of the South Carolina Jockey Club, Irving won a local reputation as writer of sporting sketches. His books include *A Day on the Cooper River* (1842), *Local Events and Incidents at Home* (1850), and *The South Carolina Jockey Club* (1857), but probably his best writings were those published in the New York *Spirit of the Times* in the 1840s and 1850s. Irving's son, John Beaufain Irving, Jr. (1825–77), was a genre, portrait, and historical painter of considerable note. The elder Irving, his fortune ruined by the Civil War, died February 22, 1881, at Bergen, New Jersey.

A Day in the Reserve

WRITTEN FOR THE "SPIRIT OF THE TIMES," BY A SOUTH CAROLINIAN

"They spread their ample nets, then drag'd to land
The scaly breed, all struggling, to the strand."

Not long since you honored by a place in your highly popular journal, an article of mine, entitled *"A Day in the Woods."* I now send you
the result of another day's sport, though in a different element, which I
have designated as *"A Day in the Reserve!"*

By the term *Reserve,* we understand at the South any collection of
water, kept back for agricultural purposes. These reserves of water being
indispensable to the successful culture of many rice plantations, they
are very common in the low country. As they are seldom entirely drawn
off, they usually contain an abundance of the finest fish, trout, bream,
perch, &c., affording at all seasons opportunities for the best of sport to
those who delight in practising the piscatorial art!

The custom of having Reserves for field culture is not of modern
invention—it is of great antiquity—*classical* in its origin. Virgil, I
remember, recommends the husbandmen of his day to form reservoirs,
or ponds, by collecting the water that fell in the rainy season, so that
in dry weather, when the fields were parched, and the plants dying, the
water might be led from the brow of each hilly tract in gently flowing
streams upon the sown corn

"Deinde satis fluvium inducit, rivosque sequentes?
Et cum exustus ager morientibus æstuat herbis,
Ecce, supercilio clivosi tramitis undam
Elicit: illa cadens raucum per levia murmur
Saxa ciet, scatebusque arentia temperat arva.
Quid, qui, ne gravidis procumbat culmus aristis,
Luxuriem segetum tenerà depascit in herbâ,
Cum primum sulcos æquant sata? quique paludis
Collectum humorem bibulà deducit arenâ?
Prœsertim incertis si mensibus amnis abundans
Exit, et obducto late tenet omnia limo,
Unde cavæ tepido sudant humore lacunæ."

My young friend K. S. B., Esq., having recently taken possession of his patrimonial estate, on which there are several of these reserves for flowing his fields, invited a large party to what he was pleased to say should be a regular fishing frolic. As there is no gentleman in his neighborhood but is *a devil of a fellow for fish,* his invitation was very generally accepted. The name of his estate is "Coming-tee"; it is situated in St. John's Parish, South Carolina, on the western branch of *Cooper River* (called by the Indians *the Etiwan River*). I have said that Coming-tee is on the western branch of the river, and properly speaking it is so, for the great bulk of the property lies in that direction; yet it commences at a point where the main body of Cooper river divides into its eastern and western branches, forming a resemblance to the letter T: hence its name of Coming-*tee;* Mr. COMING, an ancestor of the present proprietor, having been the first settler that took out a grant of this land. On the opposite sides of the river, occupying the two angles formed by the figure I have drawn, may be seen, to the left, the estate of the "Hagin," and to the right "Dean Hall." The former (his paternal residence), owned by John Huger, Esq., the descendant of an illustrious Huguenot family, and near relative of the gallant officer of the same name, of "Olmutz" fame. The latter is now the property of Col. Carson, but formerly belonged to Sir John Nesbit, a Scotch Baronet, of the ancient house of Nesbits, who called it after his family seat near Edinburgh.

Coming-tee is one of those estates we Carolinians regard with some degree of pride. It is not only a very noble inheritance, but has descended from sire to son through successive generations since the earliest settlement of the country. The great grandfather of the present proprietor was born there in 1709. In reviewing the history of the many virtues of his ancestry, and the good example they have left behind them, well may the present owner of this wide domain ruminate upon, and lay to heart, the touching sentiment contained in that good old English ballad, familiar to every good old English gentleman of the good old English school.

"Ere around the huge oak that o'ershadows yon mill
The fond ivy had dared to entwine:

Ere the church was a ruin, that nods on the hill,
Or a rook built its nest on the pine;
Could I trace back the time to a far distant date,
    Since my forefathers toil'd in this field:
And the land I now hold by *God's blessings so great*
    Is the same that my grandfather till'd.
He dying, bequeath'd to his son a good name,
    Which unsullied descended to me;
For my child I've preserved it, unblemish'd with shame,
    And it still from a spot shall be free."

Oh! yes, dead to every sentiment of good, and of filial gratitude, must be that heart that cannot be touched by the voice that calls to us from the home of our Fathers—the spot where our parents dwelt, and where they blest and nurtured us. It is a beautiful, no less than a holy superstition, depend upon it, that makes a virtuous ancestry the *Household Gods* of the living!

I don't know how others may feel, but I candidly confess it would be impossible for me to rise from the old arm chair, with its red morocco cushions, which my father used, and which has happily descended to me, to go and do a deliberate wrong to any one!

Before I proceed to give the result of our day in the Reserve at Coming-tee, it may not prove uninteresting, as it is by no means irrelevant to say a word or two upon the Philosophy of the sport we were invited to participate in.

It has been remarked that no man can really love fishing who does not possess, in some degree, a poetical temperament. There is no doubt (we judge from our own experience) that angling must most especially recommend itself as a recreation to those who love Nature, and can *feel* its influence—who like sometimes to be alone, and to commune with themselves in solitary places—those to whom high mountains are a feeling, and for whom the gently rippling stream has a voice of companionship, as grateful to the ear as the still small voice of whispered friendship.

Burton, in his Anatomy of Melancholy, introduces a very quaint but beautiful passage, elucidating our idea, and giving at the same time the pastime of fishing a very decided preference over all the other field sports.

He remarks that it is not the only commendation to fishing that the Angler must be a lover of Nature, or lose half the pleasure of his art; but he adds, when we consider the variety of baits for all seasons, and the devices which anglers have invented—the lines and flies to catch each kind of fish—much study and perspicuity is required, and it is an amusement greatly to be preferred over many other sports of the day. Hunting, for instance, Burton thinks is laborious: much riding and many dangers accompanying the diversion, but angling, he says, is *still* and *quiet*. Again, he thinks that if the angler catch no fish—does not feel even so much as a glorious nibble for his pains and his patience —he may, nevertheless, get a pleasant walk by the brook side, and find reviving shade by the cooling stream, or the rapid torrent: besides, he enjoys good air, and

> "The ripe harvest of the new-mown hay
> Gives it a sweet and wholesome odor."

Added to this, he hears the sweet melody of tuneful birds around him, which is better than the noise of hounds, and the blast of horns.

It would be almost impossible to enumerate all the different modes of fishing, as practised by the lovers of the sport at the present day.

Some delight in ensnaring fish, others in *shooting* them, others again confine themselves, poacher-like, to setting night lines; whilst the more scientific and artist like votary of old Izaak Walton, takes pleasure alone in the most legitimate branch of the Art, that of Angling, gracefully throwing his line with a straight eye, and steady hand into the shady brook, a fine trout occasionally rising from his deep hiding place, with open mouth at the well selected fly, or live bait. At first, but a slight dimple on the surface of the stream, indicates his approach: then, from a too eager desire to secure the tempting bait, he jumps clear out of the water, or with a greater regard to prudence, more wary and cunning, he quietly retires two or three times before he is hooked: when, like a high mettled racer, that for the first time feels the prick of the spur, he dashes off; awhile disappearing in the deep eddies, then rising and lashing the surface of the water into foam, as he plunges to escape from his tormentors!

One of the most extraordinary methods of fishing I ever heard of, or met with in the course of my reading, is related by the celebrated Alexander Dumas, in one of his well written stories. He says, in the valleys of the Alps—those regions of eternal snow, of eagles, and of freedom, it is quite common to catch trout after the following marvellous fashion. The fisherman provides himself only *with a lantern and a large knife,* sallying *out at night* in quest of victims. The lantern is described, as a globe of horn, to which is affixed a tube of any metallic substance three feet long, and an inch and a half in diameter. The junction between the tube and the globe being hermetically sealed, the oiled wick within the lantern, after having been lighted, receiving air only from the top of the tube, cannot be acted upon, and extinguished by either air or water. The knife used is a very sharp instrument, but usually more resembling a gardener's knife than any thing else.

On reaching the stream, where the fish are known to abound, the fisherman, no matter how inclement the night, or the season of the year, promptly removes his nether garments, "stripping to the buff," as far as his extremities are concerned, then plunges up to his waist in the water, "tho' icy cold by day it ran." With his left hand the fisherman then lowers the lantern into the water, to about two feet, thus producing a dim circle of light in the bed of the stream. The trout attracted by the light, crowd around the globe in the centre, as moths around a candle. The lantern being gently raised, the fish closely follow it. As they reach the surface of the water, they are struck on the head with the knife—they sink—but soon rise again bloody and dead, when they are *basketed* without further trouble.

Certain other modes have at different times been resorted to by sporting men for taking fish—more for diversion, perhaps, than for profit. It was not uncommon at one time in Scotland on the Lakes, which abound with large perch and pike, to append to the legs of a goose, a line about two feet long, with a baited hook at the end of it. The geese were then taken to the opposite side of the Lake from home, and driven into the water. The bait was soon swallowed by the greedy fish, when a violent struggle immediately took place. The frightened geese, of course, after a while proving the stronger of the two, made the best of their way homewards, pulling along with them the astonished fish to shore.

This was a literal verification of Dr. Johnson's definition of the sport, that fishery was nothing more, *than a long line with a goose at one end of it, and a worm at the other!*

On the smaller Lakes and Ponds in the upper part of the State of New York and in Canada, during the winter months, when the Lakes are frozen over, it is very common for persons living in the neighborhood to bore small holes in the ice;—a thin shingle is then perforated about three inches from one end of it;—a baited line is run through the hole in the shingle, and tied to a stick on the other side, long enough to prevent the line slipping back again. The shingle is placed over the hole that is made in the ice, the end of the shingle that has the line fastened to it being directly in the hole, and the line dropt into the water through the ice to a considerable depth. If a fish lays well hold and pulls strong, up raises of course, the shingle perpendicularly in the air, dancing a merry jig to the tune of "Yankee Doodle frizzle up"—(that is, if the fish happen to be on the American side of the line). As it is customary to have several lines set at the same time in this manner, when the fish bite fast, the amusement of this mode of catching fish, consists in the exercise and excitement of running from one shingle to another as they are put in motion on the ice, by the biting of the fish below.

A celebrated sporting character of Devonshire, in England, is said to have succeded in catching large quantities of fish, by conveying into a wide piece of water in that county, otherwise unapproachable, a baited line, *by means of a paper kite.* It was certainly a very novel expedient. Its success must have been highly amusing.

Now the different modes I have mentioned, are all very well in their way, as far as diversion goes—for procuring that excitement which is the main spring of every pastime, but of all methods ever devised for catching fish, for doing a *quick and profitable business,* either in this country or any other, commend me to a Seine, hauled through a well stocked Reserve in South Carolina. For the *quality* and *quantity* of the fish caught in this way, it immeasurably surpasses all other modes of fishing.

On the memorable day at *Coming-tee,* I alluded to in the beginning of this article, Jan. 24, 1842, a very large party assembled about nine o'clock. We found in readiness on the bank of the largest Reserve, two very capacious nets, long enough to have surrounded, if it had been necessary, a German Principality; certainly all the real estate of Prince Albert, before he possessed himself of the *nett* proceeds of Victoria's purse; also, instead of a boy (as I have remarked on some fishing excursions, with a basket slung around his waist to carry the fish), twelve of as prime looking fellows were detailed for that duty, as ever took a hoe in hand, or had reason to thank "Massa" for the comforts that surrounded them. These fellows instead of carrying baskets, were provided with large tubs of immense dimensions, which they arranged, longo ordine, along the margin of the Reserve, filled with clean water to receive the larger fish. The day appointed was rather unpropitious for dabbling in water. The wind was from the North, and although it was not freezing, it was quite cold enough to make additional clothing desirable, instead of pulling off that which we already had on. Nothing daunted, however, some of the more zealous of the party were soon up to their middles in the Reserves, jumping up and down like dolphins, either encouraging those who had the direction of the Seine, or amusing themselves by picking up such of the larger trout as were trying to make their escape from the net as it was hauled nearer the shore, into shallower water. The very first haul was successful. As the Seine was drawn nearer and nearer to the land, the agitation of the water increased, becoming every moment greater and greater—a splash here, and a plunge there, showed the crowded condition of the fish within the circumference of the net, and clearly indicated *"the miraculous draft"* at hand. In a few moments fish of all kinds, like leaves in Autumn time, were strewn thickly upon the ground. Before they were disentangled from the net, as they kept floundering about, I could not help likening the confusion of the poor devils, to that which prevails with a dense populace in a large assembly room, the alarm of fire having been suddenly given, every one tries to escape at the same time, through the same door, which they find cannot be opened, and the more they push against it, the more firmly it encloses them.

A second and third haul were attended with equal success—it seemed only necessary to *drag* the Seine, to *drag* out every variety of the finny tribe common to these waters.

Not the least agreeable circumstance connected with our day's re-creation, was to see the deep interest all concerned, blacks and whites, or to write more in conformity with the humbug of the age, the *Peasantry* and *Feudal Lords,* took in the business. I saw one "nigger feller" (one of the *Peasantry,* I mean), run an enormous trout into shallow water, and then pounce upon him, like a crane upon a minnow, first gouging him, and then bringing him in triumph to land.

In less than three hours, we hauled in *three cart loads of fish,* consisting principally of brim, perch and trout. I was induced to weigh some of the heaviest. Having selected thirty five of the finest from the crowd, I submitted in the first place *six of the biggest* to the scales, and found that they weighed *fifty one pounds!* Two out of the six being perceptibly heavier than the other four, I weighed them separately, and found each to be a little over *ten pounds!* They were 25½ inches in length, and 21 inches round the belly. Nine of the next size weighed forty pounds, and twenty of the smallest seventy-eight pounds!

I do not recollect ever having seen finer trout than the two heaviest we caught, nor have I seen on record any account of heavier fish of the true trout species being taken any where—the nearest approach to them was a "monarch of the brook" hooked in the river Stour in England, in 1839, by a celebrated angler named Lamberton, using a rod and line, and a common ground bait. It weighed 9½ lbs., and measured two feet two inches in length, and twenty inches in girth. There was not much difference, therefore, in the size of the fish caught by us, and that of Mr. Lamberton—ours had the advantage only by about half a pound in weight. It is much to be regretted, however, that they were caught so early in the year, as I have no doubt, if they had been permitted to remain until the height of the season, the end of May or thereabouts, their bulk and weight would have been considerably increased.

Whilst I was engaged weighing the fish, surrounded by the whole party, another personage was added to our number—a very important character at that stage of the business, and at that hour of the day—it was no less a functionary than the Master of the kitchen, the *chef de*

Cuïsine of my friend Mr. B. Dressed in the cleanest manner possible, a long white apron pendant from his neck to his feet, he approached with a very respectful air to receive his orders, as to which of the fish should be prepared for dinner. A very judicious selection having been made, I must not omit to mention, that as "there was enough and to spare," our worthy host forgot not the divine injunction—"Master's give unto your servants that which is just and equal." It was quite gratifying to witness, as is always the case on these occasions at the South, every man, woman, and child on the plantation carrying away for his own use a supply that would furnish to the kindest feeder in the world *"bittle"* (as the negroes call all kinds of *victuals*) for a week.

These out-door arrangements having been satisfactorily got through, we repaired to the old family mansion to finish the day. Dinner was announced in due course of time, and a more sumptuous repast never was placed before those whose

> "Good digestion waits on appetite,
> And health on both!"

We commenced with a very delicious soup, following it up not with a glass of Sherry or Madeira, according to a custom that has long prevailed, but with a goblet of *iced Punch!* Reader, did you ever *experiment* upon a glass of cold punch after soup? if not, live no longer in *your sins* (for there are in this world sins of *omission* as well as commission), and give the Punch a trial tomorrow, prepared according to the following receipt:—

Put the outer peel of a lemon, with a table spoonful of the juice of the lemon into a mug—add half a pint of gin—a glass of Maraschino and two table spoonsful of powdered White Rock sugar candy—then add four large tumblers of soda water, or a bottle and a half of seltzer water, shake the ingredients well together, and ice them thoroughly.

Our next course was composed altogether of fish—of the largest trout taken in the morning. What Epicure could desire a greater treat than the head and shoulders of a *ten pound trout,* bathing in a plate of melted fresh butter—the butter discolored by two table spoonsful of mushroom catchup, a piece of the Roe, and about twenty grains of red pepper —by the bye, writing of pepper, puts me in mind to mention, that if there is one spot in our country where that article is procurable, finer than another, it is on the estate of a very dear friend of mine, hard by, called "Longwood." It is so finely prepared in the process it is subjected to, so volatilized, so impalpable it becomes, that I believe it would be quite enough in the preparation of any dish for a cook only to keep a bottle of it by her in the kitchen, *with the stopper out,* to have the dish properly seasoned: something like the virtues of Saunders' Razor Strops, of which it is said, it is only necessary to put a razor over night in the same drawer with one of them, to have it ready sharpened by the morning.

A gentle squeeze of a lemon is no bad addition to the ingredients already mentioned, but I greatly prefer cutting a very thin slice or two of the lemon, by which a little of the essential oil of the rhine is obtained, imparting a very agreeable flavor. An Irish potatoe steamed and dropping to pieces is, also, an excellent adjunct, and should never be omitted if at hand. During the enjoyment of this dish—for it must not be hastily despatched—one or two glasses of "the best of Rhenish wine," are indispensable. A French gastronome, if M. Gregnon and others "have writ their annals true," would prefer a glass of *Chablis* in the interims of their mastification—interims, which must necessarily occur to every man who wishes not only to prolong a pleasure, but properly to enjoy it.

After our fish course, a "noble bird" of the wild Turkey breed, was put upon the table—a slice from the *"bosom,"* with a little white sauce, and a glass of Champagne agreeably occupied us for a while, until a pair of wild ducks, English, or canvass back ducks as they are called in these parts, smoking hot at the foot of the table, attracted general attention. Longitudinal incisions having been made in their breasts, parallel to the breast bone, and a lemon squeezed over them, with a rather *leetle sprinkle* of the "Longwood pepper," then well basted from the gravy in the dish, offered as tempting a morceau as our jaded appetites could desire. It was highly relished, and another glass of Champagne quaffed, "an all rounder" by general consent. The tables were then cleared—Regalias produced, and our senses regaled with the delightful odor of the balsamic weed. "The joke and song prevailed," and decided indications manifested on all sides to do honor to the occasion, and to the jolly God, who

> "Drinking joys did first ordain!"

To judge from the good-humored merriment that was abounding more and more every moment, a looker on of the Old School, might have supposed that the whole party belonged to that *severe sect* of philosophers, the stoics, who considered it was absolutely indispensable to human happiness, as well as to human health, to get drunk occasionally. Hippocrates and other ancient sages taught, that *monthly* excesses (hence the origin, no doubt, of *monthly* clubs in the country) in eating and drinking, were good for the spleen, and to drive away dull care and melancholy from the soul, which they contended was as liable to disease as the body. Solomon sung continually of wine and its blessings!

Thinking of these things we have often wondered how the *Tee-Totallers* of the modern school, can reconcile the new-fangled theory of their *"Reformed Inebriates,"* to the wisdom of the wise of old!

It is said, that a man during his life must eat a peck of dirt, and drink his *butt;* now is it fair that those who have such capacious swallows, as to be able to accomplish this *their destiny,* in a few years, should, during the residue of their lives *butt* at those who desire to be more moderate in their indulgences. I would not be thought illiberal, but I must ask, who ever saw an over-zealous temperance Lecturer that had not been a drunkard in his time—a regular *whale, spouting* furiously in all directions, his own merits, and the demerits of every thing intemperate; as if it was worth while in these days to try and persuade the peep-o'day-boys, that paradise was a tea-garden, and not a dram shop!

There is no doubt that some of the tee-totallers are carrying the joke a little too far. I am willing to admit that to be an admirable species of moral reform, a proud triumph of weak human nature, which enables us to relinquish one vice without substituting another in its place. Does tee-totalism do this? I believe not. An eminent practitioner of medicine has discovered that the majority of tee-totallers that are reformed dram drinkers, become either *opium eaters,* or *tobacco chewers,* which amounts pretty much to the same thing; the latter is an indulgence—a vice we may call it, of equal magnitude with the former—*both are the means of intoxication!*

But the great objection to tee-totalism, is, that it is a very *expensive virtue,* one that few honest men can afford to practise. The young, and the unwary, therefore, cannot be too cautious how they imbibe so costly a virtue as sobriety, that is, if they possess not means adequate to all its exigencies.

I have heard, or read, I do not recollect which, a capital story on this subject. It was something to this effect. A tee-totaller making one of a large dinner party, most unreflectingly endeavored to carry out his principles. Being only "half teas over," he was the only one of the party at the glorious finish of the frolic, that could say he was sober; the others all talked too thick to be understood, and not a soul among them *could unbutton a breeches pocket!* As not a purse could be produced, the tee-totaller *had to pay the bill for the party,* for the waiter, as well as "Melancholy, had long marked him for his own," and would not let him depart in peace, without first planking up the pewter!

Seeing, then, from this instance, as well as many others I could cite, that in this world *Virtue is not always its own reward,* and that opium and tobacco are poor substitutes for good old wine that "maketh the heart glad" let us pity the infirmities of those who cannot use the blessings of this world without abusing them, and be satisfied to go on our own way rejoicing, like social beings as we are formed by nature, content occasionally in a gentlemanly quiet way

> To honor the grape's ruby Nectar,
>   All sportingly, laughingly gay;
> And tho' it may call down a Lecture
>   Drive sometimes Dame WISDOM away!!

St. Thomas Parish, S.C., 1842

William Gilmore Simms (1806–70)

The outstanding man-of-letters of the Old South, William Gilmore Simms was born in Charleston on April 17, 1806, the son of William Gilmore Simms, Sr., and Harriet Ann Augusta Singleton Simms. Though his formal education ended when he was twelve, young Simms studied law in Charleston and was admitted to the bar on his twenty-first birthday. Even earlier, however, he had displayed his literary propensities—having edited the *Album* (1825), a Charleston literary journal, when he was nineteen. He first became known nationally with the publication of *Martin Faber* (1833), and for the remainder of his life he was a prolific writer of stories, novels, poetry, drama, essays, criticism, history, biography, and geography. Though he is now best known for the fifteen or sixteen novels included in his Revolutionary Romances and his Border Romances series, Simms' forte actually lay in short fiction, some of which he collected in *The Wigwam and the Cabin* (1845), but the best of which is being collected for the first time in *The Centennial Edition of the Writings of William Gilmore Simms* (University of South Carolina Press). He died in his native Charleston on June 11, 1870.

Mighty Is the Yemassee

Mighty is the Yemassee,
Strong in the trial,
Fearless in the strife,
Terrible in wrath—
Look, Opitchi-Manneyto—
He is like the rush of clouds,
He is like the storm by night,
When the tree-top bends and shivers,
When the lodge goes down.
The Westo and the Edisto,
What are they to him?—
Like the brown leaves to the cold,
Look, they shrink before his touch,
Shrink and shiver as he comes—
Mighty is the Yemassee.

The Syren of Tselica

A TRADITION OF THE FRENCH BROAD

The tradition of the Cherokees asserts the existence of a Syren, in the French Broad, who implores the Hunter to the stream, and strangles him in her embrace, or so infects him with some mortal disease, that he invariably perishes. The story, stripped of all poetry, would seem to be that of a youth, who, overcome with fatigue and heat together, sought the cool waters of the river, and was seized with cramp or spasms; or, too much exhausted for reaction, sunk under the shock. It does not much concern us, however, what degree of faith is due to the tradition. Enough that such exists, and that its locality is one of the most magnificent regions, for its scenery, in the known world. Tselica is the Indian name of the river. [Simms' note]

'Twas in summer prime, the noontide hour,
    Sleep lay heavy o'er the sunny vale;
Droop'd the sad leaves 'neath the fiery vapor,
    Droop'd and panted for the evening gale.

Gloomy, lonely, and with travail weary,
    Down the mountain slopes the stranger came;
Droop'd his eyes, and in his fainting bosom
    Lay the pulsing blood, a lake of flame.

Oh, how cool in sight the rushing river,
    With its thousand barrier-rocks at strife,
All its billows tossing high their foam wreaths,
    As if maddening with the impatient life.

Wild, with ceaseless shout they hurried onward,
    Laughing ever with their cheerful glee,
O'er the antique rocks their great limbs flinging,
    With a frantic joy was strange to see.

They, of all, possess'd the life and action,
    Silence else had sovereign sway alone,
All the woods were hush'd, and the gray mountain
    Look'd with stony eyes from crumbling throne.

Sad the youth sank down in the great shadows,
    Close beside the waters as they ran,
Very hopeless was he of his travail,
    Very weary since it first began.

Friends and fortune he had none to cheer him,
    And the growing sorrow at his heart
Wrought the bitter thought to bitter feeling,
    And he yearn'd to perish and depart.

"Why," he murmurs, "still in toil unresting,
    Should I strive for aye in fruitless strife;
Where the hopes and loves that used to glad me,
    When I first began the race of life?

"Where's the pride of triumph that was promised,
    That should crown me with the immortal wreath;
Where the fond heart that in youth embraced me—
    Gone, forever gone—and where is Death?

"Give me peace, ye skies and rocks: ye waters,
    Peace yourselves ye know not, but your flow
Tells of calm and rest beneath your billows—
    Coolness, for the fiery griefs I know."

Thus, with languid soul beside the river,
    Gazed he sadly as that hour he lay;
Gloomy with the past, and the future
    Hopeless,—hence his guilty prayer that day.

Brooding thus, and weary, a song rises,
    From the very billows, soft and clear;
Such as evening bird, with parting ditty,
    Pours at twilight to the floweret's ear.

Wild and sweet, and passionate and tender;
    Now full, now faint; with such a touching art,
His soul dissolves in weakness, and his spirit
    Goes with the throbbing sweetness at his heart.

He looks with strain'd eyes at the lapsing waters,
    And gleaming bright beneath the billows, lo!
Flashes white arms, and glides a lovely damsel,
    Bright eyes, dark locks, and bosom white as snow.

He sees, but still in moment glimpses only,
    Gleams of strange beauty, from an eye all bright,—
As when some single star, at midnight, flashes
    From the cold cloud, above the mountain's height.

As raven black as night float free her tresses,
    Outflung above the waves by snowy arms,
Now o'er her bosom spread, and half betraying,
    While half concealing still her sunny charms.

And then again ascends her song of pleading—
    "Ah, but thou failest with the noonday heat,
Thy brow is pale with care, thine eyelids drooping,
    Thy soul is sad, and weary-worn thy feet.

"Oh! come to me, and taste my waves of cooling;
    I'll soothe thy sorrows; I will bring thee rest;
Thy fainting limbs grow strong in my embraces,
    Thy burning cheek find pillow on my breast.

"Oh! come to me!" was still the loving burden,
    With charm of such a sweetness in its swell,
That every fancy in his bosom kindled,
    And every feeling woke to work the spell.

Wild was the dreamy passion that possess'd him;
    Won by the syren song, and glimpsing charms,
He leapt to join her in the wave, but shudder'd
    At the first foldings of her death-cold arms.

Fiercely against her own she press'd his bosom;—
    'Tis the ice-mountain whose embrace he feels;
Within his eyes she shot her dazzling glances:
    'Tis Death's own stony stare the look reveals.

He breaks away, the shore in horror seeking;
  But all too late,—the doom is in his heart:
He sinks beside the fatal stream, and dying,
  Deplores the prayer that pleaded to depart.

His dying sense still hears the fatal Syren;
  She sings her triumph now, her love no more:
A fearful hate was in the eldritch music,
  And terror now, where beauty sway'd before.

No more the pleasing wile, the plaintive ditty:
  He strives in vain the wizard strain to flee;
"Death," ran the song,—no more of peace and pity,
  "To him who madly seeks embrace with me!"

The Lost Pleiad

I

Not in the sky,
Where it was seen
So long in eminence of light serene,—
Nor on the white tops of the glistering wave,
Nor down, in mansions of the hidden deep,
Though beautiful in green
And crystal, its great caves of mystery,—
Shall the bright watcher have
Her place, and, as of old, high station keep!

II

Gone! gone!
Oh! never more, to cheer
The mariner, who holds his course alone
On the Atlantic, through the weary night,
When the stars turn to watchers, and do sleep,
Shall it again appear,
With the sweet-loving certainty of light,
Down shining on the shut eyes of the deep!

III

The upward-looking shepherd on the hills
Of Chaldea, night-returning, with his flocks,
He wonders why his beauty doth not blaze,
Gladding his gaze,—
And, from his dreary watch along the rocks,
Guiding him homeward o'er the perilous ways!
How stands he waiting still, in a sad maze,
Much wondering, while the drowsy silence fills
The sorrowful vault!—how lingers, in the hope that **night**
May yet renew the expected and sweet light,
So natural to his sight!

IV

And lone,
Where, at the first, in smiling love she shone,
Brood the once happy circle of bright stars:
How should they dream, until her fate was known,
That they were ever confiscate to death?
That dark oblivion the pure beauty mars,
And, like the earth, its common bloom and breath,
That they should fall from high;
Their lights grow blasted by a touch, and die,—
All their concerted springs of harmony
Snapt rudely, and the generous music gone!

V

Ah! still the strain
Of wailing sweetness fills the saddening sky;
The sister stars, lamenting in their pain
That one of the selectest ones must die,—
Must vanish, when most lovely, from the rest!
Alas! 'tis ever thus the destiny.
Even Rapture's song hath evermore a tone
Of wailing, as for bliss too quickly gone.
The hope most precious is the soonest lost,
The flower most sweet is first to feel the frost.
Are not all short-lived things the loveliest?
And, like the pale star, shooting down the sky,
Look they not ever brightest, as they fly
From the lone sphere they blest!

The Eutaw Maid

The battle of the Eutaw Springs, one of the most brilliant events of the Revolution, is well known in the history of the partisan warfare carried on in the southern department. [Simms' note]

I

It was in Eutaw's covert shade, and on a hill-side stood
A young and gentle Santee maid, who watch'd the distant wood,
Where he, the loved one of her heart, in fearful battle then,
Had gone to flesh his maiden sword with Albion's martial men:
Untaught in fight, and all unused to join the strife of blows,—
Oh! can there be a doubt with her how the deadly battle goes?

II

And wild the din ascends from far, and high in eddying whirls,
Above the forest trees and wide, the sulphur storm-cloud curls,
And fast and thick upon her ear the dreadful cries of pain,
The groan, the shriek, the hoarse alarm, run piercing to her brain:
She may not hope that he is safe when thousands fall around,
But looks to see his bloody form outstretch'd upon the ground.

III

There's a cry of conquest on the breeze, the cannon's roar is still,—
She dares not look, she does not weep, her trembling heart is chill:
The tramplings of the victors come in triumph through the glade,
She hears the loud note of the drum, the clattering of the blade:
Perchance that very blade is red with the blood of him, her love;—
The thought is death, and down she sinks within the woodland grove.

IV

But, a gentle arm entwines her form—a voice is in her ear,
Which, even in death's cold grasp itself, 'twould win her back to hear;
Her lips unclose, her eyes unfold once more upon the light,
And he is there, that gallant youth, unharm'd, before her sight!
Now happy is that Santee maid, and proudly blest is he,
And in her face the tear and smile are strangely sweet to see.

The Edge of the Swamp

'Tis a wild spot, and even in summer hours,
With wondrous wealth of beauty and a charm
For the sad fancy, hath the gloomiest look,
That awes with strange repulsion. There, the bird
Sings never merrily in the sombre trees,
That seem to have never known a term of youth,
Their young leaves all being blighted. A rank growth
Spreads venomously round, with power to taint;
And blistering dews await the thoughtless hand
That rudely parts the thicket. Cypresses,
Each a great ghastly giant, eld and gray,
Stride o'er the dusk, dank tract,—with buttresses
Spread round, apart, not seeming to sustain,
Yet link'd by secret twines, that, underneath,
Blend with each arching trunk. Fantastic vines,
That swing like monstrous serpents in the sun,
Bind top to top, until the encircling trees
Group all in close embrace. Vast skeletons
Of forests, that have perish'd ages gone,
Moulder, in mighty masses, on the plain;
Now buried in some dark and mystic tarn,
Or sprawl'd above it, resting on great arms,
And making, for the opossum and the fox,
Bridges, that help them as they roam by night.
Alternate stream and lake, between the banks,
Glimmer in doubtful light: smooth, silent, dark,
They tell not what they harbor; but, beware!
Lest, rising to the tree on which you stand,
You sudden see the moccasin snake heave up
His yellow shining belly and flat head
Of burnish'd copper. Stretch'd at length, behold
Where yonder Cayman, in his natural home,
The mammoth lizard, all his armor on,
Slumbers half-buried in the sedgy grass,
Beside the green ooze where he shelters him.

The place, so like the gloomiest realm of death,
Is yet the abode of thousand forms of life,—
The terrible, the beautiful, the strange,—
Wingéd and creeping creatures, such as make
The instinctive flesh with apprehension crawl,
When sudden we behold. Hark! at our voice
The whooping crane, gaunt fisher in these realms,
Erects his skeleton form and shrieks in flight,
On great white wings. A pair of summer ducks,
Most princely in their plumage, as they hear
His cry, with senses quickening all to fear,
Dash up from the lagoon with marvellous haste,
Following his guidance. See! aroused by these,
And startled by our progress o'er the stream,
The steel-jaw'd Cayman, from his grassy slope,
Slides silent to the slimy green abode,
Which is his province. You behold him now,
His bristling back uprising as he speeds
To safety, in the centre of the lake,
Whence his head peers alone,—a shapeless knot,
That shows no sign of life; the hooded eye,
Nathless, being ever vigilant and sharp,
Measuring the victim. See! a butterfly,
That, travelling all the day, has counted climes
Only by flowers, to rest himself a while,
And, as a wanderer in a foreign land,
To pause and look around him ere he goes,
Lights on the monster's brow. The surly mute
Straightway goes down; so suddenly, that he,
The dandy of the summer flowers and woods,
Dips his light wings, and soils his golden coat,
With the rank waters of the turbid lake.
Wondering and vex'd, the pluméd citizen
Flies with an eager terror to the banks,
Seeking more genial natures,—but in vain.
Here are no gardens such as he desires,

No innocent flowers of beauty, no delights
Of sweetness free from taint. The genial growth
He loves, finds here no harbor. Fetid shrubs,
That scent the gloomy atmosphere, offend
His pure patrician fancies. On the trees,
That look like felon spectres, he beholds
No blossoming beauties; and for smiling heavens,
That flutter his wings with breezes of pure balm,
He nothing sees but sadness—aspects dread,
That gather frowning, cloud and fiend in one,
As if in combat, fiercely to defend
Their empire from the intrusive wing and beam.
The example of the butterfly be ours.
He spreads his lacquer'd wings above the trees,
And speeds with free flight, warning us to seek
For a more genial home, and couch more sweet
Than these drear borders offer us to-night.

The Lay of the Carib Damsel

I

Come, seek the ocean's depths with me,
For there are joys beneath the sea,—
Joys, that when all is dark above,
Make all below a home of love!

II

In hollow bright and fountain clear,
Lo! thousand pearl await us there;
And amber drops that sea-birds weep
In sparry caves along the deep.

III

A crystal chamber there I know,
Where never yet did sunshaft go;
The soft moss from the rocks I take,
Of this our nuptial couch to make.

IV

There, as thou yieldest on my breast,
My songs shall soothe thy happy rest,—
Such songs as still our prophets hear,
When winds and stars are singing near.

V

These tell of climes, whose deep delight
Knows never change from day to night;
Where, if we love, the blooms and flowers,
And fruits, shall evermore be ours.

VI

Oh! yield thee to the hope I bring,
Believe the truth I feel and sing,
Nor teach thy spirit thus to weep
Thy Christian home beyond the deep.

VII

'Tis little,—ah! too well I know,
The poor Amaya may bestow,—
But if a heart that's truly thine
Be worthy thee, oh! cherish mine!

VIII

My life is in thy look—for thee
I bloom, as for the sun, the tree;
My hopes, when thou forget'st thy woes,
Unfold as flowers, when winter goes.

IX

And though, as our traditions say,
There bloom the worlds of endless day,
I would not care to seek the sky,
If there thy spirit did not fly.

Ballad. The Big Belly

As I walked out one morning in May
As pretty a little girl as ever I did see,
Came trudging alone by the side of me—
Crying O Lawd! my big belly!
What will my mammy say to me,
When I go home with a big belly.
    Bis.————Olaw! my big belly!

When my belly lay so low,
The boys they came through rain and snow;
But now my belly is up to my chin
They all pass by and ne'er come in.
   Olaw! my big belly.

I wish my sweet little babe was born,
A-setting on its father's knee
And I poor girl was dead & gone,
And the green grass growing over me.
   Olaw! my big belly &c.

The Late Henry Timrod *

We had but just published the name of Henry Timrod, of South-Carolina, as one of those fine contributors of the South upon whom we should rely in making our work a just type and representation of Southern intellect and society. We are now painfully required to record his premature death. Cut off in the prime of life, by the inexorable shears of Fate, he is lost to us and to the country. But not without having left a beautiful and worthy record. His memory is preserved to us in harmonious verse, in chaste thought, in the music of a fine fancy, and an ingenuous nature. As Milton sings:

> —Lycidas is dead; dead ere his prime,
> Young Lycidas; and hath not left his peer;—
> Who would not sing for Lycidas? He knew
> Himself to sing and build the lofty rhyme;
> He must not *slumber on his lowly bier,*
> Unwept,—
> Without the meed of some melodious tear!

Literary men, in the South, have always laboured under great difficulties in finding an audience. An appreciative audience, rather than a numerous one, was what Milton craved.

> Give me an audience *fit* though *few.*

Henry Timrod necessarily laboured under all the disadvantages of his people. An agricultural population is rarely susceptible to the charms of art and literature. He had his audience, however, and it *was* fit, capable, appreciative—though few. There were thousands that felt quickly and keenly his chaste sentiment, always pure; his gentle and winning thought; his beguiling fancy, his delicate art, and his ever fond and virtuous intercourse with nature. Such was his genius. He was not passionate; he was not profound; he laboured in no fields of metaphysics; he simply sang—"sang as the birds do when they would re-

William Gilmore Simms, "The Late Henry Timrod" in *The Last Years of Henry Timrod,* ed. Jay B. Hubbell (Durham, N.C.: Duke University Press, 1941), pp. 153–65. Copyright 1941 by The Duke University Press. Reprinted by permission of The Duke University Press.
*This article first appeared in the Baltimore *Southern Society,* I, 18–19 (October 12, 1867), only five days after Timrod's death.

joice"—with a native gift, of the things, the beauties, and the charms
of nature. He belonged, in the classification of literary men, to the order that we call the contemplative; and without the deeper studies and
aims of Wordsworth, he yet belonged to his school.—He was observ-
ant, meditative, and amiable. He avoided all strifes of parties and poli-
tics—all strong and gusty passions. The fields, the wayside, the evening twilight, stars and moon, and faint warblings of the birds in
green thickets—these were the attractions for his muse. These he
meditated in song and sonnet, and his songs emulated all the gentle
intuitions of nature.

Yet he could be lyrical, as well as contemplative.—His verse was
smooth and soft, with gentle cadences of rhyme and rhythm. His fancies were lively, with most felicitous turns of thought and expression,
and he was never monotonous and never dull. Nor was he overstrained
in the measure, either of thought or expression. He possessed the most
exquisite sense of propriety, and, whether he dealt in song or sonnet,
his thought was always appropriate to the theme, and his Fancy, a
happy page, was always obedient, waiting upon the thought, and nim-
ble in attendance. Such was the muse of Henry Timrod, and whether
he sang of his own or the loves of others, the open purity of his genius
refined equally the thought which he expressed and the verse in which
he clothed it.

His genius was, in some degree, inherited. His father—William H.
Timrod—was a poet before him. He was a man whom we knew well,
and whom we met, for many years, almost daily, in the intercourse of
life. He was a strong man, of quick intellect, at once sparkling and sensitive. He conducted a literary paper in Charleston more than forty
years ago, which he enriched with bold thoughts and generous fancies,
taken from the rough of the mine, careless perhaps of art, though sometimes her absolute master. He wrote freely and frequently. He published a volume of poems in Charleston some fifty years ago, the general characteristics of which somewhat resembled those of his son. He,
too, was a lover of nature, and his poems were meant frequently to
illustrate her phases. He was finely musical in his writings. His rhythm
was perfect, while his utterance was frequent and copious. His musings
were so many genial and generous aspirations to the superior nature,

the pure tastes and generous affections. We remember some of his *dramatic* fragments, published in the Charleston magazines, which were marked by a singular grace as well as power. His works, with those of his son, would form a valuable and beautiful contribution to the library of the South. Why should they not be blended in a new edition?

Henry Timrod received a good education at primary schools, and (we believe) finally, at the Charleston College [*sic*]. He attracted attention at an early period, by his proficiency of attainment and by the development of his poetical genius. Not that he showed himself precocious; not that he exhibited himself frequently, or in ostentatious exhibitions of performance. His muse was rather reticent. She required soliciting. As Mr. Timrod has frequently told us, he wrote with great painstaking and labour. He lacked in that readiness which belongs solely to a different temperament. His temperament was morbid. It was diseased from the beginning. He belonged to the lymphatic temperament, or rather to that which the medical men describe as the scrofulous. He was slow, timid, sensitive, and always suffering. Give him a good condition, under any circumstances, and this temperament would always work to his discomfort and disquietude. His hope was small. He had none of the sanguine in his system. His blood worked languidly and gave no proper support, stimulus, or succour to his brain.

But, that he *should* work, was the necessity of his condition. He was poor, and his brains, and the acquisitions of his brains, were required to be put in requisition for his support. He became a teacher of the young. He prepared lads and young men for school and college. He taught in schools and in private families. He was a good Latin scholar, something of a Grecian, and possessed a fair general acquaintance with some of the Continental languages.—But, whatever his acquisitions, he was always slow in asserting them. His temperament made him modest—made him distrustful of himself—and he undertook all his educational tasks with fear and trembling. How long he laboured in these fields we do not now remember. He passed from them into those of pure literature, and in 1860—as we think—a volume of his poems was published (nominally) by Ticknor & Fields, of Boston. This was published at the request of friends, and by the aid of friends. The publishers did nothing for the work, as they rarely will do where they are not themselves the proprietors. Recently a copy was sought for at the shop of the publishers, and, for awhile, they knew nothing about it. It was finally discovered on an obscure shelf, and that it was so found was owing, no doubt, to the pertinacity of the applicant.

The contents of this volume sufficed, or should suffice, to establish the fame of Timrod as a pure, chaste, graceful, fanciful, and most exquisite writer of felicitous verse—verse far superior to anything that could or can be done in Boston, by any or all of the sweet-singing swans of that American Olympus. But, save with the friends of the author, his book may be said to have fallen dead from the press. It yielded him no returns in money. Northern criticism was silent.—New England criticism is always silent in respect to the swans of other regions. Its own geese are its sufficient swans. The parish absorbs all the praise which its naturally costive character is able to bestow.

But Timrod had many admirers in the North as well as in the South. He had friends, also, who were quite willing to expend money in his behalf. At a certain period in the war he was an assistant editor in the office of the Charleston *Mercury*. About this period Mr. Vigateley [Vizetelly], an employee of the British press, was in Charleston, and employed in taking notes of the events of the war. He was engaged to produce a volume of Timrod's poems, handsomely illustrated, in England. Money was subscribed for this object here, but the scheme, we know not why, came to nothing. Money was raised for it, we know. Subsequently to his employment on the *Mercury*, Mr. Timrod became a joint editor, in charge of the *South Carolinian* newspaper at Columbia, and funds for which paper were also largely subscribed in Charleston. His assumption of the duties of this charge was coeval with his marriage. He married Miss Goodwyn [*sic*], a lovely English girl, the sister-in-law of his widowed sister. By her he had one lovely child, who died prematurely.—The death of this child affected the sensitive nature of the father to a very serious extent—far more than usual with men. His muse poured forth some of his most mournful lamentings on the subject, and his genius, never remarkable for its playfulness, acquired a more sombrous tinge from this visitation of death in his little family. His own health was impaired, and gradually he began to exhibit those shows of feebleness which awakened the liveliest fears among his friends. For the last three years he had been struggling with the adverse influences of poverty and physical prostration. His friends, themselves most generally overborne by the cruel fortune which has prostrated all the South, could do but little for his relief; and though the philanthropic and able physician watched and waited by his bed-side, with liberal and scientific service, it was probably, all the while, with the most painful misgivings that all effort would be made in vain. Day by day found him feebler; his vitality, always feeble, did not read-ily rally to the relief of nature; and his letters to his friends were im-bued with a gloomy tone which indicated his own unexpressed convic-tions of his certain decline. It was in this mood that he gave out a beautiful and touching little fancy, which prefigured the hour of parting and escape for the over-wearied soul. The reader of this little poem needs not that its delicate grace and fine fancy, and the sweet spirit of resignation which it embodies, should be pointed out to him. The pic-ture, so exquisitely touched in the lines which follow, has been realized, and the whispers of beloved ones by his couch of dying, have mur-mured mournfully and lowlily the sad, unavoidable words—"He is gone!" Was there a single moment of breathing consciousness left to the moribund, in which the senses, at such a moment, perhaps, sin-gularly acute, might enable the escaping spirit to take in the sounds? Did his darkening eyesight take in the melancholy aspects of the loved ones weeping around him?

[A COMMON THOUGHT]

Somewhere on this earthly planet,
    In the dust of flowers to be,
In the dew-drop, in the sunshine,
    Sleeps a solemn day for me.

At this wakeful hour of midnight,
    I behold it dawn in mist,
And I hear a sound of sobbing
    Through the darkness—hist! oh, hist!

In a dim and murky chamber,
    I am breathing life away;
Some one draws a curtain softly
    And I watch the broadening day.

> As it purples in the zenith,
>   As it brightens on the lawn,
> There's a hush of death about me,
>   And a whisper, "He is gone!"

The last poem from his pen, a sonnet, written literally on his dying bed, embodied a graceful tribute to the memory of a friend, in which it will not be difficult to trace the working of a thought, shadowing the presage of his own approaching fate. It will be read now, irrespective of its pure poetic merits, with a sad interest, by all those who loved the man and esteemed the genius of the poet.

IN MEMORIAM—HARRIS SIMONS

> True Christian, tender husband, gentle sire,
>   A stricken household mourns thee, but its loss
>   Is Heaven's gain and thine; upon the cross
> God hangs the crown, the pinion and the lyre;
> And thou hast won them all. Could we desire
>   To quench that diadem's celestial light,
>   To hush thy song and stay thy heavenward flight,
> Because we miss thee by this autumn fire?
> Ah, no! ah, no!—chant on!—soar on!—reign on!
>   For we are better—thou art happier thus!
> And haply from the splendour of thy throne,
>   Or haply from the echoes of thy psalm,
>   Something may fall upon us like the calm
> To which thou shalt hereafter welcome us.

We have before us a few of his later poems, the last croppings of that bright field of cultured thought and fancy from which our Southern society gathered so many lovely flowers. They indicate no decay or decline of the poetic vein. The verse flows freely and triumphantly. The fancies are sown thick upon the groundwork of the thought. They have all the airy grace and animation which distinguished his lyrical poetry in its hours of best strength and enthusiasm. What more full of freshness, life and spirit, grace and tenderness, than this spontaneous lay upon so simple a subject as ["A Summer Shower"?]

· · ·

What more dainty and felicitous than the string of triplets in the following ["The Rosebuds"]—the fancies so happily wedded to the most delicate of human sensibilities?

. . .

Of a sterner mood and character is the following poem ["Storm and Calm"], having its birth, most probably, in the melancholy condition of his native land, born down by a brutal tyranny, which threatens the moral as well as political atmosphere with the upas of degradation as well as death; the putridity of the worst corruption, prefacing the pangs of a prolonged dying.

. . .

Our last selection [sonnet beginning, "I know not why, but all this weary day"] from these later writings, most of which were contributed to the *Southern Opinion* newspaper, at Richmond, expresses that numbness of the heart, if not the head—that sense of weariness and exhaustion under which in later years he was so frequent a sufferer—a numbness of the hopes, which does not subdue the fancies, but endows them with shapes of doubt, and dread, and terror, filling the brain with such images as come to us in the demoniac dreams engendered by the Incubi.

. . .

The poems and other writings of Henry Timrod, to be dealt with justly, require more space and time than we can accord them here. We trust, however, that even here we have truly described their chief characteristics. We may add that his prose writings, which were mostly essayical, and were drawn forth mostly to meet the demands of a daily paper, were characterized by like qualities with his poetry. They were remarkable for their grace, ease, purity, and polish; for gentleness of thought and manner, frankness of spirit, and a lively fancy. His writings are not numerous; and a single duodecimo of three to four hundred pages would suffice to contain not only his poems, but a fair selection from his prose writings, including one or more lectures, and a few samples of elaborate criticism. The preparation of such a volume might well be confided to his friend and brother poet, Paul H. Hayne, who, with kindred tastes and genius, a loving nature, and a sympathizing attachment, would find the labour of such a work a labour of love.

Henry Timrod was born in Charleston, S.C., somewhere about 1830.

He was, we believe, just entered on his thirty-eighth year, at the time of his death.—This event took place in Columbia on the 7th instant. He died a Christian. We are told that, while he clung to life, and to all whom he had ever loved, with wonderful tenacity—as how should it be otherwise in the case of one who was so exquisitely sensible to the charms of life and nature?—yet his faith was firm, and he met the trying hour with unflinching fortitude. Some one remarked to him while he was under the agonies of dissolution—"You will soon have rest, Harry." "Ah, yes!" was the reply, *"but love is stronger than rest!"* A little later, and he had found both! His remains were attended at the grave by the leading citizens of Columbia, including some of our most eminent of Southern names. It was a spontaneous tribute of society and country to genius—that genius, so little honoured while it lives, but to which society owes its best and most enduring treasures.—The grave has closed its portals upon the form of the mortal; his immortal nature has its reflex in the ever-living song, which was its soul-utterance and beautiful voice on earth. He lies in consecrated soil—in the graveyard of Trinity church, Columbia. It will be for his admirers and friends to see that a graceful tablet shall indicate to posterity the sleeping place of the bard. "After life's fitful fever he sleeps well!"

How Sharp Snaffles Got His Capital and Wife

I

The day's work was done, and a good day's work it was. We had bagged a couple of fine bucks and a fat doe; and now we lay camped at the foot of the "Balsam Range" of mountains in North Carolina, preparing for our supper. We were a right merry group of seven; four professional hunters, and three amateurs—myself among the latter. There was Jim Fisher, Aleck Wood, Sam or Sharp Snaffles, *alias* "Yaou," and Nathan Langford, *alias* the "Pious."

These were our *professional* hunters. Our *amateurs* may well continue nameless, as their achievements do not call for any present record. Enough that we had gotten up the "camp hunt," and provided all the creature comforts except the fresh meat. For this we were to look to the mountain ranges and the skill of our hunters.

These were all famous fellows with the rifle—moving at a trot along the hill-sides, and with noses quite as keen of scent as those of their hounds in rousing deer and bear from their deep recesses among the mountain laurels.

A week had passed with us among these mountain ranges, some sixty miles beyond what the conceited world calls "civilization."

Saturday night had come; and, this Saturday night closing a week of exciting labors, we were to carouse.

We were prepared for it. There stood our tent pitched at the foot of the mountains, with a beautiful cascade leaping headlong toward us, and subsiding into a mountain runnel, and finally into a little lakelet, the waters of which, edged with perpetual foam, were as clear as crystal.

Our baggage wagon, which had been sent round to meet us by trail routes through the gorges, stood near the tent, which was of stout army canvas.

That baggage wagon held a variety of luxuries. There was a barrel of the best bolted wheat flour. There were a dozen choice hams, a sack of coffee, a keg of sugar, a few thousand of cigars, and last, not least, a corpulent barrel of Western uisquebaugh,* vulgarly, "whisky;" to say

---

*"Uisquebaugh," or the "water of life," is Irish. From the word we have dropped the last syllable. Hence we have "uisque," or, as it is commonly

nothing of a pair of demijohns of equal dimensions, one containing peach brandy of mountain manufacture, the other the luscious honey from the mountain hives.

Well, we had reached Saturday night. We had hunted day by day from the preceding Monday with considerable success—bagging some game daily, and camping nightly at the foot of the mountains. The season was a fine one. It was early winter, October, and the long ascent to the top of the mountains was through vast fields of green, the bushes still hanging heavy with their huckleberries.

From the summits we had looked over into Tennessee, Virginia, Georgia, North and South Carolina. In brief, to use the language of Natty Bumppo, we beheld "Creation." We had crossed the "Blue Ridge;" and the descending water-courses, no longer seeking the Atlantic, were now gushing headlong down the western slopes, and hurrying to lose themselves in the Gulf Stream and the Mississippi.

From the eyes of fountains within a few feet of each other we had blended our *eau de vie* with limpid waters which were about to part company forever—the one leaping to the rising, the other to the setting of the sun.

And buoyant, full of fun, with hearts of ease, limbs of health and strength, plenty of venison, and a wagon full of good things, we welcomed the coming of Saturday night as a season not simply of rest, but of a royal carouse. We were decreed to make a night of it.

But first let us see after our venison.

The deer, once slain, is, as soon after as possible, clapped upon the fire. All the professional hunters are good butchers and admirable cooks—of bear and deer meat at least. I doubt if they could spread a table to satisfy Delmonico; but even Delmonico might take some lessons from them in the preparation for the table of the peculiar game which they pursue, and the meats on which they feed. We, at least, rejoice at the supper prospect before us. Great collops hiss in the frying-pan, and finely cut steaks redden beautifully upon the flaming coals. Other portions of the meat are subdued to the stew, and make a very

---

written, "whisky"—a very able-bodied man-servant, but terrible as a mistress or housekeeper.

delightful dish. The head of the deer, including the brains, is put upon a flat rock in place of gridiron, and thus baked before the fire—being carefully watched and turned until every portion has duly imbibed the necessary heat, and assumed the essential hue which it should take to satisfy the eye of appetite. This portion of the deer is greatly esteemed by the hunters themselves; and the epicure of genuine stomach for the *haut gout* takes to it as an eagle to a fat mutton, and a hawk to a young turkey.

The rest of the deer—such portions of it as are not presently consumed or needed for immediate use—is cured for future sale or consumption; being smoked upon a scaffolding raised about four feet above the ground, under which, for ten or twelve hours, a moderate fire will be kept up.

Meanwhile the hounds are sniffing and snuffing around, or crouched in groups, with noses pointed at the roast and broil and bake; while their great liquid eyes dilate momently while watching for the huge gobbets which they expect to be thrown to them from time to time from the hands of the hunters.

Supper over, and it is Saturday night. It is the night dedicated among the professional hunters to what is called "The Lying Camp!"

"The Lying Camp!" quoth Columbus Mills, one of our party, a wealthy mountaineer, of large estates, of whom I have been for some time the guest.

"What do you mean by the 'Lying Camp,' Columbus?"

The explanation soon followed.

Saturday night is devoted by the mountaineers engaged in a camp hunt, which sometimes contemplates a course of several weeks, to stories of their adventures—"long yarns"—chiefly relating to the objects of their chase, and the wild experiences of their professional life. The hunter who actually inclines to exaggeration is, at such a period, privileged to deal in all the extravagances of invention; nay, he is *required* to do so! To be literal, or confine himself to the bald and naked truth, is not only discreditable, but a *finable* offense! He is, in such a case, made to swallow a long, strong, and difficult potation! He can not be too extravagant in his incidents; but he is also required to exhibit a certain degree of *art,* in their use; and he thus frequently rises into a certain realm of fiction, the ingenuities of which are made to compensate for the exaggerations, as they do in the "Arabian Nights," and other Oriental romances.

This will suffice for explanation.

Nearly all our professional hunters assembled on the present occasion were tolerable *raconteurs*. They complimented Jim Fisher, by throwing the raw deer-skin over his shoulders; tying the antlers of the buck with a red handkerchief over his forehead; seating him on the biggest boulder which lay at hand; and, sprinkling him with a stoup of whisky, they christened him "The Big Lie," for the occasion. And in this character he complacently presided during the rest of the evening, till the company prepared for sleep, which was not till midnight. He was king of the feast.

It was the duty of the "Big Lie" to regulate proceedings, keep order, appoint the *raconteurs* severally, and admonish them when he found them foregoing their privileges, and narrating bald, naked, and uninteresting truth. They must deal in fiction.

Jim Fisher was seventy years old, and a veteran hunter, the most famous in all the country. He *looked* authority, and promptly began to assert it, which he did in a single word:

"Yaou!"

II

"Yaou" was the *nom de nique* of one of the hunters, whose proper name was Sam Snaffles, but who, from his special smartness, had obtained the farther sobriquet of "*Sharp* Snaffles."

Columbus Mills whispered me that he was called "Yaou" from his frequent use of that word, which, in the Choctaw dialect, simply means "Yes." Snaffles had rambled considerably among the Choctaws, and picked up a variety of their words, which he was fond of using in preference to the vulgar English; and his common use of "*Yaou*," for the affirmative, had prompted the substitution of it for his own name. He answered to the name.

"Ay—yee, Yaou," was the response of Sam. "I was *afeard*, 'Big Lie,' that you'd be hitching me up the very first in your team."

"And what was you afeard of? You knows as well how to take up a crooked trail as the very best man among us; so you go ahead and spin your thread a'ter the best fashion."

"What shill it be?" asked Snaffles, as he mixed a calabash full of peach and honey, preparing evidently for a long yarn.

"Give's the history of how you got your capital, Yaou!" was the cry from two or more.

"O Lawd! I've tell'd that so often, fellows, that I'm afeard you'll sleep on it; and then agin, I've tell'd it so often I've clean forgot how it goes. Somehow it changes a leetle every time I tells it."

"Never you mind! The Jedge never haird it, I reckon, for one; and I'm not sure that Columbus Mills ever did."

So the "Big Lie."

The "Jedge" was the *nom de guerre* which the hunters had conferred upon me; looking, no doubt, to my venerable aspect—for I had traveled considerably beyond my teens—and the general dignity of my bearing.

"Yaou," like other bashful beauties in oratory and singing, was disposed to hem and haw, and affect modesty and indifference, when he was brought up suddenly by the stern command of the "Big Lie," who cried out:

"Don't make yourself an etarnal fool, Sam Snaffles, by twisting your mouth out of shape, making all sorts of redickilous ixcuses. Open upon the trail at onst and give tongue, or, dern your digestion, but I'll fine you to hafe a gallon at a single swallow!"

Nearly equivalent to what Hamlet says to the conceited player:

"Leave off your damnable faces and begin."

Thus adjured with a threat, Sam Snaffles swallowed his peach and honey at a gulp, hemmed thrice lustily, put himself into an attitude, and began as follows. I shall adopt his language as closely as possible; but it is not possible, in any degree, to convey any adequate idea of his *manner,* which was admirably appropriate to the subject matter. Indeed, the fellow was a born actor.

III

"You see, Jedge," addressing me especially as the distinguished stranger, "I'm a telling this hyar history of mine jest to please *you,* and

I'll try to please you ef I kin. These fellows hyar have hearn it so often that they knows all about it jest as well as I do my own self, and they knows the truth of it all, and would swear to it afore any hunters' court in all the county, ef so be the affidavy was to be tooken in camp and on a Saturday night.

"You see then, Jedge, it's about a dozen or fourteen years ago, when I was a young fellow without much beard on my chin, though I was full grown as I am now—strong as a horse, ef not quite so big as a buffalo. I was then jest a-beginning my 'prenticeship to the hunting business, and looking to sich persons as the 'Big Lie' thar to show me how to take the track of b'ar, buck, and painther.

"But I confess I weren't a-doing much. I hed a great deal to l'arn, and I reckon I miss'd many more bucks than I ever hit—that is, jest up to that time—"

"Look you, Yaou," said "Big Lie," interrupting him, "you're gitting too close upon the etarnal stupid truth! All you've been a-saying is jest nothing but the naked truth as I knows it. Jest crook your trail!"

"And how's a man to lie decently onless you lets him hev a bit of truth to go upon? The truth's nothing but a peg in the wall that I hangs the lie upon. A'ter a while I promise that you sha'n't see the peg."

"Worm along, Yaou!"

"Well, Jedge, I warn't a-doing much among the *bucks* yit—jest for the reason that I was quite too eager in the scent a'ter a sartin *doe!* Now, Jedge, you never seed my wife—my Merry Ann, as I calls her; and ef you was to see her *now*—though she's prime grit yit—you would never believe that, of all the womankind in all these mountains, she was the very yaller flower of the forest; with the reddest rose cheeks you ever did see, and sich a mouth, and sich bright curly hair, and so tall, and so slender, and so all over beautiful! O Lawd! when I thinks of it and them times, I don't see how 'twas possible to think of buck-hunting when thar was sich a doe, with sich eyes shining me on!

"Well, Jedge, Merry Ann was the only da'ter of Jeff Hopson and Keziah Hopson, his wife, who was the da'ter of Squire Claypole, whose wife was Margery Clough, that lived down upon Pacolet River—"

"Look you, Yaou, ain't you gitting into them derned facts agin, eh?"

"I reckon I em, 'Big Lie!' Scuse me: I'll kiver the pegs *direct-lie,* one a'ter t'other. Whar was I? Ah! Oh! Well, Jedge, poor hunter and poor man—jest, you see, a squatter on the side of a leetle bit of a mountain close on to Columbus Mills, at Mount Tryon, I was all the time on a hot trail a'ter Merry Ann Hopson. I went thar to see her a'most every night; and sometimes I carried a buck for the old people, and sometimes a doe-skin for the gal, and I do think, bad hunter as I then was, I pretty much kept the fambly in deer meat through the whole winter."

"Good for you, Yaou! You're a-coming to it! That's the only fair trail of a lie that you've struck yit!"

So the "Big Lie," from the chair.

"Glad to hyar you say so," was the answer. "I'll git on in time! Well, Jedge, though Jeff Hopson was glad enough to git my meat always, he didn't affection me, as I did his da'ter. He was a sharp, close, money-loving old fellow, who was always considerate of the main chaince; and the old lady, his wife, who hairdly dare say her soul was her own, she jest looked both ways, as I may say, for Sunday, never giving a fair look to me or my chaínces, when his eyes were sot on *her*. But 'twa'n't so with my Merry Ann. She hed the eyes for me from the beginning, and soon she hed the feelings; and, you see, Jedge, we sometimes did git a chaince, when old Jeff was gone from home, to come to a sort of onder-standing about our feelings; and the long and the short of it was that Merry Ann confessed to me that she'd like nothing better than to be my wife. She liked no other man but me. Now, Jedge, a'ter that, what was a young fellow to do? That, I say, was the proper kind of incouragement. So I said, 'I'll ax your daddy.' Then she got scary, and said, 'Oh, don't; for somehow, Sam, I'm a-thinking daddy don't like you enough *yit*. Jest hold on a bit, and come often, and bring him venison, and try to make him laugh, which you kin do, you know, and a'ter a time you kin try him.' And so I did—or rether I didn't. I put off the axing. I come con-stant. I brought venison all the time, and b'ar meat a plenty, a'most three days in every week."

"That's it, Yaou. You're on trail. That's as derned a lie as you've tell'd yit; for all your hunting, in them days, didn't git more meat than you could eat your one self."

"Thank you, 'Big Lie.' I hopes I'll come up in time to the right meas-ure of the camp.

"Well, Jedge, this went on for a long time, a'most the whole winter, and spring, and summer, till the winter begun to come in agin. I carried 'em the venison, and Merry Ann meets me in the woods, and we hes sich a pleasant time when we meets on them little odd chainces that I gits hot as thunder to bring the business to a sweet honey finish.

"But Merry Ann keeps on scary, and she puts me off; ontil, one day, one a'ternoon, about sundown, she meets me in the woods, and she's all in a flusteration. And she ups and tells me how old John Grimstead, the old bachelor (a fellow about forty years old, and the dear gal not yet twenty), how he's a'ter her, and bekaise he's got a good fairm, and mules and horses, how her daddy's giving him the open mouth incouragement.

"Then I says to Merry Ann:

" 'You sees, I kain't put off no longer. I must out with it, and ax your daddy at onst.' And then her scary fit come on again, and she begs me not to—not *jist yit*. But I swears by all the Hokies that I won't put off another day; and so, as I haird the old man was in the house that very hour, I left Merry Ann in the woods, all in a trimbling, and I jist went ahead, determined to have the figure made straight, whether odd or even.

"And Merry Ann, poor gal, she wrings her hainds, and cries a smart bit, and she wouldn't go to the house, but said she'd wait for me out thar. So I gin her a kiss into her very mouth—and did it over more than onst—and I left her, and pushed headlong for the house.

"I was jubous; I was mighty oncertain, and a leetle bit scary myself; for, you see, old Jeff was a fellow of tough grit, and with big grinders; but I was so oneasy, and so tired out waiting, and so desperate, and so fearsome that old bachelor Grimstead would get the start on me, that nothing could stop me now, and I jist bolted into the house, as free and easy and bold as ef I was the very best customer that the old man wanted to see."

Here Yaou paused to renew his draught of peach and honey.

IV

"Well, Jedge, as I tell you, I put a bold face on the business, though my hairt was gitting up into my throat, and I was almost a-gasping for my breath, when I was fairly in the big room, and standing up before the old Squire. He was a-setting in his big squar hide-bottom'd arm-chair, looking like a jedge upon the bench, jist about to send a poor fellow to the gallows. As he seed me come in, looking queer enough, I reckon, his mouth put on a sort of grin, which showed all his grinders, and he looked for all the world as ef he guessed the business I come about. But he said, good-natured enough:

" 'Well, Sam Snaffles, how goes it?'

"Says I:

" 'Pretty squar, considerin'. The winter's coming on fast, and I reckon the mountains will be full of meat before long.'

"Then says he, with another ugly grin, 'Ef 'twas your smoke-house that had it all, Sam Snaffles, 'stead of the mountains, 'twould be better for you, I reckon.'

" 'I 'grees with you,' says I. 'But I rether reckon I'll git my full shar' of it afore the spring of the leaf agin.'

" 'Well, Sam,' says he, 'I hopes, for your sake, 'twill be a big shar'. I'm afeard you're not the pusson to go for a big shar', Sam Snaffles. Seems to me you're too easy satisfied with a small shar'; such as the fence-squarrel carries onder his two airms, calkilating only on a small corn-crib in the chestnut-tree.'

" 'Don't you be afeard, Squire. I'll come out right. My cabin sha'n't want for nothing that a strong man with a stout hairt kin git, with good working—enough and more for himself, and perhaps another pusson.'

" 'What other pusson?' says he, with another of his great grins, and showing of his grinders.

" 'Well,' says I, 'Squire Hopson, that's jest what I come to talk to you about this blessed Friday night.'

"You see '*twas* Friday!

" 'Well,' says he, 'go ahead, Sam Snaffles, and empty your brain-basket as soon as you kin, and I'll light my pipe while I'm a-hearing you.'

"So he lighted his pipe, and laid himself back in his chair, shet his eyes, and begin to puff like blazes.

"By this time my blood was beginning to bile in all my veins, for I seed that he was jest in the humor to tread on all my toes, and then ax a'ter my feelings. I said to myself:

" 'It's jest as well to git the worst at onst, and then thar'll be an eend of the oneasiness.' So I up and told him, in pretty soft, smooth sort of speechifying, as how I was mighty fond of Merry Ann, and she, I was a-thinking, of me; and that I jest come to ax ef I might hev Merry Ann for my wife.

"Then he opened his eyes wide, as ef he never ixpected to hear sich a proposal from me.

" 'What!' says he. 'You?'

" 'Jest so, Squire,' says I. 'Ef it pleases you to believe me, and to consider it reasonable, the axing.'

"He sot quiet for a minit or more, then he gits up, knocks all the fire out of his pipe on the chimney, fills it, and lights it agin, and then comes straight up to me, whar I was a-setting on the chair in front of him, and without a word he takes the collar of my coat betwixt the thumb and forefinger of his left hand, and he says:

" 'Git up, Sam Snaffles. Git up, ef you please.'

"Well, I gits up, and he says:

" 'Hyar! Come! Hyar!'

"And with that he leads me right across the room to a big looking-glass that hung agin the partition wall, and thar he stops before the glass, facing it and holding me by the collar all the time.

"Now that looking-glass, Jedge, was about the biggest I ever did see! It was a'most three feet high, and a'most two feet wide, and it had a bright, broad frame, shiny like gold, with a heap of leetle figgers worked all round it. I reckon thar's no sich glass now in all the mountain country. I 'member when first that glass come home. It was a great thing, and the old Squire was mighty proud of it. He bought it at the sale of some rich man's furniter, down at Greenville, and he was jest as fond of looking into it as a young gal, and whenever he lighted his pipe, he'd walk up and down the room, seeing himself in the glass.

"Well, thar he hed me up, both on us standing in front of this glass, whar we could a'most see the whole of our full figgers, from head to foot.

"And when we hed stood thar for a minit or so, he says, quite solemn like:

" 'Look in the glass, Sam Snaffles.'

"So I looked.

" 'Well,' says I. 'I sees you, Squaire Hopson, and myself, Sam Snaffles.'

" 'Look good,' says he, *'obzarve* well.'

" 'Well,' says I, 'I'm a-looking with all my eyes. I only sees what I tells you.'

" 'But you don't *obzarve,'* says he. 'Looking and seeing's one thing,' says he, 'but obzarving's another. Now *obzarve.'*

"By this time, Jedge, I was getting sort o' riled, for I could see that somehow he was jest a-trying to make me feel redickilous. So I says:

" 'Look you, Squaire Hopson, ef you thinks I never seed myself in a glass afore this, you're mighty mistaken. I've got my own glass at home, and though it's but a leetle sort of a small, mean consarn, it shows me as much of my own face and figger as I cares to see at any time. I never cares to look in it 'cept when I'm brushing, and combing, and clipping off the straggling beard when it's too long for my eating.'

" 'Very well,' says he; 'now obzarve! You sees your own figger, and your face, and you air obzarving as well as you know how. Now, Mr. Sam Snaffles—now that you've hed a fair look at yourself—jest now answer me, from your honest conscience, a'ter all you've seed, ef you honestly thinks you're the sort of pusson to hev *my* da'ter!'

"And with that he gin me a twist, and when I wheeled round he hed wheeled round too, and thar we stood, full facing one another.

"Lawd! how I was riled! But I answered, quick:

" 'And why not, I'd like to know, Squaire Hopson? I ain't the handsomest man in the world, but I'm not the ugliest; and folks don't generally consider me at all among the uglies. I'm as tall a man as you, and as stout and strong, and as good a man o' my inches as ever stepped in shoe-leather. And it's enough to tell you, Squaire, whatever *you* may think, that Merry Ann believes in me, and she's a way of thinking that I'm jest about the very pusson that ought to hev her.'

" 'Merry Ann's thinking,' says he, 'don't run all fours with her fayther's thinking. I axed you, Sam Snaffles, to *obzarve* yourself in the glass. I telled you that seeing warn't edzactly obzarving. You seed only the inches; you seed that you hed eyes and mouth and nose and the airms and legs of the man. But eyes and mouth and legs and airms don't make a man!'

" 'Oh, they don't!' says I.

"'No, indeed,' says he. 'I seed that you hed all them; but then I seed thar was one thing that you hedn't got.'

"'Jimini!' says I, mighty conflustered. 'What thing's a-wanting to me to make me a man?'

"'*Capital!*' says he, and he lifted himself up and looked mighty grand.

"'Capital!' says I; 'and what's that?'

"'Thar air many kinds of capital,' says he. 'Money's capital, for it kin buy every thing. House and lands is capital; cattle and horses and sheep—when thar's enough on 'em—is capital. And as I obzarved you in the glass, Sam Snaffles, I seed that *capital* was the very thing that you wanted to make a man of you! Now I don't mean that any da'ter of mine shall marry a pusson that's not a *parfect* man. I obzarved you long ago, and seed whar you was wanting. I axed about you. I axed your horse.'

"'Axed my horse!' says I, pretty nigh dumbfoundered.

"'Yes; I axed your horse, and he said to me: "Look at me! I hain't got an ounce of spar' flesh on my bones. You kin count all my ribs. You kin lay the whole length of your airm betwixt any two on 'em, and it'll lie thar as snug as a black snake betwixt two poles of a log-house." Says he, "Sam's got *no capital!* He ain't got, any time, five bushels of corn in his crib; and he's such a monstrous feeder himself that he'll eat out four bushels, and think it mighty hard upon him to give *me* the other one." Thar, now, was your horse's testimony, Sam, agin you. Then I axed about your cabin, and your way of living. I was curious, and went to see you one day when I knowed you waur at home. You hed but one chair, which you gin me to set on, and you sot on the eend of a barrel for yourself. You gin me a rasher of bacon what hedn't a streak of fat in it. You hed a poor quarter of a poor doe hanging from the rafters— a poor beast that somebody hed disabled—'

"'I shot it myself,' says I.

"'Well, it was a-dying when you shot it; and all the hunters say you was a poor shooter at any thing. You cooked our dinner yourself, and the hoe-cake was all dough, not hafe done, and the meat was all done as tough as ef you had dried it for a month of Sundays in a Flurriday sun! Your cabin had but one room, and that you slept in and ate in; and the floor was six inches deep in dirt! Then, when I looked into your garden,

I found seven stalks of long collards only, every one seven foot high, with all the leaves stript off it, as ef you wanted 'em for broth; till thar waur only three top leaves left on every stalk. You hedn't a stalk of corn growing, and when I scratched at your turnip-bed I found nothing bigger that a chestnut. Then, Sam, I begun to ask about your fairm, and I found that you was nothing but a squatter on land of Columbus Mills, who let you have an old nigger pole-house, and an acre or two of land. Says I to myself, says I, "This poor fellow's got *no capital;* and he hasn't the head to git *capital;*" and from that moment, Sam Snaffles, the more I obzarved you, the more sartin 'twas that you never could be a man, ef you waur to live a thousand years. You may think, in your vanity, that you air a man; but you ain't, and never will be, onless you kin find a way to git *capital;* and I loves my gal child too much to let her marry any pusson whom I don't altogether consider a man!'

"A'ter that long speechifying, Jedge, you might ha' ground me up in a mill, biled me down in a pot, and scattered me over a manure heap, and I wouldn't ha' been able to say a word!

"I cotched up my hat, and was a-gwine, when he said to me, with his derned infernal big grin:

" 'Take another look in the glass, Sam Snaffles, and obzarve well, and you'll see jest whar it is I thinks that you're wanting.'

"I didn't stop for any more. I jest bolted, like a hot shot out of a shovel, and didn't know my own self, or whatever steps I tuk, tell I got into the thick and met Merry Ann coming towards me.

"I must liquor now!"

V

"Well, Jedge, it was a hard meeting betwixt me and Merry Ann. The poor gal come to me in a sort of run, and hairdly drawing her breath, she cried out:

" 'Oh, Sam! What does he say?'

"What could I say? How tell her? I jest wrapped her up in my airms, and I cries out, making some violent remarks about the old Squaire.

"Then she screamed, and I hed to squeeze her up, more close than ever, and kiss her, I reckon, more than a dozen times, jest to keep her from gwine into historical fits. I telled her all, from beginning to eend.

"I telled her that thar waur some truth in what the old man said: that I hedn't been keerful to do the thing as I ought; that the house *was* mean and dirty; that the horse was mean and poor; that I hed been thinking too much about her own self to think about other things; but that I would do better, would see to things, put things right, git corn in the crib, git 'capital,' ef I could, and make a good, comfortable home for *her*.

" 'Look at me,' says I, 'Merry Ann. Does I look like a man?'

" 'You're all the man I wants,' says she.

" 'That's enough,' says I. 'You shall see what I kin do, and what I *will* do! That's ef you air true to me.'

" 'I'll be true to you, Sam,' says she.

" 'And you won't think of nobody else?'

" 'Never,' says she.

" 'Well, you'll see what I kin do, and what I *will* do. You'll see that I *em* a man; and ef thar's capital to be got in all the country, by working and hunting, and fighting, ef that's needful, we shill hev it. Only you be true to me, Merry Ann.'

"And she threw herself upon my buzzom, and cried out:

" 'I'll be true to you, Sam. I loves nobody in all the world so much as I loves you.'

" 'And you won't marry any other man, Merry Ann, no matter what your daddy says?'

" 'Never,' she says.

" 'And you won't listen to this old bachelor fellow, Grimstead, that's got the "capital" already, no matter how they spurs you?'

" 'Never!' she says.

" 'Sw'ar it!' says I—'sw'ar it, Merry Ann—that you will be my wife, and never marry Grimstead!'

" 'I sw'ars it,' she says, kissing *me,* bekaize we had no book.

" 'Now,' says I, 'Merry Ann, that's not enough. Cuss him for my sake, and to make it sartin. Cuss that fellow Grimstead.'

" 'Oh, Sam, I kain't cuss,' says she; 'that's wicked.'

" 'Cuss him on my account,' says I—'to my credit.'

" 'Oh,' says she, 'don't ax me. I kain't do that.'

"Says I, 'Merry Ann, if you don't cuss that fellow, some way, I do believe you'll go over to him a'ter all. Jest you cuss him, now. Any small cuss will do, ef you're in airnest.'

" 'Well,' says she, 'ef that's your idee, then I says, *"Drot his skin,** and drot *my* skin, too, ef ever I marries any body but Sam Snaffles." '

" 'That'll do, Merry Ann,' says I. 'And now I'm easy in my soul and conscience. And now, Merry Ann, I'm gwine off to try my best, and git the "capital." Ef it's the "capital" that's needful to make a man of me, I'll git it, by all the Holy Hokies, if I kin.'

"And so, after a million of squeezes and kisses, we parted; and she slipt along through the woods, the back way to the house, and I mounted my horse to go to my cabin. But, afore I mounted the beast, I gin him a dozen kicks in his ribs, jest for bearing his testimony agin me, and telling the old Squaire that I hedn't 'capital' enough for a corn crib."

VI

"I was mightily let down, as you may think, by old Squaire Hopson; but I was mightily lifted up by Merry Ann.

"But when I got to my cabin, and seed how mean every thing was there, and thought how true it was, all that old Squaire Hopson had said, I felt overkim, and I said to myself, 'It's all true! How kin I bring that beautiful yaller flower of the forest to live in sich a mean cabin, and with sich poor accommydations? She that had everything comforting and nice about her.'

"Then I considered all about 'capital;' and it growed on me, ontil I begin to see that a man might hev good legs and arms and thighs, and a good face of his own, and yit not be a parfect and proper man a'ter all! I hed lived, you see, Jedge, to be twenty-three years of age, and was living no better than a three-old-year b'ar, in a sort of cave, sleeping on shuck and straw, and never looking after to-morrow.

---

*"Drot," or "Drat," has been called an American vulgarism, but it is genuine old English, as ancient as the days of Ben Jonson. Originally the oath was, "God rot it;" but Puritanism, which was unwilling to take the name of God in vain, was yet not prepared to abandon the oath, so the pious preserved it in an abridged form, omitting the G from God, and using, "Od rot it." It reached its final contraction, "Drot," before it came to America. "Drot it," "Drat it," "Drot your eyes," or "Drot his skin," are so many modes of using it among the uneducated classes.

"I couldn't sleep all that night for the thinking, and obzarvations. That impudent talking of old Hopson put me on a new track. I couldn't give up hunting. I knowed no other business, and I didn't hafe know that.

"I thought to myself, 'I must l'arn my business so as to work like a master.'

"But then, when I considered how hard it was, how slow I was to git the deers and the b'ar, and what a small chaince of money it brought me, I said to myself:

" 'Whar's the "capital" to come from?'

"Lawd save us! I ate up the meat pretty much as fast as I got it!

"Well, Jedge, as I said, I had a most miserable night of consideration and obzarvation and concatenation accordingly. I felt all over mean, 'cept now and then, when I thought of dear Merry Ann, and her felicities and cordialities and fidelities; and then, the cuss which she gin, onder the kiver of 'Drot,' to that dried up old bachelor Grimstead. But I got to sleep at last. And I hed a dream. And I thought I seed the prettiest woman critter in the world, next to Merry Ann, standing close by my bedside; and, at first, I thought 'twas Merry Ann, and I was gwine to kiss her agin; but she drawed back and said:

" 'Scuse me! I'm not Merry Ann; but I'm her friend and your friend; so don't you be down in the mouth, but keep a good hairt, and you'll hev help, and git the "capital" whar you don't look for it now. It's only needful that you be datermined on good works and making a man of yourself.'

"A'ter that dream I slept like a top, woke at day-peep, took my rifle, called up my dog, mounted my horse, and put out for the laurel hollows.

"Well, I hunted all day, made several *starts,* but got nothing; my dog ran off, the rascally pup, and, I reckon, ef Squaire Hopson had met him he'd ha' said 'twas bekaise I starved him! Fact is, we hedn't any on us much to eat that day, and old mar's ribs stood out bigger than ever.

"All day I rode and followed the track and got nothing.

"Well, jest about sunset I come to a hollow of the hills that I hed never seed before; and in the middle of it was a great pond of water, what you call a lake; and it showed like so much purple glass in the sunset, and 'twas jest as smooth as the big looking-glass of Squaire Hopson's. Thar wa'n't a breath of wind stirring.

"I was mighty tired, so I eased down from the mar', tied up the bridle and check, and let her pick about, and laid myself down onder a tree, jest about twenty yards from the lake, and thought to rest myself ontil the moon riz, which I knowed would be about seven o'clock.

"I didn't mean to fall asleep, but I did it; and I reckon I must ha' slept a good hour, for when I woke the dark hed set in, and I could only see one or two bright stars hyar and thar, shooting out from the dark of the heavens. But, ef I seed nothing, I haird; and jest sich a sound and noise as I hed never haird before.

"Thar was a rushing and a roaring and a screaming and a plashing, in the air and in the water, as made you think the universal world was coming to an eend!

"All that set me up. I was waked up out of sleep and dream, and my eyes opened to every thing that eye could see; and sich another sight I never seed before! I tell you, Jedge, ef there was one wild-goose settling down in that lake, thar was one hundred thousand of 'em! I couldn't see the eend of 'em. They come every minit, swarm a'ter swarm, in tens and twenties and fifties and hundreds; and sich a fuss as they did make! sich a gabbling, sich a splashing, sich a confusion, that I was fairly conflusterated; and I jest lay whar I was, a-watching 'em.

"You never seed beasts so happy! How they flapped their wings; how they gabbled to one another; how they swam hyar and thar, to the very middle of the lake and to the very edge of it, jest a fifty yards from whar I lay squat, never moving leg or arm! It was wonderful to see! I wondered how they could find room, for I reckon thar waur forty thousand on 'em, all scuffling in that leetle lake together!

"Well, as I watched 'em, I said to myself:

" 'Now, if a fellow could only captivate all them wild-geese—fresh from Canniday, I reckon—what would they bring in the market at Spartanburg and Greenville? Walker, I knowed, would buy 'em up quick at fifty cents a head. Forty thousand geese at fifty cents a head. Thar was "capital!" '

"I could ha' fired in among 'em with my rifle, never taking aim, and killed a dozen or more, at a single shot; but what was a poor dozen geese, when thar waur forty thousand to captivate?

"What a haul 'twould be, ef a man could only get 'em all in one net! Kiver 'em all at a fling!

"The idee worked like so much fire in my brain.

"How kin it be done?

"That was the question!

" 'Kin it be done?' I axed myself.

" 'It kin,' I said to myself; 'and I'm the very man to do it!' Then I begun to work away in the thinking. I thought over all the traps and nets and snares that I hed ever seen or haird of; and the leetle eends of the idee begun to come together in my head; and, watching all the time how the geese flopped and splashed and played and swum, I said to myself:

" 'Oh! most beautiful critters! ef I don't make some "capital" out of you, then I'm not dezarving sich a beautiful yaller flower of the forest as my Merry Ann!'

"Well, I watched a long time, ontil dark night, and the stars begun to peep down upon me over the high hill-tops. Then I got up and tuk to my horse and rode home.

"And thar, when I hed swallowed my bit of hoe-cake and bacon and a good strong cup of coffee, and got into bed, I couldn't sleep for a long time, thinking how I was going to git them geese.

"But I kept nearing the right idee every minit, and when I was fast asleep it comes to me in my dream.

"I seed the same beautifulest young woman agin that hed given me the incouragement before to go ahead, and she helped me out with the idee.

"So, in the morning, I went to work. I rode off to Spartanburg, and bought all the twine and cord and hafe the plow-lines in town; and I got a lot of great fishhooks, all to help make the tanglement parfect; and I got lead for sinkers, and I got cork-wood for floaters; and I pushed for home jist as fast as my poor mar' could streak it.

"I was at work day and night, for nigh on to a week, making my net; and when 'twas done I borrowed a mule and cart from Columbus Mills, thar;—he'll tell you all about it—he kin make his affidavy to the truth of it.

"Well, off I driv with my great net, and got to the lake about noon-day. I knowed 'twould take me some hours to make my fixings parfect, and get the net fairly stretched across the lake, and jest deep enough to do the tangling of every leg of the birds in the very midst of their swimming and snorting and splashing and cavorting! When I hed fixed it all fine, and jest as I wanted it, I brought the eends of my plow-lines up to where I was gwine to hide myself. This was onder a strong sapling, and my calkilation was when I hed got the beasts all hooked, forty thousand, more or less—and I could tell how that was from feeling on the line—why, then, I'd whip the line round the sapling, hitch it fast, and draw in my birds at my own ease, without axing much about their comfort.

" 'Twas a most beautiful and parfect plan, and all would ha' worked beautiful well but for one leetle oversight of mine. But I won't tell you about that part of the business yit, the more pretickilarly as it all turned out for the very best, as you'll see in the eend.

"I hedn't long finished my fixings when the sun suddenly tumbled down the heights, and the dark begun to creep in upon me, and a pretty cold dark it waur! I remember it well! My teeth begun to chatter in my head, though I was boiling over with inward heat, all jest coming out of my hot eagerness to be captivating the birds.

"Well, Jedge, I hedn't to wait overlong. Soon I haird them coming, screaming fur away, and then I seed them pouring, jest like so many white clouds, straight down, I reckon, from the snow mountains off in Canniday.

"Down they come, millions upon millions, till I was sartin thar waur already pretty nigh on to forty thousand in the lake. It waur always a nice calkilation of mine that the lake could hold fully forty thousand, though onst, when I went round to measure it, stepping it off, I was jubous whether it could hold over thirty-nine thousand; but, as I tuk the measure in hot weather and in a dry spell, I concluded that some of the water along the edges hed dried up, and 'twa'n't so full as when I made my first calkilation. So I hev stuck to that first calkilation ever since.

"Well, thar they waur, forty thousand, we'll say, with, it mout be, a few millions and hundreds over. And Lawd! how they played and splashed and screamed and dived! I calkilated on hooking a good many of them divers, in pretickilar, and so I watched and waited, ontil I thought I'd feel of my lines; and I begun, leetle by leetle, to haul in, when, Lawd love you, Jedge, sich a ripping and raging, and bouncing and flouncing, and flopping and splashing, and kicking and screaming, you never did hear in all your born days!

"By this I knowed that I hed captivated the captains of the host, and a pretty smart chaince, I reckoned, of the rigilar army, ef 'twa'n't edzactly forty thousand; for I calkilated that some few would git away —run off, jest as the cowards always does in the army, jest when the shooting and confusion begins; still, I reasonably calkilated on the main body of the rigiments; and so, gitting more and more hot and eager, and pulling and hauling, I made one big mistake, and, instid of wrapping the eends of my lines around the sapling that was standing jest behind me, what does I do but wraps 'em round my own thigh— the right thigh, you see—and some of the loops waur hitched round my left arm at the same time!

"All this come of my hurry and ixcitement, for it was burning like a hot fever in my brain, and I didn't know when or how I hed tied myself up, ontil suddently, with an all-fired scream, all together, them forty thousand geese rose like a great black cloud in the air, all tied up, tangled up—hooked about the gills, hooked and fast in some way in the beautiful leetle twistings of my net!

"Yes, Jedge, as I'm a living hunter to-night, hyar a-talking to you, they riz up all together, as ef they hed consulted upon it, like a mighty thunder-cloud, and off they went, screaming and flouncing, meaning, I reckon, to take the back track to Canniday, in spite of the freezing weather.

"Before I knowed whar I was, Jedge, I was twenty feet in the air, my right thigh up and my left arm, and the other thigh and arm a-dangling useless, and feeling every minit as ef they was gwine to drop off.

"You may be sure I pulled with all my might, but that waur mighty leetle in the fix I was in, and I jest hed to hold on, and see whar the infernal beasts would carry me. I couldn't loose myself, and ef I could I was by this time quite too fur up in the air, and darsn't do so, onless I was willing to hev my brains dashed out, and my whole body mashed to a mammock!

"Oh, Jedge, jest consider my sitivation! It's sich a ricollection, Jedge, that I must rest and liquor, in order to rekiver the necessary strength to tell you what happened next."

VII

"Yes, Jedge," said Yaou, resuming his narrative, "jest stop whar you air, and consider my sitivation!

"That I was dangling, like a dead weight, at the tail of that all-fired cloud of wild-geese, head downward, and gwine, the Lawd knows whar!—to Canniday, or Jericho, or some other heathen territory beyond the Mississipp, and it mout be, over the great etarnal ocean!

"When I thought of *that,* and thought of the plow-lines giving way, and that on a suddent I should come down plump into the big sea, jest in the middle of a great gathering of shirks and whales, to be dewoured and tore to bits by their bloody grinders, I was ready to die of skeer outright. I thought over all my sinnings in a moment, and I thought of my poor dear Merry Ann, and I called out her name, loud as I could, jest as ef the poor gal could hyar me or help me.

"And jest then I could see we waur a drawing nigh a great thundercloud. I could see the red tongues running out of its black jaws; and 'Lawd!' says I, 'ef these all-fired infarnal wild beasts of birds should carry me into that cloud to be burned to a coal, fried, and roasted, and biled alive by them tongues of red fire!'

"But the geese fought shy of the cloud, though we passed mighty nigh on to it, and I could see one red streak of lightning run out of the cloud and give us chase for a full hafe a mile; but we waur too fast for it, and, in tearing passion bekaise it couldn't ketch us, the red streak struck its horns into a great tree jest behind us, that we hed passed over, and tore it into flinders, in the twink of a musquito.

"But by this time I was beginning to feel quite stupid. I knowed that I waur fast gitting onsensible, and it did seem to me as ef my hour waur come, and I was gwine to die—and die by rope, and dangling in the air, a thousand miles from the airth!

"But jest then I was roused up. I felt something brush agin me; then my face was scratched; and, on a suddent, thar was a stop put to my travels by that conveyance. The geese had stopped flying, and waur in a mighty great conflusteration, flopping their wings, as well as they could, and screaming with all the tongues in their jaws. It was clar to me now that we hed run agin something that brought us all up with a short hitch.

"I was shook roughly agin the obstruction, and I put out my right arm and cotched a hold of a long arm of an almighty big tree; then my legs waur cotched betwixt two other branches, and I rekivered myself, so as to set up a leetle and rest. The geese was a tumbling and flopping among the branches. The net was hooked hyar and thar; and the birds waur all about me, swinging and splurging, but onable to break loose and git away.

"By leetle and leetle I come to my clar senses, and begun to feel my sitivation. The stiffness was passing out of my limbs. I could draw up my legs, and, after some hard work, I managed to onwrap the plow-lines from my right thigh and my left arm, and I hed the sense this time to tie the eends pretty tight to a great branch of the tree which stretched clar across and about a foot over my head.

"Then I begun to consider my sitivation. I hed hed a hard riding, that was sartin; and I felt sore enough. And I hed hed a horrid bad skear, enough to make a man's wool turn white afore the night was over. But now I felt easy, bekaise I considered myself safe. With day-peep I calkilated to let myself down from the tree by my plow-lines, and thar, below, tied fast, warn't thar my forty thousand captivated geese?

" 'Hurrah!' I sings out. 'Hurrah, Merry Ann; we'll hev the "capital" now, I reckon!'

"And singing out, I drawed up my legs and shifted my body so as to find an easier seat in the crutch of the tree, which was an almighty big chestnut oak, when, O Lawd! on a suddent the stump I hed been a-setting on give way onder me. 'Twas a rotten jint of the tree. It give way, Jedge, as I tell you, and down I went, my legs first and then my whole body—slipping down not on the outside, but into a great hollow of the tree, all the hairt of it being eat out by the rot; and afore I knowed whar I waur, I waur some twenty foot down, I reckon; and by the time I touched bottom, I was up to my neck in honey!

"It was an almighty big honey-tree, full of the sweet treacle; and the bees all gone and left it, I reckon, for a hundred years. And I in it up to my neck.

"I could smell it strong. I could taste it sweet. But I could see nothing.

"Lawd! Lawd! From bad to worse; buried alive in a hollow tree with never a chaince to git out! I would then ha' given all the world ef I was only sailing away with them bloody wild-geese to Canniday, and Jericho, even across the sea, with all its shirks and whales devouring me.

"Buried alive! O Lawd! O Lawd! 'Lawd save me and help me!' I cried out from the depths. And 'Oh, my Merry Ann,' I cried, 'shill we never meet agin no more!' Scuse my weeping, Jedge, but I feels all over the sinsation, fresh as ever, of being buried alive in a beehive tree and presarved in honey. I must liquor, Jedge."

VIII

Yaou, after a great swallow of peach and honey, and a formidable groan after it, resumed his narrative as follows:

"Only think of me, Jedge, in my sitivation! Buried alive in the hollow of a mountain chestnut oak! Up to my neck in honey, with never no more an appetite to eat than ef it waur the very gall of bitterness that we reads of in the Holy Scripters!

"All dark, all silent as the grave; 'cept for the gabbling and the cackling of the wild-geese outside, that every now and then would make a great splurging and cavorting, trying to break away from their hitch, which was jist as fast fixed as my own.

"Who would git them geese that hed cost me so much to captivate? Who would inherit my 'capital?' and who would hev Merry Ann? and what will become of the mule and cart of Mills fastened in the woods by the leetle lake?

"I cussed the leetle lake, and the geese, and all the 'capital.'

"I cussed. I couldn't help it. I cussed from the bottom of my hairt, when I ought to ha' bin saying my prayers. And thar was my poor mar' in the stable with never a morsel of feed. She had told tales upon me to Squaire Hopson, it's true, but I forgin her, and thought of her feed, and nobody to give her none. Thar waur corn in the crib and fodder, but it warn't in the stable; and onless Columbus Mills should come looking a'ter me at the cabin, thar waur no hope for me or the mar'.

"Oh, Jedge, you couldn't jedge of my sitivation in that deep hollow, that cave, I may say, of mountain oak! My head waur jest above the honey, and ef I backed it to look up, my long ha'r at the back of the neck a'most stuck fast, so thick was the honey.

"But I couldn't help looking up. The hollow was a wide one at the top, and I could see when a star was passing over. Thar they shined, bright and beautiful, as ef they waur the very eyes of the angels; and, as I seed them come and go, looking smiling in upon me as they come, I cried out to 'em, one by one:

" 'Oh, sweet sperrits, blessed angels! ef so be thar's an angel sperrit, as they say, living in all them stars, come down and extricate me from this fix; for, so fur as I kin see, I've got no chaince of help from mortal man or woman. Hairdly onst a year does a human come this way; and ef they did come, how would they know I'm hyar? How could I make them hyar me? O Lawd! O blessed, beautiful angels in them stars! O give me help! Help me out!' I knowed I prayed like a heathen sinner, but I prayed as well as I knowed how; and thar warn't a star passing over me that I didn't pray to, soon as I seed them shining over the opening of the hollow; and I prayed fast and faster as I seed them passing away and gitting out of sight.

"Well, Jedge, suddently, in the midst of my praying, and jest after one bright, big star hed gone over me without seeing my sitivation, I hed a fresh skeer.

"Suddent I haird a monstrous fluttering among my geese—my 'capital.' Then I haird a great scraping and scratching on the outside of the tree, and, suddent, as I looked up, the mouth of the hollow was shet up.

"All was dark. The stars and sky waur all gone. Something black kivered the hollow, and, in a minit a'ter, I haird something slipping down into the hollow right upon me.

"I could hairdly draw my breath. I begun to fear that I was to be siffocated alive; and as I haird the strange critter slipping down, I shoved out my hands and felt ha'r—coarse wool—and with one hand I cotched hold of the ha'ry leg of a beast, and with t'other hand I cotched hold of his tail.

" 'Twas a great b'ar, one of the biggest, come to git his honey. He knowed the tree, Jedge, you see, and ef any beast in the world loves honey, 'tis a b'ar beast. He'll go his death on honey, though the hounds are tearing at his very haunches.

"You may be sure, when I onst knowed what he was, and onst got a good gripe on his hindquarters, I warn't gwine to let go in a hurry. I knowed that was my only chaince for gitting out of the hollow, and I do believe them blessed angels in the stars sent the beast, jest at the right time, to give me human help and assistance.

"Now, yer see, Jedge, thar was no chaince for him turning round upon me. He pretty much filled up the hollow. He knowed his way, and slipped down, eend foremost—the latter eend, you know. He could stand up on his hind-legs and eat all he wanted. Then, with his great sharp claws and his mighty muscle, he could work up, holding on to the sides of the tree, and git out a'most as easy as when he come down.

"Now, you see, ef he weighed five hundred pounds, and could climb like a cat, he could easy carry up a young fellow that hed no flesh to spar', and only weighed a hundred and twenty-five. So I laid my weight on him, eased him off as well as I could, but held on to tail and leg as ef all life and etarnity depended upon it.

"Now I reckon, Jedge, that b'ar was pretty much more skeered than I was. He couldn't turn in his shoes, and with something fastened to his ankles, and, as he thought, I reckon, some strange beast fastened to his tail, you never seed beast more eager to git away, and git upwards. He knowed the way, and stuck his claws in the rough sides of the hollow, hand over hand, jest as a sailor pulls a rope, and up we went. We hed, howsomdever, more than one slip back; but, Lawd bless you! I never let go. Up we went, I say, at last, and I stuck jest as close to his haunches as death sticks to a dead nigger. Up we went. I felt myself moving. My neck was out of the honey. My airms were free. I could feel the sticky thing slipping off from me, and a'ter a good quarter of an hour the b'ar was on the great mouth of the hollow; and as I felt that I let go his tail, still keeping fast hold of his leg, and with one hand I cotched hold of the outside rim of the hollow; I found it fast, held on to it; and jest then the b'ar sat squat on the very edge of the hollow, taking a sort of rest a'ter his labor.

"I don't know what 'twas, Jedge, that made me do it. I warn't a-thinking at all. I was only feeling and drawing a long breath. Jest then the b'ar sort o' looked round, as ef to see what varmint it was a-troubling him, when I gin him a mighty push, strong as I could, and he lost his balance and went over outside down cl'ar to the airth, and I could hyar his neck crack, almost as loud as a pistol.

"I drawed a long breath a'ter that, and prayed a short prayer; and feeling my way all the time, so as to be sure agin rotten branches, I got a safe seat among the limbs of the tree, and sot myself down, detarmined to wait tell broad daylight before I tuk another step in the business."

IX

"And thar I sot. So fur as I could see, Jedge, I was safe. I hed got out of the tie of the flying geese, and thar they all waur, spread before me, flopping now and then and trying to ixtricate themselves; but they couldn't come it! Thar they waur, captivated, and so much 'capital' for Sam Snaffles.

"And I hed got out of the lion's den; that is, I hed got out of the honey-tree, and warn't in no present danger of being buried alive agin. Thanks to the b'ar, and to the blessed, beautiful angel sperrits in the stars, that hed sent him thar seeking honey, to be my deliverance from my captivation!

"And thar he lay, jest as quiet as ef he waur a-sleeping, though I knowed his neck was broke. And that b'ar, too, was so much 'capital.'

"And I sot in the tree making my calkilations. I could see now the meaning of that beautiful young critter that come to me in my dreams. I was to hev the 'capital,' but I was to git it through troubles and tribulations, and a mighty bad skeer for life. I never knowed the valley of 'capital' till now, and I seed the sense in all that Squaire Hopson told me, though he did tell it in a mighty spiteful sperrit.

"Well, I calkilated.

"It was cold weather, freezing, and though I had good warm clothes on, I felt monstrous like sleeping, from the cold only, though perhaps the tire and the skeer together hed something to do with it. But I was afeard to sleep. I didn't know what would happen, and a man has never his right courage ontil daylight. I fou't agin sleep by keeping on my calkilation.

"Forty thousand wild-geese!

"Thar wa'n't forty thousand, edzactly—very far from it—but thar they waur, pretty thick; and for every goose I could git from forty to sixty cents in all the villages in South Carolina.

"Thar was 'capital!'

"Then thar waur the b'ar.

"Jedging from his strength in pulling me up, and from his size and fat in filling up that great hollow in the tree, I calkilated that he couldn't weigh less than five hundred pounds. His hide, I knowed, was worth twenty dollars. Then thar was the fat and tallow, and the biled marrow out of his bones, what they makes b'ars grease out of, to make chicken whiskers grow big enough for game-cocks. Then thar waur the meat, skinned, cleaned, and all; thar couldn't be much onder four hundred and fifty pounds, and whether I sold him a fresh meat or cured, he'd bring me ten cents a pound at the least.

"Says I, 'Thar's capital!'

" 'Then,' says I, 'thar's my honey-tree! I reckon thar's a matter of ten thousand gallons in this hyar same honey-tree; and if I kint git fifty to seventy cents a gallon for it thar's no alligators in Flurriday!'

"And so I calkilated through the night, fighting agin sleep, and thinking of my 'capital' and Merry Ann together.

"By morning I had calkilated all I hed to do and all I hed to make.

"Soon as I got a peep of day I was bright on the look-out.

"Thar all around me were the captivated geese critters. The b'ar laid down perfectly easy and waiting for the knife; and the geese, I reckon they waur much more tired than me, for they didn't seem to hev the hairt for a single flutter, even when they seed me swing down from the tree among 'em, holding on to my plow-lines and letting myself down easy.

"But first I must tell you, Jedge, when I seed the first signs of daylight and looked around me, Lawd bless me, what should I see but old Tryon Mountain, with his great head lifting itself up in the east! And beyant I could see the house and fairm of Columbus Mills; and as I turned to look a leetle south of that, thar was my own poor leetle log-cabin standing quiet, but with never a smoke streaming out from the chimbley.

" 'God bless them good angel sperrits,' I said, 'I ain't two miles from home!' Before I come down from the tree I knowed edzactly whar I waur. 'Twas only four miles off from the lake and whar I hitched the mule of Columbus Mills close by the cart. Thar, too, I hed left my rifle. Yit in my miserable fix, carried through the air by them wild-geese, I did think I hed gone a'most a thousand miles towards Canniday.

"Soon as I got down from the tree I pushed off at a trot to git the mule and cart. I was pretty sure of my b'ar and geese when I come back. The cart stood quiet enough. But the mule, having nothing to eat, was sharping her teeth upon a boulder, thinking she'd hev a bite or so before long.

"I hitched her up, brought her to my bee-tree, tumbled the b'ar into the cart, wrung the necks of all the geese that waur thar—many hed got away—and counted some twenty-seven hundred that I piled away atop of the b'ar."

"Twenty-seven hundred!" cried the "Big Lie" and all the hunters at a breath. "Twenty-seven hundred! Why, Yaou, whenever you telled of this thing before you always counted them at 3150!"

"Well, ef I did, I reckon I was right. I was sartinly right then, it being all fresh in my 'membrance; and I'm not the man to go back agin his own words. No, fellows, I sticks to first words and first principles. I scorns to eat my own words. Ef I said 3150, then 3150 it waur, never a goose less. But you'll see how to 'count for all. I reckon 'twas only 2700 I fotched to market. Thar was 200 I gin to Columbus Mills. Then thar was 200 more I carried to Merry Ann; and then thar waur 50 at least, I reckon, I kep for myself. Jest you count up, Jedge, and you'll see how to squar' it on all sides. When I said 2700 I only counted what I sold in the villages, every head of 'em at fifty cents a head; and a'ter putting the money in my pocket I felt all over that I hed the 'capital.'

"Well, Jedge, next about the b'ar. Sold the hide and tallow for a fine market-price; sold the meat, got ten cents a pound for it fresh—'twas most beautiful meat; biled down the bones for the marrow; melted down the grease; sold fourteen pounds of it to the barbers and apothecaries; got a dollar a pound for that; sold the hide for twenty dollars; and got the cash for every thing.

"Thar warn't a fambly in all Greenville and Spartanburg and Asheville that didn't git fresh, green wild-geese from me that season, at fifty cents a head, and glad to git, too; the cheapest fresh meat they could buy; and, I reckon, the finest. And all the people of them villages, ef they hed gone to heaven that week, in the flesh, would have carried nothing better than goose-flesh for the risurrection! Every body ate goose for a month, I reckon, as the weather was freezing cold all the

time, and the beasts kept week after week, ontil they waur eaten. From
the b'ar only I made a matter of full one hundred dollars. First, thar
waur the hide, $20; then 450 pounds of meat, at 10 cents, was $45;
then the grease, 14 pounds, $14; and the tallow, some $6 more; and
the biled marrow, $11.

"Well, count up, Jedge; 2700 wild-geese, at 50 cents, you sees, must
be more than $1350. I kin only say, that a'ter all the selling—and I
driv at it day and night, with Columbus Mills's mule and cart, and
went to every house in every street in all them villages. I hed a'most
fifteen hundred dollars, safe stowed away onder the pillows of my bed,
all in solid gould and silver.

"But I warn't done! Thar was my bee-tree. Don't you think I waur
gwine to lose that honey! no, my darlint! I didn't beat the drum about
nothing. I didn't let on to a soul what I was a-doing. They axed me
about the wild-geese, but I sent 'em on a wild-goose chase; and 'twa'n't
till I hed sold off all the b'ar meat and all the geese that I made ready to
git at that honey. I reckon them bees must ha' been making that honey
for a hundred years, and was then driv out by the b'ars.

"Columbus Mills will tell you; he axed me all about it; but, though
he was always my good friend, I never even telled it to him. But he lent
me his mule and cart, good fellow as he is, and never said nothing more;
and, quiet enough, without beat of drum, I bought up all the tight-
bound barrels that ever brought whisky to Spartanburg and Greenville,
whar they hes the taste for that article strong; and day by day I went off
carrying as many barrels as the cart could hold and the mule could draw.
I tapped the old tree—which was one of the oldest and biggest chestnut
oaks I ever did see—close to the bottom, and drawed off the beautiful
treacle. I was more than sixteen days about it, and got something over
two thousand gallons of the purest, sweetest, yellowest honey you ever
did see. I could hairdly git barrels and jimmyjohns enough to hold it;
and I sold it out at seventy cents a gallon, which was mighty cheap. So
I got from the honey a matter of fourteen hundred dollars.

"Now, Jedge, all this time, though it went very much agin the grain,
I kept away from Merry Ann and the old Squaire, her daddy. I sent
him two hundred head of geese—some fresh, say one hundred, and
another hundred that I hed cleaned and put in salt—and I sent him

three jimmyjohns of honey, five gallons each. But I kept away and said nothing, beat no drum, and hed never a thinking but how to git in the 'capital.' And I did git it in!

"When I carried the mule and cart home to Columbus Mills I axed him about a sartin farm of one hundred and sixty acres that he hed to sell. It hed a good house on it. He selled it to me cheap. I paid him down, and put the titles in my pocket. 'Thar's capital!' says I.

"*That* waur a fixed thing for ever and ever. And when I hed moved every thing from the old cabin to the new farm, Columbus let me hev a fine milch cow that gin eleven quarts a day, with a beautiful young caif. Jest about that time thar was a great sale of the furniter of the Ashmore family down at Spartanburg, and I remembered I hed no decent bedstead, or any thing rightly sarving for a young woman's chamber; so I went to the sale, and bought a fine strong mahogany bedstead, a dozen chairs, a chist of drawers, and some other things that ain't quite mentionable, Jedge, but all proper for a lady's chamber; and I soon hed the house fixed up ready for any thing. And up to this time I never let on to any body what I was a-thinking about or what I was a-doing, ontil I could stand up in my own doorway and look about me, and say to myself—this is my 'capital,' I reckon; and when I hed got all that I thought a needcessity to git, I took 'count of every thing.

"I spread the title-deeds of my fairm out on the table. I read 'em over three times to see ef 'twaur all right. Thar was my name several times in big letters, 'to hev and to hold.'

"Then I fixed the furniter. Then I brought out into the stable-yard the old mar'—you couldn't count her ribs *now,* and she was spry as ef she hed got a new conceit of herself.

"Then thar was my beautiful cow and caif, sealing fat, both on 'em, and sleek as a doe in autumn.

"Then thar waur a fine young mule that I bought in Spartanburg; my cart, and a strong second-hand buggy, that could carry two pussons convenient of two different sexes. And I felt big, like a man of consekence and capital.

"That warn't all.

"I had the shiners, Jedge, besides—all in gould and silver—none of your dirty rags and blotty spotty paper. That was the time of Old Hickory—General Jackson, you know—when he kicked over Nick Biddle's consarn, and gin us the beautiful Benton Mint Drops, in place of rotten paper. You could git the gould and silver jest for the axing, in them days, you know.

"I hed a grand count of my money, Jedge. I hed it in a dozen or twenty little bags of leather—the gould—and the silver I hed in shot-bags. It took me a whole morning to count it up and git the figgers right. Then I stuffed it in my pockets, hyar and thar, every whar, whar-ever I could stow a bag; and the silver I stuffed away in my saddle-bags, and clapped it on the mar'.

"Then I mounted myself, and sot the mar's nose straight in a bee-line for the fairm of Squaire Hopson.

"I was a-gwine, you see, to supprise him with my 'capital;' but, fust, I meant to give him a mighty grand skeer.

"You see, when I was a-trading with Columbus Mills about the fairm and cattle and other things, I ups and tells him about my courting of Merry Ann; and when I told him about Squaire Hopson's talk about 'capital,' he says:

" 'The old skunk! What right hes he to be talking big so, when he kain't pay his own debts. He's been owing me three hundred and fifty dollars now gwine on three years, and I kain't git even the *intrust* out of him. I've got a mortgage on his fairm for the whole, and ef he won't let you hev his da'ter, jest you come to me, and I'll clap the screws to him in short order.'

"Says I, 'Columbus, won't you sell me that mortgage?'

" 'You shill hev it for the face of the debt,' says he, 'not considerin' the intrust.'

" 'It's a bargain,' says I; and I paid him down the money, and he signed the mortgage over to me for a vallyable consideration.

"I hed that beautiful paper in my breast pocket, and felt strong to face the Squaire in his own house, knowing how I could turn him out of it! And I mustn't forget to tell you how I got myself a new rig of clothing, with a mighty fine over-coat, and a new fur cap; and as I looked in the glass I felt my consekence all over at every for'a'd step I tuk; and I felt my inches growing with every pace of the mar' on the high-road to Merry Ann and her beautiful daddy!"

X

"Well, Jedge, before I quite got to the Squaire's farm, who should come out to meet me in the road but Merry Ann, her own self! She hed spied me, I reckon, as I crossed the bald ridge a quarter of a mile away. I do reckon the dear gal hed been looking out for me every day the whole eleven days in the week, counting in all the Sundays. In the mountains, you know, Jedge, that the weeks sometimes run to twelve, and even fourteen days, specially when we're on a long camp-hunt!

"Well, Merry Ann cried and laughed together, she was so tarnation glad to see me agin. Says she:

" 'Oh, Sam! I'm so glad to see you! I was afeard you had clean gin me up. And thar's that fusty old bachelor Grimstead, he's a-coming here a'most every day; and daddy, he sw'ars that I shill marry him, and nobody else; and mammy, she's at me too, all the time, telling me how fine a fairm he's got, and what a nice carriage, and all that; and mammy says as how daddy'll be sure to beat me ef I don't hev him. But I kain't bear to look at him, the old griesly!'

" 'Cuss him!' says I. 'Cuss him, Merry Ann!'

"And she did, but onder her breath—the old cuss.

" 'Drot him!' says she; and she said louder, 'and drot me, too, Sam, ef I ever marries any body but you.'

"By this time I hed got down and gin her a long strong hug, and a'most twenty or a dozen kisses, and I says:

" 'You sha'n't marry nobody but me, Merry Ann; and we'll hev the marriage this very night, ef you says so!'

" 'Oh! psho, Sam! How you does talk!'

" 'Ef I don't marry you to-night, Merry Ann, I'm a holy mortar, and a sinner not to be saved by any salting, though you puts the petre with the salt. I'm come for that very thing. Don't you see my new clothes?'

" 'Well, you hev got a beautiful coat, Sam; all so blue, and with sich shiny buttons.'

" 'Look at my waistcoat, Merry Ann! What do you think of that?'

" 'Why, it's a most beautiful blue welvet!'

" 'That's the very article,' says I. 'And see the breeches, Merry Ann; and the boots!'

" 'Well,' says she, 'I'm fair astonished, Sam! Why whar, Sam, did you find all the money for these fine things?'

" 'A beautiful young woman, a'most as beautiful as you, Merry Ann, come to me the very night of that day when your daddy driv me off with a flea in my ear. She come to me to my bed at midnight—'

" 'Oh, Sam! *ain't* you ashamed!'

" ' 'Twas in a dream, Merry Ann; and she tells me something to incourage me to go for'a'd, and I went for'a'd, bright and airly next morning, and I picked up three sarvants that hev been working for me ever sence.'

" 'What sarvants?' says she.

" 'One was a goose, one was a b'ar, and t'other was a bee!'

" 'Now you're a-fooling me, Sam.'

" 'You'll see! Only you git yourself ready, for, by the eternal Hokies, I marries you this very night, and takes you home to *my* fairm bright and airly to-morrow morning.'

" 'I do think, Sam, you must be downright crazy.'

" 'You'll see and believe! Do you go home and git yourself fixed up for the wedding. Old Parson Stovall lives only two miles from your daddy, and I'll hev him hyar by sundown. You'll see!'

" 'But ef I waur to b'lieve you, Sam—'

" 'I've got on my wedding-clothes o' purpose, Merry Ann.'

" 'But *I* hain't got no clothes fit for a gal to be married in,' says she.

" 'I'll marry you this very night, Merry Ann,' says I, 'though you hedn't a stitch of clothing at all!'

" 'Git out, you sassy Sam,' says she, slapping my face. Then I kissed her in her very mouth, and a'ter that we walked on together, I leading the mar'.

"Says she, as we neared the house, 'Sam, let me go before, or stay hyar in the thick, and you go in by yourself. Daddy's in the hall, smoking his pipe and reading the newspapers.'

" 'We'll walk in together,' says I, quite consekential.

"Says she, 'I'm so afeard.'

" 'Don't you be afeard, Merry Ann,' says I; 'you'll see that all will come out jest as I tells you. We'll be hitched to-night, ef Parson Stovall, or any other parson, kin be got to tie us up!'

"Says she, suddenly, 'Sam, you're a-walking lame, I'm a-thinking. What's the matter? Hev you hurt yourself any way?'

"Says I, 'It's only owing to my not balancing my accounts even in my pockets. You see I feel so much like flying in the air with the idee of marrying you to-night that I filled my pockets with rocks, jest to keep me down.'

" 'I do think, Sam, you're a leetle cracked in the upper story.'

" 'Well,' says I, 'ef so, the crack has let in a blessed chaince of the beautifulest sunlight! You'll see! Cracked, indeed! Ha, ha, ha! Wait till I've done with your daddy! I'm gwine to square accounts with *him,* and, I reckon, when I'm done with him, you'll guess that the crack's in *his* skull, and not in mine.'

" 'What! you wouldn't knock my father, Sam!' says she, drawing off from me and looking skeary.

" 'Don't you be afeard; but it's very sartin, ef our heads don't come together, Merry Ann, you won't hev me for your husband to-night. And that's what I've swore upon. Hyar we air!'

"When we got to the yard I led in the mar', and Merry Ann she ran away from me and dodged round the house. I hitched the mar' to the post, took off the saddle-bags, which was mighty heavy, and walked into the house stiff enough I tell you, though the gould in my pockets pretty much weighed me down as I walked.

"Well, in I walked, and thar sat the old Squire smoking his pipe and reading the newspaper. He looked at me through his specs over the newspaper, and when he seed who 'twas his mouth put on that same conceited sort of grin and smile that he ginerally hed when he spoke to me.

" 'Well,' says he, gruffly enough, 'it's you, Sam Snaffles, it it?' Then he seems to diskiver my new clothes and boots, and he sings out, 'Heigh! you're tip-toe fine to-day! What fool of a shop-keeper in Spartanburg have you tuk in this time, Sam?'

"Says I, cool enough, 'I'll answer all them iligant questions a'ter a while, Squire; but would prefar to see to business fust.'

" 'Business!' says he; 'and what business kin you hev with me, I wants to know?'

" 'You shill know, Squaire, soon enough; and I only hopes it will be to your liking a'ter you l'arn it.'

"So I laid my saddle-bags down at my feet and tuk a chair quite at my ease; and I could see that he was all astare in wonderment at what he thought my sassiness. As I felt I had my hook in his gills, though he didn't know it yit, I felt in the humor to tickle him and play him as we does a trout.

"Says I, 'Squaire Hopson, you owes a sartin amount of money, say $350, with intrust on it for now three years, to Dr. Columbus Mills.'

"At this he squares round, looks me full in the face, and says:

" 'What the old Harry's that to you?'

"Says I, gwine on cool and straight, 'You gin him a mortgage on this fairm for security.'

" 'What's that to you?' says he.

" 'The mortgage is over-due by two years, Squaire,' says I.

" 'What the old Harry's all that to you, I say?' he fairly roared out.

" 'Well, nothing much, I reckon. The $350, with three years' intrust at seven per cent., making it now—I've calkelated it all without compounding—something over $425—well, Squaire, that's not much to *you*, I reckon, with your large capital. But it's something to me.'

" 'But I ask you again, Sir,' he says, 'what is all this to you?'

" 'Jist about what I tells you—say $425; and I've come hyar this morning, bright and airly, in hope you'll be able to square up and satisfy the mortgage. Hyar's the dockyment.'

"And I drawed the paper from my breast pocket.

" 'And you tell me that Dr. Mills sent you hyar,' says he, 'to collect this money?'

" 'No; I come myself on my own hook.'

" 'Well,' says he, 'you shill hev your answer at onst. Take that paper back to Dr. Mills and tell him that I'll take an airly opportunity to call and arrange the business with him. You hev your answer, Sir,' he says, quite grand, 'and the sooner you makes yourself scarce the better.'

" 'Much obleeged to you, Squaire, for your ceveelity,' says I; 'but I ain't quite satisfied with that answer. I've come for the money due on this paper, and must hev it, Squaire, or thar will be what the lawyers call *four closures* upon it!'

" 'Enough! Tell Dr. Mills I will answer his demand in person.'

" 'You needn't trouble yourself, Squaire; for ef you'll jest look at the back of that paper, and read the 'signmeant, you'll see that you've got to settle with Sam Snaffles, and not with Columbus Mills!'

"Then he snatches up the dockyment, turns it over, and reads the rigilar 'signmeant, writ in Columbus Mills's own handwrite.

"Then the Squaire looks at me with a great stare, and he says, to himself like:

" 'It's a *bonny fodder* 'signmeant.'

" 'Yes,' says I, 'it's *bonny fodder*—rigilar in law—and the titles all made out complete to me, Sam Snaffles; signed, sealed, and delivered, as the lawyers says it.'

" 'And how the old Harry come you by this paper?' says he.

"I was gitting riled, and I was detarmined, this time, to gin my hook a pretty sharp jerk in his gills; so I says:

" 'What the old Harry's that to *you*, Squaire? Thar's but one question 'twixt us two—air you ready to pay that money down on the hub, at onst, to me, Sam Snaffles?'

" 'No, Sir, I am not.'

" 'How long a time will you ax from me, by way of marciful indulgence?'

" 'It must be some time yit,' says he, quite sulky; and then he goes on agin:

" 'I'd like to know how you come by that 'signmeant, Mr. Snaffles.'

"Mr. Snaffles! Ah! ha!

" 'I don't see any neecessity,' says I, 'for answering any questions. Thar's the dockyment to speak for itself. You see that Columbus Mills 'signs to me for full *con*sideration. That means I paid him!'

" 'And why did you buy this mortgage?'

" 'You might as well ax me how I come by the money to buy any thing,' says I.

" 'Well, I do ax you,' says he.

" 'And I answers you,' says I, 'in the very words from your own mouth, What the old Harry's that to you?'

" 'This is hardly 'spectful, Mr. Snaffles,' says he.

"Says I, ' 'Spectful gits only what 'spectful gives! Ef any man but you, Squire, hed been so onrespectful in his talk to me as you hev been I'd ha' mashed his muzzle! But I don't wish to be onrespectful. All I axes is the civil answer. I wants to know when you kin pay this money?'

" 'I kain't say, Sir.'

" 'Well, you see, I thought as how you couldn't pay, spite of all your "capital," as you hedn't paid even the *intrust* on it for three years; and, to tell you the truth, I was in hopes you couldn't pay, as I hed a liking for this fairm always; and as I am jest about to git married, you see—'

" 'Who the old Harry air you gwine to marry?' says he.

" 'What the old Harry's that to you?' says I, giving him as good as he sent. But I went on:

" 'You may be sure it's one of the woman kind. I don't hanker a'ter a wife with a beard; and I expects—God willing, weather premitting, and the parson being sober—to be married this very night!'

" 'To-night!' says he, not knowing well what to say.

" 'Yes; you see I've got my wedding-breeches on. I'm to be married to-night, and I wants to take my wife to her own fairm as soon as I kin. Now, you see, Squire, I all along set my hairt on this fairm of yourn, and I determined, ef ever I could git the "capital," to git hold of it; and that was the idee I hed when I bought the 'signmeant of the mortgage from Columbus Mills. So, you see, ef you kain't pay a'ter three years, you never kin pay, I reckon; and ef I don't git my money this day, why—I kain't help it—the lawyers will hev to see to the *four closures* to-morrow!'

" 'Great God, Sir!' says he, rising out of his chair, and crossing the room up and down, 'do you coolly propose to turn me and my family headlong out of my house?'

" 'Well now,' says I, 'Squire, that's not edzactly the way to put it. As I reads this dockyment'—and I tuk up and put the mortgage in my pocket—'the house and fairm are *mine* by law. They onst was yourn; but it wants nothing now but the *four closures* to make 'em mine.'

" 'And would you force the sale of property worth $2000 and more for a miserable $400?'

" 'It must sell for what it'll bring, Squire; and I stands ready to buy it for my wife, you see, ef it costs me twice as much as the mortgage.'

" 'Your wife!' says he; 'who the old Harry is she? You once pertended to have an affection for my da'ter.'

" 'So I hed; but you hedn't the proper affection for your da'ter that I hed. You prefar'd money to her affections, and you driv me off to git "capital!" Well, I tuk your advice, and I've got the capital.'

" 'And whar the old Harry,' said he, 'did you git it?'

" 'Well, I made good tairms with the old devil for a hundred years, and he found me in the money.'

" 'It must hev been so,' said he. 'You waur not the man to git capital in any other way.'

"Then he goes on: 'But what becomes of your pertended affection for my da'ter?'

" ' 'Twa'n't pertended; but you throwed yourself betwixt us with all your force, and broke the gal's hairt, and broke mine, so far as you could; and as I couldn't live without company, I hed to look out for myself and find a wife as I could. I tell you, as I'm to be married to-night, and as I've swore a most etarnal oath to hev this fairm, you'll hev to raise the wind to-day, and square off with me, or the lawyers will be at you with the *four closures* to-morrow, bright and airly.'

" 'Dod dern you!' he cries out. 'Does you want to drive me mad!'

" 'By no manner of means,' says I, jest about as cool and quiet as a cowcumber.

"But he was at biling heat. He was all over in a stew and a fever. He filled his pipe and lighted it, and then smashed it over the chimbly. Then he crammed the newspaper in the fire, and crushed it into the blaze with his boot. Then he turned to me, suddent, and said:

" 'Yes, you pertended to love my da'ter, and now you are pushing her father to desperation. Now ef you ever did love Merry Ann, honestly, raally, truly, and *bonny fodder,* you couldn't help loving her yit. And yit, hyar you're gwine to marry another woman, that, prehaps, you don't affection at all.'

" 'It's quite a sensible view you takes of the subject,' says I; 'the only pity is that you didn't take the same squint at it long ago, when I axed you to let me hev Merry Ann. *Then* you didn't valley her affections or mine. You hed no thought of nothing but the "capital" then, and the affections might all go to Jericho, for what you keered! I'd ha' married Merry Ann, and she me, and we'd ha' got on for a spell in a log-cabin, for, though I was poor, I hed the genwine grit of a man, and would come to something, and we'd ha' got on; and yit, without any "capital" your own self, and kivered up with debt as with a winter over-coat, hyar, you waur positive that I shouldn't hev your da'ter, and you waur a-preparing to sell her hyar to an old sour-tempered bachelor, more than double her age. Dern the capital! A man's best capital for any woman, ef so be he *is* a man. Bekaise, ef he be a man, he'll work out cl'ar, though he may hev a long straining for it through the sieve. Dern the capital! You've as good as sold that gal child to old Grimstead, jest from your love of money!'

" 'But she won't hev him,' says he.

" 'The wiser gal child,' says I. 'Ef you only hed onderstood me and that poor child, I hed it in me to make the "capital"—dern the capital! —and now you've ruined her, and yourself, and me, and all; and dern my buttons but I must be married to-night, and jest as soon a'ter as the lawyers kin fix it I must hev this fairm for my wife. My hairt's set on it, and I've swore it a dozen o' times on the Holy Hokies!'

"The poor old Squire fairly sweated; but he couldn't say much. He'd come up to me and say:

" 'Ef you only did love Merry Ann!'

" 'Oh,' says I, 'what's the use of your talking that? Ef you only hed ha' loved your own da'ter!'

"Then the old chap begun to cry, and as I seed that I jest kicked over my saddle-bags lying at my feet, and the silver Mexicans rolled out—a bushel on 'em, I reckon—and, O Lawd! how the old fellow jumped, staring with all his eyes at me and the dollars!

" 'It's money!' says he.

" 'Yes,' says I, 'jest a few hundreds of thousands of *my* "capital." ' I didn't stop at the figgers, you see.

"Then he turns to me and says, 'Sam Snaffles, you're a most wonderful man. You're a mystery to me. Whar, in the name of God, hev you been?

and what hev you been doing? and whar did you git all this power of capital?'

"I jest laughed, and went to the door and called Merry Ann. She come mighty quick. I reckon she was watching and waiting.

"Says I, 'Merry Ann, that's money. Pick it up and put it back in the saddle-bags, ef you please.'

"Then says I, turning to the old man, 'Thar's that whole bushel of Mexicans, I reckon. Thar monstrous heavy. My old mar'—ax her about her ribs now!—she fairly squelched onder the weight of me and that money. And I'm pretty heavy loaded myself. I must lighten; with your leave, Squaire.'

"And I pulled out a leetle doeskin bag of gould half eagles from my right-hand pocket and poured them out upon the table; then I emptied my left-hand pocket, then the side pockets of the coat, then the skairt pockets, and jist spread the shiners out upon the table.

"Merry Ann was fairly frightened, and run out of the room; then the old woman she come in, and as the old Squaire seed her, he tuk her by the shoulder and said:

" 'Jest you look at that thar.'

"And when she looked and seed, the poor old hypercritical scamp sinner turned round to me and flung her airms round my neck, and said:

" 'I always said you waur the only right man for Merry Ann.'

"The old spooney!

"Well, when I hed let 'em look enough, and wonder enough, I jest turned Merry Ann and her mother out of the room.

"The old Squaire, he waur a-setting down agin in his airm-chair, not edzactly knowing what to say or what to do, but watching all my motions, jest as sharp as a cat watches a mouse when she is hafe hungry.

"Thar was all the Mexicans put back in the saddle-bags, but he hed seen 'em, and thar was all the leetle bags of gould spread upon the table; the gould—hafe and quarter eagles—jest lying out of the mouths of the leetle bags as ef wanting to creep back agin.

"And thar sot the old Squaire, looking at 'em all as greedy as a fish-hawk down upon a pairch in the river. And, betwixt a whine and a cry and a talk, he says:

" 'Ah, Sam Snaffles, ef you ever did love my leetle Merry Ann, you would never marry any other woman.'

"Then you ought to ha' seed me. I felt myself sixteen feet high, and jest as solid as a chestnut oak. I walked up to the old man, and I tuk him quiet by the collar of his coat, with my thumb and forefinger, and I said:

" 'Git up, Squire, for a bit.'

"And up he got.

"Then I marched him to the big glass agin the wall, and I said to him: 'Look, ef you please.'

"And he said, 'I'm looking.'

"And I said, 'What does you see?'

"He answered, 'I sees you and me.'

"I says, 'Look agin, and tell me what you *obzarves.'*

" 'Well,' says he, 'I obzarves.'

"And says I, 'What does your *obzarving* amount to? That's the how.'

"And says he, 'I sees a man alongside of me, as good-looking and handsome a young man as ever I seed in all my life.'

" 'Well,' says I, 'that's a correct obzarvation. But,' says I, 'what does you see of *your own self?'*

" 'Well, I kain't edzackly say.'

" 'Look good!' says I. 'Obzarve.'

"Says he, 'Don't ax me.'

" 'Now,' says I, 'that won't edzactly do. I tell you now, look good and ax yourself ef you're the sawt of looking man that hes any right to be a feyther-in-law to a fine, young, handsome-looking fellow like me, what's got the "capital?" ' "

"Then he laughed out at the humor of the sitivation; and he says, 'Well, Sam Snaffles, you've got me dead this time. You're a different man from what I thought you. But, Sam, you'll confess, I reckon, that ef I hedn't sent you off with a flea in your ear when I hed you up afore the looking-glass, you'd never ha' gone to work to git in the "capital." '

" 'I don't know *that*, Squire,' says I. 'Sarcumstances sarve to make a man take one road when he mout take another; but when you meets a man what has the hairt to love a woman strong as a lion, and to fight an inimy big as a buffalo, he's got the raal grit in him. You knowed I was young, and I was poor, and you knowed the business of a hunter is a mighty poor business ef the man ain't born to it. Well, I didn't do much at it jest bekaise my hairt was so full of Merry Ann; and you should ha' made a calkilation and allowed for *that*. But you poked your fun at me and riled me consumedly; but I was detarmined that you shouldn't break *my* hairt or the hairt of Merry Ann. Well, you hed your humors, and I've tried to take the change out of you. And now, ef you raaly thinks, a'ter that obzarvation in the glass, that you kin make a respectable feyther-in-law to sich a fine-looking fellow as me, what's got the "capital," jest say the word, and we'll call Merry Ann in to bind the bargain. And you must talk out quick, for the wedding's to take place this very night. I've swore it by the etarnal Hokies.'

" 'To-night!' says he.

" 'Look at the "capital" ' says I; and I pinted to the gould on the table and the silver in the saddle-bags.

" 'But, Lawd love you, Sam,' says he, 'it's so suddent, and we kain't make the preparations in time.'

"Says I, 'Look at the "capital," Squaire, and dern the preparations!'

" 'But,' says he, 'we hain't time to ax the company.'

" 'Dern the company!' says I; 'I don't b'lieve in company the very night a man gits married. His new wife's company enough for him ef he's sensible.'

" 'But, Sam,' says he, 'it's not possible to git up a supper by to-night.'

"Says I, 'Look you, Squaire, the very last thing a man wants on his wedding night is supper.'

"Then he said something about the old woman, his wife.

"Says I, 'Jest you call her in and show her the "capital." ' '

"So he called in the old woman, and then in come Merry Ann, and thar was great hemmings and hawings; and the old woman she said:

" 'I've only got the one da'ter, Sam, and we *must* hev a big wedding! We must spread ourselves. We've got a smart chaince of friends and ac-quaintances, you see, and 'twon't be decent onless we axes them, and they won't like it! We *must* make a big show for the honor and 'spectability of the family.'

"Says I, 'Look you, old lady! I've swore a most tremendous oath, by the Holy Hokies, that Merry Ann and me air to be married this very night, and I kain't break sich an oath as that! Merry Ann,' says I, 'you wouldn't hev me break sich a tremendous oath as that?'

"And, all in a trimble, she says, 'Never, Sam! No!'

" 'You hyar that, old lady!' says I. 'We marries to-night, by the Holy Hokies! and we'll hev no company but old Parson Stovall, to make the hitch; and Merry Ann and me go off by sunrise to-morrow morning—you hyar?—to my own fairm, whar thar's a great deal of furniter fixing for her to do. A'ter that you kin advertise the whole county to come in, ef you please, and eat all the supper you kin spread! Now hurry up,' says I, 'and git as ready as you kin, for I'm gwine to ride over to Parson Stovall's this minit. I'll be back to dinner in hafe an hour. Merry Ann, you gether up that gould and silver, and lock it up. It's *our* "capital!" As for you, Squire, thar's the mortgage on your fairm, which Merry Ann shill give you, to do as you please with it, as soon as the parson has done the hitch, and I kin call Merry Ann, Mrs. Snaffles—Madam Merry Ann Snaffles, and so forth, and aforesaid.'

"I laid down the law that time for all parties, and showed the old Squire sich a picter of himself, and me standing aside him, looking seven foot high, at the least, that I jest worked the business 'cording to my own pleasure. When neither the daddy nor the mammy hed any thing more to say, I jumped on my mar' and rode over to old Parson Stovall.

"Says I, 'Parson, thar's to be a hitch to-night, and you're to see a'ter the right knot. You knows what I means. I wants you over at Squire Hopson's. Me and Merry Ann, his da'ter, mean to hop the twig to-night, and you're to see that we hop squar', and that all's even, 'cording to the law, Moses, and the profits! I stand treat, Parson, and you won't be the worse for your riding. I pays in gould!'

"So he promised to come by dusk; and come he did. The old lady hed got some supper, and tried her best to do what she could at sich short notice. The venison ham was mighty fine, I reckon, for Parson Stovall played a great stick at it; and ef they hedn't cooked up four of my wild-geese, then the devil's an angel of light, and Sam Snaffles no better than a sinner! And thar was any quantity of jimmyjohns, peach and honey considered. Parson Stovall was a great feeder, and I begun to think he never would be done. But at last he wiped his mouth, swallowed his fifth cup of coffee, washed it down with a stiff dram of peach and honey, wiped his mouth agin, and pulled out his prayer-book, psalmody, and Holy Scrip—three volumes in all—and he hemmed three times, and begun to look out for the marriage text, but begun with giving out the 100th Psalm.

" 'With one consent, let's all unite—'

" 'No,' says I, 'Parson; not all. It's only Merry Ann and me what's to unite to-night!'

"Jest then, afore he could answer, who should pop in but old bachelor Grimstead! and he looked round 'bout him, specially upon me and the parson, as ef to say:

" 'What the old Harry's they doing hyar!'

"And I could see that the old Squire was oneasy. But the blessed old Parson Stovall, he gin 'em no time for ixplanation or palaver; but he gits up, stands up squar', looks solemn as a meat-axe, and he says:

" 'Let the parties which I'm to bind together in the holy bonds of wedlock stand up before me!'

"And, Lawd bless you, as he says the words, what should that old skunk of a bachelor do, but he gits up, stately as an old buck in spring time, and he marches over to my Merry Ann! But I was too much and too spry for him. I puts in betwixt 'em, and I takes the old bachelor by his coat-collar, 'twixt my thumb and forefinger, and afore he knows whar he is, I marches him up to the big looking-glass, and I says:

" 'Look!'

" 'Well,' says he, 'what?'

" 'Look good,' says I.

" 'I'm looking,' says he. 'But what do you mean, Sir?'

"Says I, 'Obzarve! Do you see yourself? Obzarve!'

" 'I reckon I do,' says he.

" 'Then,' says I, 'ax yourself the question, ef you're the sawt of looking man to marry my Merry Ann.'

"Then the old Squire burst out a-laughing. He couldn't help it.

" 'Capital!' says he.

" 'It's capital,' says I. 'But hyar we air, Parson. Put on the hitch, jest as quick as you kin clinch it; for thar's no telling how many slips thar may be 'twixt the cup and the lips when these hungry old bachelors air about.'

" 'Who gives away this young woman?' axes the parson; and the Squire stands up and does the thing needful. I hed the ring ready, and before the parson had quite got through, old Grimstead vamoosed.

"He waur a leetle slow in understanding that he warn't wanted, and warn't, nohow, any party to the business. But he and the Squire hed a mighty quarrel a'terwards, and ef 't hedn't been for me, he'd ha' licked the Squire. He was able to do it; but I jest cocked my cap at him one day, and, says I, in the Injin language:

" 'Yaou!' And he didn't know what I meant; but I looked toma- hawks at him, so he gin ground; and he's getting old so fast that you kin see him growing downwards all the time.

"All that, Jedge, is jest thirteen years ago; and me and Merry Ann git on famously, and thar's no eend to the capital! Gould breeds like the cows, and it's only needful to squeeze the bags now and then to make Merry Ann happy as a tomtit. Thirteen years of married life, and look at me! You see for yourself, Jedge, that I'm not much the worse for wear, and I kin answer for Merry Ann, too, though, Jedge, we hev hed thirty-six children."

"What!" says I, "thirty-six children in thirteen years!"

The "Big Lie" roared aloud.

"Hurrah, Sharp! Go it! You're making it spread! That last shot will make the Jedge know that you're a right truthful sinner, of a Saturday night, and in the 'Lying Camp.' "

"To be sure! You see, Merry Ann keeps on. But you've only got to do the ciphering for yourself. Here, now, Jedge, look at it. Count for yourself. First we had *three* gal children, you see. Very well! Put down three. Then we had *six* boys, one every year for four years; and then, the fifth year, Merry Ann throwed deuce. Now put down the six boys a'ter the three gals, and ef that don't make thirty-six, thar's no snakes in all Flurriday!

"Now, men," says Sam, "let's liquor all round, and drink the health of Mrs. Merry Ann Snaffles and the thirty-six children, all alive and kicking; and glad to see you, Jedge, and the rest of the company. We're doing right well; but I hes, every now and then, to put my thumb and forefinger on the Squire's collar, and show him his face in the big glass, and call on him for an *obzarvation*—for he's mighty fond *of go- ing shar's* in my 'capital.' "

Mary Boykin Chesnut (1823–86)

Mary Boykin Chesnut provided an invaluable record of the death agonies of the Old South through her literate and understandably biased diary. Born on March 31, 1823, she represented the cream of Southern society. The daughter of Stephen Decatur Miller, who served South Carolina as governor, U.S. Senator, and U.S. Representative, in 1840 married James Chesnut, Jr., U.S. Senator from South Carolina, 1859–61, and brigadier general in the Confederate army. Mrs. Chesnut lived for many years at Mulberry plantation, near Camden, the home of her husband's parents, dying at Sarsfield, also near Camden, in 1886. Her diary, which she began about 1860 and continued through 1865, was not published until 1905. A more recent edition of *A Diary from Dixie,* edited by Ben Ames Williams, appeared in 1949.

From *A Diary from Dixie*

February 15th, 1861.—I came to Charleston on November 7th and then went to Florida to see my mother. On the train, just before we reached Fernandina, a woman called out: "That settles the hash!" Tanny touched me on the shoulder and said: "Lincoln's elected." "How do you know?" "The man over there has a telegram." Someone cried: "Now that the black radical Republicans have the power I suppose they will Brown* us all."

I have always kept a journal, with notes and dates and a line of poetry or prose, but from today forward I will write more. I now wish I had a chronicle of the two delightful and eventful years that have just passed. Those delights have fled, and one's breath is taken away to think what events have since crowded in.

It was while I was in Florida, on November 11th that (alas!) my husband resigned his seat in the Senate of the United States. I might not have been able to influence him, but I should have tried.

In Florida I spent two weeks amid hammocks and everglades, oppressed and miserable. One evening while we were at dinner, Stephen brought in some soldiers from an encampment near there, the Montgomery Blues. The poor fellows said they were "very soiled blues." They had been a month before Fort Pickens and not allowed to attack it. Colonel Chase, who commanded the Alabama troops there, they accused of too great affection for the Fort. He built it himself, and could not bear it should be proved not impregnable. Colonel Lomax telegraphed Governor Moore if he might not try "Chase or no Chase." The Governor of Alabama was inexorable. They said "we have been down there and worked like niggers, and as soon as the fun seems about to begin, we are replaced by regulars." Sadly discomfited they were. My mother packed a huge hamper of eatables for the Colonel, and the subalterns amiably played a game of billiards. I dare say they would fight, as they eat, like Trojans.

---

*John Brown's seizure of Harper's Ferry and his attempt to set up a slave republic had revived throughout the South the ever-present fear of a slave rebellion.

Mary Boykin Chesnut, *A Diary from Dixie,* ed. Ben Ames Williams (Boston: Houghton Mifflin Company, 1961), pp. 1–2, 10–11, 163–64, 527–28. Copyright 1905 by D. Appleton and Company. Copyright 1949 by Houghton Mifflin Company. Reprinted by permission of Houghton Mifflin Company.

Colonel Chase had blazed out a road behind them. The Montgomery Blues had gone there to take Fort Pickens, and here was a road ready for them to retreat if they were attacked! They resented the insulting insinuation which they scented in the "blazing" of that road. Indeed it was not needed, if they felt an inclination to run. Stephen took a servant there who had never seen anything larger than a double barrel shotgun. When they fired the evening gun, he dashed off for home and got there by daybreak next day, cured of all tendency toward soldiering forever.

I saw a few men running up a wan Palmetto flag, and shouting, though prematurely: "South Carolina has seceded!" I was overjoyed to find Florida so sympathetic, but Tanny told me the young men were Gadsdens, Porchers and Gourdins, names as inevitably South Carolinian as Moses and Lazarus are Jewish.

March 4th.—I have seen a Negro woman sold upon the block at auction. I was walking. The woman on the block overtopped the crowd. I felt faint, seasick. The creature looked so like my good little Nancy. She was a bright mulatto, with a pleasant face. She was magnificently gotten up in silks and satins. She seemed delighted with it all, sometimes ogling the bidders, sometimes looking quite coy and modest; but her mouth never relaxed from its expanded grin of excitement. I dare say the poor thing knew who would buy her. My very soul sickened. It was too dreadful. I tried to reason. "You know how women sell themselves and are sold in marriage, from queens downwards, eh? You know what the Bible says about slavery, and marriage. Poor women, poor slaves."

November 28th.—"Ye who listen with credulity to the whispers of fancy"—pause, and look on this picture and that.

On one side Mrs. Stowe, Greeley, Thoreau, Emerson, Sumner. They live in nice New England homes, clean, sweet-smelling, shut up in libraries, writing books which ease their hearts of their bitterness against us. What self-denial they do practice is to tell John Brown to come down here and cut our throats in Christ's name. Now consider what I have seen of my mother's life, my grandmother's, my mother-in-law's. These people were educated at Northern schools, they read the same books as their Northern contemporaries, the same daily papers, the same Bible. They have the same ideas of right and wrong, are high-bred, lovely, good, pious, doing their duty as they conceive it. They live in Negro villages. They do not preach and teach hate as a gospel, and the sacred duty of murder and insurrection; but they strive to ameliorate the condition of these Africans in every particular. They set them the example of a perfect life, a life of utter self-abnegation. Think of these holy New Englanders forced to have a Negro village walk through their houses whenever they see fit, dirty, slatternly, idle, ill-smelling by nature. These women I love have less chance to live their own lives in peace than if they were African missionaries. They have a swarm of blacks about them like children under their care, not as Mrs. Stowe's fancy painted them, and they hate slavery worse than Mrs. Stowe does. Book-making which leads you to a round of visits among crowned heads is an easier way to be a saint than martyrdom down here, doing unpleasant duty among the Negroes with no reward but the threat of John Brown hanging like a drawn sword over your head in this world, and threats of what is to come to you from blacker devils in the next.

The Mrs. Stowes have the plaudits of crowned heads; we take our chances, doing our duty as best we may among the woolly heads. My husband supported his plantation by his law practice. Now it is running him in debt. Our people have never earned their own bread. Take this estate, what does it do, actually? It all goes back in some shape to what are called slaves here, called operatives, or tenants, or peasantry elsewhere. I doubt if ten thousand in money ever comes to this old gentleman's hands. When Mrs. Chesnut married South, her husband was as wealthy as her brothers-in-law. How is it now? Their money has accumulated for their children. This old man's goes to support a horde of idle dirty Africans, while he is abused as a cruel slave owner. I say we are no better than our judges in the North, and no worse. We are human beings of the nineteenth century and slavery has to go, of course. All that has been gained by it goes to the North and to Negroes. The slave owners, when they are good men and women, are the martyrs. I hate slavery. I even hate the harsh authority I see parents think it their duty to exercise toward their children.

May 2nd, 1865.—I am writing from the roadside below Blackstock's, *en route* to Camden. Since we left Chester, solitude; nothing but tall, blackened chimneys to show that any man has ever trod this road before us. This is Sherman's track! It is hard not to curse him.

I wept incessantly at first. "The roses of the gardens are already hiding the ruins," said Mr. Chesnut, trying to say something. Then I made a vow. If we are a crushed people, I will never be a whimpering, pining slave.

We heard loud explosions of gunpowder in the direction of Chester. I suppose the destroyers are at it there. We met William Walker. Mr. Preston left him in charge of a carload of his valuables. Mr. Preston was hardly out of sight before poor helpless William had to stand by and see the car plundered. "My dear Missis, they have cleaned me out, nothing left," moaned William the faithful.

May 4th.—From Chester to Winnsboro, we did not see one living thing, man, woman or animal, except poor William trudging home after his sad disaster. The blooming of the gardens had a funereal effect. Nature is so luxuriant here; she soon covers the ravages of savages. The last frost occurred the seventh of March, so that accounts for the wonderful advance of vegetation. It seems providential to these starving people; so much that is edible has grown in two months.

At Winnsboro, to my amazement, the young people had a May Day amidst the smoking ruins. Irrepressible youth! The fidelity of the Negroes is the principal topic everywhere. There seems not a single case of a Negro who betrayed his master; and yet they showed a natural and exultant joy at being free. In the fields we saw them plowing and hoeing corn as always. The fields in that respect looked quite cheerful.

May 9th.—Anne Bailey said Godard had gone North. "Where he ought to have stayed," she added venomously. "For we are behaving down here like beaten curs." The cool Captain wants to go across the Mississippi with Hampton. "I do not think Hampton will go," said Dr. Boykin. "They could only fight as partisans, guerillas."

Mary Kirkland had an experience with Yankees. When they came, Monroe, their Negro man-servant, told her to stand up and keep her children in her arms. She stood against the wall with her baby in her arms, and the other two as closely pressed against her knees as they could get. Mammy Selina and Lizzie stood grimly on each side of their young missis and her children. For four mortal hours the soldiers surged through this room, and the Yankee soldiers reviled the Negro women for their foolishness in standing by their cruel slave owners and they taunted Mary with being glad of the protection of her poor ill-used slaves. Monroe had one leg bandaged, and pretended to be lame, so that he might not be enlisted as a soldier. He kept making pathetic appeals to Mary. "Don't answer 'em back, Miss Mary. Let them say what they want to. Don't give em any chance to say you are impudent to 'em."

Finally poor Aunt Betsey fainted from pure fright and exhaustion. Mary put down her baby and sprang to her mother, lying limp on a chair, and called to them: "Leave this room, you wretches! Do you mean to kill my mother!" Without a word, they all slunk out, ashamed.

Mrs. Bartow drove with me to our house at Mulberry. On one side of the house, every window was broken, every bell torn down, every piece of furniture destroyed, every door smashed in. The other side was intact. Maria Whitaker and her mother explained this odd state of things. "They were working like regular carpenters, destroying everything, when the General came in. He said it was a shame, and he stopped them; he said it was a sin to destroy a fine old house like this, whose owner was over ninety years old. He would not have done it for the world. It was wanton mischief."

Henry Timrod (1828–67)

Henry Timrod, the son of minor poet William Henry Timrod (1792–1838), was born in Charleston in 1828, attended Franklin College (now the University of Georgia) for two years, and took up the study of law for a while before attempting to earn his living by writing and teaching. Timrod's first poem appeared in a Charleston newspaper in 1846, and he later joined forces with his old friend and classmate, Paul Hamilton Hayne, in making *Russell's Magazine* (1857–60, edited by Hayne) the best literary journal in the South. In 1859 Timrod published the only volume of his lifetime, *Poems,* but after his death (in Columbia on October 6, 1867) Hayne collected his friend's best work in another volume, again simply entitled *Poems* (1873). Though primarily known as "the laureate of the Confederacy," Timrod would not have been pleased with the title, for he wanted to be remembered as a universal poet.

The Cotton Boll

While I recline
At ease beneath
This immemorial pine,
Small sphere!
(By dusky fingers brought this morning here
And shown with boastful smiles),
I turn thy cloven sheath,
Through which the soft white fibres peer,
That, with their gossamer bands,
Unite, like love, the sea-divided lands,
And slowly, thread by thread,
Draw forth the folded strands,
Than which the trembling line,
By whose frail help yon startled spider fled
Down the tall spear-grass from his swinging bed,
Is scarce more fine;
And as the tangled skein
Unravels in my hands,
Betwixt me and the noonday light,
A veil seems lifted, and for miles and miles
The landscape broadens on my sight,
As, in the little boll, there lurked a spell
Like that which, in the ocean shell,
With mystic sound,
Breaks down the narrow walls that hem us round,
And turns some city lane

Henry Timrod, "Lines: There Was a Fire Within My Brain," in *The Uncollected Poems of Henry Timrod,* ed. Guy Cardwell, Jr. (Athens: University of Georgia Press, 1942), pp. 83–84. Copyright © 1942 by The University of Georgia Press. Reprinted by permission of The University of Georgia Press. Henry Timrod, "Sonnet: I Know Not Why," "Sonnet: Most Men Know Love," "Ethnogenesis," "Spring," "Carolina," "The Unknown Dead," "Ode" in *The Collected Poems of Henry Timrod,* A Variorum Edition, ed. Edd Winfield Parks and Aileen Wells Parks (Athens: University of Georgia Press, 1965), pp. 79–80, 92–95, 100, 109–11, 122–24, 126–27, 129–30. Copyright © 1965 by The University of Georgia Press. Reprinted by permission of The University of Georgia Press.

Into the restless main,
With all his capes and isles!

Yonder bird,
Which floats, as if at rest,
In those blue tracts above the thunder, where
No vapors cloud the stainless air,
And never sound is heard,
Unless at such rare time
When, from the City of the Blest,
Rings down some golden chime,
Sees not from his high place
So vast a cirque of summer space
As widens round me in one mighty field,
Which, rimmed by seas and sands,
Doth hail its earliest daylight in the beams
Of gray Atlantic dawns;
And, broad as realms made up of many lands,
Is lost afar
Behind the crimson hills and purple lawns
Of sunset, among plains which roll their streams
Against the Evening Star!
And lo!
To the remotest point of sight,
Although I gaze upon no waste of snow,
The endless field is white;
And the whole landscape glows,
For many a shining league away,
With such accumulated light
As Polar lands would flash beneath a tropic day!
Nor lack there (for the vision grows,
And the small charm within my hands—
More potent even than the fabled one,
Which oped whatever golden mystery
Lay hid in fairy wood or magic vale,
The curious ointment of the Arabian tale—

Beyond all mortal sense
Doth stretch my sight's horizon, and I see,
Beneath its simple influence,
As if with Uriel's crown,
I stood in some great temple of the Sun,
And looked, as Uriel, down!)
Nor lack there pastures rich and fields all green
With all the common gifts of God,
For temperate airs and torrid sheen
Weave Edens of the sod;
Through lands which look one sea of billowy gold
Broad rivers wind their devious ways;
A hundred isles in their embraces fold
A hundred luminous bays;
And through yon purple haze
Vast mountains lift their plumed peaks cloud-crowned;
And, save where up their sides the ploughman creeps,
An unhewn forest girds them grandly round,
In whose dark shades a future navy sleeps!
Ye Stars, which, though unseen, yet with me gaze
Upon this loveliest fragment of the earth!
Thou Sun, that kindlest all thy gentlest rays
Above it, as to light a favorite hearth!
Ye Clouds, that in your temples in the West
See nothing brighter than its humblest flowers!
And you, ye Winds, that on the ocean's breast
Are kissed to coolness ere ye reach its bowers!
Bear witness with me in my song of praise,
And tell the world that, since the world began,
No fairer land hath fired a poet's lays,
Or given a home to man!

But these are charms already widely blown!
His be the meed whose pencil's trace
Hath touched our very swamps with grace,
And round whose tuneful way

All Southern laurels bloom;
The Poet of "The Woodlands," unto whom
Alike are known
The flute's low breathing and the trumpet's tone,
And the soft west wind's sighs;
But who shall utter all the debt,
O Land wherein all powers are met
That bind a people's heart,
The world doth owe thee at this day,
And which it never can repay,
Yet scarcely deigns to own!
Where sleeps the poet who shall fitly sing
The source wherefrom doth spring
That mighty commerce which, confined
To the mean channels of no selfish mart,
Goes out to every shore
Of this broad earth, and throngs the sea with ships
That bear no thunders; hushes hungry lips
In alien lands;
Joins with a delicate web remotest strands;
And gladdening rich and poor,
Doth gild Parisian domes,
Or feed the cottage-smoke of English homes,
And only bounds its blessings by mankind!
In offices like these, thy mission lies,
My Country! and it shall not end
As long as rain shall fall and Heaven bend
In blue above thee; though thy foes be hard
And cruel as their weapons, it shall guard
Thy hearth-stones as a bulwark; make thee great
In white and bloodless state;
And haply, as the years increase—
Still working through its humbler reach
With that large wisdom which the ages teach—
Revive the half-dead dream of universal peace!
As men who labor in that mine

Of Cornwall, hollowed out beneath the bed
Of ocean, when a storm rolls overhead,
Hear the dull booming of the world of brine
Above them, and a mighty muffled roar
Of winds and waters, yet toil calmly on,
And split the rock, and pile the massive ore,
Or carve a niche, or shape the archëd roof;
So I, as calmly, weave my woof
Of song, chanting the days to come,
Unsilenced, though the quiet summer air
Stirs with the bruit of battles, and each dawn
Wakes from its starry silence to the hum
Of many gathering armies. Still,
In that we sometimes hear,
Upon the Northern winds, the voice of woe
Not wholly drowned in triumph, though I know
The end must crown us, and a few brief years
Dry all our tears,
I may not sing too gladly. To Thy will
Resigned, O Lord! we cannot all forget
That there is much even Victory must regret.
And, therefore, not too long
From the great burthen of our country's wrong
Delay our just release!
And, if it may be, save
These sacred fields of peace
From stain of patriot or of hostile blood!
Oh, help us, Lord! to roll the crimson flood
Back on its course, and, while our banners wing
Northward, strike with us! till the Goth shall cling
To his own blasted altar-stones, and crave
Mercy; and we shall grant it, and dictate
The lenient future of his fate
There, where some rotting ships and crumbling quays
Shall one day mark the Port which ruled the Western seas.

La Belle Juive

Is it because your sable hair
Is folded over brows that wear
At times a too imperial air;

Or is it that the thoughts which rise
In those dark orbs do seek disguise
Beneath the lids of Eastern eyes;

That choose whatever pose or place
May chance to please, in you I trace
The noblest woman of your race?

The crowd is sauntering at its ease,
And humming like a hive of bees—
You take your seat and touch the keys:

I do not hear the giddy throng;
The sea avenges Israel's wrong,
And on the wind floats Miriam's song!

You join me with a stately grace;
Music to Poesy gives place;
Some grand emotion lights your face:

At once I stand by Mizpeh's walls:
With smiles the martyred daughter falls,
And desolate are Mizpeh's halls!

Intrusive babblers come between,
With calm, pale brow and lofty mien,
You thread the circle like a queen!

Then sweeps the royal Esther by;
The deep devotion in her eye
Is looking "If I die, I die!"

You stroll the garden's flowery walks;
The plants to me are grainless stalks,
And Ruth to old Naomi talks.

Adopted child of Judah's creed,
Like Judah's daughters, true at need,
I see you mid the alien seed.

I watch afar the gleaner sweet;
I wake like Boaz in the wheat,
And find you lying at my feet!

My feet! Oh! if the spell that lures
My heart through all these dreams endures,
How soon shall I be stretched at yours!

The Arctic Voyager

Shall I desist, twice baffled? Once by land,
And once by sea, I fought and strove with storms,
All shades of danger, tides, and weary calms;
Head-currents, cold and famine, savage beasts,
And men more savage; all the while my face
Looked northward toward the pole; if mortal strength
Could have sustained me, I had never turned
Till I had seen the star which never sets
Freeze in the Arctic zenith. That I failed
To solve the mysteries of the ice-bound world,
Was not because I faltered in the quest.
Witness those pathless forests which conceal
The bones of perished comrades, that long march,
Blood-tracked o'er flint and snow, and one dread night
By Athabasca, when a cherished life
Flowed to give life to others. This, and worse,
I suffered—let it pass—it has not tamed
My spirit nor the faith which was my strength.
Despite of waning years, despite the world
Which doubts, the few who dare, I purpose now—
A purpose long and thoughtfully resolved,
Through all its grounds of reasonable hope—
To seek beyond the ice which guards the Pole,
A sea of open water; for I hold,
Not without proofs, that such a sea exists,
And may be reached, though since this earth was made
No keel hath ploughed it, and to mortal ear
No wind hath told its secrets. . . . With this tide
I sail; if all be well, this very moon
Shall see my ship beyond the southern cape
Of Greenland, and far up the bay through which,
With diamond spire and gorgeous pinnacle,
The fleets of winter pass to warmer seas.
Whether, my hardy shipmates! we shall reach
Our bourne, and come with tales of wonder back,

Or whether we shall lose the precious time,
Locked in thick ice, or whether some strange fate
Shall end us all, I know not; but I know
A lofty hope, if earnestly pursued,
Is its own crown, and never in this life
Is labor wholly fruitless. In this faith
I shall not count the chances—sure that all
A prudent foresight asks we shall not want,
And all that bold and patient hearts can do
Ye will not leave undone. The rest is God's!

There Was a Fire Within My Brain!

There was a fire within my brain!
I did not mean to give thee pain.
I looked, I spoke—I know not what—
I loved, and felt—that thou did'st not;
And I was mad—perhaps was weak,
The consciousness is on my cheek
In blushes hot as molten lead,
And tears I blush as hot to shed.
God! that I could not hide my shame!
But needs must bare my heart of flame
To hearts so cold and minds so tame.
Aye think me weak, and smile with those
Who saw and jested with my woes.
Such still has been, such still must be
The doom, the meed of Misery,
When Misery permits the crowd
To guess the woe it strives to shroud.
That night indeed—it was not long—
I had no sense of right or wrong;
That night indeed—thank God 'tis past!
How could the reckless madness last
And I be breathing here!
Henceforth I shut within my breast
A ghastly and eternal guest—
Its deep and dark despair.
And thou and God alone shall know
The inextinguishable woe,
Intense, unmitigated pain
Which weighs on sense, and soul, and brain.
Oh, I will carry on my brow,
A smile like that thou wearest now,
As careless and as gay
As if this heart were brimmed with mirth—

And had no cares upon the earth
Which earth could not allay.
Yet if the smile I'll strive to wear,
Should sometimes wither to a sneer,
If what I look and what I say,
Have aught that's bitter in its play,
Forgive it and forget—
And think I speak not as I feel—
I would not pain, but must conceal
And cannot kill regret.
Aye think me weak, and yet—and yet—
What eyes have seen these eyelids wet,
Though I have wept as guilt might weep
When Hell reveals itself in sleep.

Sonnet: I Know Not Why

I know not why, but all this weary day,
Suggested by no definite grief or pain,
Sad fancies have been flitting through my brain:
Now it has been a vessel losing way
Rounding a stormy headland; now a gray
Dull waste of clouds above a wintry main;
And then a banner drooping in the rain,
And meadows beaten into bloody clay.
Strolling at random with its shadowy woe
At heart, I chanced to wander hither! Lo!
A league of desolate marsh-land, with its lush,
Hot grasses in a noisome, tide-left bed,
And faint, warm airs, that rustle in the hush
Like whispers round the body of the dead!

Sonnet: Most Men Know Love

Most men know love but as a part of life;
They hide it in some corner of the breast,
Even from themselves; and only when they rest
In the brief pauses of that daily strife,
Wherewith the world might else be not so rife,
They draw it forth (as one draws forth a toy
To soothe some ardent, kiss-exacting boy)
And hold it up to sister, child, or wife.
Ah me! why may not love and life be one?
Why walk we thus alone, when by our side,
Love, like a visible God, might be our guide?
How would the marts grow noble! and the street,
Worn like a dungeon-floor by weary feet,
Seem then a golden court-way of the Sun!

Ethnogenesis

WRITTEN DURING THE MEETING OF THE FIRST SOUTHERN CONGRESS,
AT MONTGOMERY, FEBRUARY, 1861

I

Hath not the morning dawned with added light?
And shall not evening call another star
Out of the infinite regions of the night,
To mark this day in Heaven? At last, we are
A nation among nations; and the world
Shall soon behold in many a distant port
      Another flag unfurled!
Now, come what may, whose favor need we court?
And, under God, whose thunder need we fear?
      Thank Him who placed us here
Beneath so kind a sky—the very sun
Takes part with us; and on our errands run
All breezes of the ocean; dew and rain
Do noiseless battle for us; and the Year,
And all the gentle daughters in her train,
March in our ranks, and in our service wield
      Long spears of golden grain!
A yellow blossom as her fairy shield,
June flings her azure banner to the wind,
    While in the order of their birth
Her sisters pass, and many an ample field
Grows white beneath their steps, till now, behold
      Its endless sheets unfold
THE SNOW OF SOUTHERN SUMMERS! Let the earth
Rejoice! beneath those fleeces soft and warm
      Our happy land shall sleep
      In a repose as deep
    As if we lay intrenched behind
Whole leagues of Russian ice and Arctic storm!

II

And what if, mad with wrongs themselves have wrought,
    In their own teachery caught,

By their own fears made bold,
And leagued with him of old,
Who long since in the limits of the North
Set up his evil throne, and warred with God—
What if, both mad and blinded in their rage,
Our foes should fling us down their mortal gage,
And with a hostile step profane our sod!
We shall not shrink, my brothers, but go forth
To meet them, marshaled by the Lord of Hosts,
And overshadowed by the mighty ghosts
Of Moultrie and of Eutaw—who shall foil
Auxiliars such as these? Nor these alone,
But every stock and stone
Shall help us; but the very soil,
And all the generous wealth it gives to toil,
And all for which we love our noble land,
Shall fight beside, and through us, sea and strand,
The heart of woman, and her hand,
Tree, fruit, and flower, and every influence,
Gentle, or grave, or grand;
The winds in our defence
Shall seem to blow; to us the hills shall lend
Their firmness and their calm;
And in our stiffened sinews we shall blend
The strength of pine and palm!

III

Nor would we shun the battle-ground,
Though weak as we are strong;
Call up the clashing elements around,
And test the right and wrong!
On one side, creeds that dare to teach
What Christ and Paul refrained to preach;
Codes built upon a broken pledge,
And Charity that whets a poniard's edge;
Fair schemes that leave the neighboring poor
To starve and shiver at the schemer's door,

While in the world's most liberal ranks enrolled,
He turns some vast philanthropy to gold;
Religion, taking every mortal form
But that a pure and Christian faith makes warm,
Where not to vile fanatic passion urged,
Or not in vague philosophies submerged,
Repulsive with all Pharisaic leaven,
And making laws to stay the laws of Heaven!
And on the other, scorn of sordid gain,
Unblemished honor, truth without a stain,
Faith, justice, reverence, charitable wealth,
And, for the poor and humble, laws which give,
Not the mean right to buy the right to live,
     But life, and home, and health!
To doubt the end were want of trust in God,
      Who, if he has decreed
   That we must pass a redder sea
Than that which rang to Miriam's holy glee,
     Will surely raise at need
     A Moses with his rod!

IV

But let our fears—if fears we have—be still,
And turn us to the future! Could we climb
Some mighty Alp, and view the coming time,
     The rapturous sight would fill
     Our eyes with happy tears!
Not for the glories which a hundred years
Shall bring us; not for lands from sea to sea,
And wealth, and power, and peace, though these shall be;
But for the distant peoples we shall bless,
And the hushed murmurs of a world's distress:
   For, to give labor to the poor,
     The whole sad planet o'er,
And save from want and crime the humblest door,
Is one among the many ends for which

     God makes us great and rich!
The hour perchance is not yet wholly ripe
When all shall own it, but the type
Whereby we shall be known in every land
Is that vast gulf which laves our Southern strand,
And through the cold, untempered ocean pours
Its genial streams, that far off Arctic shores
May sometimes catch upon the softened breeze
Strange tropic warmth and hints of summer seas!

Spring

Spring, with that nameless pathos in the air
Which dwells with all things fair,
Spring, with her golden suns and silver rain,
Is with us once again.

Out in the lonely woods the jasmine burns
Its fragrant lamps, and turns
Into a royal court with green festoons
The banks of dark lagoons.

In the deep heart of every forest tree
The blood is all aglee,
And there's a look about the leafless bowers
As if they dreamed of flowers.

Yet still on every side we trace the hand
Of Winter in the land,
Save where the maple reddens on the lawn,
Flushed by the season's dawn;

Or where, like those strange semblances we find
That age to childhood bind,
The elm puts on, as if in Nature's scorn,
The brown of Autumn corn.

As yet the turf is dark, although you know
That, not a span below,
A thousand germs are groping through the gloom,
And soon will burst their tomb.

Already, here and there, on frailest stems
Appear some azure gems,
Small as might deck, upon a gala day,
The forehead of a fay.

In gardens you may see, amid the dearth,
The crocus breaking earth;
And near the snowdrop's tender white and green,
The violet in its screen.

But many gleams and shadows need must pass
Along the budding grass,
And weeks go by, before the enamored South
Shall kiss the rose's mouth.

Still there's a sense of blossoms yet unborn
In the sweet airs of morn;
One almost looks to find the very street
Grow purple at his feet.

At times a fragrant breeze comes floating by,
And brings, you know not why,
A feeling as when eager crowds await
Before a palace gate

Some wondrous pageant; and you scarce would start,
If from a beech's heart
A blue-eyed Dryad, stepping forth, should say,
"Behold me! I am May!"

Ah! who would couple thoughts of war and crime
With such a blessed time!
Who in the west-wind's aromatic breath
Could hear the call of Death!

Yet not more surely shall the Spring awake
The voice of wood and brake
Than she shall rouse, for all her tranquil charms,
A million men to arms.

There shall be deeper hues upon her plains
Than all her sunlit rains,
And every gladdening influence around,
Can summon from the ground.

Oh! standing on this desecrated mould,
Methinks that I behold,
Lifting her bloody daisies up to God,
Spring kneeling on the sod,

And calling with the voice of all her rills
Upon the ancient hills,
To fall and crush the tyrants and the slaves
Who turn her meads to graves.

Carolina

I

The despot treads thy sacred sands,
Thy pines give shelter to his bands,
Thy sons stand by with idle hands,
           Carolina!
He breathes at ease thy airs of balm,
He scorns the lances of thy palm;
Oh! who shall break thy craven calm,
           Carolina!
Thy ancient fame is growing dim,
A spot is on thy garment's rim;
Give to the winds thy battle hymn,
           Carolina!

II

Call on thy children of the hill,
Wake swamp and river, coast and rill,
Rouse all thy strength and all thy skill,
           Carolina!
Cite wealth and science, trade and art,
Touch with thy fire the cautious mart,
And pour thee through the people's heart,
           Carolina!
Till even the coward spurns his fears,
And all thy fields and fens and meres,
Shall bristle like thy palm with spears,
           Carolina!

III

Hold up the glories of thy dead;
Say how thy elder children bled,
And point to Eutaw's battle-bed,
           Carolina!

Tell how the patriot's soul was tried,
And what his dauntless breast defied;
How Rutledge ruled and Laurens died,
                    Carolina!
Cry! till thy summons, heard at last,
Shall fall like Marion's bugle-blast
Re-echoed from the haunted Past,
                    Carolina!

IV

I hear a murmur as of waves
That grope their way through sunless caves,
Like bodies struggling in their graves,
                    Carolina!
And now it deepens; slow and grand
It swells, as, rolling to the land,
An ocean broke upon the strand,
                    Carolina!
Shout! let it reach the startled Huns!
And roar with all thy festal guns!
It is the answer of thy sons,
                    Carolina!

V

They will not wait to hear thee call;
From Sachem's Head to Sumter's wall
Resounds the voice of hut and hall,
                    Carolina!
No! thou hast not a stain, they say,
Or none save what the battle-day
Shall wash in seas of blood away,
                    Carolina!
Thy skirts indeed the foe may part,
Thy robe be pierced with sword and dart,
They shall not touch thy noble heart,
                    Carolina!

VI

Ere thou shalt own the tyrant's thrall
Ten times ten thousand men must fall;
Thy corpse may hearken to his call,
                    Carolina!
When by thy bier in mournful throngs
The women chant thy mortal wrongs,
'T will be their own funereal songs,
                    Carolina!
From thy dead breast by ruffians trod
No helpless child shall look to God;
All shall be safe beneath thy sod,
                    Carolina!

VII

Girt with such wills to do and bear,
Assured in right, and mailed in prayer,
Thou wilt not bow thee to despair,
                    Carolina!
Throw thy bold banner to the breeze!
Front with thy ranks the threatening seas
Like thine own proud armorial trees,
                    Carolina!
Fling down thy gauntlet to the Huns,
And roar the challenge from thy guns;
Then leave the future to thy sons,
                    Carolina!

The Unknown Dead

The rain is plashing on my sill,
But all the winds of Heaven are still;
And so it falls with that dull sound
Which thrills us in the church-yard ground,
When the first spadeful drops like lead
Upon the coffin of the dead.
Beyond my streaming window-pane,
I cannot see the neighboring vane,
Yet from its old familiar tower
The bell comes, muffled, through the shower.
What strange and unsuspected link
Of feeling touched, has made me think—
While with a vacant soul and eye
I watch that gray and stony sky—
Of nameless graves on battle-plains
Washed by a single winter's rains,
Where, some beneath Virginian hills,
And some by green Atlantic rills,
Some by the waters of the West,
A myriad unknown heroes rest.
Ah! not the chiefs who, dying, see
Their flags in front of victory,
Or, at their life-blood's noble cost
Pay for a battle nobly lost,
Claim from their monumental beds
The bitterest tears a nation sheds.
Beneath yon lonely mound—the spot
By all save some fond few forgot—
Lie the true martyrs of the fight,
Which strikes for freedom and for right.
Of them, their patriot zeal and pride,
The lofty faith that with them died,
No grateful page shall farther tell
Than that so many bravely fell;
And we can only dimly guess

What worlds of all this world's distress,
What utter woe, despair, and dearth,
Their fate has brought to many a hearth.
Just such a sky as this should weep
Above them, always, where they sleep;
Yet, haply, at this very hour,
Their graves are like a lover's bower;
And Nature's self, with eyes unwet,
Oblivious of the crimson debt
To which she owes her April grace,
Laughs gaily o'er their burial place.

Ode

SUNG ON THE OCCASION OF DECORATING THE
GRAVES OF THE CONFEDERATE DEAD, AT
MAGNOLIA CEMETERY, CHARLESTON, S.C., 1866

Sleep sweetly in your humble graves,
  Sleep, martyrs of a fallen cause!—
Though yet no marble column craves
  The pilgrim here to pause.

In seeds of laurels in the earth,
  The garlands of your fame are sown;
And, somewhere, waiting for its birth,
  The shaft is in the stone.

Meanwhile, your sisters for the years
  Which hold in trust your storied tombs,
Bring all they now can give you—tears,
  And these memorial blooms.

Small tributes, but your shades will smile
  As proudly on these wreaths to-day,
As when some cannon-moulded pile
  Shall overlook this Bay.

Stoop, angels, hither from the skies!
  There is no holier spot of ground,
Than where defeated valor lies
  By mourning beauty crowned.

Paul Hamilton Hayne (1830–86)

Paul Hamilton Hayne, son of an officer in the United States Navy and nephew of the orator Robert Y. Hayne, was born in Charleston on January 1, 1830. As a youth he attended private school in Charleston. Henry Timrod sat next to him, and a lifelong friendship began. Graduating in 1850 from the College of Charleston, he studied law with Timrod, then threw himself into a literary career, his "doom." As editor of *Russell's Magazine* (1857–60), modeled upon *Blackwood's,* Hayne worked earnestly to establish a Southern rival to the *Atlantic Monthly.* His publications include *Poems* (1855), *Sonnets and Other Poems* (1857), *Avolio* (1860), *Legends and Lyrics* (1872), and *Collected Poems* (1882). He also edited Timrod's poems (1873) and wrote a life of *Hugh Swinton Legaré* (1878). After Simms' death, Hayne "inherited his position as chief literary representative of the South" (Jay B. Hubbell, *The South in American Literature, 1607–1900,* p. 743). Hayne died at Copse Hill, Grovetown, Georgia, on July 6, 1886.

Vicksburg—A Ballad

For sixty days and upwards,
    A storm of shell and shot
Rained round us in a flaming shower,
    But still we faltered not.
"If the noble city perish,"
    Our grand young leader said,
"Let the only walls the foe shall scale
    "Be ramparts of the dead!"

For sixty days and upwards,
    The eye of heaven waxed dim;
And e'en throughout God's holy morn,
    O'er Christian prayer and hymn,
Arose a hissing tumult,
    As if the fiends in air
Strove to engulf the voice of faith
    In the shrieks of their despair.

There was wailing in the houses,
    There was trembling on the marts,
While the tempest raged and thundered,
    'Mid the silent thrill of hearts;
But the Lord, our shield, was with us,
    And ere a month had sped,
Our very women walked the streets
    With scarce one throb of dread.

And the little children gambolled,
    Their faces purely raised,
Just for a wondering moment,
    As the huge bombs whirled and blazed,
Then turned with silvery laughter
    To the sports which children love,
Thrice-mailed in the sweet, instinctive thought
    That the good God watched above.

Yet the hailing bolts fell faster,
    From scores of flame-clad ships,

Yet the hailing bolts fell faster,
    From scores of flame-clad ships,
And about us, denser, darker,
    Grew the conflict's wild eclipse,
Till a solid cloud closed o'er us,
    Like a type of doom and ire,
Whence shot a thousand quivering tongues
    Of forked and vengeful fire.

But the unseen hands of angels
    Those death-shafts warned aside,
And the dove of heavenly mercy
    Rules o'er the battle tide;
In the houses ceased the wailing,
    And though the war-scarred marts
The people strode, with step of hope,
    To the music in their hearts.

Under the Pine

TO THE MEMORY OF HENRY TIMROD

The same majestic pine is lifted high
  Against the twilight sky,
The same low, melancholy music grieves
  Amid the topmost leaves,
As when I watched, and mused, and dreamed with him,
  Beneath these shadows dim.

O Tree! hast thou no memory at thy core
  Of one who comes no more?
No yearning memory of those scenes that were
  So richly calm and fair,
When the last rays of sunset, shimmering down,
  Flashed like a royal crown?

And he, with hand outstretched and eyes ablaze,
  Looked forth with burning gaze,
And seemed to drink the sunset like strong wine,
  Or, hushed in trance divine,
Hailed the first shy and timorous glance from far
  Of evening's virgin star?

O Tree! against thy mighty trunk he laid
  His weary head; thy shade
Stole o'er him like the first cool spell of sleep:
  It brought a peace *so* deep
The unquiet passion died from out his eyes,
  As lightning from stilled skies.

And in that calm he loved to rest, and hear
  The soft wind-angels, clear
And sweet, among the uppermost branches sighing:
  Voices he heard replying
(Or so he dreamed) far up the mystic height,
  And pinions rustling light.

O Tree! have not his poet-touch, his dreams
  So full of heavenly gleams,

Wrought through the folded dullness of thy bark,
　　And all thy nature dark
Stirred to slow throbbings, and the fluttering fire
　　Of faint, unknown desire?

At least to me there sweeps no rugged ring
　　That girds the forest-king
No immemorial stain, or awful rent
　　(The mark of tempest spent),
No delicate leaf, no lithe bough, vine-o'ergrown,
　　No distant, flickering cone,

But speaks of him, and seems to bring once more
　　The joy, the love of yore;
But most when breathed from out the sunset-land
　　The sunset airs are bland,
That blow between the twilight and the night,
　　Ere yet the stars are bright;

For then that quiet eve comes back to me,
　　When, deeply, thrillingly,
He spake of lofty hopes which vanquish Death;
　　And on his mortal breath
A language of immortal meanings hung,
　　That fired his heart and tongue.

For then unearthly breezes stir and sigh,
　　Murmuring, "Look up! 'tis I:
Thy friend is near thee! Ah, thou canst not see!"
　　And through the sacred tree
Passes what seems a wild and sentient thrill—
　　Passes, and all is still!—

Still as the grave which holds his tranquil form,
　　Hushed after many a storm,—
Still as the calm that crowns his marble brow,
　　No pain can wrinkle now,—
Still as the peace—pathetic peace of God—
　　That wraps the holy sod,

Where every flower from our dead minstrel's dust
  Should bloom, a type of trust,—
That faith which waxed to wings of heavenward might
  To bear his soul from night,—
That faith, dear Christ! whereby we pray to meet
  His spirit at God's feet!

The Spirea

Of all the subtle fires of earth
   Which rise in form of spring-time flowers,
Oh, say if aught of purer birth
   Is nursed by suns and showers

Than this fair plant, whose stems are bowed
   In such lithe curves of maiden grace,
Veiled in white blossoms like a cloud
   Of daintiest bridal lace?

So rare, so soft, its blossoms seem
   Half woven of moonshine's misty bars,
And tremulous as the tender gleam
   Of the far Southland stars.

Perchance—who knows?—some virgin bright,
   Some loveliest of the Dryad race,
Pours through these flowers the kindling light
   Of her Arcadian face.

Nor would I marvel overmuch
   If from yon pines a wood-god came,
And with a bridegroom's lips should touch
   Her conscious heart to flame;

While she, revealed at that strange tryst,
   In all her mystic beauty glows,
Lifting the cheek her Love had kissed,
   Paled like a bridal rose.

My Mother-Land

"Animis Opibusque Parati."

My Mother-land! thou wert the first to fling
Thy virgin flag of freedom to the breeze,
The first to front along thy neighboring seas,
The imperious foeman's power;
But long before that hour,
While yet, in false and vain imagining,
Thy sister nations would not own their foe,
And turned to jest thy warnings, though the low,
Portentous mutterings, that precede the throe
Of earthquakes, burdened all the ominous air;
While yet they paused in scorn,
Of fatal madness born,
Thou, oh, my mother! like a priestess bless'd
With wondrous vision of the things to come,
Thou couldst not calmly rest
Secure and dumb—
But from thy borders, with the sounds of drum
And trumpet rose the warrior-call,—
(A voice to thrill, to startle, to appall!) —
"Prepare! the time grows ripe to meet our doom!"

Thy careless sisters frowned, or mocking said:
"We see no threatening tempest overhead,
Only a few pale clouds, the west wind's breath
Will sweep away, or melt in watery death."
"Prepare! the time grows ripe to meet our doom!"
Alas! it was not till the thunder-boom
Of shell and cannon shocked the vernal day,
Which shone o'er Charleston Bay,
That startled, roused, the last scale fallen away
From blinded eyes, our South, erect and proud,
Fronted the issue, and, though lulled too long,
Felt her great spirit nerved, her patriot valor strong.

· · ·

Death! What of death?—
Can he who once drew honorable breath
  In liberty's pure sphere,
  Foster a sensual fear,
When death and slavery meet him face to face,
Saying: "Choose thou between us; here, the grace
Which follows patriot martyrdom, and there,
Black degradation, haunted by despair."

The very thought brings blushes to the cheek!
I hear all 'round about me murmurs run,
Hot murmurs, but soon merging into one
Soul-stirring utterance—hark! the people speak:

"Our course is righteous, and our aims are just!
  Behold, we seek
Not merely to preserve for noble wives
The virtuous pride of unpolluted lives,
To shield our daughters from the servile hand,
And leave our sons their heirloom of command,
  In generous perpetuity of trust;
Not only to defend those ancient laws,
Which Saxon sturdiness and Norman fire
Welded forevermore with freedom's cause,
And handed scathless down from sire to sire—
Nor yet our grand religion, and our Christ,
Unsoiled by secular hates, or sordid harms,
(Though these had sure sufficed
To urge the feeblest Sybarite to arms)—
But more than all, because embracing all,
Ensuring all, self-government, the boon
Our patriot statesmen strove to win and keep,
From prescient Pinckney and the wise Calhoun
  To him, that gallant knight,
The youngest champion in the Senate hall,
Who, led and guarded by a luminous fate,
His armor, Courage, and his war-horse, Right,

Dared through the lists of eloquence to sweep
Against the proud Bois Guilbert of debate!

"There's not a tone from out the teeming past,
Uplifted once in such a cause as ours,
Which does not smite our souls
In long reverberating thunder-rolls,
From the far mountain-steeps of ancient story,
Above the shouting, furious Persian mass,
Millions arrayed in pomp of Orient powers,
Rings the wild war-cry of Leonidas
Pent in his rugged fortress of the rock;
And o'er the murmurous seas,
Compact of hero-faith and patriot bliss
(For conquest crowns the Athenian's hope at last),
Come the clear accents of Miltiades,
Mingled with cheers that drown the battle-shock
Beside the wave-washed strand of Salamis.

"Where'er on earth the self-devoted heart
Hath been by worthy deeds exalted thus,
We look for proud exemplars; yet for us
    It is enough to know
Our fathers left us freemen; let us show
The will to hold our lofty heritage,
The patient strength to act our father's part.

    "Yea! though our children's blood
Rain 'round us in a crimson-swelling flood,
Why pause or falter?—that red tide shall bear
    The ark that holds our shrinèd liberty,
    Nearer, and yet more near
Some height of promise o'er the ensanguined sea.

    "At last, the conflict done,
The fadeless meed of final victory won,
Behold! emerging from the rifted dark
Athwart a shining summit high in heaven,

That delegated Ark!
No more to be by vengeful tempests driven,
But poised upon the sacred mount, whereat
The congregated nations gladly gaze,
Struck by the quiet splendor of the rays
That circle freedom's blood-bought Ararat!"

Thus spake the people's wisdom; unto me
Its voice hath come, a passionate augury!
Methinks the very aspect of the world
Changed to the mystic music of its hope.
For, lo! about the deepening heavenly cope
The stormy cloudland banners all are furled,
 And softly borne above
Are brooding pinions of invisible love,
 Distilling balm of rest and tender thought
 From fairy realms, by fairy witchery wrought:
O'er the hushed ocean steal ethereal gleams
 Divine as light that haunts an angel's dreams:
 And universal nature, wheresoever
My vision strays—o'er sky, and sea, and river—
 Sleeps, like a happy child,
 In slumber undefiled,
A premonition of sublimer days,
When war and warlike lays
At length shall cease,
Before a grand Apocalypse of Peace,
Vouchsafed in mercy to all human kind—
A prelude and a prophecy combined!

Fire-Pictures

O! the rolling, rushing fire!
  O! the fire!
 How it rages, wilder, higher,
 Like a hot heart's fierce desire,
 Thrilled with passion that appalls us,
 Half appalls, and yet enthralls us,
  O! the madly mounting fire!

Up it sweepeth,—wave and quiver,—
Roaring like an angry river,—
  O! the fire!
Which an earthquake backward turneth,
Backward o'er its riven courses,
Backward to its mountain sources,
While the blood-red sunset burneth,
Like a God's face grand with ire,
  O! the bursting, billowy fire!

Now the sombre smoke-clouds thicken
To a dim Plutonian night;—
  O! the fire!
How its flickering glories sicken,
Sicken at the blight!
Pales the flame, and spreads the vapor,
Flares the waning, struggling light:
O! thou wan, faint-hearted fire,
  Sadly darkling,
  Weakly sparkling,
Rise! assert thy might!
  Aspire! aspire!

At the word, a vivid lightning,
Threatening, swaying, darting, brightening,
Where the loftiest yule-log towers,—
  Bursts once more,
Sudden bursts the awakened fire;

Hear it roar!
Roar, and mount high, high, and higher,
Till beneath,
Only here and there a wreath
Of the passing smoke-cloud lowers,—
Ha! the glad, victorious fire!

Oh! the fire!
How it changes,
Changes, ranges
Through all phases fancy-wrought,
Changes like a wizard thought;
See Vesuvian lavas rushing
'Twixt the rocks! the ground asunder
Shivers at the earthquake's thunder;
And the glare of Hell is flushing
Startled hill-top, quaking town;
Temples, statues, towers go down,
While beyond that lava flood,
Dark-red like blood,
I behold the children fleeting
Clasped by many a frenzied hand;
What a flight, and what a meeting,
On the ruined strand!

O! the fire!
Eddying higher, higher, higher
From the vast volcanic cones;
O! the agony, the groans
Of those thousands stifling there!
"Fancy," say you? but how near
Seem the anguish and the fear!
Swelling, turbulent, pitiless fire:
'Tis a mad northeastern breeze
Raving o'er the prairie seas;
How, like living things, the grasses
Tremble as the storm-breath passes,

Ere the flames' devouring magic
Coils about their golden splendor,
        And the tender
Glory of the mellowing fields
To the wild destroyer yields;
Dreadful waste for flowering blooms,
Desolate darkness, like the tomb's,
Over which there broods the while,
Instead of daylight's happy smile,
A pall malign and tragic!

        Marvellous fire!
        Changing, ranging
Through all phases fancy-wrought,
Changing like a charmèd thought;
A stir, a murmur deep,
Like airs that rustle over jungle-reeds,
Where the gaunt tiger breathes but half asleep;
        A bodeful stir,—
And then the victim of his own pure deeds,
        I mark the mighty fire
Clasps in its cruel palms a martyr-saint,
        Christ's faithful worshipper;
One mortal cry affronts the pitying day,
One ghastly arm uplifts itself to heaven—
When the swart smoke is riven,—
Ere the last sob of anguish dies away,
The worn limbs droop and faint,
And o'er those reverend hairs, silvery and hoary,
Settles the semblance of a crown of glory.

        Tireless fire!
        Changing, ranging
Through all phases fancy-wrought,
Changing like a Prótean thought;
Here's a glowing, warm interior,
A Dutch tavern, rich and rosy

With deep color,—sill and floor
Dazzling as the white seashore,
Where within his armchair cozy
Sits a toper, stout and yellow,
Blinking o'er his steamy bowl;
           Hugely drinking,
           Slyly winking,
As the pot-house Hebe passes,
With a clink and clang of glasses;
Ha! 'tis plain, the stout old fellow—
As his wont is—waxes mellow,
Nodding 'twixt each dreamy leer,
Swaying in his elbow chair,
Next to one,—a portly peasant,—
Pipe in hand, whose swelling cheek,
Jolly, rubicund, and sleek,
Puffs above the blazing coal;
While his heavy, half-shut, eyes
Watch the smoke-wreaths evanescent,
Eddying lightly as they rise,
Eddying lightly and aloof
Toward the great, black, oaken roof!

Dreaming still, from out the fire
Faces grinning and grotesque,
Flash an eery glance upon me;
Or, once more, methinks I sun me
On the breadths of happy plain
Sloping towards the southern main,
Where the inmost soul of shadow
           Wins a golden heat,
And the hill-side and the meadow
(Where the vines and clover meet,
Twining round the virgins' feet,
While the natural arabesque
Of the foliage grouped above them
Droops, as if the leaves did love them,

Over brow, and lips, and eyes)
Gleam with hints of Paradise!

Ah! the fire!
Gently glowing,
Fairly flowing,
Like a rivulet rippling deep
Through the meadow-lands of sleep,
Bordered where its music swells,
By the languid lotos-bells,
And the twilight asphodels;
Mingled with a richer boon
Of queen-lilies, each a moon,
Orbèd into white completeness;
O! the perfume! the rare sweetness
Of those grouped and fairy flowers,
Over which the love-lorn hours
Linger,—not alone for them,
Though the lotos swings its stem
With a lulling stir of leaves,—
Though the lady-lily waves,
And a silvery undertune
From some mystic wind-song grieves
Dainty sweet amid the bells
Of the twilight asphodels;
But because a charm more rare
Glorifies the mellow air,
In the gleam of lifted eyes,
In the tranquil ecstasies
Of two lovers, leaf-embowered,
Lingering there,
Each of whose fair lives hath flowered,
Like the lily-petals finely,
Like the asphodel divinely.

Titan arches!
Titan spires!
Pillars whose vast capitals

Tower toward Cyclopean halls,
And whose unknown bases pierce
Down the nether universe;
Countless coruscations glimmer,
Glow and darken, wane and shimmer,
'Twixt majestic standards, swooping,—
Like the wings of some strange bird
By mysterious currents stirred
Of great winds,—or darkly drooping,
In a hush sublime as death,
When the conflict's quivering breath
Sobs its gory life away,
At the close of fateful marches,
On an empire's natal day:
Countless coruscations glimmer,
Glow and darken, wane and shimmer,
Round the shafts, and round the walls,
Whence an ebon splendor falls
On the scar-seamed, angel bands,—
   (Desolate bands!)
Grasping in their ghostly hands
Weapons of an antique rage,
From some lost, celestial age,
When the serried throngs were hurled
Blasted to the under world:
Shattered spear-heads, broken brands,
And the mammoth, moonlike shields,
Blazoned on their lurid fields,
With uncouth, malignant forms,
   Glowering, wild,
Like the huge cloud-masses piled
Up a Heaven of storms!

     . . .

Ah, the faint and flickering fire!
   Ah, the fire!

Like a young man's transient ire,
Like an old man's last desire,
Lo! it falters, dies!
Still, through weary, half-closed lashes,
        Still I see,
    But brokenly, but mistily,
        Fall and rise,
        Rise and fall,
    Ghosts of shifting fantasy;
Now the embers, smouldered all,
Sink to ruin; sadder dreams
Follow on their vanished gleams;
Wailingly the spirits call,
Spirits on the night-winds solemn,
Wraiths of happy Hopes that left me;
(Cruel! why did ye depart?)
Hopes that sleep, their youthful riot
Mergèd in an awful quiet,
With the heavy grief-moulds pressed
On each pallid, pulseless breast,
In that graveyard called THE HEART,
        Stern and lone.
    Needing no memorial stone,
    And no blazoned column:
        Let them rest!
        Let them rest!
Yes, 't is useless to remember
May-morn in the mirk December;
Still, O Hopes! because ye were
Beautiful, and strong, and fair,
Nobly brave, and sweetly bright,
        Who shall dare
Scorn me, if through moistened lashes,
Musing by my hearthstone blighted,
Weary, desolate, benighted,—
I, because those sweet Hopes left me,

I, because my fate bereft me,
Mourn my dead,
Mourn,—and shed
Hot tears in the ashes?

Beyond the Potomac

They slept on the field which their valor had won,
But arose with the first early blush of the sun,
For they knew that a great deed remained to be done,
    When they passed o'er the river.

They arose with the sun, and caught life from his light,
Those giants of courage, those Anaks in fight,
And they laughed out aloud in the joy of their might,
    Marching swift for the river.

On, on! like the rushing of storms through the hills;
On, on! with a tramp that is firm as their wills;
And the one heart of thousands grows buoyant, and thrills,
    At the thought of the river.

Oh, the sheen of their swords! the fierce gleam of their eyes!
It seemed as on earth a new sunlight would rise,
And, king-like, flash up to the sun in the skies,
    O'er their path to the river.

But their banners, shot-scarred, and all darkened with gore,
On a strong wind of morning streamed wildly before,
Like wings of death-angels swept fast to the shore,
    The green shore of the river.

As they march, from the hillside, the hamlet, the stream,
Gaunt throngs whom the foemen had manacled, teem,
Like men just aroused from some terrible dream,
    To cross sternly the river.

They behold the broad banners, blood-darkened, yet fair,
And a moment dissolves the last spell of despair,
While a peal, as of victory, swells on the air,
    Rolling out to the river.

And that cry, with a thousand strange echoings, spread,
Till the ashes of heroes were thrilled in their bed,
And the deep voice of passion surged up from the dead,
    "Ay, press on to the river!"

On, on! like the rushing of storms through the hills,
On, on! with a tramp that is firm as their wills;
And the one heart of thousands grows buoyant and thrills,
    As they pause by the river.

Then the wan face of Maryland, haggard and worn,
At this sight lost the touch of its aspect forlorn,
And she turned on the foemen, full-statured in scorn,
    Pointing stern to the river.

And Potomac flowed calmly, scarce heaving her breast,
With her low-lying billows all bright in the west,
For a charm as from God lulled the waters to rest
    Of the fair rolling river.

Passed! passed! the glad thousands march safe through the tide;
Hark, foeman, and hear the deep knell of your pride,
Ringing weird-like and wild, pealing up from the side
    Of the calm-flowing river.

'Neath a blow swift and mighty the tyrant may fall;
Vain, vain! to his gods swells a desolate call;
Hath his grave not been hollowed, and woven his pall,
    Since they passed o'er the river?

The Voice in the Pines

The morn is softly beautiful and still,
　　Its light fair clouds in pencilled gold and gray
Pause motionless above the pine-grown hill,
Where the pines, tranced as by a wizard's will,
　　Uprise as mute and motionless as they!

Yea! mute and moveless; not one flickering spray
　　Flashed into sunlight, nor a gaunt bough stirred;
Yet, if wooed hence beneath those pines to stray,
We catch a faint, thin murmur far away,
　　A bodiless voice, by grosser ears unheard.

What voice is this? what low and solemn tone,
　　Which, though all wings of all the winds seem furled,
Nor even the zephyr's fairy flute is blown,
Makes thus forever its mysterious moan
　　From out the whispering pine-tops' shadowy world?

Ah! can it be the antique tales are true?
　　Doth some lone Dryad haunt the breezeless air,
Fronting yon bright immitigable blue,
And wildly breathing all her wild soul through
　　That strange unearthly music of despair?

Or can it be that ages since, stormtossed,
　　And driven far inland from the roaring lea,
Some baffled ocean-spirit, worn and lost,
Here, through dry summer's dearth and winter's frost,
　　Yearns for the sharp, sweet kisses of the sea?

Whate'er the spell, I hearken and am dumb,
　　Dream-touched, and musing in the tranquil morn;
All woodland sounds—the pheasant's gusty drum,
The mock-bird's fugue, the droning insect's hum—
　　Scarce heard for that strange, sorrowful voice forlorn!

Beneath the drowsèd sense, from deep to deep
   Of spiritual life its mournful minor flows,
Streamlike, with pensive tide, whose currents keep
Low murmuring 'twixt the bounds of grief and sleep,
   Yet locked for aye from sleep's divine repose.

The Arctic Visitation

Some air-born genius, with malignant mouth,
Breathed on the cold clouds of an Arctic zone—
Which o'er long wastes of shore and ocean blown
Swept threatening, vast, toward the amazèd South:

Over the land's fair form at first there stole
A vanward host of vapors, wild and white;
Then loomed the main cloud cohorts, massed in might,
Till earth lay corpse-like, reft of life and soul;

Death-wan she lay, 'neath heavens as cold and pale;
All nature drooped toward darkness and despair;
The dreary woodlands, and the ominous air
Were strangely haunted by a voice of wail.

The woeful sky slow passionless tears did weep,
Each shivering rain-drop frozen ere it fell;
The woodman's axe rang like a muffled knell;
Faintly the echoes answered, fraught with sleep.

The dawn seemed eve; noon, dawn eclipsed of grace;
The evening, night; and tender night became
A formless void, through which no starry flame
Touched the veiled splendor of her sorrowful face;

Like mourning nuns, sad-robed, funereal, bowed,
Day followed day; the birds their quavering notes
Piped here and there from feeble, querulous throats.
Fierce cold beneath—above, one riftless cloud

Wrapped the mute world—for now all winds had died—
And, locked in ice, the fettered forests gave
No sign of life; as silent as the grave
Gloomed the dim, desolate landscape far and wide.

Gazing on these, from out the mist one day
I saw, a shadow on the shadowy sky,
What seemed a phantom bird, that faltering nigh,
Perched by the roof-tree on a withered spray;

With drooping breast he stood, and drooping head;
This fateful time had wrought the minstrel wrong;
Even as I gazed, our southland lord of song
Dropped through the blasted branches, breathless, dead!

Yet chillier grew the gray, world-haunting shade,
Through which, methought, quick, tremulous wings were heard;
Was it the ghost of that heartbroken bird
Bound for a land where sunlight cannot fade?

To Algernon Charles Swinburne

Not since proud Marlowe poured his potent song
Through fadeless meadows to a marvelous main,
Has England hearkened to so sweet a strain—
So sweet as thine, and ah! so subtly strong!
Whether sad love it mourns, or wreaks on wrong
The rhythmic rage of measureless disdain,
Dallies with joy, or swells in fiery pain,
What ravished souls the entrancing notes prolong!
At thy charmed breath pale histories blush once more:
See! Rosamond's smile! drink love from Mary's eyes;
Quail at the foul Medici's midnight frown.
Or hark to black Bartholomew's anguished cries!
Blent with far horns of Calydon widely blown
O'er the grim death-growl of the ensanguined boar!

But crowned by hope, winged with august desire,
Thy muse soars loftiest, when her breath is drawn
In stainless liberty's ethereal dawn,
And "songs of sunrise" her warm lips suspire:
High in auroral radiance, high and higher,
She buoys thee up, till, earth's gross vapors gone,
Thy proud, flame-girdled spirit gazes on
The unveiled fount of freedom's crystal fire.
When thou hast drained deep draughts divinely nurst
'Mid lucid lustres, and hale haunts of morn,
On lightning thoughts thy choral thunders burst
Of rapturous song! Apollo's self, newborn,
Might thus have sung from his Olympian sphere;
All hearts are thrilled; all nations hushed to hear!

Midsummer in the South

I love Queen August's stately sway,
And all her fragrant south winds say,
With vague, mysterious meanings fraught,
Of unimaginable thought;
Those winds, 'mid change of gloom and gleam,
Seem wandering thro' a golden dream
The rare midsummer dream that lies
In humid depths of nature's eyes,
Weighing her languid forehead down
Beneath a fair but fiery crown:
Its witchery broods o'er earth and skies,
Fills with divine amenities
The bland, blue spaces of the air,
And smiles with looks of drowsy cheer
'Mid hollows of the brown-hued hills;
And oft, in tongues of tinkling rills,
A softer, homelier utterance finds
Than that which haunts the lingering winds!

I love midsummer's azure deep,
Whereon the huge white clouds, asleep,
Scarce move through lengths of trancéd hours;
Some, raised in forms of giant towers—
Dumb Babels, with ethereal stairs
Scaling the vast height—unawares
What mocking spirit, æther-born,
Hath built those transient spires in scorn,
And reared towards the topmost sky
Their unsubstantial fantasy!
Some stretched in tenuous arcs of light
Athwart the airy infinite,
Far glittering up yon fervid dome,
And lapped by cloudland's misty foam,
Whose wreaths of fine sun-smitten spray
Melt in a burning haze away:

Some throned in heaven's serenest smiles,
Pure-hued, and calm as fairy isles,
Girt by the tides of soundless seas—
The heavens' benign Hesperides.

I love midsummer uplands, free
To the bold raids of breeze and bee,
Where, nested warm in yellowing grass,
I hear the swift-winged partridge pass,
With whirr and boom of gusty flight,
Across the broad heath's treeless height:
Or, just where, elbow-poised, I lift
Above the wild flower's careless drift
My half closed eyes, I see and hear
The blithe field-sparrow twittering clear
Quick ditties to his tiny love;
While, from afar, the timid dove,
With faint, voluptuous murmur, wakes
The silence of the pastoral brakes.

I love midsummer sunsets, rolled
Down the rich west in waves of gold,
With blazing crests of billowy fire.
But when those crimson floods retire,
In noiseless ebb, slow-surging, grand,
By pensive twilight's flickering strand,
In gentler mood I love to mark
The slow gradations of the dark;
Till, lo! from Orient's mists withdrawn,
Hail! to the moon's resplendent dawn;
On dusky vale and haunted plain
Her effluence falls like balmy rain;
Gaunt gulfs of shadow own her might;
She bathes the rescued world in light,
So that, albeit my summer's day,
Erewhile did breathe its life away,
Methinks, whate'er its hours had won

Of beauty, born from shade and sun,
Hath not perchance so wholly died,
But o'er the moonlight's silvery tide
Comes back, sublimed and purified!

Shelley

Because they thought his doctrines were not just,
　Mankind assumed for him the chastening rod,
And Tyrants reared in pride, and strong in lust,
　Wounded the noblest of the sons of God;
The heart's most cherished benefactions riven,
　They strove to humble, blacken and malign,
A soul whose charities were wide as Heaven,
　Whose *deeds,* if not his *doctrines,* were divine;
And in the name of HIM, whose sunshine warms
　The evil as the righteous, deemed it good
To wreak their bigotry's relentless storms
　On one whose nature was not understood.
Ah! well! God's ways are wondrous,—it may be
　HIS seal hath not been set to man's decree.

Aspects of the Pines

Tall, sombre, grim, against the morning sky
    They rise, scarce touched by melancholy airs,
Which stir the fadeless foliage dreamfully,
    As if from realms of mystical despairs.

Tall, sombre, grim, they stand with dusky gleams
    Brightening to gold within the woodland's core,
Beneath the gracious noontide's tranquil beams—
    But the weird winds of morning sigh no more.

A stillness, strange, divine, ineffable,
    Broods round and o'er them in the wind's surcease,
And on each tinted copse and shimmering dell
    Rests the mute rapture of deep hearted peace.

Last, sunset comes—the solemn joy and might
    Borne from the West when cloudless day declines—
Low, flutelike breezes sweep the waves of light,
    And lifting dark green tresses of the pines,

Till every lock is luminous—gently float,
    Fraught with the hale odors up the heavens afar
To faint when twilight on her virginal throat
    Wears for a gem the tremulous vesper star.

The Mocking-Bird

[At night]

A golden pallor of voluptuous light
Filled the warm southern night:
The moon, clear orbed, above the sylvan scene
Moved like a stately queen,
So rife with conscious beauty all the while,
What could she do but smile
At her own perfect loveliness below,
Glassed in the tranquil flow
Of crystal fountains and unruffled streams?
Half lost in waking dreams,
As down the loneliest forest dell I strayed,
Lo! from a neighboring glade,
Flashed through the drifts of moonshine, swiftly came
A fairy shape of flame.
It rose in dazzling spirals overhead,
Whence to wild sweetness wed,
Poured marvellous melodies, silvery trill on trill;
The very leaves grew still
On the charmed trees to hearken; while for me,
Heart-trilled to ecstasy,
I followed—followed the bright shape that flew,
Still circling up the blue,
Till as a fountain that has reached its height,
Falls back in sprays of light
Slowly dissolved, so that enrapturing lay,
Divinely melts away
Through tremulous spaces to a music-mist,
Soon by the fitful breeze
    How gently kissed
Into remote and tender silences.

Face to Face

Sad mortal! couldst thou but know
  What truly it means to die,
The wings of thy soul would glow,
  And the hopes of thy heart beat high;
Thou wouldst turn from the Pyrrhonist schools,
  And laugh their jargon to scorn,
As the babble of midnight fools
  Ere the morning of Truth be born:
But I, earth's madness above,
  In a kingdom of stormless breath—
I gaze on the glory of love
  In the unveiled face of Death.

I tell thee his face is fair
  As the moon-bow's amber rings,
And the gleam in his unbound hair
  Like the flush of a thousand Springs;
His smile is the fathomless beam
  Of the star-shine's sacred light,
When the Summers of Southland dream
  In the lap of the holy Night:
For I, earth's blindness above,
  In a kingdom of halcyon breath–
I gaze on the marvel of love
  In the unveiled face of Death.

In his eyes a heaven there dwells—
  But they hold few mysteries now—
And his pity for earth's farewells
  Half furrows that shining brow;
Souls taken from Time's cold tide
  He folds to his fostering breast,
And the tears of their grief are dried
  Ere they enter the courts of rest:
And still, earth's madness above
  In a kingdom of stormless breath,

I gaze on a light that is love
　In the unveiled face of Death.

Through the splendor of stars impearled
　In the glow of their far-off grace,
He is soaring world by world,
　With the souls in his strong embrace;
Lone ethers, unstirred by a wind,
　At the passage of Death grow sweet,
With the fragrance that floats behind
　The flash of his wingèd retreat:
And I, earth's madness above,
　'Mid a kingdom of tranquil breath,
Have gazed on the lustre of love
　In the unveiled face of Death.

But beyond the stars and the sun
　I can follow him still on his way,
Till the pearl-white gates are won
　In the calm of the central day.
Far voices of fond acclaim
　Thrill down from the place of souls,
As Death, with a touch like flame,
　Uncloses the goal of goals;
And from heaven of heavens above
　God speaketh with bateless breath—
My angel of perfect love
　Is the angel men called Death!

Julia Peterkin (1880–1961)

Pulitzer Prize-winning novelist Julia Mood Peterkin was born in Laurens County, on October 31, 1880. She received both her B.A. and M.A. degrees from Converse College and in 1903 married William George Peterkin of Lang Syne Plantation, where she spent most of her life writing and becoming familiar with the language and folklore of the Gullah Negroes. Her novels include *Black April* (1927); *Scarlet Sister Mary* (1928), which won the Pulitzer Prize for 1929; and *Bright Skin* (1932). *Green Thursday* (1924) is a collection of her short stories, and *Roll, Jordan, Roll* (1933) consists of descriptive narrative accompanying photographs. After a period of long neglect, Mrs. Peterkin's works are arousing renewed interest. Since her death in 1961 serious scholarly and critical attention has focused on her for the first time.

The Red Rooster

The night was hot. The heavy fragrance of the blossoms in the china-berry tree near Killdee's cabin door thickened the air and made it more difficult to breathe.

The red rooster sleeping high up on one of its limbs stirred uneasily and crowed in a dull hoarse voice.

Killdee lying beside Rose inside moved restlessly. He tried to keep still. He didn't want to wake Rose. She went hard as she could at her work all day long. When night came, she was tired. Worn out. Glad to go to bed and rest. He must keep still and let her sleep.

She had not mended just right after Sis was born. Maum Hannah said it was the warm weather. Maybe so. But Rose stayed downhearted some-how. Dissatisfied. He felt she had lost faith in him.

To-night he went to meeting because Rose wanted him to go. She wanted him to get religion and join the Church. Rose thought if he'd be a member they might have better luck. Killdee pondered over it.

Being a member could not make old Mike, the mule, younger; or Mike's teeth sound, so he could chew corn and get fat. Mike was too old and slow to keep up with the grass, especially when dog days came and it rained every day God sent. Being a member could not stop that.

The air in the cabin was close. Killdee got up softly and took the bar down and opened the door wide. Baby Sis moved. Her ears were keen. She had never been as sound a sleeper as Jim.

Killdee stood perfectly still until she seemed quiet, then he stepped out and stood on the doorstep. He breathed deep and looked up at the stars. How thick and bright they were! A sign of rain to-morrow. More rain. Always rain. And the grass had already wound its strong roots around the tender cotton. He would ruin the stand trying to kill the grass out. Why couldn't the sun shine awhile?

A glittering sliver of light shining through the china-berry tree caught his eyes. He instinctively turned them away from it—then with a wry smile he turned them back again.

Julia Peterkin, "The Red Rooster" and "Son" in *Green Thursday* (New York: Alfred A. Knopf, 1924), pp. 103–14, 132–42. Copyright 1924 and renewed 1952 by Alfred A. Knopf, Inc. Reprinted by permission of William G. Peter-kin, Jr., and William G. Peterkin, III.

No use to look away now. He had seen it. He couldn't fool himself. No. He knew well enough what it was. The new moon. He had seen it *through trees*. More bad luck for a month. More bad luck. Of course. He had nothing else. Never. He'd cut that tree down and be rid of it. It was always screening the moon.

He moved to the side of the door where he could see the moon clear. There it was. Thin and white.

Something in his heart felt sick. Why did he always see the new moon through trees? To-night he had been out in the open field. Why didn't he see it then?

He didn't mind work. Nor doing without things for Missie and Rose and Jim and Sis. The question was, why couldn't he have a chance to work and make something? That was all he wanted.

Bad luck. Shucks! Everything bad that could happen had already happened. He turned inside and closed the door and put the bar in its place. He felt in the darkness for the foot of the bed, then laid himself down again beside Rose. He listened for her breathing. She was very still. Then a sudden jerk of her body made him know she was awake. Awake and sobbing.

"Rose," he said softly, "why you duh cry, Honey? Don' do dat. Wha's de matter? I tryin' fo' do de bes' I kin. I know you ain' de one fo' complain. I know dat. Not my Rose. Ain' we got de putties' lil boy an' lil gal een de worl'? Tell me dat. Howcome you cryin', Honey? Please don' do em. Jim's a-growin' so fas', an' Sis, too. An' Missie—Missie kin hoe same ez a grown 'oman. We haffer be t'anksful. T'anksful. Da's de way. You t'ink I can' mek a good crop o' cotton? Shucks!"

Rose did not answer and Killdee put his hand on her arm and patted it gently, then let it rest there. Soon it became heavier and heavier, then it slipped down limp on the straw mattress beside her.

Killdee had seemed so downhearted that Rose made him take Missie and go to the quarter to meeting. She thought if he'd listen to the people sing and pray and see his friends and hear a sermon he'd feel better.

She had stayed at home with the children.

When Jim was asleep she put the creaky little rocking-chair close to the door where she could see out across the field while she rocked baby Sis to sleep.

How bright the stars seemed in the sky! There right up over the china-tree was a new moon. She saw it clear. Good luck! Thank God for that! Killdee was at meeting. Maybe he'd decide to pray and seek.

But Killdee came home from meeting as low-spirited as he had gone. Nothing seemed to cheer him up. He did work hard. But things kept going wrong all the time. If Killdee would do like other men——

If Killdee would seek and get religion—that might help. But he wouldn't. Rain came and made the grass eat up his cotton, and no telling what else would happen unless he changed.

The red rooster out in the china-berry tree crowed huskily. It was hot. The blossoms thick on the tree out there were too heavy sweet. Their fragrance filled the cabin. They made breathing an effort. Rose couldn't sleep. Killdee lay so quiet, he must be asleep.

Rose sent out a prayer in the darkness; a prayer for her baby, that God, wherever He was, would take care of her little girl. Then she prayed for Jim. She prayed again for herself, that she'd get well—well as she was before Sis was born——Then she prayed for Killdee, that he would have longer patience—and be happier—and get saved from sin.

But her thoughts wandered. She was praying here in the darkness. Where was God that He could hear her?

A fear of things crept into her heart—a fear of the dark, of what she didn't know. Her fear made her get closer to Killdee and, gently lifting his heavy arm, she put it over her. She somehow felt protected by it, and soon fell into a heavy sleep.

When breakfast was ready the next morning, Killdee got up and ate hurriedly and went to the field with his mule and plow. Missie followed with a hoe. Rose stood in the door and watched them going to the field. Killdee looked tired, though the day's work had not begun. His lean shoulders were stooped, and he was only a young man.

The plow was rickety. Missie did the best she could, but she was little and the grass was tough and wiry.

But this was Monday morning. Rose didn't have time to be standing there thinking foolish, useless thoughts. No! She had work to do.

First, she sat down by the hearth and ate a bite of breakfast; then covered up what was left in the pot and put it closer to the coals to keep warm until Jim woke.

She hadn't slept well last night. The china-berry blossoms were too sweet, and the red rooster kept crowing all through the night. She had never heard him crow so loud before. He woke up baby Sis two or three times. Jim never waked for anything. No. He was a good sleeper. That was why he grew so fast.

She went to the bed where he lay alseep. In the early morning light her two chubby, little black children looked almost exactly alike. One was a very little larger than the other. Rose looked with pride at Jim's soft, round chin; his curved cheek. The full lips, slightly parted, showed teeth white as new milk. A sturdy little boy, but Rose shook her head as she looked, and her eyes filled with tears. Jim's little clothes were all ragged.

The red rooster gave a shrill crow right at the doorway. Baby Sis, asleep in the cradle beside Rose's own bed, woke and cried out sharply. Rose went quickly to her and took her up and held her close and murmured:

"Did de bad ol' rooster wake up my baby? E did! E skeery 'em. Go to sleep———"

She sat in the creaky rocking-chair and crooned to the child she fed at her breast.

The sun had risen bright and hot. A light breeze fluttered through the leaves of the china-berry tree outside and came in through the door, cooler than the fire-warmed air inside the cabin.

Rose rocked back and forth till Sis's little eyelids fell, then she kissed the fuzzy little head gently and, rising carefully, tipped over to the cradle and laid the baby down.

The red rooster crowed. Baby Sis's bright eyes opened wide. Rose leaned over and patted the soft little body and rocked the cradle till the heavy eyelids closed tight again. Then she went to the door and waved her apron fiercely at the red rooster.

"Git on off!" she whispered angrily at him. "Git on off! Sometime I wish you was dead! You won' let nobody sleep een de night wid you crowin'! Now you keep wakin' my baby up! Quit you doin's! I got work fo' do! I ain' got time fo' be runnin' you 'way fom de do'! Shoo!"

He ran away cackling with terror. Rose began getting up the clothes to wash. This was Monday morning. She piled them all together in the middle of the floor. Then she took up each garment, piece by piece. She must find where there were missing buttons or torn, worn places.

A small paper box sat on the mantelshelf, a box that had once held shells for Killdee's gun. Now it held her one needle and a ball of coarse thread. She drew the rocking-chair to the door where there was light, and with her big-eyed needle and coarse thread, she repaired the clothing carefully.

The big, black, iron wash-pot sat out in the yard not far from the woodpile. Killdee and Missie had filled it on Saturday. Rose built up a hot fire under it. She took the two wooden washtubs out from under the house and put them up on a bench by the cabin, in the shade of the china-berry tree. Then she brought out the clothes and separated the white ones from the colored ones. With a tin bucket she dipped hot water from the big, iron pot and poured it into the tubs. Soon she was bending her body up and down, up and down, over the wash-board, and white soap-suds foamed through her fingers.

She sang as she worked, a low, spiritual melody. She felt happier, somehow. Work was good, after all. It helps people to shed their troubles. As she washed each garment in one tub, she dropped it into the other tub to be washed again. They'd all be clean when she finished with them.

The red rooster hopped up in the doorway. Rose did not see him. He peeped around carefully to see if she heard him, but she was thinking just then she would have to be careful or the soap would not last through this washing. Jim and Killdee used so many clothes this rainy weather. So many more than she did, or Missie. They got them so dirty too. She didn't mind that, bless their hearts, if the soap would hold out. Rubbing clothes without soap made sorry washing.

The red rooster stepped cautiously inside the cabin. He was hungry and curious, and with Rose out of sight he was bold.

He looked at the pot on the hearth. The fire coals near it blinked red and hot. He was afraid to go closer to them.

He looked all around the room. A few white threads were scattered on the floor. He pecked at one. It hung on his beak, a tasteless, annoying thing. He shook it off with a croak of disgust.

Jim was a sound sleeper. He did not wake. But Baby Sis's ears were keen. Her eyes opened wide and caught sight of the red rooster's glossy, bright feathers and his scarlet comb. She cooed with delight.

The red rooster listened and walked timidly up to the cradle. He stretched his neck and looked over the side to see what was there. Tiny dimpled fists and small black feet jerked uncertainly, quickly, Two black eyes danced and sparkled.

The red rooster leaned a little closer. The child seemed harmless enough.

He was hungry. He had not had a single grain that morning. Not a crumb. Rose and Missie and Killdee had all forgotten to feed him.

The hens were scratching for worms, but it was very hot. They had to hold their wings out away from their bodies while they scratched. A tiresome thing.

Maybe these two bright shiny eyes would be good to eat. He would have to be quick to get them. They didn't keep still like blackberries. No, but maybe they tasted better.

His yellow beak was sharp and his long neck was strong, and he gave a swift peck.

Rose outside was washing and singing, but she heard the strangled gasp of terror, the silent held breath, then the shrill, heart-breaking scream.

She flew up the cabin steps, stumbling over the frightened red rooster. He squawked and cackled with terror and tried to fly past her out through the door.

It was easy to see what had happened. A bloody hole gaped, then it poured out red tears.

Rose's eyes dazzled. She picked up the child and held her close while stumbled blindly, wildly over the soft furrows to where Killdee worked to kill grass in the field. Killdee would know what to do. He'd know.

"Killdee—Killdee——" she moaned as she went, "mah po' lil baby ——Looka wha' de rooster done to em, Killdee——"

Killdee heard her and went running to meet her. Missie ran too. Killdee looked once at Sis's poor little blood-stained face and turned away with a breath that whistled sharp through his teeth. His mouth went hard. His lips taut.

Why couldn't he speak? What was the matter with him?

Rose put out a hand to touch him, then drew it back.

He was laughing—no—not laughing, either, but his face was working curiously——

Missie followed his eyes as they looked wistfully across the fields where heat waves danced merrily in the hot sunshine. What was Killdee thinking? Why was he so quiet?

"Yinner mus' be blame me—yinner won' say nuttin'," Rose sobbed. Killdee said slowly, hoarsely:

"No—I dunno nuttin' fo' say——"

Rose turned away crying. Killdee was blaming her. She had let the rooster get in. It was Monday. She had to wash. He knew that.

"Look lak you'd come kill de rooster—Killdee——Don' look lak you'd stan' up dere an' don' say nuttin'—an' don' do nuttin'——"

Killdee held out his arms.

"Gi' Sis to me, Rose. Lemme tote em home fo' you. Missie, you go walk behime Mike. He kin keep to de row an' plow tell I git back. You des hol' de plow up fo' em."

With the child in his arms, he walked toward the cabin. Rose followed him, sobbing and saying as she went:

"I can' wash no mo' to-day. No. Not at mah baby eye done pick out——You haffer kill da rooster, Killdee. I can' stan' fo' hab em roun' de do' no mo'—no—not at e pick mah baby eye out. I know all de time somet'ing been gwine happen. Nobody wouldn' lis'n at me when I talk—nobody wouldn' pray, but me."

Killdee did not answer, but he remembered how the new moon hid behind the china-berry tree last night. Bad luck had come. Yes.

When he killed the rooster, he'd cut the damned tree down too.

Son

All night long Son was restless. Under the bed where Killdee slept, he twisted and stretched his lean neck and thin paws,—and clawed and scratched and bit and snapped at the hungry fleas that lived on his rough, yellow hide.

Killdee woke and listened and pitied and studied and tried to go back to sleep again.

Fleas had to be. Dogs always had them. Son ought to know that and keep quiet. He kept himself from sleeping with all this uneasy, impatient fidgeting. Son ought to learn to rule himself. To hold steady.

As long as Son lived, fleas would stay on his hide and lay and hatch and bite and sting and breed more fleas to keep doing it.

Killdee reached down a hand to find and pat the poor, tormented beast. But the hand couldn't see and it stirred the darkness with long, sleepy fingers, until a moist nose touched it gratefully.

Then the fingers grasped the harsh, warm hair, they tenderly felt the sharp edges of narrow bones and rubbed a limp ear.

"Son," Killdee murmured, "don' fight dem fleas too hard. You claw's mighty sharp. Dey gwine tear a crack een you hide. Den mange'll git een. Mange is wusser'n fleas. Fleas is natchel. Fleas can' do nuttin' but mek you on-res'less. Mange'll mek you ugly an' mean."

Son patted his bony string of a tail on the floor. Killdee's interest made his breathing husky with joy. Even after Killdee's hand was withdrawn, Son gave faint whimpers of pleasure.

But soon he was restless again. He got up and went to the door and whined and scratched to be let out.

Killdee followed him and took down the bar and Son slipped by and went down the steps into the night.

First he stood still and listened. Then he trotted away down the weedy path. He knew where he wanted to go. Knew exactly.

Killdee looked out and listened, too. The dwindling old moon cast a gray light that made the frosty night chillier. There were very few sounds at all.

An owl whooed far away in the river swamp, but Son cared nothing for owls.

Something rustled and scurried in the fence corner, but Son's light, patting feet went steadily on—without slacking.

Cocks near by crowed and got answers faint and far away.

Little chickens hovering under a mother hen gave a few uneasy, troubled peeps and were hushed with a drawling cluck. That was all.

Son had listened at none of these. Something else had called him. He sniffed the air and then went straight to where he wanted to go. Son had keen ears. His nose was hard to fool.

Killdee smiled to himself and closed the door and put up the bar to hold it. He went back to bed and eased himself down beside Rose. But he kept smiling to think how shrewd Son was. How wise.

Son's faithful interest in love-making made him get up and break his night's rest and go far in the cold and dark. More than likely, he'd be late getting to the lady's house. He'd have to fight other dogs there for a chance to get the lady to even notice him. Fight dogs that were younger and bigger and stronger.

If the lady happened to choose him, he'd soon come away and leave her. He'd forget all about her. He would never even know his own children.

It was hard luck to be a dog when you had as much sense as Son. If Son were a man—a man——

Something Maum Hannah said long ago came into Killdee's mind and mocked him: "It's a wise man kin tell his own chillen."

An unpleasant saying. And yet—even a man had to take somebody else's word—about children.—Whose they really were.

Of course, Rose's children were his. But Mary's—since Bully left, children had come to Mary just the same.

How did any man know if they were his or not? Did Mary herself know for certain? She always laughed and said: "My chillen daddy ain' nobody een pa-ticular."

After all, maybe fathers don't matter much. Son knew that. He went about his business and did what he thought was his duty, and then he bothered himself no more about it. Maybe Son's way was good as any.

Killdee went to sleep and forgot about Son until the next day when dinner-time came. Even then he didn't remember until his pan of peas and rice was almost empty.

It was Son's custom to sit patiently by and watch Killdee eat and catch bits of food that his master tossed to him.

Where was Son to-day?

Killdee got up and whistled and called him. He wondered and whistled and called again before Son came creeping out from under the house where a dark corner hid his fresh wounds from meddlesome flies.

Poor Son. One limp ear was torn. His wishful eyes were bloodshot and battered. His thin legs tottered unsteadily. His coarse, yellow hair was reddened and wet. Above open cuts on his body, flies hummed and buzzed and frolicked.

Killdee knelt and took Son's head ruefully in his big hands. He stroked the sensitive nose and patted a cheek and whispered sorrowful words.

"Po' ol' Son. Po' ol' man. Dey got you all cripple up, enty? It hu't me clean to my heart fo' see you all bung up like dis.—Po' ol' Son. Better lef 'oman lone, Son. Better lef em lone, ef you kin."

Rose stood in the doorway watching. She didn't love Son, and Killdee was not deceived by her show of sympathy when she suggested kindly:

"You wan' me fo' git you a clot' so you kin tie em up, enty?"

No, he didn't want a cloth. Son's hurts were better left uncovered. Son's tongue could lick them and keep them clean. Son could cure them himself. No other medicine would do as much good as the medicine within Son's own mouth.

Men have to tie up their sores and grease them. Not dogs. Dogs have learned to cure themselves. Son knew how.

Killdee went to the haystack by the barn and got a bit of fine dried grass. He crawled away back under the house and fixed Son a bed in a dark warm corner.

Son followed and laid himself down with a sigh and wagged his tail weakly.

A lump came in Killdee's throat to see him so downhearted. Son couldn't help wanting to go courting last night. Something inside him compelled him. Drove him. Son wasn't to blame.

Son wasn't to blame that he wasn't strong enough to fight other dogs away, without getting himself beat almost to death.

Who was to blame? What? Why couldn't things be fair to dogs?— And to men—and women?

A face came before Killdee's eyes—black—eager—young—with

a bluish bloom on the cheeks—a pointed chin where a dimple came and went—dark red lips where white teeth gleamed with laughter—lips that quivered in such a pitiful way when things went wrong—little Missie—good little Missie.

She was so little—so tender—so trustful. Could he ruin her because she was what he loved best?

Love was a disease. It was wilting all the joy in her—in himself. It was a poison that would burn and shrivel—that would change her clean freshness to shame.

Son could go and love when he liked. Where he liked. If he came home bruised and torn, he could go off and hide and lick his bloody hurts and get well.—But a man—has to lie—and seem hard and mean——

If a man could only learn to cure his hurts too—that would be good. Maybe a man has to learn to do it. Maybe so.

Killdee crawled out from under the house with a gloomy, frowning face. Rose turned away when she saw him and he walked slowly down the path.

Gray clouds hung low and drops of cold rain were falling on the damp ground. Dull, reddish puddles of water shivered in the wind, as if they were hurt.

Killdee gave a bitter laugh.

"Me and Son ain' de onlies' one hab trouble. Mud-puddle hab 'em too! 'E can' be still. 'E haffer stan' pain. De wind trouble em. De sun-hot'll dry em up. Po' mud puddle! Do Jedus!"

What was the use to try? To want to do anything? Something got everything. Even mud-puddles!

. . .

Heavy clouds bunched over the wide river swamp. In the distance their rough, dark edges touched the tree-tops, and the hills on the other side were hidden. Down under the trees the rivers were swollen and muddy. They swirled and lapped and rushed along disregarding their rightful channels.

Killdee stood at the edge of the steep hill and looked down. The water was rising. Everything in the swamp would be flooded. Cattle and hogs left down there would be caught soon. Traps would be washed away unless they were fastened strong to trees.

Where was Son? He'd been gone since first daylight, and his hurts were hardly well.

Thinking about him made Killdee automatically give a long, shrill whistle. He missed Son when he went away like this. Son was getting along in years. Since rations were short, Son was weak.

He wouldn't stop scratching at the fleas. Mange had him. His eyes were dimmer than when he was young. Fighting ruined them. He wouldn't stay home at night and rest. He'd rather go running around and getting into trouble with other dogs. Son was foolish. He'd be better off asleep.

Killdee whistled again before he turned towards home. He had no hogs in the swamp to bother him to-day. Cholera got them all last year. He didn't have to go hunt in the swamp for them now. That was something. Those rivers down below were mean to-day. Good all his traps were chained to trees.

The solitude was disturbing. Killdee drew his rough shirt together at the neck and buttoned it across his throat. He peered into the colorless, blurred distance. There was something troubling about it. Bare tree-tops hid wicked streams that tore at things to destroy them.

Where was Son? Son knew that swamp too well to risk it now. Killdee wanted to shout and shake those dull clouds. To make those quiet tree-tops rustle. He drew in a full breath and forced it out with all the power of his lungs.

The clouds hung still. The tree-tops did not move. Only the heavy silence was stirred. A deep echo came back to meet his cry and two voices seemed to meet. Something within his breast moved with hope and courage. If Son was down there in trouble, he'd hear that call and take heart and fight his way back home.

Something more than an echo answered. What? A faint yelping. A weak whining. Could Son make a puny yapping like that? It was almost like a fox bark.

Killdee strained his ears to hear. Yes, it was a dog calling for help. Somebody's dog. Maybe it was Son!

Killdee whistled and called and encouraged, then listened again. The sound was nearer, but still uncertain—then a sharp outcry came. And silence.

Killdee plunged down the hill in the direction of the cry. Through tangled vines and low-growing bushes he went following the bank of the foamy, trashy river, but there was nothing to be seen of Son.

He climbed slowly back up the hill and went home to Rose and the children.

It was night when a scratching at the door made him get up and take down the bar. Biting, cold rain rushed in and hurried Son with it. Wet, shivering, dirty with mud and blood, Son limped toward the fire on three legs. Red drops spattered on the floor, for the fourth leg, a front one, was gone, nipped off close to his body.

"My Gawd, Son," Killdee whispered, "who dat done you so!"

Then he knew. A trap. Nothing but cold, hard steel could cut Son's bones and meat like that. Son had gone looking for food. For meat. The trap treated all alike. Possums. Coons. Dogs. Son's leg was too thin to stand the pinch of it. It came off. Poor Son! Down in the swamp hunting something to eat. To eat!

Son might be wrong to scratch fleas and get mange, and to go fighting dogs for a mate, but Son couldn't help being hungry. He wasn't to blame because he wanted a taste of meat.

Son's hide was no good to anybody, but the trap didn't care. It caught anything that came in reach of it. Anything.

"You gwine tie 'em up wid clot', or le' 'em stay so 'e kin lick 'em?" Rose asked.

Killdee did not answer. He took Son in his arms and held him close to the fire. The poor stub trembled and bled.

Light, flickering flames gave out little warmth. Their yellow fluttering mocked. With an impatient kick, Killdee shoved the logs further back into the chimney. A shower of sparks crackled and flared.

"Son—Son——" It was all Killdee could say. The pain in his breast hurt him through.

What was the use of anything? Something always gets you. Son never harmed anybody. Never! He did his duty the best he knew how.

Fleas wouldn't let him rest. They made him scratch. His own claws tore holes in his hide and let mange get in.

Son would have stayed around home at night too, but some bitch was always calling him to come breed his kind. Son had to go. Something inside him drove him. Son had sense. He knew he would meet other dogs there. But he couldn't help taking the risk of being beat.

Son needed meat. His appetite stung him. He was too old to catch rabbits. The bait in the traps was his best chance. Son thought so. Son didn't know traps were jealous of dogs the same as of possums or coons. Son was too suspectless.

Now his front leg was gone. Cut off. Some possum had gnawed it by now.

It wasn't good to trust anything. No. Not anything. There was no escape. Some day, Son, he too, would lie still with a mouth full of dirt. Yes, dirt.

Archibald Rutledge (1883–)

South Carolina's poet laureate, Archibald Rutledge, was born at McClellanville, on October 23, 1883, attending McClellanville High School and the Porter Academy in Charleston. He graduated from Union College in Schenectady, New York, in 1904 and taught English for thirty-three years at Mercersburg Academy in Pennsylvania, retiring in 1937 to devote his efforts to full-time writing and to the restoration of his plantation home. Rutledge was appointed the first poet laureate of the state upon the establishment of that office by the South Carolina legislature in 1934. A prolific writer, he has published more than seventy books and monographs. *Deep River, The Collected Poems of Archibald Rutledge* was published in 1960.

The Tomb

When you pass out of the peach and tobacco country of North Carolina and come to the moss-hung live-oaks, the towering yellow pines,
the supine Negroes, and the dreamy waters of the coastal country between Wilmington and Charleston, the strange spell of that lonely land
begins to take hold of you—if anything can. And when you drive slowly
over the great three-mile bridge spanning the mighty delta of the
Santee, a bridge over a shimmering wilderness of greenery starred with
aquatic wild flowers, you come to the locality where old Isaac McCoy
and Dandy Davis had their deadly and memorable encounter, which
ended more strangely than anyone, however inventive, could have
planned.

From the moment you quit the main artery of traffic to Florida,
with its ceaseless roar, its general odor of whisky, gasoline, and oil, its
trumpery of flaring signs, all is green, hushed, dewy in the hale fragrance of the wilderness. Bearing westward, you will be on a road that
winds between ranks of great yellow pines—a road bedded with pinestraw, that, for the most part, lies high and level but now and then dips
into the aromatic gloom of a watery glade. On either hand, as far as
eye can see, the forest withdraws in dim fabulous aisles; and beside the
pineland road, as in the long savannas that mistily retire from it, are
the vivid green of flytraps, the late daisies, stargrass, the snowy orchids,
wild asters, tawny goldenrod.

Soon you will come to the King's Highway. Turn southward on it.
This is the ancient road connecting Georgetown and Charleston. It is
the road that Washington travelled, and Lafayette, Lord Rawdon, Tarleton, and Marion. But the new concrete highway having been laid over
an entirely new route, traffic has almost ceased on the old. In a little
while, you will come to St. James, Santee, parish church, quaint and
beautiful, built in 1760, of English brick and native black cypress. It
would have been utterly out of place beside a modern highway; but
here in the old days it was where it belonged, in this far back country,

Archibald Rutledge, "The Tomb," *The Yale Review*, XXXVII (1947), pp.
129–37. From *The Yale Review*, copyright Yale University Press. Reprinted
by permission of *The Yale Review* and Archibald Rutledge.

and here it belongs now, here where Yesterday is not too much desecrated by the clangor of Today and by the onrush of Tomorrow.

The spell of beauty and of ancient peace is upon the place. Although
you may not know it, you are miles from any human habitation, save
only the little shack where old Isaac McCoy lives. That is a half-mile
down the road. About the church is an enclosed yard some two acres in
extent, forever being encroached upon by the fecund growths of the
wilderness.

Isaac worked among the tombs of the churchyard. Once or twice a
week this old Negro walked the half-mile from his staggering cabin
among the pines to the church—ostensibly to keep the yard clean; but
most of his time he spent musing on the old days, when regular services had been held there, and when he had been the sexton, or, as the
plantation Negroes said, "the section." His sole duty now in relation to
the deserted shrine was to keep its enclosure from looking too much
like the surrounding wilderness. Only once a year, on Palm Sunday, did
the far-scattered parishioners gather here for worship. For the rest of
the time, this wayside church, which was built before our nation came
into being, slept placidly in the lonely pinelands, now shimmering in
the sunlight, now dark with sweeping rains, now silvered in moonlight.
The church slept; and those in the churchyard slept: old rice-planters
of the Santee country; old indigo-growing French Huguenots; Revolutionary patriots; women who in their day had been the belles of the
parish; men who had been the hard riders, the duellists, the great lovers
of their time. All these slumbered now, in a little dust quiescent.

Any visitor to that church is sure to be attracted by one of the
moldering tombs: a huge affair it is, of English brick, shaped like a vast
hogshead, half buried on its side in the ground. A careful observer will
notice a hole in its side flush with the ground, an aperture large enough
to admit the body of a small man; and he may muse how, in the general mutability of things, even our tombs decay! He may further notice
how little wildwood shrubs and streamers of ivy grow out of the chinks
between the bricks, almost covering with a green mantle the sacred
place. And if he reads the lichened inscription on the marble slab that
covers the top of the grave, he will discover that within this vault lie
the mortal remains of one Raven McCloud, "who was drowned at

Murphy's Island, at the mouth of the South Santee River, in the great gale of 1822."

For reasons that he kept to himself, old Isaac would never let a visitor to the church go near the McCloud tomb. If asked his reason, he would merely shake his head and look inscrutably away through the forest. Nor could the visitor fail to feel about this old pinewoods Negro something as unfathomable as the stillness, the air of eternal spiritual autumn over the church and its dead.

Old Isaac alone knew that a Thing lived in the dark and haunted depths of the tomb of Raven McCloud—a Thing incredibly beautiful, graceful, terrible, and deadly.

One day, a visitor out of the busy world, struck by the dreaming quietude of the church, said, smiling, to its keeper, "I guess nothing ever happens here, does it?"

Isaac had been trained in a school that had taught him to agree with everything a white man ever said. It was the safe and easy way through life.

"No, sah," he answered, "nothin' doan ever happen here."

But Isaac did not smile as his guest drove away. He did not exactly know what this visitor from the mysterious outer world meant by things happening, but as far as he was concerned, life was strenuous, even hectic. For the moment, he had on him the problem of Dandy Davis, probably the worst Negro that the Santee country had ever known. Just what to do about Dandy and his wickedness kept Isaac's mind in a turmoil. He had, like many other people who live close to the soil, to the trees, to the wind and the rain, a certain dim infallible wisdom; and this now seemed to tell him that the day of his final reckoning with Dandy was close at hand.

When Isaac had returned home, only the church and the dead remained; the church and the dead, and those living things of the wilderness that, when night falls over the world, come forth from their dens and their other day-time fastnesses to seek their meat from God. Had you been there, you would have seen what Isaac had several times seen: you would have seen a living Thing steal from the McCloud tomb—a thing of sinister beauty and of primeval might. And if you had asked Isaac about it, he could have told you that, at least in that stretch of coastal country, the most attractive place in all the world as a home for this formidable chimera was a moldering tomb. But he never mentioned this Presence to anyone; and he never molested it, knowing it to be an old resident, indigenous to the churchyard, and, to his dim mind, somehow related to the awful enigma of the grave and to his own solemn guardianship of the church.

Dandy Davis, that weasel of a man, that yellow weasel, had, not many months before, drifted into the Santee country out of the region near Florence and Lake City—a very modern and civilized country compared to Santee, and therefore, Isaac thought, calculated to produce Negroes of his type: furtive, sly, treacherous. A high mulatto, he could read and write, he was a flashy dresser, had five times served terms on the chain gang, had killed his man in a brawl over a crap game, would try to steal anything he wanted, had had at least six wives. He had a great way with women, especially with plantation Negro women, who sensed in Dandy a breath of the great world of glamour, society, fashion, and high romance. It was even rumored that he had been as far north as Richmond. To those who admired him for his travels Dandy did not supply the detail that while in Richmond he had spent his time in a public building at the expense of the State of Virginia. Isaac mistrusted and hated him as he mistrusted all things modern and hated all people of Dandy's kind, and he knew that this flamboyant visitor was corrupting the manners and the morals of the people of his own Johnson Hill Church. He had been especially disgusted to hear that some of the younger set had managed to get Dandy invited to preach to them. Isaac's comment on hearing this news was: "Those young people don't want to hear religion. What they want is to hear somebody who can tell them how they can sin and be happy."

Of the Johnson Hill Church Isaac was accounted the most important and trusted member; for he had been, for many years, the treasurer of the Skyrocket Resurrection Burial Society, the greatest organization in the church. In the case of all other burial societies in the Santee country, the treasurer kept the cash box, and some other member of the congregation kept the key; but in this case, he was allowed to keep both. And Isaac had never had any apprehension concerning the money entrusted to his care until Dandy Davis had come into the Santee country;

of him alone Isaac had a haunting premonition of fear. It is human nature that a native usually has far more dread of a foreigner than he ever
has of another native. In this case, you could hardly imagine two people
more different, even in appearance.

Walking down a pineland road at dusk, Isaac might easily have
been taken for a prehistoric man—with his ragged shirt open, showing
the black and hairy arch of his mighty chest, his prodigious arms and
his huge hands, with palms that turned forward, hanging below his
knees and swinging back and forth as he walked, his short, burly neck
that had the effect of burying his chin in his bosom, and a certain
shambling yet easy gait which gave the impression that he walked with
his feet rather than with his legs. He might have startled you into a
feeling that you were in the Gabon or in the Belgian Congo.

It was not only in a general moral way that Isaac disliked Dandy
Davis. He had a premonition that this suave mulatto might have de-
signs on the moneys of the Skyrocket Society, moneys entrusted to him.
Even now, in the little battered tin box hidden behind one of the big
beams in the loft of his cabin he had the savings of forty-one families
—money that would in time afford all those who had contributed to the
fund some measure of decent burial. Next Sunday the quarterly payments were to be made, and Isaac would have more responsibility on
him than ever. And, all the while, the conviction was growing on him
that Dandy was taking a sinister interest in his cash box. How to meet
the crisis, he did not know.

Isaac finally came to two decisions: he could cut for himself and
would travel with a much larger hickory stick than had been his wont;
and he would no longer keep the money in his house. He believed that
somewhere in the churchyard would be a far safer place to hide it until Dandy left the country. For he was sure that Dandy's bubble would
soon burst.

"Dat kind," he used to say, "can't last." But he might last long enough
to do irretrievable damage.

Back on the edge of Wildcat Branch, Isaac cut for his own personal
use a hickory club of imposing proportions, with a gnarled root for the
handle. Thus armed, he set out on that Sunday night for the Negro
church. It was the night when the collections would be made. Alone he

walked through the moonlight, his precious box tucked under his arm. Every few hundred yards he would pause to look about him and listen; but silence slept over the dreaming forest, and the wide sandy road was deserted. All was well.

After the service, which nearly every member of the Johnson Hill community attended, the pay-off was made in a dingy little back room. The pennies and nickels and dimes poured in apace. Once Isaac saw the leering face of Dandy Davis at the open window. The sight made him come to another decision. When all the payments were in, he asked Ben Vandross to walk home with him. Ben was the strongest Negro in the Santee country; courageous, too, except when it came to matters of superstition.

It must have been eleven o'clock, with the full moon riding almost overhead, when Isaac and Ben set out for Isaac's lonely little cabin in the pinelands. Nothing happened. They walked safely and securely until they came within sight of St. James Church, glimmering eerily in the forest.

"Well," said Ben, "I think I will leave you here. You is almost to home. You ain't got as far to go on as what I got to go back."

But distance was not the thing on Ben's mind. He did not so much mind passing the old church in Isaac's company, but he did not intend to return by it alone. What business had he, a self-respecting Negro, to prowl by churchyards in the deep and dead of night?

"Thank you for comin', Ben," Isaac said. "I think I will be all right now."

On the back-track, Ben travelled rather fast; so that he was a long way from Isaac when the treasurer of the Skyrocket Society reached the church. Isaac was not afraid of the church or of the churchyard; not even of the tomb of Raven McCloud. All he was afraid of was Dandy Davis; and he now felt in his old bones that Dandy was near. He was. Indeed, there he stood by the road just beyond the church. There was no mistaking that slim and cocky figure. He must have taken the short-cut by Elmwood to get here before Isaac did. At any rate, Ben was gone; and physically, even with his huge hickory stick, the old man was no match for Dandy—no match for him even if Dandy had no gun. But he did have one. In the moonlight the barrel of a short pistol gleamed dully.

Making sure of his quarry, Dandy sauntered forward. "Old man," he said with easy insolence, "don't make me no trouble. I got to have the box what you got. Gimme dat box, and you can go on home."

Isaac was too busy thinking to answer him. Through his mind rushed the series of places in the churchyard where he had considered hiding his trust funds. If he made a run for the enclosure, he might hide the box before Dandy laid his yellow hands on it.

With a speed surprising for his age, Isaac dashed across the road, jammed open the gate, and ran in among the tombs. But Dandy Davis was hot after him. He had clubbed his pistol, ready to deal his victim a lethal blow. Isaac ran around the McCloud tomb. Black in the moonlight yawned the singular opening at its base. Should he throw the box in there? He swung it in his right hand to do so; there was no mistaking the purpose of his movement. But in that second the butt of the pistol crashed on the back of his head, and he sprawled forward. He fell beyond the opening; and under him lay the treasury of the Skyrocket Resurrection Burial Society.

But Dandy Davis thought he had thrown the box into the tomb of Raven McCloud; and being a man with no respect for anybody, he did not even respect the dead. Also, having consumed a pint of moonshine liquor to nerve him for this especial event, he had no sense and no fear left.

"Ah, hah," he said. "You t'ink you would fool me, eh? Well, I gwine after dat money."

On all fours he backed towards the opening in the tomb. Being slight of build, he forced his body in. He let himself down into that ancient darkness. When he was once in, all he had to do, he might have thought, was to strike some matches and recover the treasure. But the tomb was deep, and he was short of stature. He let himself down to arm's length, and still found no footing. At last he dropped into the noisome depths.

If Isaac had seen what Dandy was doing, much as he hated him, he would have warned him. But he fell into a daze, and by the time he regained his senses, whatever commotion there had been was over. All was still. Isaac called, but there was no answer. And he well knew then that there would never be one.

Slowly the old Negro rose to his feet, clutching with joy the treasury of his congregation. And with prayers of thanksgiving on his lips and in his heart he passed unmolested towards his home.

An hour later, he began to think again of the Thing, and he thought he could see, as clearly as if he were still there, what was happening in the silent moonlight, by the ancient tomb. Out of it came that which, long before, the Seminoles had called the Great King of which they always went in reverent dread. As became such majesty, he advanced slowly. And, for all the horror of his wide unlidded eyes of bloodshot topaz, the sullen droop, almost human in its malice, at the corners of his mouth, the pallor of thin contemptuous lips, the powerful jaws, articulated with the strength of steel, the Banded Death was beautiful in his regal black-and-gold coloring. A savage yet graceful strength made all his movements rhythmic and flowing; a spirit of power went with him, and a spirit of awe went before him. Once clear of the den, he lay at full length, wary and still as old Isaac had so often seen him— this great diamond-back rattlesnake, more than nine feet long and as large around as a strong man's thigh, the serpent terror of the Santee world.

Since Dandy Davis had been regarded as a "floater," it was some days before anyone particularly noticed his absence. Then the gossips began, directing their remarks towards those members of the church who were suspected of having yielded their charms to him: "Ah, hah! Ain't I done tole you so? I knowed dat was a run'way nigger." "I bet you he done gone back where he done come from."

It was some time after this mysterious disappearance, when things in the Santee country had settled back to normal, that one of the Negro girls who was especially concerned over his abandonment of her asked old Isaac what he thought of the chances of Dandy's return.

"Katie, chile," he said gently, "I think Dandy is gone to come no mo'. You must git you another man. Where Dandy is now, I 'spect he don't eber eben think of you." The finality of Isaac's opinion ended

Katie's suspense, and in that way brought her comfort; and she at once energetically proceeded to the business of seeking out another lover.

A few days after he had given Katie this advice, Isaac again met at the old church the same white man who had asked him if anything ever happened there.

"Nothing happened here yet, old man?" he asked smiling.

"No, sah; nothing yet," answered Isaac. But his eyes had in them an inscrutable look.

God's Highwaymen

I

In carrying more than mortals can
John was an ordinary man;
Of cares, he was a caravan.
He staggered onward in the sun;
But for his load, he might have run;
How shamblingly his pace advanced
When joyously he might have danced!
He reached the wood at last;—and then
They ambushed him—God's highwaymen!

II

Ah, when he reached the wood at last,
Delicious rapine followed fast,
Pillage divine, celestial rape.
From which no mortal could escape.
Their purpose steeped his heart in dread;
He shivered, trembled, cried, and pled;
Had he a chance, he would have fled.
A mirthful, tolerant, lawless clan
Woe had him sure,—and had their plan
To sack the precious caravan
Of this unhappy Everyman!

III

Burdened, unarmed, he faced about;
A tall Oak robbed him of his doubt;
A Hickory hale the thieves among
Deprived him of his weakness strong;
A Holly stole his fine disdain;
A Dewdrop plundered him of pain;

Archibald Rutledge, "God's Highwaymen," "Requiem," "Lee" in *Deep River, The Complete Poems of Archibald Rutledge* (Columbia, S.C.: The R. L. Bryan Co., 1960), pp. 600–602, 398, 454. Copyright 1960, 1966 by The R. L. Bryan Company. Reprinted by permission of The R. L. Bryan Company and Archibald Rutledge.

The agate of his heart, they say,
A Sunbeam melted quite away;
His hate he suddenly let fall
Because he saw a Cardinal;
Huge Elms—those burly buccaneers—
Despoiled him of his priceless fears;
A Laurel leaned to him and took
His aching eyes, his anxious look;
From him a Cedar lifted soft
A burden that had bent him oft.
A debonair and lissome Stream
The luggage of his self-esteem
Laughed quite away; and from him bore
Pity of self, a tragic store.
A spirit of wild glamour came
And filched his sordid greed of fame;
A splendor-coronetted Pine
Has made him all his pride resign;
A lithe Birch spirited away
Forgetfulness to kneel and pray;
A poignant Perfume merciless
Preyed on his paltry thriftiness . . .
He laid sick hope that had been sleeping
Upon a Greensward's quiet keeping.

IV

O what a raid on John to stage!
O buccaneering! brigandage!
Disaster on disaster came:
Into her secret halls of flame
The stately sorrow that he kept
Closest his heart, a Wildrose swept;
His anger—he was sore beset—
He yielded to a Violet;
To many a joy his sad farewells
He lost to golden Jasmine-bells;

Surrendered to a spray of Rue
The dream that never could come true;
And with a virgin Lily left
A love whose heart long since was cleft.

V

Stripped, rifled, raided, and profaned,—
His wealth evanished,—what remained?
A dewy respite deep; a sense
Of all relaxed that had been tense;
Once more the blue of God above,
A white star looking down like love;
A delicate wild stillness sweet
In which the heart finds far retreat;
A tide of beauty flooding fair
With waves of wonder, drowning care.

VI

Pillaged and joyous, ruined, glad,
Free, naked, reft of all he had,—
John Everyman, from yonder wood,
Carried no more than mortals should:
Carried a heart for life made strong,
A hope, a faith, a friend, a song.

VII

O Traveller somewhere on the Way,
May God's good thieves your path waylay . . .
—And this with all my heart I pray.

Requiem

Under the ancient pine,
Deep in the ferny glade,
Where the wild jasmine vine
Showers a fragrant shade,
Let me be laid.

Here will the moon and star
Watch with their silver light;
Here woodland winds from far
Haunt the deep purple night
With dim delight.

Here for my watch and ward,
In place of shaft and stone,
Great oaks shall be my guard,
And the tall cypress lone.
Loving his own.

Here let the dreamer rest,
Now that the dream is o'er;
Safe on the wildwood's breast,
Calm by the river's shore,
Waking no more.

Lee

As Arthur is to England,
As Roland is to France,
Beyond the range of time and change,
Immortal as Romance,
America, whose heritage
Of heroes is your crown,
Forever shall the fame of Lee
Be one with your renown.

O Land, his chivalry of heart
In all your glory gleams;
And from afar his spirit's star
Dawns through your noblest dreams,
Who through eternal years shall mean
In your superb advance,
What Arthur is to England,
What Roland is to France.

DuBose Heyward (1885–1940)

Born in Charleston on August 31, 1885, DuBose Heyward was one of the major forces in the Charleston Poetry Society in the 1920s and won a national reputation with *Porgy* (1925), a novel of Charleston Negro life. Its dramatic version (written with his wife Dorothy) won the 1927 Pulitzer Prize, later becoming the basis for the opera *Porgy and Bess* (1935), with music by George Gershwin. Heyward's first book was a collection of poems, *Carolina Chansons* (1922), written in collaboration with Hervey Allen. Other books by Heyward include five novels—*Angel* (1926), *Mamba's Daughters* (1929), *Peter Ashley* (1932), *Lost Morning* (1936), and *Star Spangled Virgin* (1939)—and two volumes of poetry, *Skylines and Horizons* (1924) and *Jasbo Brown* (1931). Heyward died at his North Carolina home, Dawn Hill, near Hendersonville, on June 16, 1940.

The Half Pint Flask

I picked up the book and regarded it with interest. Even its format suggested the author: the practical linen covered boards, the compact and exact paragraphing. I opened the volume at random. There he was again: "There can be no doubt," "An undeniable fact," "I am prepared to assert." A statement in the preface leaped from the context and arrested my gaze:

"The primitive American Negro is of a deeply religious nature, demonstrating in his constant attendance at church, his fervent prayers, his hymns, and his frequent mention of the Deity that he has cast aside the last vestiges of his pagan background, and has unreservedly espoused the doctrine of Christianity."

I spun the pages through my fingers until a paragraph in the last chapter brought me up standing:

"I was hampered in my investigations by a sickness contracted on the island that was accompanied by a distressing insomnia, and, in its final stages, extreme delirium. But I already had sufficient evidence in hand to enable me to prove—"

Yes, there it was, fact upon fact. I was overwhelmed by the permanence, the unanswerable last word of the printed page. In the face of it my own impressions became fantastic, discredited even in my own mind. In an effort at self justification I commenced to rehearse my *impressions* of that preposterous month as opposed to Barksdale's *facts;* my feeling for effects and highly developed fiction writer's imagination on the one hand; and on the other, his cold record of a tight, three dimensional world as reported by his five good senses.

Sitting like a crystal gaze, with the book in my hand, I sent my memory back to a late afternoon in August, when, watching from the shore near the landing on Ediwander Island, I saw the "General Stonewall Jackson" slide past a frieze of palmetto trees, shut off her steam, and nose up to the tenuous little wharf against the ebb.

Two barefooted Negroes removed a section of the rail and prepared to run out the gang plank. Behind them gathered the passengers for

Ediwander landing: ten or a dozen Negroes back from town with the proceeds of a month's labor transformed into flaming calico, amazing bonnets, and new, flimsy, yellow luggage; and trailing along behind them, the single white passenger.

I would have recognized my guest under more difficult circumstances and I experienced that inner satisfaction that comes from having a new acquaintance fit neatly into a preconceived pattern. The obstinacy of which I had been warned was evident in the thin immobile line of the month over the prognathous jaw. The eyes behind his thick glasses were a bright hard blue and moved methodically from object to object, allowing each its allotted time for classification then passing unhurriedly on to the next. He was so like the tabloid portrait in the letter of the club member who had sent him down that I drew the paper from my pocket and refreshed my memory with a surreptitious glance.

"He's the museum, or collector type," Spencer had written; "spends his time collecting facts—some he sells—some he keeps to play with. Incidentally his hobby is American glass, and he has the finest private collection in the state."

We stood eyeing each other over the heads of the noisy landing party without enthusiasm. Then when the last Negro had come ashore he picked up his bag with a meticulousness that vaguely exasperated me, and advanced up the gang plank.

Perfunctory introductions followed: "Mr Courtney?" from him, with an unnecessarily rising inflection; and a conventional "Mr. Barksdale, I presume," from me in reply.

The buckboard had been jogging along for several minutes before he spoke.

"Very good of Mr. Spencer to give me this opportunity," he said in a close clipped speech. "I am doing a series of articles on Negroid Primates, and I fancy the chances for observation are excellent here."

"Negroid Primates!" The phrase annoyed me. Uttered in that dissecting voice, it seemed to strip the human from the hundred or more Negroes who were my only company except during the duck season when the club members dropped down for the shooting.

"There are lots of Negroes here," I told him a little stiffly. "Their ancestors were slaves when the island was the largest rice plantation in

South Carolina, and isolation from modern life has kept them primitive enough, I guess."

"Good!" he exclaimed. "I will commence my studies at once. Simple souls, I fancy. I should have my data within a month."

We had been traveling slowly through deep sand ruts that tugged at the wheels like an undertow. On either side towered serried ranks of virgin long-leaf pine. Now we topped a gentle rise. Before us was the last outpost of the forest crowning a diminishing ridge. The straight columned trees were bars against a released splendor of sunset sky and sea.

Impulsively I called his attention to it:

"Rather splendid, don't you think?"

He raised his face, and I was immediately cognizant of the keen methodical scrutiny that passed from trees to sea, and from sea back to that last wooded ridge that fell away into the tumble of dunes.

Suddenly I felt his wire-tight grasp about my arm.

"What's that?" he asked, pointing with his free hand. Then with an air of authority, he snapped: "Stop the cart. I've got to have a look at it."

"That won't interest you. It's only a Negro burying ground. I'll take you to the quarters tomorrow, where you can study your 'live primates'."

But he was over the wheel with surprising alacrity and striding up the slight ascent to the scattered mounds beneath the pines.

The sunset was going quickly, dragging its color from the sky and sea, rolling up leagues of delicately tinted gauze into tight little bales of primary color, then draping these with dark covers for the night. In sharp contrast against the light the burying ground presented its pitiful emblems of the departed. Under the pine needles, in common with all Negro graveyards of the region, the mounds were covered with a strange litter of half emptied medicine bottles, tin spoons, and other futile weapons that had failed in the final engagement with the last dark enemy.

Barksdale was puttering excitedly about among the graves, peering at the strange assortment of crockery and glass. The sight reminded me of what Spencer had said of the man's hobby and a chill foreboding assailed me. I jumped from the buckboard.

"Here," I called, "I wouldn't disturb those things if I were you."

But my words went unheeded. When I reached Barksdale's side, he was holding a small flat bottle, half filled with a sticky black fluid, and was rubbing the earth from it with his coat sleeve. The man was electric with excitement. He held the flask close to his glasses, then spun around upon me.

"Do you know what this is?" he demanded, then rushed on triumphantly with his answer: "It's a first issue, half pint flask of the old South Carolina state dispensary. It gives me the only complete set in existence. Not another one in America. I had hoped that I might get on the trail of one down here. But to fall upon it like this!"

The hand that held the flask was shaking so violently that the little palmetto tree and single X that marked it described small agitated circles. He drew out his handkerchief and wrapped it up tenderly, black contents and all.

"Come," he announced, "we'll go now."

"Not so fast," I cautioned him. "You can't carry that away. It simply isn't done down here. We may have our moral lapses, but there are certain things that—well—can't be thought of. The graveyard is one. We let it alone."

He placed the little linen covered package tenderly in his inside pocket and buttoned his coat with an air of finality; then he faced me truculently.

"I have been searching for this flask for ten years," he asserted. "If you can find the proper person to whom payment should be made I will give a good price. In the meantime I intend to keep it. It certainly is of no use to anyone, and I shan't hesitate for a silly superstition."

I could not thrash him for it and I saw that nothing short of physical violence would remove it from his person. For a second I was tempted to argue with him; tell him why he should not take the thing. Then I was frustrated by my own lack of a reason. I groped with my instinctive knowledge that it was not to be done, trying to embody the abstract into something sufficiently concrete to impress him. And all the while I felt his gaze upon me, hard, very blue, a little mocking, absolutely determined.

Behind the low crest of the ridge sounded a single burst of laughter,

and the ring of a trace chain. A strange panic seized me. Taking him by
the arm I rushed him across the short distance to the buckboard and into
his seat; then leaped across him and took up the lines.

Night was upon us, crowding forward from the recesses of the forest,
pushing out beyond us through the last scattered trees, flowing over the
sea and lifting like level smoke into the void of sky. The horse started
forward, wrenching the wheels from the clutching sand.

Before us, coming suddenly up in the dusk, a party of field Negroes
filled the road. A second burst of laughter sounded, warm now, volatile
and disarming. It made me ashamed of my panic. The party passed the
vehicle, dividing and flowing by on both sides of the road. The last
vestiges of day brought out high lights on their long earth-polished
hoes. Teeth were a white accent here and there. Only eyes, and fallen
sockets under the brows of the very old, seemed to defy the fading
glimmer, bringing the night in them from the woods. Laughter and
soft Gullah words were warm in the air about us.

"Howdy Boss."

"Ebenin' Boss."

The women curtsied in their high tucked up skirts; the men touched
hat brims. Several mules followed, grotesque and incredible in the
thickening dark, their trace chains dangling and chiming faintly.

The party topped the rise, then dropped behind it.

Silence, immediate and profound, as though a curtain had been run
down upon the heels of the last.

"A simple folk," clipped out my companion. "I rather envy them
starting out at zero, as it were, with everything to learn from our amazing civilization."

"Zero, hell!" I flung out. "They had created a Congo art before our
ancestors drugged and robbed their first Indian."

Barksdale consigned me to limbo with his mocking, intolerable smile.

The first few days at the club were spent by my guest in going
through the preliminary routine of the systematic writer. Books were
unpacked and arranged in the order of study, loose-leaf folders were
laid out, and notes made for the background of his thesis. He was working at a table in his bedroom which adjoined my own, and as I also

used my sleeping apartment as a study for the fabrication of the fiction which, with my salary as manager of the club, discharged my financial obligations, I could not help seeing something of him.

On the morning of the second day I glanced in as I passed his door, and surprised him gloating over his find. It was placed on the table before him, and he was gazing fixedly at it. Unfortunately, he looked up; our glances met and, with a self consciousness that smote us simultaneously, remained locked. Each felt that the subject had better remain closed—yet there the flask stood evident and unavoidable.

After a strained space of time I managed to step into the room, pick up a book and say casually:

"I am rather interested in Negroes myself. Do you mind if I see what you have here?"

While I examined the volume he passed behind me and put the flask away, then came and looked at the book with me. " 'African Religions and Superstitions'," he said, reading the title aloud; then supplemented:

"An interesting mythology for the American Negro, little more. The African Gullah Negro, from whom these are descended, believed in a God you know, but he only created, then turned his people adrift to be preyed upon by malign spirits conjured up by their enemies. Really a religion, or rather a superstition, of senseless terror."

"I am not so sure of the complete obsoleteness of the old rites and superstitions," I told him, feeling as I proceeded that I was engaged in a useless mission. "I know these Negroes pretty well. For them, Plat-eye, for instance, is a very actual presence. If you will notice the cook you will see that she seems to get along without a prayer book, but when she goes home after dark she sticks a sulphur match in her hair. Sulphur is a charm against Plat-eye."

"Tell me," he asked with a bantering light in his hard eyes, "just what is Plat-eye?"

I felt that I was being laughed at and floundered ahead at the subject, anxious to be out of it as soon as possible.

"Plat-eye is a spirit which takes some form which will be particularly apt to lure its victims away. It is said to lead them into danger or lose them in the woods and, stealing their wits away, leave them to die alone."

He emitted a short acid laugh.

"What amusing rot. And I almost fancy you believe it."

"Of course I don't," I retorted but I experienced the feeling that my voice was over-emphatic and failed to convince.

"Well, well," he said, "I am not doing folk lore but religion. So that is out of my province. But it is amusing and I'll make a note of it. Plateye, did you say?"

The next day was Thursday. I remember that distinctly because, although nearly a week's wages were due, the last servant failed to arrive for work in the morning. The club employed three of them; two women and a man. Even in the off season this was a justifiable expense, for a servant could be hired on Ediwander for four dollars a week. When I went to order breakfast the kitchen was closed, and the stove cold.

After a makeshift meal I went out to find the yard boy. There were only a few Negroes in the village and these were women hoeing in the small garden patches before the cabins. There were the usual swarms of lean mongrel hounds, and a big sow lay nourishing her young in the warm dust of the road. The women looked up as I passed. Their soft voices, as they raised their heads one after another to say "Mornin' Boss," seemed like emanations from the very soil, so much a part of the earth did they appear.

But the curs were truculent that morning: strange, canny, candid little mongrels. If you want to know how you stand with a Negro, don't ask him—pat his dog.

I found Thomas, the hired boy, sitting before his cabin watching a buzzard carve half circles in the blue.

"When are you coming to work?" I demanded. "The day's half done."

"I got de toot' ache, Boss. I can't git ober 'fore termorrer." The boy knew that I did not believe him. He also knew that I would not take issue with him on the point. No Negro on the island will say "no" to a white man. Call it "good form" if you will, but what Thomas had said to me was merely the code for "I'm through." I did not expect him and I was not disappointed.

Noon of the following day I took the buckboard, crossed the ferry to the mainland, and returned at dark with a cheerful wholesome Negress, loaned to me by a plantation owner, who answered for her faithfulness and promised that she would cook for us during the emergency. She got us a capital supper, retired to the room adjoining the kitchen that I had prepared for her, as I did not wish her to meet the Negroes in the village, and in the morning had vanished utterly. She must have left immediately after supper, for the bed was undisturbed.

I walked straight from her empty room to Barksdale's sanctum, entered, crossed to the closet where he had put the flask, and threw the door wide. The space was empty. I spun around and met his amused gaze.

"Thought I had better put it away carefully. It is too valuable to leave about."

Our glances crossed like the slide of steel on steel. Then suddenly my own impotence to master the situation arose and overwhelmed me. I did not admit it even to myself, but that moment saw what amounted to my complete surrender.

We entered upon the haphazard existence inevitable with two pre-occupied men unused to caring for their own comfort: impossible makeshift meals, got when we were hungry; beds made when we were ready to get into them; with me, hours put into work that had to be torn up and started over the next day; with Barksdale, regular tours of investigation about the island and two thousand words a day, no more, no less, written out in longhand, and methodically filed. We naturally saw less and less of each other—a fact which was evidently mutually agreeable.

It was therefore a surprise to me one night in the second week to leap from sleep into a condition of lucid consciousness and find myself staring at Barksdale who had opened the door between our rooms. There he stood like a bird of ill omen, tall and slightly stooping, with his ridiculous nightshirt and thin slightly bowed shanks.

"I'll leave this open if you don't mind," he said with a new note of apology in his voice. "Haven't been sleeping very well for a week or so, and thought the draft through the house might cool the air."

Immediately I knew that there was something behind the apparently casual action of the man. He was the type who could lie through conviction; adopt some expedient point of view, convince himself that it was the truth, then assert it as a fact; but he was not an instinctive liar, and that new apologetic note gave him away. For a while after he went back to bed, I lay wondering what was behind his request.

Then for the first time I felt it; but hemmed in by the appalling limitations of human speech, how am I to make the experience plain to others!

Once I was standing behind the organ of a great cathedral when a bass chord was pressed upon the keys; suddenly the air about me was all sound and movement. The demonstration that night was like this a little, except that the place of the sound was taken by an almost audible silence, and the vibrations were so violent as to seem almost a friction against the nerve terminals. The wave of movement lasted for several minutes, then it abated slowly. But this was the strange thing about it: the agitation was not dissipated into the air; rather it seemed to settle slowly, heavily, about my body, and to move upon my skin like the multitudinous crawling of invisible and indescribably loathsome vermin.

I got up and struck a light. The familiar disorder of the room sprang into high relief, reassuring me, telling me coolly not to be a fool. I took the lamp into Barksdale's room. There he lay, his eyes wide and fixed, braced in his bed with every muscle tense. He gave me the impression of wrenching himself out of invisible bonds as he turned and sat up on the edge of his bed.

"Just about to get up and work," he said in a voice that he could not manage to make casual. "Been suffering from insomnia for a week, and it's beginning to get on my nerves."

The strange sensation had passed from my body but the thought of sleep was intolerable. We went to our desks leaving the door ajar, and wrote away the four hours that remained until daylight.

And now a question arises of which due cognizance must be taken even though it may weaken my testimony. Is a man quite sane who has been without sleep for ten days and nights? Is he a competent witness? I do not know. And yet the phenomena that followed my first startled awakening entered into me and became part of my life experience. I live them over shudderingly when my resistance is low and memory has its way with me. I know that they transpired with that instinctive certainty which lies back of human knowledge and is immune from the skepticism of the cynic.

After that first night the house was filled with the vibrations. I closed the door to Barksdale's room, hoping a superstitious hope that I would be immune. After an hour I opened it again, glad for even his companionship. Only while I was wide awake and driving my brain to its capacity did the agitation cease. At the first drowsiness it would commence faintly, then swell up and up, fighting sleep back from the tortured brain, working under leaden eyelids upon the tired eyes.

Ten days and nights of it! Terrible for me: devastating for Barksdale. It wasted him like a jungle fever.

Once when I went near him and his head had dropped forward on his desk in the vain hope of relief, I made a discovery. He was the *centre.* The moment I bent over him my nerve terminals seemed to become living antennæ held out to a force that frayed and wasted them away. In my own room it was better. I went there and sat where I could still see him for what small solace there was in that.

I entreated him to go away, but with his insane obstinacy he would not hear of it. Then I thought of leaving him, confessing myself a coward—bolting for it. But again, something deeper than logic, some obscure tribal loyalty, held me bound. Two members of the same race; and out there the palmetto jungle, the village with its fires bronze against the midnight trees, the malign, beleaguering presence. No, it could not be done.

But I did slip over to the mainland and arrange to send a wire to Spencer telling him to come and get Barksdale, that the man was ill.

During that interminable ten days and nights the fundamental difference between Barksdale and myself became increasingly evident. He would go to great pains to explain the natural causes of our malady.

"Simple enough," he would say, while his bloodshot eyes, fixed on me, shouted the lie to his words. "One of those damn swamp fevers. Livingstone complained of them you will remember, and so did Stanley. Here in this subtropical belt we are evidently subject to the plague. Doubtless there is a serum. I should have inquired before coming down."

To this I said nothing, but I confess now, at risk of being branded a coward, that I had become the victim of a superstitious terror. Frequently when Barksdale was out I searched for the flask without finding the least trace of it. Finally I capitulated utterly and took to carrying a piece of sulphur next to my skin. Nothing availed.

The strange commotion in the atmosphere became more and more persistent. It crowded over from the nights into the days. It came at noon; any time that drowsiness fell upon our exhausted bodies it was there, waging a battle with it behind the closed lids. Only with the muscles tense and the eyes wide could one inhabit a static world. After the first ten days I lost count of time. There was a nightmare quality to its unbreakable continuity.

I remember only the night when I saw *her* in Barksdale's doorway, and I think that it must have been in the third week. There was a full moon, I remember, and there had been unusual excitement in the village. I have always had a passion for moonlight and I stood long on the piazza watching the great disc change from its horizon copper to gold, then cool to silver as it swung up into the immeasurable tranquillity of the southern night. At first I thought that the Negroes must be having a dance, for I could hear the syncopation of sticks on a cabin floor, and the palmettos and moss-draped live oaks that grew about the buildings could be seen the full quarter of a mile away, a ruddy bronze against the sky from a brush fire. But the longer I waited listening the less sure I became about the nature of the celebration. The rhythm became strange, complicated; and the chanting that rose and fell with the drumming rang with a new, compelling quality, and lacked entirely the abandon of dancers.

Finally I went into my room, stretched myself fully dressed on the bed, and almost achieved oblivion. Then suddenly I was up again, my fists clenched, my body taut. The agitation exceeded anything that I had before experienced. Before me, across Barksdale's room, were wide open double doors letting on the piazza. They molded the moonlight into a square shaft that plunged through the darkness of the room, cold, white, and strangely substantial among the half obliterated familiar objects. I had the feeling that it could be touched. That hands could be slid along its bright surface. It possessed itself of the place. It

was the one reality in a swimming, nebulous cube. Then it commenced
to tremble with the vibrations of the apartment.

And now the incredible thing happened. Incredible because belief
arises in each of us out of the corroboration of our own life experience;
and I have met no other white man who has beheld Plat-eye. I have no
word, no symbol which can awaken recognition. But who has not seen
heat shaking upward from hot asphalt, shaking upward until the things
beyond it wavered and quaked? That is the nearest approach in the
material world. Only the thing that I witnessed was colored a cold blue,
and it was heavy with the perfume of crushed jasmine flowers.

I stood, muscle locked to muscle by terror.

The centre of the shaft darkened; the air bore upon me as though
some external force exerted a tremendous pressure in an effort to render
an abstraction concrete: to mold moving unstable elements into something that could be seen—touched.

Suddenly it was done—accomplished. I looked—I saw *her.*

The shock released me, and I got a flare from several matches struck
at once. Yellow light bloomed on familiar objects. I got the fire to a
lamp wick, then looked again.

The shaft of moonlight was gone. The open doors showed only a
deep blue vacant square. Beyond them something moved. The lamp
light steadied, grew. It warmed the room like fire. It spread over the
furniture, making it real again. It fell across Barksdale's bed, dragging
my gaze with it. *The bed was empty.*

I got to the piazza just as he disappeared under a wide armed live oak.
The Spanish moss fell behind him like a curtain. The place was a
hundred yards away. When I reached it, all trace of him had vanished.

I went back to the house, built a rousing fire, lit all the lamps, and
stretched myself in a deep chair to wait until morning.

Then! an automobile horn on Ediwander Island. Imagine that! I
could not place it at first. It crashed through my sleep like the trump of
judgment. It called me up from the abysses into which I had fallen. It
infuriated me. It reduced me to tears. Finally it tore me from unutter-
able bliss, and held me blinking in the high noon, with my silly lamps
still burning palely about me.

"You're a hell of a fellow," called Spencer. "Think I've got nothing to do but come to this jungle in summer to nurse you and Barksdale."

He got out of a big muddy machine and strode forward laughing. "Oh, well," he said, "I won't row you. It gave me a chance to try out the new bus. That's why I'm late. Thought I'd motor down. Had a hell of a time getting over the old ferry; but it was worth it to see the niggers when I started up on Ediwander. Some took to trees—one even jumped overboard."

He ended on a hearty burst of laughter. Then he looked at me and broke off short. I remember how his face looked then, close to mine, white and frightened.

"My God, man!" he exclaimed, "what's wrong? You aren't going to die on me, are you?"

"Not today," I told him. "We've got to find Barksdale first."

We could not get a Negro to help us. They greeted Spencer, who had always been popular with them, warmly. They laughed their deep laughter—were just as they had always been with him. Mingo, his old paddler, promised to meet us in half an hour with a gang. They never showed up; and later, when we went to the village to find them, there was not a human being on the premises. Only a pack of curs there that followed us as closely as they dared and hung just out of boot reach, snapping at our heels.

We had to go it alone: a stretch of jungle five miles square, a large part of it accessible only with bush hooks and machettes. We dared not take the time to go to the mainland and gather a party of whites. Barksdale had been gone over twelve hours when we started and he would not last long in his emaciated condition.

The chances were desperately against us. Spencer, though physically a giant, was soft from office life. I was hanging on to consciousness only by a tremendous and deliberate effort. We took food with us, which we ate on our feet during breathing spells, and we fell in our tracks for rest when we could go no farther.

At night, when we were eating under the high, white moon, he told me more of the man for whom we were searching.

"I ought to have written you more fully at the start. You'd have been sorry for him then, not angry with him. He does not suggest Lothario now, but he was desperately in love once.

"She was the most fantastically imaginative creature, quick as light, and she played in circles around him. He was never dull in those days. Rather handsome, in the lean Gibson manner; but he was always—well —matter of fact. She had all there was of him the first day, and it was hers to do as she pleased with. Then one morning she saw quite plainly that he would bore her. She had to have someone who could *play*. Barksdale could have died for her, but he could not play. Like that," and Spencer gave a snap of his fingers, "she jugged him. It was at a house party. I was there and saw it. She was the sort of surgeon who believes in amputation and she gave it to Barksdale there without an anæsthetic and with the crowd looking on.

"He changed after that. Wouldn't have anything he couldn't feel, see, smell. He had been wounded by something elusive, intangible. He was still scarred; and he hid behind the defenses of his five good senses. When I met him five years later he had gone in for facts and glass."

He stopped speaking for a moment. The August dark crowded closer, pressing its low, insistent nocturne against our ears. Then he resumed in a musing voice: "Strange the obsession that an imaginative woman can exercise over an unimaginative man. It is the sort of thing that can follow a chap to the grave. Celia's living in Europe now, married—children—but I believe that if she called him today he'd go. She was very beautiful, you know."

"Yes," I replied, "I know. Very tall, blonde, with hair fluffed and shining about her head like a madonna's halo. Odd way of standing, too, with head turned to one side so that she might look at one over her shoulder. Jasmine perfume, heavy, almost druggy."

Spencer was startled: "You've seen her!"

"Yes, here. She came for Barksdale last night. I saw her as plainly as I see you."

"But she's abroad, I tell you.

I turned to Spencer with a sudden resolve: "You've heard the Negroes here talk of Plat-eye?"

He nodded.

"Well, I've got to tell you something whether you believe it or not.

Barksdale got in wrong down here. Stole a flask from the graveyard. There's been hell turned loose ever since: fires and singing every night in the village and a lot more. I am sure now what it all meant—conjuring, and Plat-eye, of course, to lead Barksdale away and do him in, at the same time emptying the house so that it could be searched for the flask."

"But Celia; how could they know about her?"

"They didn't. But Barksdale knew. They had only to break him down and let his old obsession call her up. I probably saw her on the reflex from him, but I'll swear she was there."

Spencer was leaning toward me, the moon shining full upon his face. I could see that he believed.

"Thank God you see it," I breathed. "Now you know why we've got to find him soon."

In the hour just before dawn we emerged from the forest at the far side of the island. The moon was low and reached long fingers of pale light through the trees. The east was a swinging nebula of half light and vapor. A flight of immense blue heron broke suddenly into the air before us, hurling the mist back into our faces from their beating wings. Spencer, who was ahead of me, gave a cry and darted forward, disappearing behind a palmetto thicket.

I grasped my machette and followed.

Our quest had ended. Barksdale lay face downward in the marsh with his head toward the east. His hands flung out before him were already awash in the rising tide.

We dragged him to high ground. He was breathing faintly in spasmodic gasps, and his pulse was a tiny thread of movement under our finger tips. Two saplings and our coats gave us a makeshift litter; and three hours of stumbling, agonizing labor brought us with our burden to the forest's edge.

I waited with him there, while Spencer went for his car and some wraps. When he returned his face was a study.

"Had a devil of a time finding blankets," he told me as we bundled Barksdale up for the race to town. "House looks as though a tornado had passed through it; everything out on the piazza, and in the front yard."

With what strength I had left I turned toward home. Behind me lay the forest, dark even in the summer noon; before me, the farthest hill, the sparse pines, and the tumble of mounds in the graveyard.

I entered the clearing and looked at the mound from which Barksdale had taken the flask. There it was again. While it had been gone the cavity had filled with water; now this had flooded out when the bottle had been replaced and still glistened grey on the sand, black on the pine needles.

I regained the road and headed for the club.

Up from the fields came the hands, dinner bound; fifteen or twenty of them; the women taking the direct sun indifferently upon their bare heads. Bright field hoes gleamed on shoulders. The hot noon stirred to deep laughter, soft Gullah accents:

"Mornin' Boss—howdy Boss."

They divided and flowed past me, women curtsying, men touching hat brims. On they went; topped the ridge; dropped from view.

Silence, immediate and profound.

Ambrose Gonzales (1857–1926)

Ambrose Elliott Gonzales, born at Adams Run on May 29, 1857, began his career as a telegraph operator, working in South Carolina from 1874 through 1878 and in New York and New Orleans from 1881 through 1885. In 1885, however, he began a long journalistic career as a correspondent for the *Charleston News and Courier*. With his brother, N. G. Gonzales, he founded the newspaper, *The State,* in Columbia, on February 18, 1891, becoming its publisher and president in March 1893. Gonzales served in the Spanish-American War as a captain of the United States Volunteers. In 1922 he published the first of his Gullah stories of the Carolina coast, *The Black Border*. Others in this series are *With Aesop Along the Black Border* (1924) and *The Captain: Stories of the Black Border* (1924). He died on July 11, 1926.

The Lion of Lewisburg

Several years ago there lived on the "Lewisburg" rice plantation of former Governor Duncan Clinch Heyward, one Monday White, a yellow negro and a persistent and imaginative practical joker. The little "Devil's Fiddles" which boys construct of empty tin cans and rosined string emit unchristian squeaks and groans when played upon with smooth hardwood sticks, and Monday believed that a similar device on a larger scale could be so manipulated as to frighten into hysterics half the negro population along Combahee River. Begging from the store a large empty powder keg, he surreptitiously rigged it up with stout twine which, well rubbed with rosin and scraped with a dry hickory stick for a bow, produced a hoarse and horrible sound which might have passed among the uninitiated for the roar of a lion—or for anything else.

Monday knew that the superstitious negroes feared most the unknown. The negro who would have taken a chance with alligator or bull, or the even more dangerous hind legs of a mule, could be scared stiff by a weird, unfamiliar sound in the woods at night. So Monday decided that the ear-jarring sound emitted by his double-bass "Devil's Fiddle" should do service for the roar of a lion, as these creatures were unknown on Combahee, and the few negroes who had once seen lions when the circus visited Walterboro, brought back marvelous tales of their ferocity and their terrible voices.

Monday baited his victims skilfully. One Saturday night when the store was crowded with trading negroes, he led the conversation lionwards. He needed tales of terror, and the two or three negroes who had once seen lions were willing to oblige. One of them had even seen them fed. "W'en uh bin Walterburruh, uh look 'puntop one dem annimel fuh call lion, en' uh shum w'en dem duh g'em 'e bittle fuh eat."

"Nigguh g'em 'e bittle?"

"No man, buckruh feed'um. Nigguh ent fuh feed'um. Da' t'ing dainjus tummuch! Nigguh duh him bittle. Lion en' nigguh alltwo come f'um Aff'iky, en' w'en dem Aff'ikin king en' t'ing hab lion een dem

Ambrose Gonzales, "The Lion of Lewisburg" in *The Black Border* (Columbia, S.C.: The State Co., 1922), pp. 35–44. Copyright 1922 by The State Company. Reprinted by permission of the publisher.

cage, 'e g'em uh nigguh fuh eat eb'ry day Gawd sen', en' 'e crack nigguh' hambone een 'e jaw sukkuh dem Beefu't nigguh crack crab claw'
w'en 'e done bile. Him *done* fuh lub nigguh! W'en dem sukkus man
fuh feed'um een Walterburruh, dem fetch half uh bull yellin' fuh 'e
bittle, en' w'en da' t'ing look 'puntop de meat, 'e tail t'rash' 'pun de flo'
sukkuh nigguh duh t'rash rice 'long flail, en' 'e gyap 'e mout' same
lukkuh Mistuh Jokok op'n 'e trunk mout' fuh t'row uh flow 'puntop
Mass Clinch' rice! 'E woice roll lukkuh t'unduh roll, en' w'en 'e holluh,
eb'ry Chryce' nigguh t'row 'e han' obuh e' two' yez en' run out de tent,
en' gone!"

"Tengk Gawd dem annimel nebbuh come 'puntop Cumbee!" a
woman fervently exclaimed.

"Yaas, tittie," said another, "ef da' t'ing ebbuh come yuh, me fuh run
Sabannuh. Uh nebbuh stop run 'tell uh done pass de Yamassee!"

Others joined in the trembling chorus and Monday, when they had
become sufficiently worked up, shrewdly spilled the first spoonful of
powder leading to his mine. "Oonuh nigguh, one buckruh binnuh talk
'puntop de flatfawm to W'ite Hall deepo dis mawnin', en' uh yeddy'um
tell dem torruh buckruh suh one sukkus hab uh acksident to Orangebu'g, en' one lion git out 'e cage en' run een de swamp en' gone, en' de
buckruh try fuh ketch'um but dem 'f'aid fuh gone een de swamp, en'
dem sen' dem dog attuhr'um, en' de lion kill t'irteen beagle one time!"

"Oh Jedus!" cried an excited woman, "Uh berry 'f'aid da' t'ing gwine
come Cumbee! Hummuch mile Orangebu'g stan' f'um yuh?"

"Uh dunno hummuch mile," Monday replied, "but uh know lion kin
mek'um 'tween middlenight en' day-clean, en' ef uh ebbuh yeddy 'e
woice roll een dish'yuh swamp, meself gwine git een me trus'me'gawd
coonoo en' uh fuh gone down Cumbee ribbuh, en' uh nebbuh stop
paddle 'tell uh git Beefu't!"

A week passed. Like the waves from a stone thrown into still waters,
the lion stories spread among the outlying plantations in all directions.
Saturday night found Monday early at the store. Another convenient
buckra at White Hall station had told that morning of the lion's escape
from the Edisto and his crossing over the intervening pinelands into the
Salkehatchie Swamp and, as most people know, the Salkehatchie River,
below the line of the Charleston and Savannah railway, becomes the

Combahee. The lion was loose, therefore, in their own proper swamp, and might even now be riding a floating log down the current of their beloved river!

Monday stealthily slipped out. An hour later, when the negroes in and about the store had worked themselves up to a delectable pitch of excitement, an unearthly groaning roar came from the woods nearby. The night was hot, but the negroes almost froze with fear, and the clerk, in whom Monday had confided, raised no objection when the negroes within the store called in their companions from the outside and asked permission to bar the door.

"Oonuh yeddy'um, enty! Wuh uh tell you 'bout da' t'ing' woice?" said the negro who had seen lions in Walterboro.

Monday's "Devil's Fiddle" groaned again, and as its dying notes trembled on the summer night, a rush was made to close and bolt the windows. The kerosene lamps smoked and flared in the fetid air. The men listened and shuddered as the recurrent roars, now muffled, reached their expectant ears. The women wailed. "O Gawd! uh lef' me t'ree chillun shet up een me house," cried one. "Uh 'spec' da' t'ing done nyam'um all by dis time!"

"Shet yo' mout', 'ooman," said a masculine comforter. "Hukkuh him kin eat en' holluh alltwo one time? Yo' chillun ent fuh eat."

"Me lef' my juntlemun een de house," said another woman, with resignation, "Uh 'spec' him done eat."

"Wuh you duh bodduh 'bout loss uh man?" said the mother. "Man easy fuh git tummuch. Me yent duh bodduh 'bout man. Uh kin git anodduh juntlemun ef da' t'ing nyam my'own, but weh uh fuh git mo' chillun?"

"Go'way, gal, ef you kin fuh git anodduh juntlemun, same fashi'n Gawd help you fuh git anodduh chilluh."

After a while the roaring ceased and the clerk, being perilously near suffocation, calmed the fears of the negroes and opened the windows. The trembling darkeys cocked their ears and listened apprehensively, but the shrilling of the Cicada among the pines and the bellowing of the bullfrogs in the distant canals were the only sounds that broke the silence of the night so recently full of terrors. After awhile the door also was unbarred and opened, and a bold man borrowed an axe from the storekeeper and adventured far enough to cut some slabs of lightwood from a familiar stump. The hero added to his popularity by splitting these up and distributing them among the members of the gentler sex, whose escorts lighted torches and convoyed them in a body back to the quarters, where the children and husbands whom they left at home were found intact.

At church on Sunday, the Lewisburg negroes spread among their brethren from the other plantations the news of the coming of the lion, and the "locus pastuh" fervently touched upon the king of beasts. "Puhtec' we, Maussuh Jedus, f'um da' t'ing oonuh call lion. Lead'um, Lawd, to weh de buckruh' cow en' t'ing' duh bite grass so him kin full 'e belly bedout haffuh nyam nigguh, en' ef 'e *yiz* haffuh tek nigguh fuh 'e bittle, do, Lawd, mek'um fuh tek dem sinful nigguh wuh ent wut, en' lef' de Lawd' renointed. Mek'um fuh do wid de good sistuh en' bredduh 'puntop dis plantesshun same lukkuh oonuh mek'um fuh do long Dannil—" "Yaas, Lawd," shouted Monday, the hypocrite, "ef 'e *yiz* fuh eat nigguh, mek'um fuh eat dem nigguh 'puntop'uh Bonny Hall 'cross de ribbuh, en' tek 'e woice out'uh we pinelan'." "Yaas, Lawd!" "Please suh fuh do'um, Lawd!" shouted the fervent brethren and sisters. And stealthily, about two hours after dark that night, while the emotional negroes were alternately laughing, shouting and praying, Monday put his Devil's Fiddle into a sack, slipped into his canoe, and, crossing to the opposite shore of the river, roared frightfully along the Bonny Hall water line, terrifying the negroes on that plantation and filling the Lewisburg darkeys with thankfulness that their prayers had been answered.

Another week passed. Monday, playing with them as a cat plays with a mouse, kept quiet, until by Saturday night, no news having come of any damage at Bonny Hall, the Lewisburg negroes hoped that the lion had been captured by "de sukkus buckruh," or had left the neighborhood, and soon after nightfall, half the plantation gathered at the store.

About nine o'clock, when the store was jammed with briskly trading negroes, from afar in the woods came the ominous roar of the handmade lion. It was distant, and the negroes, while badly frightened, stood their ground to await developments, but a few minutes later the awful sound came again from a nearer point, and by the time the roaring had come within a quarter of a mile of the place, the negroes were panic-stricken, and most of them hurried from the store and ran to the quarters, where they bolted themselves in, to pass a night in fear and trembling, for at intervals until past midnight, their ears carried terror to their souls. On Sunday, Monday, wearing the sanctimonious expression of a cat that has just swallowed the canary, moved among them, listening with sympathetic ears to the tales of perilous adventures that some of them had experienced. "Bredduh W'ite," said a church sister, "lemme tell you. Las' night uh gone to Sistuh Bulow' house attuh daa'k. Uh did'n' bin to de sto', 'cause las' week de buckruh credik me, en' uh 'f'aid 'e gwine ax'me fuh pay'um wuh uh owe'um, en' uh gi' Sistuh Bulow de money fuh buy me rashi'n' en' t'ing', en' uh seddown een 'e yaa'd fuh wait 'tell 'e come back. Him house ent dey een nigguhhouse yaa'd, 'e stan' to 'eself 'pun de aige uh de pinelan'. Bumby uh yeddy da' t'ing' woice. W'en uh yeddy'um fus', 'e bin fudduh, en' uh t'awt 'e bin Jackass duh holluh, but w'en 'e git close, uh ruckuhnize 'e woice, en' uh know 'e duh lion. Uh *dat* 'f'aid, uh cyan' talk. Uh trimble sukkuh mule' shouldduh duh shake off cowfly. W'en da' t'ing come t'ru de bush en' look 'puntop me, me two eye' pop' out me head! 'E stan' high mo'nuh Mass Clinch' mule. 'E yeye shine lukkuh dem fiah buckruh does mek 'puntop'uh Jackstan' duh pinelan' duh summuhtime fuh keep off muskittuh! W'en 'e op'n 'e jaw, 'e t'roat red lukkuh beef haslett! 'E mout' full'up wid teet' sukkuh harruh, en' blood duh drip out 'e jaw sukkuh water drap outah nigguh mout' w'en 'e look 'puntop'uh watuh-milyun! W'en uh shum stan' so, uh drap' 'puntop me two knee' en' uh baig' me Jedus fuh sabe me! Uh dat 'f'aid, uh shet me yeye', en' w'en uh done pray en' op'n'um 'gen, de t'ing gone!" And so on, each tale of dreadful experience told by one negro, being over-matched by the next, who, if one gave "free rein" to her imagination, would be sure to strip the bridle off hers and throw it away. "Meself shum," related a 20th Century Munchausen in petticoats. "Uh bin down de road uh piece 'bout two hour' attuh daa'k fuh try fuh ketch da' gal, 'cause uh kinduh 'spishun my juntlemun, en' uh binnuh folluh 'e track fuh ketch'um, but uh nebbuh ketch'um yet, but uh gwine fuh ketch'um, 'cause uh got me yeye 'puntop da' gal f'um W'ite Hall wuh tote dem bottle en' t'ing onduhneet' 'e frock fuh sell rum to all dese man eb'ry

Satt'd'y night, en' mek'um fuh t'row 'way dem money 'stead'uh g'em to dem wife en' t'ing', en' uh bin swif' 'pun da' gal track, 'cause yistiddy w'en my juntlemun git pay'off fuh 'e wu'k, 'e come en' pit half 'e money een me han' befo' uh kin ax'um fuhr'um, en' da' t'ing mek me fuh know him duh fool me. Uh look 'puntop'um en' uh shum duh grin. Sattifaction duh run roun' da' nigguh mout' same lukkuh puppy run roun' de yaa'd attuh 'e own tail! Uh know man tummuch, en' w'en 'e stan' so, 'e yent fuh trus'! Eb'ry time man gi' money to 'e lawfully lady, 'e h'aa't duh cry, en' w'en him look lukkuh 'e glad fuh g'em, 'e face duh lie, 'e try fuh kibbuh up 'e h'aa't, en' 'e done mek'up 'e min' fuh fool'um, but me! uh got uh ecknowledge fuh look t'ru 'e face, en' w'en uh look 'puntop 'e h'aa't, 'e stan' crookety ez uh cowpaat'! Da' gal kin fool some dem todduh 'ooman, but 'e yent fuh fool me! Him hab two petticoat', one mek out'uh homespun clawt', lukkuh we'own, en' todduh one hab skollup', lúkkuh buckruh lady' own. W'en him hab on de clawt' petticoat, none de man nebbuh bodduhr'um, but w'en 'e walk t'ru Lewisbu'g nigguhhouse yaa'd wid da' skollup' petticoat staa'ch' *stiff,* en' 'e frock hice up high fuh show'um, en' dem man look 'puntop de skollup en' yeddy de staa'ch duh talk *'she, she, she'* w'en 'e walk, dem *know* suh 'e got rum fuh sell—dat duh 'e sign—dem t'roat' biggin fuh dry, en' dem eb'ry Gawd' one pick uh chance fuh folluhr'um, but dem todduh 'ooman, dem t'ink suh man lub da' skollup' t'ing 'cause 'e stylish, en' dem study 'bout git skollup' petticoat demself fuh mek man fuh folluhr'um, but duh nutt'n' but de pyo' rum dem man dey attuh. Dem fuh folluh da' gal ef 'e petticoat mek out'uh grano sack!

"W'en uh did'n' ketch de gal, uh staa't' fuh gone home, en' uh look 'way off t'ru de pinelan' en' uh see two t'ing duh shine sukkuh injine headlight! Uh look 'gen, 'e come close, en' uh see 'e duh annimel eye! Bumby 'e op'n' 'e mout' fuh holluh. Spaa'k' duh come outuhr'um en' 'e woice roll 'tell de groun' shake. Uh nebbuh hab no time fuh pray. W'en uh see da' fiah come out 'e mout', uh tell'um, 'so long, bubbuh, *uh gone!'* en' uh hice me 'coat en' uh tek me two foot een me han' en' uh nebbuh study 'bout no road. Uh gone slam t'ru de bush! Briah 'cratch' me, uh dunkyuh. Jackwine' ketch' me foot en' obuht'row me, uh jump up, uh gone 'gen! One harricane tree bin 'cross de paat', uh bus' t'ru'um sukkuh fiah gone t'ru broom grass fiel'. Nutt'n' nebbuh stop me, 'cause, bubbuh, *uh run!* W'en uh git een de big road, uh hog binnuh leddown fuh tek 'e res'. W'en 'e yeddy me foot duh beat groun', 'e jump up fuh run, but uh obuhtek'um dat swif', me foot kick'um ez uh gwine, en' uh yeddy'um holluh behin' me sukkuh tarrier duh graff'um by 'e yez! Briah tayre off me frock 'tell, time uh git nigguhhouse yaa'd, uh yent hab nutt'n' lef' but me shimmy, en' w'en dem nigguh look 'puntop me dem t'ink uh sperrit come out de 'ood. Uh run een me house, uh shet me do', en' uh nebbuh come out 'gen 'tell sunhigh!"

Monday inclined his ear and listened to the negroes, but he showed them no mercy, and before the end of the third week his lion became so bold that a roar came even in broad daylight from among the reeds along the river bank, frightening the laborers out of the fields and even prompting a neighboring planter to order his foreman to lock up the mules for safety when he saw the hands flying in terror from the rice-fields! At last, to avoid industrial paralysis, the owner of the plantation, discovering Monday's plot, suppressed the powder keg lion. And the master saved his people, the Halcyon nested again on the waves of the Combahee, bringing peaceful days and peaceful ways to the Lewisburg plantation, with nothing more exciting than the quest of "da' skollup' petticoat," but—"that's another story."

Elliott White Springs (1896–1959)

Elliott White Springs was born on July 31, 1896, in Lancaster, South Carolina, and educated in England, at Princeton and at the Oxford School of Military Aeronautics. Aviation was one of the chief interests in his life, and after fifteen years' service he retired from the Air Force in 1942 as a lieutenant colonel. Also a successful businessman, he served as president of Springs Cotton Mills until his death. His books include *War Birds: The Diary of an Unknown Aviator* (1926), *Nocturne Militaire* (1927), *Above the Bright Blue Sky* (1928), *Leave Me with a Smile* (1928), *Contact* (1930), *In the Cool of the Evening* (1930), *The Rise and Fall of Carol Banks* (1931), and *Clothes Make the Man* (1949).

From *War Birds: Diary of an Unknown Aviator*

No date

War is a horrible thing, a grotesque comedy. And it is so useless.
This war won't prove anything. All we'll do when we win is to sub-
stitute one sort of Dictator for another. In the meantime we have destroyed our best resources. Human life, the most precious thing in the
world, has become the cheapest. After we've won this war by drowning
the Hun in our own blood, in five years' time the sentimental fools at
home will be taking up a collection for these same Huns that are killing
us now and our fool politicians will be cooking up another good war.
Why shouldn't they? They have to keep the public stirred up to keep
their jobs and they don't have to fight and they can get soft berths for
their sons and their friends' sons. To me the most contemptible cur in
the world is the man who lets political influence be used to keep him
away from the front. For he lets another man die in his place.

The worst thing about this war is that it takes the best. If it lasts long
enough the world will be populated by cowards and weaklings and their
children. And the whole thing is so useless, so unnecessary, so terrible!
Even those that live thru it will never be fit for anything else. Look at
what the Civil War did for the South. It wasn't the defeat that wrecked
us. It was the loss of half our manhood and the demoralization of the
other half. After the war the survivors scattered to the four corners of
the earth; they roamed the West; they fought the battles of foreign
nations; they became freebooters, politicians, prospectors, gamblers,
and those who got over it, good citizens. My great-uncle was a captain
in the Confederate Army and served thruout the war. He became a
banker, a merchant, a farmer and a good citizen, but he was always a
little different from other men and now I know where the difference lay.
At the age of seventy he hadn't gotten over those four years of misery
and spiritual damnation. My father used to explain to me that he wasn't
himself. But he was himself, that was just the trouble with him. The
rest were just out of step. My father used to always warn me about

Elliott White Springs, from *War Birds: Diary of an Unknown Aviator* (New
York: Grosset & Dunlap, 1926), pp. 268–77. Copyright 1926 by George H.
Doran Company. Copyright 1926 by Liberty Weekly, Inc. Reprinted by per-
mission of Springs Mills, Inc.

licker by telling me that uncle learned to drink in the army and it finally killed him. I always used to think myself that as long as it took forty years to do it, he shouldn't speak disrespectfully of uncle's little weakness. And as the old gentleman picked up stomach trouble from bad food in the campaign of '62, I always had a hunch that perhaps the licker had an unfair advantage of him.

The devastation of the country is too horrible to describe. It looks from the air as if the gods had made a gigantic steam roller, forty miles wide, and run it from the coast to Switzerland, leaving its spike holes behind as it went.

I'm sick. At night when the colonel calls up to give us our orders, my ears are afire until I hear what we are to do the next morning. Then I can't sleep for thinking about it all night. And while I'm waiting around all day for the afternoon patrol, I think I am going crazy. I keep watching the clock and figuring how long I have to live. Then I go out to test out my engine and guns and walk around and have a drink and try to write a little and try not to think. And I move my arms and legs around and think that perhaps to-morrow I won't be able to. Sometimes I think I am getting the same disease that Springs has when I get sick at my stomach. He always flies with a bottle of milk of magnesia in one pocket and a flask of gin in the other. If one doesn't help him he tries the other. It gives me a dizzy feeling every time I hear of the men that are gone. And they have gone so fast I can't keep track of them; every time two pilots meet it is only to swap news of who's killed. When a person takes sick, lingers in bed a few days, dies and is buried on the third day, it all seems regular and they pass on into the great beyond in an orderly manner and you accept their departure as an accomplished fact. But when you lunch with a man, talk to him, see him go out and get in his plane in the prime of his youth and the next day some one tells you that he is dead—it just doesn't sink in and you can't believe it. And the oftener it happens the harder it is to believe. I've lost over a hundred friends, so they tell me,—I've seen only seven or eight killed—but to me they aren't dead yet. They are just around the corner, I think, and I'm still expecting to run into them any time. I dream about them at night when I do sleep a little and sometimes I dream that some one is killed who really isn't. Then I don't know who is and who isn't. I saw a man in Boulogne the other day that I had dreamed I saw killed and I thought I was seeing a ghost. I can't realize that any of them are gone. Surely human life is not a candle to be snuffed out. The English have all turned spiritualistic since the war. I used to think that was sort of far fetched but now it's hard for me to believe that a man ever becomes even a ghost. I have sort of a feeling that he stays just as he is and simply jumps behind a cloud or steps thru a mirror. Springs keeps talking about Purgatory and Hades and the Elysian Fields. Well, we sure are close to something.

When I go out to get in my plane my feet are like lead—I am just barely able to drag them after me. But as soon as I take off I am all right again. That is, I feel all right, tho I know I am too reckless. Last week I actually tried to ram a Hun. I was in a tight place and it was the only thing I could do. He didn't have the nerve to stand the gaff and turned and I got him. I poured both guns into him with fiendish glee and stuck to him tho three of them were on my tail. I laughed at them. I ran into an old Harry Tate over the lines the other day where he had no business to be. He waved to me and I waved back to him and we went after a balloon. Imagine it! An R. E. Eight out balloon straffing! I was glad to find some one else as crazy as I was. And yet if I had received orders to do it the night before, I wouldn't have slept a wink and would have chewed up a good pair of boots or gotten drunk. We didn't get the balloon—they pulled it down before we got to it, but it was a lot of fun. That lad deserves the V. C. And he got all the Archie in the world on the way back. So did I, for I stayed with him. He had a high speed of about eighty and was a sitting shot for a good gunner but I don't think he got hit. I didn't.

I only hope I can stick it out and not turn yellow. I've heard of men landing in Germany when they didn't have to. They'd be better off dead because they've got to live with themselves the rest of their lives. I wouldn't mind being shot down; I've got no taste for glory and I'm no more good, but I've got to keep on until I can quit honorably. All I'm fighting for now is my own self-respect.

17 and 148 seem to get a lot of Huns these days. That's one thing about a Camel; you've got to shoot down all the Huns to get home your-self. There's not a chance to run for it. Clay, Springs and Vaughn are all piling up big scores. But their scores won't be anything to those piled up on the American and French fronts. Down there if six of them

jump on one Hun and get him, all six of them get credit for one Hun apiece. On the British front each one of them would get credit for one sixth of a Hun. Of course, what happens up here is that the man who was nearest him and did most of the shooting gets credit for one Hun and the others withdraw their claims. Either that or the C. O. decides who should get credit for it and tears up the other combat reports.

Cal has five or six now and I've got four to my credit.

Springs and Clay have been decorated by the King with the D. F. C. Hamilton and Campbell got it posthumously and Kindley and Vaughn have been put in for it. Cal is going to get it too. Springs tells me that Clay is the finest patrol leader at the front. He's certainly gotten away with some good work from all reports. And on Clerget Camels too! These boys are lucky if they just get back.

I heard unofficially that Clay and Springs are going to get squadrons of their own and that Cal and I are to take their flights. Not if we can help it! Tubby Ralston is down there in Springs's flight now and he reports hell on roller skates.

I hear that Tipton and Curtis and Tillinghast are prisoners. I'm glad they aren't done in for good.

Clay and Springs got separated from their men after a dogfight the other day and decided they'd have a look at Hunland by themselves. They found a formation of ten Hannoveranners and jumped on them. These Hannoveranners have been licking us all so regularly that they wanted to make sure of getting one so they both leapt on the rear plane to make sure of it and one took him from above and the other from below. The rest of them mixed in and they had trouble getting out of it. They kidded each other all day about what rotten shots they were and that afternoon Rainor of 56 flew over to tell them that he was down below and saw their Hannoveranner crash. They thought he was kidding them at first but he gave them the pinpoints and they flew over there again and sure enough there was the crash. Our infantry pushed the next day and they went up in a tender and got up to the crash. They were stripping it when the Hun artillery opened up on them and all they brought back was the black crosses off the fusilage and the machine guns. The pilot's seat looked like a sieve where Clay had got a burst in from below and the cowling was full of holes from above where Springs was decorating the observer. That's some shooting. They said the way the plane hit it looked like one of them must have still been alive as it wasn't smashed up badly. It had one of the new Opal motors in it. That's the hardest plane to fight on the front.

Everybody in 17 and 148 are still 1st. lieutenants. Yet all the regulars and politicians' sons stay at home and get their promotions automatically.

I heard that Ed Cronin was killed on D. H. Fours down South. He was sent out late in the afternoon and had to land in the dark when he came back and cracked up. Jake Stanley was shot down on Bristols and is in a German hospital. Anderson, Roberts, Fred Shoemaker, Wells, Leyson and Bill Mooney are all missing. Touchstone is a prisoner of war and wounded and so is Clayton Knight with a bullet in his leg. Knight got into a fight with a bunch of Fokkers and they shot his machine all to pieces. He was flying a D. H. Nine and his observer was wounded early in the fight so all he had was his front gun. They thought he went down in flames but got a postcard from him later that he was alive. Frank Sidler has been killed and so has Ritter and Perkins and Suiter and Tommy Evans and Earl Adams.

I saw Springs the other day in Boulogne. He said his girl at home sent him a pair of these Ninette and Rintintin luck charms. Since then he's lost five men, been shot down twice himself, lost all his money at blackjack and only gotten one Hun. He says he judges from that that she is unfaithful to him. So he has discarded them and says he is looking for a new charm and that the best one is a garter taken from the left leg of a virgin in the dark of the moon. I know they are lucky but I'd be afraid to risk one. Something might happen to her and then you'd be killed sure. A stocking to tie over my nose and a Columbian half dollar and that last sixpence and a piece of my first crash seem to take care of me all right, tho I am not superstitious.

EDITOR'S NOTE

Here the diary ends due to the death of its author in aerial combat. He was shot down by a German plane twenty miles behind the German lines. He was given a decent burial by the Germans and his grave was later found by the Red Cross.

John Bennett (1865–1956)

Born at Chillicothe, Ohio, on May 17, 1865, John Bennett was educated in the public schools in Chillicothe and at the Art Students' League in New York City, working as a newspaper reporter in Ohio and editing the *Chillicothe Daily News* from 1895 to 1900. Moving to Charleston in 1900, he became active in the Poetry Society of South Carolina. His publications include *Master Skylark* (1897), *Barnaby Lee* (1902), *Treasure of Peyre Galliard* (1906), *Madame Margot* (1921), *The Pigtail of Ah Lee Ben Loo* (1928), and *The Doctor to the Dead* (1946). He died in Charleston on December 28, 1956, and is buried in Magnolia Cemetery.

The Thirsty Dead

Before Trumbo Street ran through the old Gardiner property from Trapman Street west, the dead-end roadway was known as Columbus Trumbo's Court. At the corner stood the building afterward known as the Trapman Street Hospital. This was not Dr. Ogier's hospital for colored folk in Wilson Street, where the Methodist church is now, but Dr. Chisolm's, afterward a soldiers' hospital during the Confederate War. It stood on the southwest corner of Trapman Street and Trumbo's Court, halfway between Broad and Queen Streets.

It was a long, low, wooden building, quite unbeautiful. Its north wall abutted on the pavement in Trumbo's Court, so that a girl could chat with a friend in the street from the lower floor windows. There were piazzas along the south side of the house, low built, with boxed wooden columns painted white. The house itself was painted a dull slate blue or leaden gray, one cannot be sure just which; but it makes no difference. When the tenants in Trumbo's Court looked out of their windows at night the hospital building was just the color of fog, only a little more solid. There were eighteen rooms in the building; and under them a basement for storage. It was into the basement they carried the dead, and set them in rows on stretchers.

The old house is gone now; a cyclone wrecked its roof, and an earthquake shook the chimneys down. A tenement took the place where the hospital had stood; and the people living in the tenement did not like to mention the subject.

Nothing ever grew where the hospital stood; not a green leaf or blade of grass; not even vetch grew there, though vetch will grow almost anywhere.

It was a private hospital until after the savage fight at Secessionville. Many young men from the town died there, or were brought back to town covered with wounds. The hospital was a shambles; for the young men were shot, cut with sabers, stabbed, torn and run through by bayo-

John Bennett, "Tales from the Trapman Street Hospital," in *The Doctor to the Dead* (New York: Rinehart & Co., 1946), pp. 123–35. Copyright 1943, 1946 by John Bennett. Reprinted by permission of Susan Adger Bennett and Russell & Volkening, Inc.

nets, their faces were beaten in by gun butts, and their lips were often
already black with mortification; all were white from loss of blood.
There was time neither for mercy nor delay in that place: there were
sixteen rooms full.

For lack of proper surgical instruments wounds were probed with
straws snapped from the brooms which swept the hospital floors; there
were no anodynes to ease their agony. There was no laudanum, no morphine, no opiates of any sort; there was not even whisky: the blockade
had prevented their entry. A little to ease the festering wounds the sur-
geons gathered the jelly bags of the ladies of the town, filled them with
moss or cotton, soaked them in cool well water, and hung them so that
the slow drip from their evaporating damp might fall upon the in-
flamed wounds and cool them if but a trifle. But the weather was intensely hot; gangrene is swift; the wounded died like flies. Death stood
waiting in the piazza.

Afterward the house was sold. Nobody would move into it, until,
long after, a poor colored washerwoman, attracted by the low rent,
moved into a room on the upper floor with her lazy bitch of a daughter.
There was nobody else lodged in the house but a colored harlot or two,
who also had rooms on the upper floor.

At the end of the lower piazza a flight of wooden steps went down
to the ground; and a few yards from the steps was an old well from
which the household drew its supply of water. It was an old-time well,
such as one may still find in old yards about the city, closed by a shield-
shaped cast-iron lid, lifted by an iron ring. The lid was too heavy for a
dead man to lift. So that the drinks of the dead were long between and
their thirst very great.

One close, hot night in midsummer, the upper rooms were full of
choking heat and steam. The women were trying to finish a two weeks'
wash in one, a wash already overdue. They were behind with the rent,
also, and were working hard to be done. Thirsty with the heat, the
steam and the toil, the old woman said to her daughter, "Go fetch a
bucket of water from the well, that we all may drink." The daughter, a
perverse, bitchy girl, said "No; I won't carry water for harlots or horses
. . . you may go get it yourself." So the woman herself took the bucket,

and went down alone through the dark house and along the piazza to the well.

As she lifted the heavy iron lid and the cold, stagnant smell of the water puffed up into her face, something behind her heaved a long sigh. Startled, she looked behind her; but there was nobody. She let the bucket down into the well, gave a jerk, let it fill, drew it up brimming full, and started back to the house.

As she came to the piazza steps and lifted her arm before her, so that, by lifting the bucket, the water might not be spilled by the bucket striking the steps, something she could not see took the bucket out of her hand. The starlight was bright in the open, bright enough for her to have seen anyone there. She saw nothing. But something took the bucket out of her hand.

She saw it go up the steps, one, two, three . . . and then, as she stared dumfounded, she saw it go along the piazza, lifting, tipping, and swinging along in scallops through the air, where was nothing but the empty wind, while she stood gasping at the piazza steps.

At the peak of each long scallop, the bucket paused, stood still, tipped sidewise; and then went swinging on again in swooping scallops. After each pause she heard, there in the empty piazza, long-drawn breaths and deep, contented sighs, such as thirsty men heave when, after long hours of waiting, their thirst at last has been quenched. All the while not one drop of water was spilled from the bucket's rim.

Then the bucket came back, swinging, scalloping, rising and tipping, down the outer side of the piazza, turned itself in the air, with never a visible hand to hold it, and offered itself, handle-to, for her taking.

Knowing that the dead had taken it out of her hand to quench their thirst, she durst not touch the handle; but cried out, "Oh, Jesus! No. Take the bucket away!"

The women upstairs heard her cry out, and hurried down to see what had befallen. They found her crouched against the piazza steps on her knees; and, beside her, on the steps, the bucket, still wet, but without a drop of water in it.

The woman who had borne the bucket and drawn the water was taken by a long trembling which lasted three days.

If ever a woman told the truth, this is true; I was there, and saw it. I was the perverse bitch of a daughter. And the man from whom we rented those rooms was Henry Gardiner whom everybody knows.

As told by Mary Simmons, cook and washerwoman

There were many odd things about the old hospital known to folk living in Trapman Street, particularly a woman called "Dirty Dolly," and the baker's wife who owned the house but refused to live in it. Those who lived in the building were chary of information, and answered curtly and evasively when they answered at all. They admitted sulkily that sometimes at twilight the piazzas were filled by a sound of men's voices and the tread of heavy feet going up and down, and sometimes the sound of laughter when nobody was there. But Mary Simmons told me the tale of

The Little Harlot and Her Broken Pitcher

She was not a good girl. She lived in the old hospital barracks at the corner of Trumbo's Court. Her business was known to all. She was not a bad girl. She was just a whore by the name of Daphne Trenholm . . . men called her "The Marsh Hen" . . . she was just one of those women who get swept behind the door.

One night, after all the lights in the barracks were out and the town asleep, having no patron and being out of luck, her rent to pay and no money, she got up from her bed and walked the floor, to and fro, to and fro, much troubled in her mind. It being a very hot summer night and sleepless, she grew thirsty, and went down to the yard cistern to get a pitcher of water. When she got to the cistern she could not fill her pitcher full because its mouth was broken, and the water spilled over the broken rim, ran down her nightdress, and wet her bare feet. "Even my pitcher is broken!" she said.

She sat down again in her room, tired, anxious and overwrought. As she sat there, troubling, she heard, coming up Trapman Street, the sound of scuffling feet and a pitiful voice, crying over and over: "Just one grain, for Christ's sake! Only one grain!" Startled out of her own trouble, she listened to the footsteps and the voice coming up Trapman Street. The footfalls came nearer and nearer. They stopped at the barrack-yard gate. She heard the latch click and the hinges creak. The shuffling feet and pitiful voice came on through the yard to the piazza steps, and up the steps into the piazza. Then there were no more footfalls; only the pitiful voice, crying over and over: "Just one grain, for Christ's sake! Only one grain!"

Curious to know what caused this pitiful outcry, she went out to the piazza. Of the men whose footfalls she had heard there was nothing to be seen. But in the piazza stood a stretcher; and on the stretcher at full length lay a young man, scarcely more than a boy of twenty, his eyes staring up out of cruelly darkened hollows. He was half covered by a greatcoat; his shirt was torn and stained red above his heart, and just over his heart his breast was pierced through and through; and as his breast rose and fell the wound whispered and bubbled.

She saw at once that the young fellow was already as good as dead; no man could live with a wound like that . . . his face was already ghastly white and bloodless; but his chin was firmly set, and between his clenched teeth he continued to moan: "Just one grain, for Christ's sake! Only one grain!"

She was a careless, light-minded girl; and what to do she did not know; she had not one grain of morphine to her name. She shrank back, frightened and trembling, for his face was like that of a dead man. But he, speaking clearly, though with a queer voice, like that of someone far off, said: "Don't be afraid. I come not for evil; but for unbearable thirst. I am dying of thirst that is greater than my wounds. Give me a drink of water, for Christ's sake!"

She ran for her pitcher, and kneeling beside the stretcher, lifted his head to rest upon her breast where so many heads had carelessly rested, and put the pitcher to his lip.

But its mouth was broken and the lip gone. She had to hold it carefully sidewise not to spill water upon him. He drank greedily, with the choked, gurgling sound so often heard in a dying man's throat. Then, turning his eyes up to her face, he said, "Thank you!" "It was nothing," she said . . . and gasped . . . for there was nothing there in the piazza but herself, on her knees, pouring water out of a broken pitcher which there was no one there to drink.

Trembling with fear, she ran to her room, shut and barred the door, and spent the rest of the night crying and praying beside her bed.

When morning came she rose and looked around. Everything in the room was just as it had been. But the water pitcher was whole, and the broken lip was silver.

Some have pardon by word; some have pardon by deed; some have pardon vouchsafed from Heaven. So Daphne, the harlot, though her sins had been many and her faults great, knew by the lip on her broken pitcher that her transgressions had been forgiven.

But how she paid her room rent I have no means of knowing.

The Army of the Dead

At the time of the Confederate War, Trumbo's Court was a dead-end street. But Trapman ran from Broad to Queen; and as that section of the city was beyond the range of the Federal siege guns, a constant traffic, both by night and by day, flowed up and down the little street.

After the war was over the traffic left the little street, and the dust and sand lay deep and still till midnight.

Then, at the stroke of twelve, the quiet street awoke to the sound of wheels rolling by . . . and the sound of wheels passing by in the night is a curious and intriguing sound.

A moment before, except for the rustle of the palmettos and the light pattering of the dew upon the roof, there was no sound whatever. But on the twelfth stroke everywhere came the sound of heavily burdened wheels far too heavy for common wagon wheels; not even the night-soil wagon wheels could bring such a rumble from the earth, like far-off thunder out at sea; and, every now and then, the sonorous sound of metal heavily smitten.

Every now and then the iron lid of the manhole of the sewer at the corner lifted with the force of the air beneath it compressed by the rising tide . . . the lid lifted . . . pff-ff-ff! a gust of air blew out like the blast from a gun, and with a loud clang of metal the manhole lid fell back again upon its iron ring.

But the sound in the street was another sound, utterly different . . . a rumble and a clang, heavy and deep. Every night the laundress who lodged on the upper floor was wakened by that sound. Night after night, weary after the hard day, her sleep was broken. At last, spent by broken rest, she said to her husband: "Can't you do something to stop that noise in the night? It breaks my sleep, and I get no rest."

Her husband answered angrily: "Jesus! Woman, don't ask me that. It is no business of mine, or yours. Don't speak of it."

"Why should I not speak of it?"

"Because it is their affair and God's. I advise you to let it alone."

So she did, for a time. But still it troubled her . . . who and what was it went by in the night, night after night, endlessly faring, whither and whence? It troubled her the more since she was quite often alone.

One night when, at the stroke of twelve, the noise began, she got up from the bed and went to the window to open the shutter and look out into the street. She had taken but two steps when her husband overtook her, and snatched her from the window, angry and trembling: "Use what little sense God gave you, woman," he said, "and let what you do not know alone!"

So that night also she let it alone. But next day she said to the woman at the next tub: "What is it goes by in the night?"

The woman looked at her gravely; then said: "I take it that your heart is sincere in asking; and that you truly desire to know. For that reason, and that reason only, I speak: it is the Army of the Dead going by."

"Where on earth are they going?"

"To reinforce Lee in Virginia. They are the dead who died in the hospital here before the war came to an end.

"At the end of the war came peace for the living. But no one could sign a peace for the dead. So they, not knowing that peace has come, rise from their graves at midnight and march off, forever, until Judgment Day, to reinforce Lee in Virginia.

"While all still went well for the South, they slept and rested from battle. But when the armies of the North came crowding down and the army of the South began to bend, they who lay dead in the hospital yard pushed off their coffin lids, rose from their graves, and marched to strengthen the bending battle line.

"They do not know that peace has come, and so, until the last trump sounds, they rise and march to Virginia forever."

That was what the woman at the next tub said.

I am not bold. Nor have I looked out my window to see that army marching by; only fools meddle with things like that. But a woman in Trumbo's Court looked out one night when the Army of the Dead went by. All she saw at first was the gray fog drifting in from the river, and the mist lying cold and low in the hollow street among the gray tenements, the trees overhead only bunches of shadow in the fog, and the shredded fog drifting and trailing like smoke over the fence tops . . . nothing more. There was no sound anywhere but the rustle of the palmettos and the dripping of the dew on the roof.

But at the stroke of twelve came the sound of heavy wheels rolling, and a smell in the fog of horses and wet leather. The sound was a rumble heavy and deep: there is no other sound like it . . . it is the sound of cannon rolling along uneven ground.

She could hear the horses grunt as they heaved their burden through the heavy sand and over the obstructing roots of the trees; she could hear the horses panting; and the fog grew thick with the hot steam rising from their lathered flanks . . . and with the panting of the horses there was a sound of rough human voices distinctly audible. She could hear the saddle leathers squeak and the trace chains rattle, and the crack of the drivers' whips.

For hours the rumble and the rattle kept on, with the stamping of the horses, the shouts of the teamsters, the chink of metal bits, and the jingle of chains. Team after team came snorting by, the horses straining against the breast leathers, tugging at their rumbling burden, the gray steam rising like fog from their flanks.

And, behind the sound of horses and cannon, and through it, the tramp of marching feet . . . rr-r-r-r-r-rup, rr-r-r-r-r-rup, rr-r-r-r-r-rup!

Hosts of horsemen went riding by, with flags and banners trailing like fog; and rank after rank of foot soldiers in gray, their long, uncut hair and beards dripping with the gathered mist.

All night they marched, horse, foot, wagons, ambulances, cannon . . . and at the last a belated wagon driving at a gallop to overtake the rest, whips crick-cracking and horses snorting for wind.

Then, far away, and thin, and faint, somewhere beyond Gadsden's Green, shrill, but muffled by the fog, came the notes of a bugle blowing . . . then a cock crew . . . and all suddenly was still.

Dazed and bewildered she went back to her bed. When she woke in the morning one arm was paralyzed, so that she never again could do a good day's wash.

That is the legend of the Army of the Dead. Their names were not written in the book of peace. They ride as they rode, unrested ghosts, through the gray mist, with banners as gray as the gray sea fog.

They ride as they rode, and stride as they strode, with the tireless swing of veteran soldiery. Through the night they pass like the wind through a bystreet, marching to reinforce Lee in Virginia until the Judgment Day.

These were men who were hard to stop, who would not stay dead when slain, still hoping to wring desperate victory from the jaws of defeat. An unnumbered host, rising like the mist from their scattered graves to the sound of far-off trumpets calling, the muffled beat of ghostly drums setting their step, the long, distance-destroying step of veteran soldiers. Horse, foot and artillery, with sabers and carbines clattering, with muskets over their thin shoulders, and bayonets slapping their thighs, clad in coats as gray as the mist of the night. Death clapped them into medlied graves, after their victories and defeats; their bloody battles and weary marches unfinished behind them, and all unfinished before, they still march to reinforce Lee in Virginia.

The Army of the Dead.

As told by Mary Simmons

Josephine Pinckney (1895–1957)

One of the founders of the Poetry Society of South Carolina, Josephine Lyons Scott Pinckney was born in Charleston on January 25, 1895, and studied at Ashley Hall, the College of Charleston, Columbia University, and Radcliffe College. Her volume of poetry, *Sea-drinking Cities,* was published in 1927. She also wrote four novels: *Hilton Head* (1941), *Three O'Clock Dinner* (1945), *Great Mischief* (1948), and *My Son and Foe* (1952). She died on October 4, 1957.

Sea-drinking Cities

Sea-drinking cities have a moon-struck air;
Houses are topped with look-outs; as a dog
Looks up with dumb eyes asking, dormers stare
At stranger-vessels and swart cunning faces.
They are touched with long sleeping in the sea-born moon;
They have heard fabled sails slatting in the dark,
Clearing with no papers, unwritten in any log,
Light as thin leaves before the rough typhoon;
Keels trace a phospher-mark,
To follow to old ocean-drowned green places.

They never lose longing for the never-known,
These ocean-townships moored and hawsered fast,
They welcome ships, salt-jewelled venturers
That up over the curve of the world are blown
With sun-rise in their sails and gold-topped mast;
And in the evening they let them go again
With a twisted lip of pain,
Into the cavernous fog that folds and stirs;
They have not even a faint tenderness
For their own loveliness.

Their loveliness, as of an old tale told . . .
A harbor-goblet with wide-brimming lip
Where morning tumbles in shaken red and gold,
Trinketed and sun-bedizened they sip;
Their tiny tiles all twinkle, fire-bright;
Their strong black people bargain on the docks
In gaudy clothes that catch the beating light . . .
But all betwitched, old cities sit at gaze
Toward the wharves of Mogador . . . Gibraltar,
Where the shawl-selling Arab piles a blaze

Of fiery birds and flowers on Trade's heaped altar.
Sea-drunken sure are these,—
Towns that doze—dream—and never wake at all,
While the soft supple wind slides through the trees,
And the sun sleeps against the yellow wall.

The Misses Poar Drive to Church

Out from the tall plantation gate
Issue the Misses Poar in state.
Neatly darned are their black silk mitts,
And straight each stately sister sits.
Their carriage-dresses, brushed and steamed,
Cover their decent limbs; they seemed
No finer, really, before the War
When money was free in the house of Poar.
The negro coachman in beaver hat,
Slightly nibbled by moth and rat,
Smooths his frock-coat of greenish hue,—
But fitting as trim as when it was new—
With which he stiffens his spine of pride
By tightly buttoning himself inside
To drive in this elegant equipage
A yoke of oxen of doubtful age.
(They've had no horses since sixty-four
When the Yankees stopped at the house of Poar.)

The ladies move to the square front pew,
Their Christian meekness in ample view,
And follow the youthful parson's word
With reverence meet for a legate of God
Up to the moment when he prates
Of the President of the United States;
Then, knowing full well that Heaven can't
Expect them to pray for General Grant,
They bury their noses' patrician hook
In dear Great-grand-papa's prayer-book,
Wherein are found urbane petitions
To guard the Crown against seditions
And rest King Charles the Martyr's soul.
Not that they hold King Charles so dear,
Although their blood is Cavalier,
But it suits their piety, on the whole,
Better to pray for the Restoration
Than the overseer of a patch-work nation.

Street Cries

The dreamer turns.
Clear tones zig-zag like lightning
Through soft black sleep.
Thick walls of sleep are cracking. . . .
From streets immeasurably below
The vendors' voices leap,
The cool tunes flow:
"Turtle-eggs—turtle-eggs!"
Delicious quiet:
The sleeper turns . . .
"Turtle-eggs . . ."
Dreaming of steaming beaches . . .
The warm sand is wet,
Diggers' bodies bow
Clammy with salt and sweat;
Nests are hidden deep,
. . . turtle-eggs . . .
Round, creamy curds.
How good to dig in the fresh morning
While rosy beaches whiten
Quick with the young sea-birds!
Through glassy heat the beach-lines run
Quiver in misty sea and sun,
Gently-rocking sea and sun.

"I got honey,
I got um in de comb!"
June is honey-gold,
Oozing through shutters;
"Honey in de comb—"
An impish whistling tickles
The dreamer's muffled ears:
"I'm a po' boy long ways fum home—"
A clack and a clack of feet,
Words fountain up and fall,
Plash in the stony street;

Slow-dripping music trickles,—
"Honey . . . in . . . comb . . ."

Soft black sleep
Is barred with amber light;
The sleeper sighs . . .
Oh, sweet delight of love
Where is there such delight
As to love blindly—
Shut-eyed as flowers are at night!

A chorus sings,
A negro chorus, stately-moving,
Fruit-piled basket on head,
And perfect balancings,
Paeans to ripe earth harvested.
"Melons . . . musk-melons . . ."
Strophe—curve—return.

Round tones rolling,
Like fruit from horns of plenty,
Spiral down—lie mute,
Trampled by idle strolling
"Water-water-water-melons . . .
Musk . . ."
Oh, such is love—dream-fruit!
On it the sleeper feeds
And loses all content
With daylight things,
Like Proserpine who ate pomegranate seeds
And back to darkness went . . .
And back to darkness went.

Beatrice Ravenel (1870–1956)

Beatrice Witte Ravenel, born in Charleston on August 24, 1870, studied as a special student at Radcliffe College for five years until 1897. She married twice—Francis Gualdo Ravenel of Charleston on November 21, 1900, and, six years after his death in 1920, S. Priouleau Ravenel. Mrs. Ravenel was an active member of the Poetry Society of South Carolina and the winner of one of its major prizes, publishing her one volume of poetry, *The Arrow of Lightning,* in 1926. In August of 1969 the University of North Carolina Press published a reprint of this volume with uncollected poems, edited by Louis D. Rubin. Beatrice Ravenel died in Charleston on March 15, 1956, and lies in Magnolia Cemetery.

Poe's Mother

It's something to be born at sea, as I
Was born. Earth fails to get full clutch on you.
You keep a certain cleanliness of depths—
Soul, self-respect, you call it what you like.
There's evil in the sea, but cleaner evil,
Chasms of swallowing ultramarine, cold, cold,
Where pulsing moons and devil-fish like stars
May eat you, but crystal-blooded, without passion.
The ocean always keeps about your neck
One tentacle, sucks gently at your veins
Until you yield and lapse to him once more.

I love such crazy fancies, early mornings,
When nothing's very real. The babies sleeping
Safe islanded in small worlds of their own;
And two good hours before the wench comes in
With tea (her tea *tastes* surly), and the *Courier;*
The sea-breeze, slitting through the broken shutter,
Magnolias, too far off to sicken one,
Across the balcony where, strung with vines,
The metal twists a lyre! Eddie saw it—
That child sees everything. This is the hour
I love, the unrealest hour of all the day,
When beauty's more than stage-plays, when ill-will
And debts and duns, and even the superbities
Of that damned Beaumont woman (not a chance
Of any decent part with her), and even—
And even David—O God, where is he now?—
Forsake me like a tide that's going out.

My cough itself grows better in this air;
Mild, vivid Charleston April, lax and salty
As gusts from sea-flowers. Lying half-alive
I watch the sky grow saffron, bluish-pink,
Like colored drawings travelers bring from Venice
Or pearl-crimped shells from Caribbean islands.

For these two hours I can forgive the world,
Forgive myself. Why, when my mind needs comfort
Must it flow always to that same old season
Two years ago, as though that promised me
Some unsuspected, some—*foreboding* good—
Good prismed with darkness? *Yes.* We played in Boston
Together. Eddie came. I hardly rested.
Oh, gentles, think that I played Juliet!
Would you believe it? Could you fancy it?

Juliet, the girl whom everybody loves.
Why has the world conspired to clothe its dream
Of utter beauty in a velvet pall,
With pallid velvet tapers, head and feet,
In Capulet's monument? Perhaps to claim
That beauty is real, the flaws are accidents.
Or, it may be, since this world must be damned,
A foredoomed planet (that's what Beaumont tells me),
To stand (I love that) on the defiant thesis
That death itself can be adorable.

Two years ago I never had such thoughts.
It seemed quite natural the world should love us—
Juliet was I and I was Juliet,
Not dead but dreaming, living, to bring forth life.
(If ever there was a love-child it was Eddie.)
We quarreled and we hated but, merciful heaven,
What difference does that make when people love
Each other? Yes, and Juliet too—who knows,
Who knows that she was not a rose in bud
As well?

    Oh, elegant and poetic way
To put the ugliest miracle in life!
Don't let me think of that—that's waiting for me!
Ungainliness and sickness, sickness, anguish,
And David gone, and grinding weariness

Of making both ends meet. Let me get the good
Of these two unreal hours. Let me be quiet.
The only bearable things in life are dreams.

A queer man, that man Beaumont, brittle, white
As chalk without his make-up, with an ear
Cocked over his shoulder, listening, so you'd say,
For that strange slow disease that's killing him.
Always implying, surmising love to me—
Well, heaven knows, he must be sick enough
Of second fiddle to his Olympian missus,
New-lighted, like a goddess from her car,
From Covent Garden. Most, he slinks aside,
A well-kicked dog, to work on plays no playhouse
Will risk. I dropped a friendly word one day.
He smiled. "Don't pity me, my lovely Betsey,
Blood of its martyrs is the seed of art . . .
Has it occurred to you that Something throws
Our moods at us, our churning, troubled backgrounds,
As stage mechanics throw their rays and shadows,
To work, not good to us, but His effects?"
I asked, "Do you mean God?" He laughed this time.
And I: "If trouble's all the gifts it takes
Someday I'll try my hand at plays myself."
"Women write plays? God gave them His first law
Of self-expression, never gave a second:
'Ladies, I beg you'll have the condescension—
Forgive my taste—to increase and multiply!' "
With such a grand Lord Orville kind of bow,
I had to laugh, though I was angry too.

Beaumont, the least attaching sort of man,
Why must he draw me? He takes me from myself?
His bitterness is whole as other's passion
And modulates his love, as wind and water
Enrich each other in a stormy picture.
Women he scorns, they barely save themselves

By being mothers. Once, he said, some poet
Proclaimed the sea the chariot of nature.
Was I, sea-born, meant only for the bringer,
The chariot of children? Will's no care,
All day he's with the young ones of the house,
But this strange other baby—

      They talked of changelings,
Born with old memories. No child should live
The moods—they can't be thoughts—behind his eyes;
Crushed mulberry shadows washed around the lids.
I almost could believe God threw His shadows
Across my skies and worked my cloudy ferment
To shape this child.

      He's born of Juliet's body!

It isn't me he wants, it's only love,
To feel himself alive in someone else.
He holds me off even while he clings to me,
His fingers on my mouth: "Sing, sing—not talk!"
What will become of him? I know, I know
The child's *alone!*

What will become of them? Two helpless children
And one more coming.—I mustn't think of that!
I mustn't cry. I'll wake them. Where's the paper,
The yesterday's, the slattern wench forgot?
Behind the bureau. Can I reach it? There.
Of course there's nothing but the bare announcement
Of our next play. The perfect Charleston manner,
To look with distant, not unfriendly eyes
On those quaint animals, the player-folk,
But scarcely serve them with the gentry's breakfast;
No puffs nor praises, though there have been pleas
That gentlemen who cluster in the wings
Should go, nor discommode the actresses.
Here's what I'm looking for. *"The Winter's Tale."*

(I'm Mopsa). "Mrs. Beaumont's Benefit."
When will that woman go and let me play
More than a maid, a Mog, a mountebank?
Before she came they gave me *Lady Teazle,*
Lydia.

      Oh God, I once was Juliet!

Don't think of that! What else? A hundred boxes
Of Cheese, true Paté-Grasse. And, Lor', I wish
Some friend remembered me! *Lines to a Chimney Sweeper.*
The Lottery for the Presbyterian Church,
To "raise an edifice to the most HIGH."
Some likely negro wenches to be hired.
I wish I had one. I'd dress her to the life
As Beaumont-Roxalana in *The Sultan.*
Oh look! At Mrs. Henry's, Elliot Street,
Brought by the brig *Eliza,* straight from London,
Rosettes and Silver Bandoes, Jaconet,
Gauze, Lawns and Tiffany, and Garden fans
With sticks of ivory, and Brunswick Slippers.
White Brunswick Slippers! Mine are over-run
And both the buckles tarnished. Jaconet,
So sweet for tunics with a Highland ribbon
On little boys. Oh Lord, oh Lord—

               That's me!
I'll cry as hard as that for anything:
My cough, a part, David, my soul's salvation,
Or all the sorrows of this wicked world,
As for a length of gauze! That's Betsey Arnold.
I know how those Aeolean things must feel
They rig on our piazza. Any breath
Will set me off. Oh hush, you idiot fool!
You couldn't tell to save your precious neck
Which one you're crying for. Most like the slippers,
With heels to challenge feathers in your hair
Which is the lightest; so that Beaumont's eyes

May follow you with human moisture in them.
What would it be to love a man like that,
A man who works, who's bitter-true and genuine
As men are only in romantic plays?
As real as unreality.

                    We hate
His wife with perfect and voluptuous hatred . . .
But what's the good? He wouldn't be the end.
I'd hanker after some archangel next,
Riding his fiery charger through the sunset.
All, all my life I've wanted the next highest
To feel myself dragged back—the silver chains
Of seas, or jet-black chains of this vile earth!
How many, many things one mustn't think of!
A ravening horde of thoughts that long to stamp
Above my pitiful drift-fire, put it out—

There now, I've waked him!
                    No, he mustn't cry!
Don't cry, my little, little, darling lamb!
His mother'll wrap him in the counterpane,
The pretty white-and-purple patchwork thing,
And rock him on the balcony. She'll sing
Of cities in the water, just like this,
And flowers that bloom when everyone's asleep;
And he shall watch the steeples, and the point
Of that long heaving island, and the sunrise
That catches every color on the marsh.
She'll make the whole world pretty for him! Yes—
We'll sing—not talk . . . we'll sing . . .

The Alligator

He roars in the swamp.
For two hundred years he has clamored in Spring;
He is fourteen feet long, and his track scars the earth in the night-time,
His voice scars the air.

Oak-boughs have furred their forks, are in velvet;
Jessamine crackle their fire-new sparks;
The grass is full of a nameless wildness of color, of flowers in solution.
The glass-blower birds twist their brittle imaginings over the multi-
  plied colors of water.

But the counterpoint of the Spring—
Exacerbate, resonant,
Raw like beginnings of worlds,
Cry of the mud made flesh, made particular, personal,
Midnight assailing the morning, myopic sound, blinded by sun,—
Roars from the swamp.
A thing in itself,
Not only alive, but the very existence of death would be news to it.
Will—
Will without inflection,
Making us shudder, ashamed of our own triviality—
The bull alligator roars in the swamp.

This is queer country.
One does not walk nor climb for a view;
It comes right up to the porch, like a hound to be patted.
Under our hog-back
The swamp, inchoate creature, fumbles its passage, still nearer;
Puffing a vapor of flowers before it.

This week there are ponds in the woods, vertiginous skies underfoot,
Pondering heaven.
Next week, in the pashing mud of the footpath
Fish may be gasping, baffled in semi-solids.
The negroes will eat them.

This is queer country.
Thick-blooded compulsive sound,
Like scum in the branch, chokes, mantles the morning.

Sangarrah! . . . Sangarrah! . . . Sangarrah! . . .

Two hundred years back—
And the medicine-man of the Yemassee
Sat in the thick of the swamp, on the ridge where the cypresses flung
Their elfin stockade.
Wrinkled his chest as the cast-off skin of the blacksnake,
The hide of his cheeks hung square and ridged as the hide
Of the grown alligator.
A young alligator squirmed on his naked knees
While he muttered its lesson.

That was strong medicine. Over the old man's eyes
    Drooped the holy beloved crest of the swan-plumes;
Otter-skin straps cut under his arms
From the breastplate of conch-shells.
Fawn-trotters fell from his boot-tops; the white beloved mantle
Lined with raw scarlet, hung on the gum-tree, along with the ocelot
    quiver
And locust-wood bow.
He had fasted, drinking the dark button snake-root. He shuddered,
Calling the secret name, the name of the Manneyto,
Y-O-He,
Never known by the people.

On the infant saurian, long-lived, ruled into patterns, his hands
Moved, taking the shape of a sharp-curved arrow;
He spoke, teaching its lesson, calling its name;
"Nanneb-Chunchaba,
Fish-like-a-Mountain,
Remember!

"By the day-sun and the night-sun,
By the new beloved fire of the corn-feast;

By the Arrow of Lightning, that came from the storm,
From the Spirit of Fire to the ancient chief of the Yemassee—
Totem of Yemassee!
Let our voice be remembered.

"We go from the hunting-grounds of our fathers,
The lands that we took, fighting north through the man-eating
    Westoes,
Fall from our hands.
In the hills of our dead, in the powdering flesh that conceived us,
    Shall the white man plant corn.

"The trails where we fought with the fierce Tuscarora
Will call us in vain;
No pictures of skillful canoemen will green Isundiga paint clear in
    his waters.
We shall be cut from the land as the medicine-man cuts the totem
From the arm of the outcast.

"From the sky they cannot cut our totem!

"My name too shall vanish.
When the drums and the music for three days are silent
And men praise me under the peach-trees,
My over-wise spirit
Shall root itself here, as the oak-tree takes hold.
Who will wait for me? Which of the spirits
That have made of my body a lodge, that have twisted my sinews
As women twist withes for their baskets, will claim habitation,
That have spoken their wisdom
Out of my mouth?
I shall hide from them all, as the war-chiefs
Cover their lives with the tree-tops,
Leaving them safe when they go on the war-path.
I shall sleep in this place.

In the new days,
The days when our voice shall be silent,

Speak for the Yemassee!
Nanneb-Chunchaba, you, little Fish-like-a-Mountain,
Shout through the forest the terrible war-cry of Yemassee!

"Sangarrah! . . . Sangarrah-me! . . . Sangarrah-me!
Shout! I shall hear you!
Sangarrah! . . ."

For two hundred years—
Will, without inflexion—
The bull alligator
Roars from the swamp
In the Spring.

The Yemassee Lands

I

In the Yemassee Lands
Peace-belts unwind in the Spring on the banks of Savannah;
Flowers like wampum weave in the grass
Reiterate beads of pink-orange, of clouded white, of pale, shimmerless
    ochre,
Mile after mile.

II

Round the curve of the river,
Meshed by conniving impatient shoots of the gum tree,
Streamers of silver dart, muffled lapping of paddles.
Always, just round the turning, the stealthy canoe with its naked up-
    standing warrior
Comes . . . for the wild-fowl rise in a hurtling of startled feathers;
Never comes into sight.

III

In the Yemassee Lands
Cypress roots, at the edge of the swamp, roughly fluted, age-wrinkled,
Have budded their rufous knobs like dim and reptilian eyes,
That watch.
Orchids, liquid gold, bend from cylindrical sheaths
Under a phantom moccasined tread.
Gossamer webs, barring the overgrown way through the woods,
Shudder but do not break, betraying the passage
Of footsteps gone by.

IV

In the undulant mist of the sunsets of summer
Slim pines stand with scarlet and quivering outlines—
Initiate boys whose whipped young blood leaps up
Now, the first time, to the war-path.
Shadows of red, shadows of bronze and of copper
Disengage from the wood-growth;

Cowering, melting, lost, reappearing,
One after one, the long, lithe, menacing war-line
Loops through the stems.
Light cups the crouching knees,
Splinters on polished shoulders,
Ravels in towering head-plumes.

V

In the Yemassee Lands
When with blowing of wood-smoke and throbbing of hidden drums
Indian Summer fashions its spell,
Trembling falls on the air.
Wild things flatten themselves in the jeopardy of the shade.
Out of the snarling keen-toothed vines
Berries wink with the cunning obsidian gleam
Of the arrow-head, and deep in the shuddering fern
The rattlesnake coils his pattern of war.
Silence, inimical, lurks in the dark:
Softly on buckskinned soles, halting a step behind,
Something follows and waits . . .
And will not be appeased.

VI

But when Autumn unleashes the winds
And storm treads the lowlands,
Trees, like a panic of horses galloping over the sky-line,
(Charging of chestnut and roan and bay,
Tossing their frantic forelocks)
Flee from the rush
Of invisible hunters.

VII

Stars in the coppery afterglow of the sundown
Hang like strings of teeth on the savage breast of a warrior;
Water-willows trail in the shadowy depths of Savannah,
Draggle like scalps from the war-belt;
And the night-wind sings overhead

Like arrows on deadly sendings,
In the Yemassee Lands.

VIII

Gray through young leaves blows the smoke from the ancient fires;
The thud of the young men's dances troubles the earth.
Shadows from ambushed boughs
Reach with a plucking hand for the hair.
The lightning-set pine far away blazes with hideous cracklings,
Remembering the long black tresses of captive squaws
Tied to the death-pyre.

IX

After two hundred years
Has the forest forgotten?
Always the trees are aware
(Significant, perilous, shaken with whispers of dread and of welcome)
Of the passage of urgent feet.
Violent shoots strain up to the air and the sunshine
Of cut-over land;
Leaves crowd over the barrows of last year's skeleton leaves.
Ever and ever again
The Red Man comes back to his own
In the Yemassee Lands.

The Humming-Bird

The sundial makes no sign
At the point of the August noon.
The sky is of ancient tin,
And the ring of the mountains diffused and unmade
(One always remembers them).
On the twisted dark of the hemlock hedge
Rain, like a line of shivering violin-bows
Hissing together, poised on the last turgescent swell,
Batters the flowers.
Under the trumpet-vine arbor,
Clear, precise as an Audubon print,
> The air is of melted glass,
> Solid, filling interstices
Of leaves that are spaced on the spines
> Like a pattern ground into glass;
> Dead, as though dull red glass were poured into the mouth,
Choking the breath, molding itself into the creases of soft red tissues.

And a humming-bird darts head first,
Splitting the air, keen as a spurt of fire shot from the blowpipe,
Cracking a star of rays; dives like a flash of fire,
Forked tail lancing the air, into the immobile trumpet;
Stands on the air, wings like a triple shadow
Whizzing around him.

Shadows thrown on the midnight streets by a snow-flecked arc-light,
Shadows like sword-play,
Splinters and spines from a thousand dreams
Whizz from his wings!

E. C. L. Adams (1876–1946)

Edward Clarkson Leverett Adams was born in Weston (Richland County) on January 5, 1876. He graduated from Clemson College and the Medical College of South Carolina, and, after service in the Spanish-American War and World War I, practiced medicine in Columbia, dying on November 1, 1946. His interests were wide-ranging: he served as president of the South Carolina Audubon Society, twice ran unsuccessfully for the office of lieutenant governor, and traveled widely through Europe and the Near East. Adams published two collections of folktales of lower Carolina Negroes, *Congaree Sketches* (1927) and *Nigger to Nigger* (1928), and a three-act play, *Potee's Gal* (1929).

Jeff's Funeral Sermon

Reverend:

Oh, Lord, dis man was born in sin, an' he died in Christ.

He sold his lot in Egypt, an' he bought a lot in Paradise.

Watch wey you put your foot-steps,

Don' put 'em in de mud.

Kiver up your tracks,

'En look out for de serpents dat's lyin' all 'bout.

Don' tell your secrets,

Don' put your trus' in mens,

But put your faith in Jesus,

He is de only fren' you got.

Keep your eye upon your foot-steps,

Kiver up your tracks,

Don' walk in de mud.

Old Lucy: (Walking up and down the aisles, waving her hand and hollering at the top of her voice)

Great God, Reverend, hold your holt! I'm gwine to my Jesus! I'll bus' heben wide open wid a trail of light leading to my Lord. Great God, Reverend, hold your holt!

Jeff's Son: (Standing by the coffin, bending up and down and hollering)

Pa, Oh, Pa! Pa gone. I de last one talked wid Pa. Pa tell me, he say tear down dis shed an' buil' a better one. Pa, Oh, Pa! Ain't you hear me? I goin' do what you say.

Feminine voice in back of congregation shrieking:

Jesus, Jesus, gone to Jesus!

Reverend:

Oh, Lord, dis man was born in sin an' he died in Christ.

He sold his lot in Egypt, an' he bought a lot in Paradise.

For he watch where he put he foot-steps.

E. C. L. Adams, "Jeff's Funeral Sermon," "Fragment of a Negro Sermon," "His Day Is Done" in *Congaree Sketches* (Chapel Hill: University of North Carolina Press, 1927), pp. 41–49. Copyright 1927 by The University of North Carolina Press. Reprinted by permission of George C. S. Adams and Stephen B. Adams.

An' he kiver up he tracks.

He place his faith in God, an' he walk aroun' de serpents that was
  lyin' all 'bout.

He put his faith in Jesus, an' he trusted in he God.

He kept his eye upon he foot-steps.

He kivered up he tracks, an' he never put 'em in de mud,

For he put he faith in God.

Oh, Lord, he born in sin, an' he died in Christ,

He sold he lot in Egypt an' he bought a lot in Paradise.

Old Lucy: Great God, Reverend, hold your holt! I'm goin' to bus'
  heben wide open wid a trail of light leadin' to de throne.

Voice: (of sister, in middle of congregation)

> Lead us, Sister Lucy,
> Lead us to de light.
> Lead us from de darkness,
> Lead us from de night.
> Lead us toward de throne,
> Where all is snowy white.

Reverend:

Our deceased brother was born in sin, an' he died in Christ.

He sold his lot in Egypt,

An' he bought a lot in Paradise.

He has placed his foot-steps on de golden stairs,

He never put 'em in de mud.

He has kivered up his tracks.

He's up in heben.

He is on his way to Jesus.

He has throwed away his crown of thorns.

He has shunned the path of serpents.

He steps beneath the silver lights,

He is walking on the golden stairs,

He is climbing to the pearley throne.

He'll set up a foot-stool at the feet of Jesus.

He'll tell to him the secrets

That he didn't tell to mens,

For he is walkin' up the golden stairs,

He is climbing to the pearley throne,
And he will set upon a foot-stool in spotless-white,
Beneath the bright and shining lights of heben.
And he will tell his troubles to his God,
For he was born in sin,
An' he died in Christ.
He sold his lot in Egypt,
An' he bought a lot in Paradise.

Old Lucy:

Great God, Reverend, hold your holt!
I'm goin' to bus heben wide open,
I'm goin' to the throne of Christ.
I'm goin' to make a trail of light.
I'm goin' out of darkness,
I'm goin' to lef' behind de night.
I'm on my way to Jesus,
I'm goin' to my Christ,
I'm goin' to shout my way theu Paradise,
Great God, Reverend, hold your holt!

Fragment of a Negro Sermon

Our Brother is dead,
He rests from he labor
An' he sleeps,—
    (Shrill voice of Sister)   He sleeps, Oh, he sleeps!
Wey de tall pines grow,
    (Another voice)   On the banks of a river.
On the banks of a river.
    (Several voices)   On the banks of a river.

He trouble is done,
He's left dis world
On the wings of glory.
    (Voice)   On the wings of glory!
Out of life's storm,
    (Another voice)   On the wings of glory!
Out of life's darkness,
    (Several voices)   On the wings of glory!
He sails in the light,
Of the Lamb.
Away from his troubles,
Away from the night
    (Congregation)   In the light!
                    In the light!
                    Of the Lamb.

He's gone to the kingdom above,
In the raiment of angels,
    (Voice of Sister)   In the raiment!
                    In the raiment of angels!
To the region above,
An' he sleeps,—
    (Voices chanting throughout congregation)
                    Oh, he sleeps,—
                    Oh, he sleeps!
                    On the banks of a river.
Way de tall pines grow,
On the banks of a river.
    (Congregation)   With the starry crowned angels,

On the banks of a river.

An' the flowers is bloomin'
In the blood of the Lamb.
>   (*Shrill voice of Sister and taken up by congregation chanting and
>   swaying*)   The blood of the Lamb!
>   In the blood of the Lamb!

An' the birds is singin'
Wey de wind blows soft,
As the breath of an angel,
An' he sleeps!
Wey de tall pines grow,
On the banks of a river.
>   (*Voice*)   An' he sleeps!
>   (*Another voice*) Wey de tall pines grow.

An' his sperrit is guarded,
>   (*Several voices*) On the banks of a river.

By a flaming-faced angel.
>   (*Sister*)   Yes, Jesus, of a flaming-faced angel
>   On the banks of a river.

Standing on mountains of rest.
An' he sleeps way de tall pines grow,
On the banks of a river.
>   (*Congregation*)   Oh, he sleeps!
>   He sleeps!

His Day Is Done

His day is done,
His work is over,
And he is riding through the sky,
 (*Shrill voice of Sister*) He is riding, Oh, yes, he's riding, through the
            sky.
To his home in the heavens,
Just above the thunder,
 (*Another voice*) Just above the thunder.
In a golden chariot,
 (*Another voice*) In a chariot,
        In a chariot.
Just above the thunder.
 (*Other voices*) In a golden chariot,
       Just above the thunder.

Jesus waits for him,
At his home in the sky,
There's wings on his chariot,
 (*Sister*) There's wings on his chariot, on his chariot, on
      his chariot,
And a light around his head,
 (*Another voice*) A light, a light, a light around his head
Just above the thunder,
In a golden chariot,
 (*Other voices*) In a golden chariot,
      Just above the thunder.
Just above the thunder.

His life was weary,
But he's done his duty,
And now his road's beyond the clouds,
 (*Several voices*) Beyond the clouds,
      Beyond the clouds,
      Beyond the clouds.
In a golden chariot,
Just above the thunder,
In a golden chariot,
 (*Another voice*) In a golden chariot,
      In a golden chariot.

Just above the thunder.
 (*Congregation*)   Just above the thunder.
He does not dread the lightning,
From sin his soul is free,
 (*Several voices*)   His soul is free, free,
           Oh, his soul is free.
He sweeps across the skies,
With Jesus as his guide,
Just above the thunder,
In a golden chariot,
Just above the thunder.
 (*Congregation*)   Yes, Jesus is his guide.
           Just above the thunder,
           In a golden chariot,
           Just above the thunder.

And he looks with pity upon the world,
 (*Voice*)   Pity, pity, he looks with pity upon the world.
That he has left so far below,
He's flying in a chariot,
 (*Another voice*)   He's flying in a chariot.
And angels is his horses in the sky,
 (*Shrill voice*)   And angels is his horses, in the sky.
Just above the thunder,
 (*Sister*)   Angels is his horses.
In a golden chariot,
Just above the thunder.
 (*Congregation*)   Just above the thunder
           In a chariot,
           A golden chariot,
           Just above the thunder.

William Watts Ball (1868–1952)

Born in Laurens County, December 9, 1868, William Watts Ball graduated from South Carolina College in 1887 and studied at the University of Pennsylvania Law School before being admitted to the South Carolina bar in 1890. In that year, he began a long career in journalism as editor and publisher of the Columbia *Journal.* Ball also served as editor of the Greenville *Daily News* in 1897, of the Charleston *News and Courier* (1909–13), and as managing editor of the Columbia *State* (1913–23), before he became dean of the school of journalism at the University of South Carolina in 1923, though he returned, in 1927, to the *News and Courier* as editor. His book, *The State That Forgot,* was published in 1932. Ball died on October 14, 1952.

A Log-Cabin Law Office

The frame house with stone steps, of nine or ten rooms, built in 1852, was set in a grove of oaks about fifty yards from the Spartanburg road on its northern side, and a wide "front walk" flanked by boxwood hedges and crêpe-myrtles led to the front gate which was a mile and a thousand yards (my "Uncle Larry" measured it) north of the court-house steps in the village of Laurens. The house stands now, remodeled, in the middle of a cotton-mill village. I was born in it, December 9, 1868 (Scott, the Carpetbagger, was governor). I mention my birth because of its relevance, not its importance, for who I was and am it is prudent to write that the reader may have understanding of this book. It is a blend ("pudding" would better phrase it) of history, biography and opinion, and the design is to tell of the South Carolina that I have seen. My father was the lens through which I saw it. The lens is gone, the beauty and the strength of the state are gone, but the heritage of a picture is mine.

Beaufort Watts Ball was my father, thirty-eight when I was born, and Eliza Watts, not yet twenty-one, his second cousin, whom he had married the year before, is my mother. He was a lawyer and landowner, and had been a slave owner and Confederate soldier. Hereafter when I shall speak of the "Colonel" it will mean him. From the time that I remember I trudged over the fields with him, rode on his shoulders when I was tired or on a pillow on the pommel of his saddle to go a-fishing for hornyheads and perch in the creek beyond the "Farley Woods," growing up in his friendship, sharing his thoughts and drawing from him what he knew of things and men and books.

Some of these Wattses of Laurens have long memories, too long it may be sometimes for the convenience of other folk, and my mother, now eighty-four, is of them. Late at night on April 17, 1916, Duncan Clinch Heyward, who had been governor ten years before, and I sat in my library in Columbia (I was then editor of *The State*), as we did once a week; as we talked he said, "Ball, you have a good memory, you should keep a diary," and I said I would. It is voluminous now, and in it are most of the reminiscent anecdotes that are written in this book, which I had from my mother, from her double first cousin, William Augustine Watts, a Confederate veteran of eighty-five years, her youngest brother, James Dunklin Watts, too young to have been a soldier and still young at seventy-eight, and from many others. If these things about my family, who are unpretentious people and not prominent, are trivial, they are nevertheless guide-posts for readers.

The years we lived on the plantation, my father and his mother-in-law, Sarah Speake Watts, planting it in partnership, I was a grand duke. The negroes were free, but "Little Nathe" and "Johnny" and eight or ten other little black boys, some of them much older (Jefferson Davis Watts must have been twelve) were my faithful vassals and retainers. The day that I pulled the big splinter from my foot and Little Nathe carried me on his shoulders to my mother, all my liegemen shouting triumphantly as they ran at his heels, was the great day of my reign. When I was six we left the plantation, and since then I have not been a grand duke.

Most of the prominent men of the state were the Colonel's friends, or acquaintances, and judges, visiting lawyers, ministers, captains, colonels, sometimes a general, came to our house in the village, and so did hundreds of his friends of the county, from out in the country. I knew them all, even if when there were half a dozen for dinner I had to "wait" and eat at the second table. It embittered me toward them, but I soon got over it.

So I grew up among the "Bourbon Democrats," steeped in their opinions and prejudices, which I honor and cherish, in maturer years rejecting nothing. Of these men I shall write, of all kinds and conditions of them, briefly of their origins, in chapters about the settlement of the Colony, and I shall write something of the plantation life and of the political conditions before and after the Confederate War as they were reflected through experiences of my own kindred and friends, saying here that the anecdotes, with occasional concealment of real names, are true.

My political thesis is that the Federal Government, by means of armed forces, placed South Carolina on the operating table in 1867, that in 1868 the Carpetbaggers made an incision in its body, and, by the constitution they adopted, injected into it the deadly and foreign poison of democracy which, after causing the loathsome ulcers of Reconstruction, subtly spread through the blood-stream of the white people and killed for ever in it the inherited corpuscles of political and social health. I begin the book with description of the villages and counties, using Laurens as representative of those of the "Upcountry." The Upcountry, in my meaning, is the whole state except five coastal counties.

The guests gathered for the wedding. They were about one hundred, three-fourths of them merchants, clerks, lawyers, loafers; the others negroes. The party stuffed the eastern room of the one-story log house and the open way between it and the Colonel's law office on the other end, while a dozen on the long piazza in front peered through the windows. The year was 1878, the month June and warm, Hampton was governor, times were easy, cotton was fetching more than it sometimes had (though the price has never been high enough), the "Yankee" garrison had left fourteen months before, and the eight hundred people in the village had settled down to the quiet life at last.

Hence the wedding, a serious wedding to the bride and bridegroom, but to the white guests, from the stores and offices about the square, who invited themselves, it was what one of the town's most respected citizens called a "cockaded affair" to expose Captain John Watts as scared for once. They looked to see him tremble.

John Watts, "Citadel man," handsome, gay fellow, had a hand in most of the village fun, and was in good humor except on rare occasions. Angered, he was dangerous. Two years before he had commanded the village company of "Red Shirts," and before that, in the war he had commanded the "Briars," Company G, Third South Carolina, Kershaw's brigade. A Minié ball had struck him under the cheek-bone and when he had been carried from a bloody field on the North Anna, Surgeon James Evans had cut it out under the other eye. He was not a lawyer or reading man, but General Hampton had appointed him justice of the peace, and "the boys" around town, when they heard that "Mat" Sullivan and Mary Mack wanted to marry, arranged that Mat ask the Captain to perform the ceremony.

Mat, a light brown youth, was in a neat black coat and trousers, and Mary, coal black, of trim figure, a comely girl, was in starched calico and white apron with broad strings. The guests, jamming the room and perspiring, craned their necks as the couple entered and stood before the table—to see the "Judge" faint.

The Judge lifted his right hand, his left resting on the Bible which the witnesses kissed when they were sworn, and there was a great silence.

"Mary," he said, in his steady voice, "do you take this man to be your lawfully wedded husband?"

"Ya-as, sir," Mary lisped, her eyes downcast.

"Matthew, do you take this woman to be your lawfully wedded wife?"

"Yas, sir," said Mat, looking straight at the Captain, who looked on both and said:

> "Under this roof and in this hot weather,
> I join this man and woman together,
> Let none but Him who rules the thunder
> Sever this man and woman asunder————

"Matthew and Mary, I pronounce you man and wife. Amen."

The guests, the merchants, the lawyers, the clerks, the loafers, scattered—the Captain had been too much for them, but they explained that of course the Colonel had got his brother-in-law out of the scrape, for they well knew that the Colonel was up to such things. The Colonel said the credit was "John's," he had not coached him, though he thought that the verse was somewhere in one of the Elizabethan or Queen Anne authors—likely Swift. That afternoon he searched his Swift and Johnson, too, for it, but without success. John Watts had picked it up (he was no student but he was not a forgetter), and forty-seven years later one ran upon it in a life of Swift—the Dean stopped under a tree in a thunder-storm and improvised the rhyme when a damsel and swain, on their way to his parish church to be married, also took refuge under the tree, the bridegroom appealing to him because the damsel's clothes were drenched, and she would go no farther in a wet frock. The Dean said "stormy" where the Captain said "hot."

At the time of the wedding Laurens had about four hundred and fifty white people and three hundred and fifty negroes. Now it is a factory as well as court-house town and has five thousand people. A mid-northwestern county, it lies between the Saluda and the Enoree, shoaly rivers, and the village sprawls over tumbling hills and hollows. Little River (over which one could jump in a dry time but which swells furiously in a rainy spell) runs through it. There were springs and little meadows, cane-brakes and even farms within the village limits, and ground level enough for baseball was hard to find.

One saw South Carolina in counties from the log-cabin law office. A wide roofed hallway open from front to rear separated the two rooms. Behind the house fine corn, sometimes barley, grew in the half-acre lot, and in front looking south one hundred feet to the imposing brick court-house, brown plastered, stretched a long broad piazza. Here the Bradfords were cut in August, four or five at a time, that "Uncle Andy" had hauled in the one-horse wagon from the spring-house where they had reposed three or four days in a stone trough over which the cold water trickled. The judge presiding at court (perhaps General William H. Wallace of Union or Colonel "Josh" Hudson of Bennettsville), a visiting lawyer or two, and half a dozen other gentlemen were there. The Colonel split the long, dark, cloudily striped melons in halves, then cut the halves across—a quarter of a twenty-five or thirty pound melon was a "portion" and the guests sat on split-bottom chairs and ate and talked. These Bradfords were the best melons in town, but Dr. "Billy" Irby at Clinton had Bradfords too.

Or on summer afternoons, when court was not in session, the Colonel and three of his friends, one or two of them factors or traveling salesmen from Charleston, sat about a pine table and played whist according to Hoyle—with the innovations of Pole. They were, all of them, Confederate veterans, lawyers and "traveling men," middle-aged and vigorous.

Through his eyes a boy saw Greenville and Spartanburg, our neighbor counties to the north on the North Carolina border, to the west of them Pickens and Oconee, mountainous like Greenville, and to the east of Spartanburg, York, Lancaster, Chesterfield and Marlboro.

Union, Newberry and Abbeville were our neighbors northeast, southeast and southwest. Beyond Newberry were Richland, Lexington, Orangeburg, Sumter, Kershaw, middle country counties, with pinelands, sand-hills, wide streams and ponds with bream in them. Chester and

Fairfield, hill counties of the Catawba and Wateree, were between Richland and York and Lancaster, beyond them to the east were Darlington and Marion, and they, with Marlboro and Chesterfield, were Peedee counties (their people notoriously flocked together in elections), and farther to the south were Clarendon and Williamsburg.

The "Independent Republic of Horry" lay on the coast next to North Carolina, and its members of the Legislature had to travel two days by boat and rail to Columbia. Then came Georgetown, Charleston, Colleton, Beaufort, southerly along the coast to the Savannah, and above Beaufort, up the Savannah, Hampton, Barnwell, Aiken, Edgefield (which always seemed very close to Laurens), Abbeville and Anderson. Hampton was brand-new; one of the first acts of the Democrats when they came into power in 1877 was to carve it out of the great domain of Beaufort and name it for the General. The counties are forty-six now, but in those days they were only thirty-three.

One saw the counties focused in the court-house towns, and of the towns one thought in pictures of men in them, General Johnson Hagood when Barnwell was mentioned, for example, General Kershaw and General Kennedy if it were Camden, Major Hart of "Hart's Battery" if York, or Captain "Dick" Howard if it were Marion. But General John Bratton, of whom one came to think as the flawless man and soldier, did not live in Winnsboro, he was a countryman and farmer (in the Upcountry the word "planter" was used sparingly) of Fairfield.

Of Charleston one did not think as a county at all. Charleston was the "city" where the "grand lodge" met, where one could have fresh oysters sold by negro women who carried them in pails on their heads and uttered cries that no one understood, and where was the "ocean" which the boy was told stretched thousands of miles but which in his mind he compared with Badgett's mill-pond.

Columbia was a place where Governor Hampton lived, where the "College" was to which one of course would go some day and be "freshed," which one would not greatly mind if one did not whimper or make an uproar about it. It was also the place where the Legislature and the supreme court met, and the state Democratic conventions, which were more important. That it was in a county named Richland, one learned later at school. In most of the counties the court-house towns have the same names, but in North Carolina many of them have been misplaced; for instance, Rockingham ought not to be in Richmond but in Rockingham, and how Albemarle got out of Albemarle into Stanley remains a mystery.

One first suspected that the people of the coast counties were not quite like "our people" when Jim Irby, the colored barber, brought his ten-year-old orphan nephew, Will Bowman, from one of them and the negroes in Laurens as well as the white people could not easily make out his talk—he talked "Gullah." Anyway, Will also grew up to be a barber and a good man, speaking the language of the Upcountry. How different had been the Lowcountrymen and the Upcountrymen and how the differences had slowly faded (though never entirely) is a story to be told.

The people of the counties and their towns, except five or six along the coast, had had for the most part the same origins, the early mixtures of blood had long been blended and forgotten, but with all their resemblance they had features of their own.

Greenville was Baptist, having Baptist colleges, with a dilution of Episcopalians, in the town, who came early from Charleston and the Lowcountry. Dancing was never as heinous a sin in Greenville as in other Upcountry towns, indeed the dances in Greenville were more delightful than elsewhere in the state, except Charleston. The Presbyterians were prone to be led astray by the Episcopalians; they seemed to like it.

In Spartanburg one was more fortunate to be a Methodist, for there Benjamin Wofford, a native, had left the money upon which Wofford College was started; Dr. James H. Carlisle, a truly glorious old saint and professor of mathematics, was its president, and the Reverend Coke Smith, a great preacher and later bishop, was another member of the faculty. John S. Reynolds, newspaper man and lawyer, produced "patent outsides" for the weeklies and moved his plant from another town to Spartanburg. After two months one of his friends, meeting him in Columbia, said, "Why, John, I thought you had gone to Spartanburg to grow up with the town—now I hear you are back to stay—what's the matter?"

"Yes, I've come to stay."

"Well, what's the matter with Spartanburg?"

"Spartanburg is all right, George, but I found I couldn't live there without accepting three dogmas."

"Yes; what were they?"

"The first was that Wofford College is a greater institution than Oxford, the second that Doctor Carlisle is a greater mathematician than Copernicus was, and the third is that Coke Smith is a greater pulpit orator than the Apostle Paul—and I'll be damned if I could subscribe to them."

In the hill town of York, with King's Mountain and its battleground in the county and in sight, is a Presbyterian aristocracy who worship in a fine old gray church built in the 'fifties, and to the town came in the 'eighties Count von Moltke, nephew of the great field-marshal. He had married in Germany out of his class and by some chance drifted to this, one of the loveliest villages in all the world, a village of Witherspoons, Brattons, McCorkles, McDows, McNeells, McCaws and Moores—not German. The Count applied for membership in the Presbyterian church and was summoned before the elders, the session, for what is usually a perfunctory examination.

After a brief prayer, an elder began: "Count, do you believe in the final perseverance of the saints?"

"By no means," said the pudgy Count.

The elders lifted their eyebrows slightly.

Another said: "You accept the doctrine of justification by faith?"

"Not at all, not at all, I know nothing about it," the Count replied, with no effort to conceal impatience.

The eyebrows of the elders went higher, but one of them persisted: "At the basis of our church is the doctrine of election and foreordination—you are prepared to accept that tenet, Count?"

"No," said the Count, "none of that nonsense interests me."

The elders were taken aback, but the venerable pastor rallied and inquired:

"May I ask, Count, since you reject so many of the essentials of our church, what led you to seek membership with us?"

"Certainly," said the Count. "I have been here a year now and it seems to me you are the best people in York and I want to be one of you."

The Count never became a Presbyterian. In three or four years he died, and one may see, in York's graveyard, his grave with a stone bearing his name and the dates of his birth and death. His family returned to Germany.

Camden is in Kershaw, of the middle-eastern counties. It has produced a pattern of gentlemen singularly sweet and gracious of manner, it contributed six general officers to the Confederate armies, two of its lads won the Congressional medal in the World War—and Camden's soft-spoken men of earlier times probably fought more duels than did the men of any other village of the state.

In the Piedmont counties and towns where the Scotch-Irish have so long been ascendent life was taken more seriously than in the counties of the plains east, south and west. The gentlemen drank harder liquors and more of them, they played milder poker and less of it, and ever have been more strenuous in prayer. They vote "dry" nowadays scathingly, that is, so they vote.

Edgefield on the Savannah, until 1895, included the present areas of four counties, and should have a book of its own. It has had more dashing, brilliant, romantic figures, statesmen, orators, soldiers, adventurers, daredevils than any county of South Carolina, if not of any rural county in America. James Bonham and William Barrett Travis, leaders of the Texan defenders of the Alamo, the American Thermopylæ that "had no messenger to tell its story," were born on its soil. Edmund Bacon, the "Ned Brace" of Judge A. B. Longstreet's *Georgia Scenes,* was one of the earliest of a family of brilliant Edgefieldians. The Brookses, Simkinses, Pickenses, Butlers, were Edgefield families. All of these were kin, by blood or marriage, and they and other related families gave to their village and county a character that was South Carolinian, more intense, more fiery, than was found elsewhere. Not less cultivated and courtly than the men of Camden or the "Old Cheraws," they seemed to be, if they were not, harder riders, bolder hunters, more enterprising and masterly politicians. Their virtues were shining, their vices flamed. They were not careful reckoners of the future, sometimes they spoke too quickly, and so acted, yet in crises an audacity that might have been called imprudence by milder men made them indispensable to the state. Martin Witherspoon Gary, stormiest leader of the Hampton campaign, born in Abbeville, "belonged" in Edgefield where his life as a lawyer was spent. The Tillmans also were of Edgefield, established as planters and slaveholders, but were not of the accepted tribal chiefs— wherein is one of the keys to the political revolution that Benjamin R. Tillman engineered in 1890.

So from town to town and county to county one might go in this day, to find each with its savor, however they be of one blood. They seemed tied together with an affection like that among grown-up sons and daughters having families of their own, and the state was the mother. Other states, even the Southern States, except Virginia, seemed a long way off. With the growth of population and the mobility of the twentieth century the sharpness of the differences is vanishing, and it is with an older life that this book is concerned.

With their differences the counties and villages are steeped in the individuality that is South Carolina's, and that is reflected peculiarly and intensely in the state's rigid attitude in respect of marriage. It binds in South Carolina. Mat and Mary might have had the "knot tied" by a plain citizen instead of Trial Justice Watts and it would have held—it would have held not more firmly had bishop or governor officiated. A new statute forbids, with penalties, a marriage unless the parties have obtained a license, but the marriage is not the less legal or honorable without it. It is not good manners in South Carolina to refer to a "common-law marriage" as if a stigma attached, and informed South Carolinians resent it. Recourse to clergyman or magistrate is the custom, so general that most South Carolinians think it necessary, and it is advisable, for clear evidence of the contract is important and observance of formality preserves and fixes it. Only in a year or two of the "Radical" or "Reconstruction" Government was divorce permitted, that was alien government, it is of the life of the people to hate its memories; hence indulgence of divorce made it more hateful in the years that have followed.

In the village nearly forty years before the wedding of Mat and Mary, a tall, handsome, clever girl of sixteen, the daughter of English immigrants, married a man of another county and they went to the Southwest where they swam rivers horseback and endured the frontier's perils. The husband was cruel, and, when in a few years they returned to South Carolina, a legal separation was had. The laws were cruel too and the husband was given the baby, the mother being allowed to see it once a year, at the husband's gate, after she had traveled fifty miles by horse and buggy for the purpose.

Now "Miss Martha" was a dashing young woman in her twenties, she sang in the choir, she wore flounces, ribbons and gauds, and, though there was no breath of scandal, a fine-looking young grass widow was a vexation to the elders, some of whom had wives and maiden sisters who would talk. (They still do.) Relief arrived in the person of a little gentleman, a journeyman tailor he was and a Jew, and boarding at the same house with Miss Martha, the two fell in love, as the angels would have it. But the husband was living, there could be no divorce. The elders took counsel and it was agreed that it would be nonsense to remember the marriage. So one of them, the "ordinary" of the county, a friend of all good people in Laurens, arranged that a magistrate who was a relative of the young woman should come and join Miss Martha and Mr. Lucius, and was present to bless the transaction—not religiously for he was a member of no communion. A few years later the first husband died and, the news of it coming to the village, the elders again consulted, the ordinary arranged for a second marriage ceremony (it might avoid legal complications in the event of children), and again he was present when the same magistrate "said the words," to join the "happy twain."

Never was a more successful marriage in Laurens, though there were no children. Miss Martha and Mr. Lucius lived happily ever after, she five feet ten and weighing two hundred and he five feet four and weighing one hundred and twenty, she the very pattern of colossal starchiness among women, he the model of trigness, dignity among small gentlemen. Of him one has a picture in mind: he is wearing his flat, little, black-banded straw hat and alpaca coat, he is carrying, as the oldest Mason, the great open Bible at a Masonic funeral ("Mason walks" they were called), and with one is another picture of the two as they trimmed their roses in the garden, as prim as both were, in Laurens Street.

Yet, for years, two or three, they had been "married" when there was no marriage, when their companionship was in defiance and violation of law, they had so lived to the improvement of the morals of the community, to the laying of the ghost of gossip about "grass widows," exemplifying the decorum of the marriage estate. If there was no divorce, neither were there railroads or telegraph lines or newspaper correspondents in Laurens, and the elders were men of good sense and good will. The ordinary, or judge of probate, who directed this assault on the majesty of the law, was the father of the Captain who officiated for Mat and Mary.

Still, we South Carolinians are content without a divorce law, in not one of the forty-six counties could a candidate be elected to the General Assembly if known to be unorthodox on the subject, and "companionate marriage" is scarcely mentioned in polite company.

William Hance was a saddler and a good man in the village long ago. He died, leaving a widow, a daughter and three sons. Three tombstones stand in a row in the graveyard, on the hillside, that slopes to the meadow of Little River, and beneath them are buried the three sons. They were Lieutenant-Colonel James Hance, Captain William Hance and Sergeant Theodore Hance. They were soldiers of the Confederacy. They were killed in battle.

Mrs. Hance lived in a three-room cottage close to the "Double Chimneys" where the Colonel lived, and when James Hance's widow came out from the Georgia town where he had been a lawyer and was married, the Colonel's wife went to see her. She was sick that day, in 1869, but old Mrs. Hance invited the caller into the room where her daughter-in-law was lying down. The Colonel's wife noticed on the bed a quilt upon which was stitched, not embroidered, the name ANDREW JOHNSON, and said, "Oh, that is the Andrew Johnson quilt that he gave you when you were engaged?"

"Oh, no," said old Mrs. Hance, with her gentle dignity, "that was only a girl-and-boy affair—there was nothing in it." So Mrs. Hance dismissed the subject and Andrew Johnson was at the time President of the United States. Miss Mary Word and Andrew Johnson had been sweethearts, they were engaged, when he was a journeyman tailor in Laurens, and Mrs. Sallie Bolt, her granddaughter, has the keepsakes to this day that he gave her when he left Laurens. One of them is a tailor's goose. As for Mrs. Hance, she lived to be old in Laurens and loved the village, tending the graves of her boys who had died for love of the state, which they had from her.

Such was the village and such was the life of it in which the Colonel, through whose eyes my gaze on South Carolina was fixed, began his career as a country lawyer about 1854. He had just been admitted to practise, about the same time he had his military title as a member of Governor John L. Manning's staff, and the presiding judge appointed him to defend a friendless white man (it was his first case) charged with stealing a bushel of oats from a wealthy planter "down in Jacks." (Jacks is one of the nine townships in Laurens.) The evidence was conclusive, the verdict was guilty, and the minimum sentence was ninety days in jail and so many lashes on the bare back on the first Monday ("sales day") in each month. The man got the sentence.

The Solicitor (State's Attorney), after a whispered conversation with the Judge, called the young lawyer aside and said: "The Judge and I think it just as well that this young fellow be not publicly whipped—it might have a bad effect. If you will advise your client to drop a few yards behind the Sheriff when the court recesses for dinner and he takes the prisoners back to jail and then as he reaches the alley that leads out of the Square to break and run and not to stop till he gets to Georgia, and not to come back to South Carolina, there will be a hue and cry, but it won't amount to much, and he will get away—I'll arrange that."

The Colonel explained, delightedly, the plan to his client, who was delighted too, apparently. As court rose, he walked to the northern portico which commanded a view of the alley to see the chase. The Sheriff walked the thirty yards to the entrance to the alley, the client dropped three yards behind, the sheriff did not look back, and the client —looking not to right or left—followed the Sheriff down the alley and into the jail. He served his term and took his three whippings "like a man," but the Colonel was disgusted with such devotion to South Carolina and Laurens County.

Herbert Ravenel Sass (1884–1958)

Herbert Ravenel Sass, born in Charleston on November 2, 1884, received both his B.A. and M.A. degrees from the College of Charleston. A prolific writer of nature tales and historical novels, he is the author of *The Way of the Wild* (1926), *Adventures in Green Places* (1926), *Gray Eagle* (1927), *War Drums* (1928), *On the Wings of a Bird* (1929), *Look Back to Glory* (1933), *Hear Me, My Chiefs* (1940), and *Emperor Brims* (1956). With DuBose Heyward he wrote *Fort Sumter* (1938). He died in Charleston on September 18, 1958.

Charleston

At ten minutes before three o'clock the first ironclad in the line, the monitor *Weehawken,* having an Ericsson torpedo-searcher raft attached to her bow, was directly opposite Fort Moultrie at the northern entrance of the harbor. Richard Acton saw white smoke roll in a curling cloud above the parapet of Moultrie and the next moment the stillness of the bay was broken by a heavy detonation. The range was too great for Moultrie's smooth-bore columbiads; after a few rounds they suspended their fire. One shot from the *Passaic,* the second vessel in the line, was fired in contemptuous reply.

It was plain that the shore batteries on either side of the entrance were not seriously considered by Admiral DuPont. Fort Sumter, in the middle of the harbor mouth, was the lion in his path, and against it his effort was to be directed. The black ominous ships held steadily on their way, biding their time. But those opening guns had sent their message rolling above the calm waters of the inner bay. The roofs of Charleston and the long reach of the sea-wall promenade were thronged with thousands gathering to witness the battle upon which their fate depended.

At three minutes after three o'clock, the *Weehawken,* still leading the line, had approached within fourteen hundred yards of Fort Sumter. Two puffs of white smoke leaped from her turret, instantly merging to form a single snowy cloud. Richard heard the heavy report of the simultaneous discharges, he heard a humming sound increasing to a roar, followed immediately by the crash of a bursting shell, then silence.

The silence lengthened; he could hear the quick breathing of the men near him. A gunner behind him laughed nervously. There was another heavy report; the turret of the second ironclad was enveloped in smoke.

"Too high," a voice whispered hoarsely. "And one of 'em didn't burst. Look at that flag." Acton saw that there was a clean hole through the regimental colors flying above the gorge wall.

"Rhett better come down," another voice said. "If that damned thing had been lower . . ."

Colonel Rhett and his aides were still standing on the southeast parapet fully exposed. Rhett, conspicuous in his parade uniform, was bending slightly forward. He was watching the *Weehawken* intently. He hadn't, Acton realized, so much as turned his head when the shell burst.

Acton's gaze remained fixed upon the tall figure sharply outlined upon the parapet. He hadn't in the old days known Alfred Rhett well. In a duel in the second year of the war Rhett had killed Colonel Ransom Calhoun, at one time commander of Fort Sumter, and later had succeeded to the post which Calhoun had held. The affair had caused bitter feeling—Calhoun had been exceedingly popular—but the prescriptions of the code had been followed strictly, and no one had questioned Rhett's fitness to command. He was fearless, a born soldier, a strict disciplinarian, and he had taught the Sumter artillerists how to shoot. Under his rigid training, the First South Carolina Regiment had become one of the best artillery commands in the Confederate service. A man at Richard Acton's elbow, a bearded private from the up-country, was muttering to himself.

"Why the hell don't he come down?" the man was saying. "I aim to kill him myself when the war's over on account o' Ransom Calhoun, and ef he stays up thar, the Yanks'll kill him fust."

Richard Acton found himself wishing with an increasing intensity that Colonel Rhett would descend from the exposed parapet. The other officers with him didn't matter so much, but for the moment the whole fate of Fort Sumter and of Charleston seemed comprehended in the fate of Alfred Rhett. At any moment the next salvo from the ironclads might come. He saw that Rhett was still watching the *Weehawken* closely; he knew that the Sumter battery commanders had been ordered to withhold their fire until the leading Federal ship had reached a certain buoy.

A tall man, in the uniform of a cavalry colonel, his left arm supported in a sling, ran up the narrow brick stairway leading to the parapet where Rhett stood. He saluted the officers there and moved forward to Rhett's side. Richard recognized James Hail. He was conscious of a sudden hot flare of resentment, anger. So that was why Diane was in Charleston. Evidently Hail had been wounded and had come home from Virginia on leave. He must have hurried down to Sumter from Charleston by boat to offer Rhett his services. Acton heard Captain Mazÿck Marion speaking in a low voice to the men of the battery.

"That's Colonel Hail, men," Marion said; "Hail of Wade Hampton's cavalry—we can't lose now."

There was a general craning of necks. In two years of war James Hail had become a legendary figure, one of those celebrated and romantic leaders in whose individual brilliance the passionately individualistic South found warrant for that faith which had dared challenge an adversary of three times its strength. There was the beginning of a cheer which Captain Marion quickly suppressed. Hail nodded, smiling; he lifted his unwounded arm in salute. Suddenly Richard saw Colonel Rhett raise his hand.

The *Weehawken* had reached the buoy upon which the eastern barbette guns of Sumter had previously been trained. With a deafening crash the whole front of the fort burst into flame. Crash followed crash; dense clouds of smoke rolled up above the rampart. Firing by battery, the guns of Sumter, combined at first upon the *Weehawken* and then upon the *Passaic,* ripped and churned the blue waters of the bay.

Richard Acton lost all knowledge, all consciousness, of what was happening beyond the sphere of his immediate action; his whole being was concentrated upon the swift and machine-like handling of the powder charges for the eight-inch gun to which he had been assigned.

He was filled with an exaltation, a happiness, surpassing anything he had ever known. It came somehow from Diane; she flashed in and out of his thoughts, but he had no clear vision of her. He saw, too—a momentary flash, as of lightning—the columns of Avalon far off through a shadowy vista of overarching oaks; he seemed to hear again a golden tinkling of cow-bells. But presently all this passed; the exaltation left him. Abruptly, as though until that moment he had been utterly deaf, he became aware of the infernal and intolerable din of the guns.

He couldn't stand it, he felt; it would drive him mad; the smoke in his nostrils and throat was strangling him. There was a heavy shock; the whole massive rampart of Fort Sumter rocked and trembled. He heard the crash of a falling wall, followed by screams and groans. The smoke around him cleared suddenly; beyond a space of blue water he saw the ironclads.

The funnel of one was black with a red band around the top—the *Weehawken;* another's funnel was gray with a green band; a third was enveloped in the smoke of her own guns. Out of that smoke he saw clearly a great black sphere, apparently as large as a flour barrel, burst suddenly. It sped in full view across the intervening space. He realized with an intense surprise that his eye had followed the shell as it bounded from the port of the monitor's turret to the wall of the fort, and in the same instant he felt another mighty shock and again the fort shook to its foundations.

He wondered whether Rhett and Hail were still on the exposed parapet; thick smoke now obscured the spot where they had been standing. He smiled faintly. James Hail had always excelled him, defeated him. He, Richard Acton, was one of five hundred private soldiers serving the guns of Fort Sumter; but Colonel James Hail, lustrous with the glory he had won in Virginia, was up there in the battle-smoke. Up there with Rhett on the highest parapet, the point of utmost danger. In front and near at hand he saw a waterspout rise from the surface of the bay. A mortar shell had exploded just beneath the water; a blue and white column heaved upward to twice the height of the fort and, breaking, deluged the rampart with spray. A man beside Acton cursed shrilly and snatched off his scarlet cap; he saw that the crown of the man's cap had been filled with water.

He laughed; the man's solicitude for his cap seemed indescribably humorous. A runner came racing up the spiral stairway leading to the parapet battery and spoke to Captain Marion. Acton heard Marion's voice, issuing an order; he couldn't distinguish the words.

The awful shocks, the more awful trembling of the fort, continued. The concussions were coming at shorter intervals; the Federal gunners were shooting more accurately. With a swift and horrible fear he realized presently that the firing of Sumter was perceptibly slower. The conviction came to him that the huge fifteen-inch guns of the turret ships were battering Fort Sumter to pieces.

He perceived in a moment, however, what had happened. Colonel Rhett had modified his plan of battle. The guns of Sumter were no longer firing by battery; they were firing piece by piece, searching out their moving targets with greater deliberation and certainty.

The *Weehawken* was backing. Evidently she had abandoned the design of breaking through the rope and boom obstructions of the inner harbor with the torpedo-defense raft brought for that purpose. She was firing vigorously; the *Passaic,* passing in front of her, fired and then moved backward in turn; the two other monitors of the first division, the *Patapsco* and the *Montauk,* were completely hidden in the smoke of their turret guns.

A heavy curtain of smoke surrounded the fort. It lifted slowly; he saw for the first time the complete panorama of the battle.

On both sides of the harbor mouth the Confederate shore batteries were firing at long range: Fort Moultrie and Batteries Bee and Beauregard on the northern shore and Battery Gregg at Cummings Point on Morris Island. As yet only the first division of the fleet was in action against Fort Sumter. The *New Ironsides,* leading the second division, had halted. She had the appearance of a ship becoming unmanageable from lack of headway; her uncertain movements threw into confusion the line of vessels behind her. She ran foul of two of them, got clear with difficulty; Richard saw that she was signaling. The ships of the second division moved forward past her. As though encouraged by their boldness, the *New Ironsides* swung round and advanced again.

Acton realized that within a few minutes the offensive power of the enemy actually engaged with Sumter would be more than doubled. The *Catskill, Nantucket* and *Nahant* of the second division, were monitors of the *Passaic* class, carrying fifteen-inch and eleven-inch guns; the *Keokuk,* with her double hull and her two sloping turrets, was an unknown quantity, while the *New Ironsides'* powerful broadside batteries of rapid-firing eleven-inch guns rendered her probably the most formidable unit of the fleet. Moultrie was firing upon the flag-ship at long range, and, although she was still twice as far distant as the first division monitors, there was for some minutes a concentration of fire upon her from the eight- and ten-inch columbiads of Sumter.

She halted and hung uncertainly in the tide. Undoubtedly she had been hit, but at that long range her armored sides could hardly have been pierced. Nevertheless, she held back; larger and more vulnerable than the monitors, she might have suffered severely in close battle with Fort Sumter, while her great size increased the hazard of maneuvering her within the arms of the bay. But the other ships of the second division were coming rapidly on. Already the first of them, the *Catskill*, was in action. Soon the *Nantucket* and the *Nahant* were hotly engaged.

The light breeze lulled; the smoke curtain shut down; it was denser than ever and it had a different smell. Again it lifted. He saw that the whole fleet was now in action. The *Nahant* and the *Keokuk,* last in the attacking line, had moved gallantly to the front. They were fighting at shorter range than any of the first division ships.

Richard Acton realized that the crisis of the battle had come; the entire force of the ironclad fleet except the flagship was concentrated against Fort Sumter.

The ceaseless and shocking uproar of the guns increased; more than a hundred of the heaviest cannon ever used in war were thundering together. The monitors were constantly in motion; each moved in an ellipse, and together they formed a wide half-circle in front of the fort. The thick walls and arches of Sumter trembled under the impact of the great fifteen-inch and eleven-inch shells; when at the moment of impact the shells burst, deep craters were blasted in the brick walls of the fort. The smoke became so dense, its acrid smell so penetrating, that breathing was almost impossible. Richard realized suddenly that Fort Sumter was on fire.

If there was talk around him, he heard little of it. A voice with the accent of the up-country cursed the *New Ironsides* because she wouldn't come closer. "The goddamned old bitch!" he heard the man say. "The pot-bellied old ———" The crash of an exploding shell obliterated the rest. A gunner beside him screamed and fell backward. He was coatless now, his face black with powder, his shirt half-torn from him. He saw faces, flitting forms, in the smoke: Mazÿck Marion, Louis Treves,

runners with ammunition. One of these shouted that the fire was close
to the magazine.

That, however, meant nothing to him. There was something else far
more important, but he couldn't fix what it was. His hands, his body,
ceaselessly engaged, seemed entirely separate from his mind. He realized
vaguely that he was trying to think of Diane. But it was as though he
couldn't now think of her. She was near him and yet immeasurably remote; she eluded even his thoughts.

Well, she was worthless. Damn her, she was worthless! He knew
her for what she was. Jacqueline had been worth ten of her. Jacqueline
Fleur. How long ago that was! Paris . . . St. Petersburg. The cafés of
the Boulevard Saint-Michel. It was all ashes. His life was ashes. Diane
had burnt him to ashes. She had consumed him. He saw her eyes; they
looked as they had looked that night in the summer-house—they were
lying now just as they had lied then.

A sudden and overwhelming sense of her enchantment, her magic,
poured through him. The rampart under him shook. In front of him
the parapet trembled, cracked; a section of it toppled over into the sea.
Another fifteen-inch shell struck the wall of the fort below the breached
parapet and exploded. . . .

The concussion stunned him momentarily; he fell sideways against
the chassis of the gun. He hung there dazed, only half-conscious. His
mind groped blindly: James Hail's bullet, he imagined, had hit him;
he was at Avalon—at Sherborne. Vienna was bringing in his supper.
It was a hot night, but that wasn't why she had bared her amber shoulders. She moved as gracefully as a cat; she was watching him out of the
corners of her eyes.

Diane, of course, had heard the talk about Vienna and himself. He
wanted her to hear it. So that she wouldn't know. . . . Ash Rowland,
he remembered suddenly, was in the Army of Northern Virginia. He
looked a little like Diane—a great deal like her. Richard Acton pushed
his hand through his hair; his head was pounding, black spheres re-
volved before his eyes.

He stood swaying, one hand clutching the gun-chassis, but presently,
almost suddenly, his vision began to clear, the pounding in his head

diminished, the revolving spheres disappeared. Through the breached parapet he could see the whole fleet, the whole battle. Except for the noise and the white jets leaping upward from the water where the shells struck, it was like a picture, a picture in a frame.

Most of the ships were hidden or half-hidden in smoke. One monitor —from her position he believed it was the *Passaic*—had retired to the eastward. Her pilot-house had been wrecked and a cloud of steam was issuing from her deck. The *Weehawken,* too, seemed to be in trouble; her funnel, painted black and red, was riddled; her side armor was cracked and split. The *Nahant* and the double-turreted *Keokuk* were sustaining the hottest fire of Sumter. All round them the water seethed with the rain of projectiles. Acton saw the *Nahant* struck three times in as many minutes; he could see the black fragments of solid shot falling back from her impenetrable turret.

It was impenetrable, but the heavy blows jammed it so that it could not revolve and her guns were rendered useless. Her steering gear apparently had also been disabled, for she was drifting helplessly. . . . The *Keokuk* turned bow-on and headed straight for Sumter. Immediately she received the concentric fire of all the fort's guns that could be brought to bear. Spouts of foam and jets of spray flooded her turtle-backed decks; in front of her and on either side the water was churned white by a deluge of shells and balls.

Firing from her forward turret, she came bravely on. Richard could see that she was being hit repeatedly. Her eleven-inch bow-gun was silenced; a solid shot crashed into her forward turret; a bolt from a Brooke rifle ripped open her hull ten feet from her stem and barely above the waterline. Her headway slackened, then ceased; she drifted toward the fort under a hail of fire.

The guns of Sumter, served with almost perfect precision, were hammering her to death. Her sloping turrets were cracked and dented; her armored hull was torn and ripped, her funnel riddled. Slowly she gathered way again. With ninety wounds in her—all the high courage of her officers and crew made fruitless by the cool skill of Sumter's gunners—the *Keokuk,* mortally stricken, moved slowly out of the fight.

The fire in the fort had been controlled; a squad under Lieutenant Inglesby had stopped its progress toward the magazines. The smoke cloud over Fort Sumter was less dense. Richard Acton saw the Confederate flag at the top of its tall staff. Through a thin white veil of drifting smoke it shone like a flame. There was a great hole through its red union with the stars of the Confederate States, but the blue flag of South Carolina at the western angle of the gorge was unscarred. Acton was conscious of a queer contraction of his throat; he was stirred strangely by the sight of the flags.

He laughed harshly. He wasn't a sentimentalist, he told himself. Flags were nothing but flags. A battle apparently was mainly a hellish noise, a bad smell and an aching head. Nevertheless, he realized presently that he was shouting, cheering. The men around him were cheering. Captain Marion was trying to stop it, but throughout the fort the consciousness of victory had overcome the rigidity of Rhett's discipline. The men of the other batteries were cheering also, waving their caps.

The half-circle of ironclads in front of the fort was shifting, breaking up. The battered *Nahant,* her steering gear repaired, was steaming slowly out of range. The other monitors, still firing sullenly, were retiring; he saw that signals were flying on the *New Ironsides*—the Admiral's order to withdraw from action.

A shirtless, powder-blackened man jigged up and down in front of Richard Acton. His grimed face was almost unrecognizable, but Acton saw in a moment that it was the up-countryman who had cursed the *New Ironsides.* He was singing in a high cracked voice:

> "King Abraham is very sick,
> DuPont has got the measles,
> Old Sumter we have got it still.
> Pop goes the weasel."

Another man joined him, two more,—half the battery. They were singing madly, waving their caps. But now it was *Dixie:*

> "I wish I was in the land of cotton,
> Old times dar am not forgotten;
> Look away, look away, look away, Dixie-Land.
> In Dixie-Land where I was born in,
> Early on a frosty mornin';
> Look away, look away, look away, Dixie-Land.

"Then I wish I was in Dixie;
Hooray! Hooray!
In Dixie-Land I'll take my stand
To live and die in Dixie. . . ."

A salvo from the big casemate columbiads of one of the second-tier batteries came like a crash of applause. The garrison of Sumter, their outburst of joy over, had returned to the service of their guns; there had been, as a matter of fact, hardly more than a momentary slackening of their fire. A rumor ran from battery to battery that the ships would return, that Rhett expected another attack at once. It was known that, so far, casualties had been few and that the fort had suffered no irreparable damage; but the walls had been weakened, a renewal of the bombardment might have serious results. Rhett's order was to continue firing as rapidly as accuracy permitted. Until they had passed beyond extreme range, the retreating ironclads were pursued by the persistent Confederate shells.

They did not turn. Few, if any, of them could have survived another half-hour in the deadly fire-zone in front of Sumter. They filed past the *New Ironsides* in slow and solemn procession, and when the last of them had passed, Admiral DuPont got his flag-ship under way and followed his broken and beaten fleet. He was wondering perhaps— Samuel F. DuPont was an old man with years of honorable service behind him—how Washington would receive the news that he had to give. Defeat instead of the victory that had seemed so sure. The invincible iron armada flung back from the gate of the hated city. The vaunted *Keokuk* sinking, four other ships disabled. The *"Rebel"* flag still flying over Sumter. . . .

Richard Acton looked westward toward Charleston. He was alone on the western rampart; the stir and excitement following the victory had in large measure subsided. Over the bay—over the whole world, he thought—a profound and serene silence reigned. In the softened afternoon light the waters of the inner harbor, barely ruffled by the faint breeze, were a delicate and luminous blue. The sun was going down behind the roofs of Charleston. The tall steeples of St. Michael's and St. Philip's were sharply drawn against a golden sky.

Charleston, with the blue water in front of it and the splendor of the sunset above . . .

He felt again, suddenly, that contraction of his throat-muscles which the sight of the flag over Sumter had caused. Damn it, he wouldn't be an ass. Charleston was—Charleston. He, or at least his brother, had property there; the Acton town-house overlooked the sea-wall promenade. It was safe. Charleston hadn't been captured; Fort Sumter had beaten back the enemy. That was all that needed to be said. So far as he was concerned, the chief result of the battle was a headache.

He saw Mazÿck Marion approaching. Thank heaven, there wouldn't be any heroics, any sentimental gush from Mazÿck. There would be plenty of patriotic eloquence in the *Charleston Mercury* in the morning, but he wouldn't have to read it. Still, what had happened this day had gone some distance toward proving that the *Mercury* and Barnwell Rhett were right—that the South might win. God, he exclaimed to himself, if only that could happen! He had differed with Barnwell Rhett, after all, on only one, but the most essential, point—the practicability of secession; it was probably true, as Rhett believed, that the South would be better off outside the Union. He had opposed Rhett and secession solely because he hadn't believed that the South could win a war against the North. But now the South seemed to be winning.

He smiled. He had perhaps helped Barnwell Rhett win the revolution that Rhett had worked all his life to launch. After opposing Rhett's secession policy, he had helped establish it. But there was a sharper irony in the fact that he had helped defend Diane. He had fought for her; he had been conscious all the while that it was she he was fighting for. Well, he was a fool, that was all . . . Mazÿck Marion was standing at his elbow. Marion said simply, "Well, Richard," then stood silent, gazing across the calm blue water.

He saw that Marion was deeply moved. Mazÿck's dark eyes, fixed upon Charleston, were strangely bright; his tanned bony face was transformed by some inner radiance.

"We've saved it," he said in a low trembling tone. "Thank God, we've saved it."

He paused. Without looking at Acton, he went on, his voice steadier. "I kept seeing her. I think I saw her the whole time. It was a strange thing, Richard, that all three of us were here. You and I and James Hail. All three of us here in Sumter and Diane yonder in Charleston. . . ."

He stopped abruptly. Richard Acton, without realizing what he was saying, replied:

"Yes, that was very strange."

Ben Robertson (1903–43)

Born at Clemson on June 22, 1903, Ben Robertson received his B.S. from Clemson College in 1923 and his bachelor of journalism degree at the University of Missouri in 1926. He worked for various newspapers—the Honolulu *Star-Bulletin* (1926–28), the Adelaide, Australia *News* (1928), the New York *Herald Tribune* (1929–34)—and as a correspondent for the Associated Press in Washington and London (1934–37). After a period of free-lancing for the *Saturday Evening Post* and other magazines, in 1940 he became London correspondent for the newspaper *PM*. While there as a war correspondent, he published a popular wartime account of the German air raids, *I Saw England* (1941). His other books are *Travelers' Rest* (1938) and his most important book, an account of life in upper South Carolina during the early twentieth century, *Red Hills and Cotton* (1941). During early 1943, while he was returning to London to become the head of the London Bureau of the New York *Herald Tribune,* his Pan-American clipper struck the water while landing at Lisbon and the plane crashed, killing Robertson and twelve other passengers.

From *Red Hills and Cotton*

I lived like a wild bird when I was growing up in our valley. All about me were my kinfolks. Old and very old and young, and still there was solitude, and in spite of all the barns and houses and cultivated fields I always had the sensation of space. I was surrounded by all sorts of restrictions—by the rules of the church, by all the personal rules of my kinfolks, by the rules of the white and colored races, but I was not aware of restriction. I thought I was free. Even time, I thought, was my own, but I realize now that it, too, was cadenced, it moved in cycles, over and over again, in the Southern rhythm. Everything with us had the beautiful motion of simple routine. I rose at daylight and started fires, and I remember how powerful it made me feel to be up before anyone else, to have in my own hands the opening control of the day. I discovered early the realness of the pleasure of getting up at daylight; it gives you a feeling of living as all life ought to live; you are surged onward and outward, beyond yourself, and you know a sense of smoothness within that is like the wind blowing and the sun shining. There is quiet and rest about everything and you feel very close to the mystery of existence.

I milked the cow and I went to the rabbit traps as the sun was rising. Five days each week I went to school, and at sundown I split kindling and brought in wood for the woodboxes, and at twilight I milked the cow. On Saturdays I cut wood and worked in the garden and roamed the woods and hunted and did nothing. I went to Sunday school on Sunday morning, to the cemetery on Sunday afternoon, and I never thought of time at all until I was about ready to go to college. I led a happy life. Time is always timeless whenever a person is happy.

I went to Charleston once when I was a small boy to see the ocean, and once I went to North Carolina and pitched pebbles into the French Broad River, but except for those excursions I stayed at home, almost within the valley. Always I knew I would go far away when the time should come, so I never bothered about going anywhere before I started to college. I was not concerned, nor were my kinfolks, about travel for a child. The travel that I knew was the roaming of fancy. My parents did not care whether I saw an opera or understood a statue; all that could be considered in time, in the future, for operas and statues belonged to urban culture, and my kinfolks said any person with any kind of background could acquire a city civilization, but that few city people could ever learn the culture of a rural country. Urban culture was wax, a polish, and was superimposed, it was gloss. They wanted to instruct me in the rural beauties, to ground me in the Southern fields, to give me an anchor that no storm could ever loose, to give me an attitude, a philosophy, a purpose. There must be an original flavor that would stay with me always, a particular savor. I was to know one special life and to know all that could be known about it. I was to understand cotton farming and how to live with tenant farmers and colored people on a cotton farm. My kinfolks did not believe in a broad education for a small child. They believed in narrowness for a child. My kinfolks were not afraid of narrowness, nor were they skittish about being called fanatics. They wanted me to have a point of view, to have my mind made up from the start on a number of things. I was to be tolerant but I was not to budge beyond a certain point, and if ever I was threatened at that point, I was to stand where I was and fight. My kinfolks thought more about character than about culture. They said culture could be acquired but character had to be formed. Character had to be hammered into shape like hot iron on an anvil. It had to be molded in the most exact and unrelenting form.

So they gave me books to read and work to do and they gave me time of my own, but always they were guiding and directing and advising and pouring their own wisdom into my growing mind. Hundreds of precious hours were devoted to my education by my parents and aunts and uncles and by my grandparents and my Great-Aunt Narcissa and by Margit and Mary and Bill. They left culture to chance—I was free to develop in that realm as I chose. They left nothing to chance about character. With that they did what they could. So they read to me from the Bible, took me through the woods, worked with me in the fields, and over and over tried to make me understand that the value I must search for was x. My kinfolks did not care a hoot that a bridge was a thousand feet long or that a tower was a hundred and two stories high. They wanted to know why the bridge was there, what purpose it served, what sort of strength the tower possessed, what beauty it held. My kinfolks were never interested in 2 plus 2; their principal interest was centered in a plus b. Over and over again they told me I had to amount to something, I had to be somebody, I had to hold on, to wait, I was to live with dignity, with honor, I was to do what was right. My kinfolks wanted me to stand like one of the mountains, like the granite of the Blue Ridge. The sculpture, the decoration, they would leave to me. What they wanted to do was to set me in the mold—to make me a Carolinian, a Democrat and a Baptist. Once they had accomplished that —well, hell and high water could try as they liked.

So I lived the cotton life. Round the clock it went, round the calendar, year after year. Our beautiful old hills were heavy clay, red and rocky, and we could never plow them when they were wet. We could never prepare the land for the cotton crop until the heavy rains of the winter were over, usually not until March. Sometimes in winter we would hear that strangers said a crow could not make a living flying through our fields, the cotton patches looked so old and poor; but we understood our land, we knew its virtues and its stored wealth; our hills could grow a bale of cotton to an acre, there was strength in the clay. Even the most eroded clay lands could be brought back into fertility if they were handled properly for a few seasons, if they were fertilized and sown in pea vines and in winter grain. In March we planted cotton and in April we planted corn. In May we hoed and chopped and thinned, and in June we hoed and ran around the cotton with a plow, and we also cut and thrashed our oats and wheat. We planted pea vines and sorghum cane, and we plowed under the stubble in the grain fields and planted corn. We liked to finish all that by the Fourth of July. Through the long hot sultry July days we plowed and hoed some more, and when August came we laid the crops by. We rested and went fishing and attended family reunions and went to camp meetings and to all-day singings, and enjoyed ourselves to the fullest. It gave us a fine feeling to look out over our well-tilled fields and to see the heat radiating upward in dazzling waves, to see the cotton blooming and the corn tasseling out. August was cotton-growing weather, and the hotter the better—cotton liked the blazing heat, chilled now and then by a short sudden August shower. The fields blossomed like islands in the South Seas, white and red splotches on a glorious green and crimson—the white and red hibiscus-like cotton flowers on the green cotton plants that spread away in long curving rows across the silky vermilion of the fields. Nothing gave us more satisfaction than to watch cotton growing in August in the fields that we ourselves had plowed and planted. Jim said he was just as satisfied in a fine cotton patch as the angels were in glory. During September we sowed the winter turnips and pulled the corn fodder and gathered in the corn. We dug sweet potatoes and picked cotton through October, and in November we went to town.

I liked to plow cotton, to stand between the swerving handles of the plow, to hold the handles lightly, to guide the shares in the smooth furrow, and to walk barefooted in the fresh earth. No wonder there is so much singing about cotton-plowing; it is a simple, complete way of work. It is hard and the sweat pours, but there is an open freedom about it, and the waterboy brings you a cool drink, and you drink and rest—it is an exquisite sensation—and at night when you come in tired, you sleep the wonderful sleep of the really weary. It is a fine sensation really to be thirsty and to drink cold water, really to be tired and to crawl into a bed and rest. The reward is worth the effort, especially if cotton is bringing ten cents a pound. Of course it is discouraging, year after year, to plant and plow and pick and to get only five cents for the crop, but even then we somehow never give up. We always expect something to come along and boost the price of cotton. Cotton is cash to us, it is faith, it is hope. We can make more money picking cow peas in the autumn than we can make picking cotton, but somehow cow-pea money has never meant to us what cotton money means. We can sell grain for cash, but we have never trusted grain as money. We do not understand grain as we understand cotton. So all summer long we plow in the cotton fields and sing and tell the mule what we intend to do when we have the cash in hand from our cotton.

Our cotton country swarms with non-producing hangers-on who scheme the year around to get their fingers on our cotton dollars. They come around throughout the spring and summer and trade on our hope; they sell us things on time, credit us against the cotton crop that we will gather in the autumn. They sell us radios and phonographs and Sunday suits, and they sell the colored people funeral insurance and enlarged photographs of themselves and their kinfolks; they even sell them fifteen-dollar Bibles. Once in the late autumn Aunt Coot dashed into the house with a Bible in her hand and breathlessly told me the Bible man was coming for his money and she would be obliged to pick cotton a few more days before she could pay him. She said maybe he would let her keep the book, maybe he would extend her time if the book was written in—would I write in it the names of her children?

"All right, Aunt Coot," said I. "How do you want me to start?"

"The first one," she said, "is John the Divine Christopher Columbus."

I had known Aunt Coot all of my life, I knew all of her children well, but never had I heard of anyone in her family with the name John the Divine Christopher Columbus.

"Aunt Coot," said I, "who in the world is that?"

"That's Son," she answered.

"All right, who comes after Son?" "Emmalina Kathaline Jollycosey Julianne."

"Which one is that?"

"That's Doll Baby."

I listed them all—the first batch, the second batch, Brother John's children, Brother Joe's—Lord Wellington Lord Nelson, Queen Victoria, Matthew Mark Luke John, Bathshebabe States Rights, Narcissa Clarissa Temperance, Miss Mary B., Miss Hattie Boone.

And Aunt Coot kept the book.

There was great commotion in the hills when at last the sweeping fields turned white. There would be frost in the air, and whole families would appear with crocker sacks slung over one shoulder—old and young would take to the cotton patch. They would bend to the stalks, picking with both hands, and they would sing old rhythmic hymns— "In grand mansions above," "Lord I want to be like Jesus," "Must Jesus bear the cross alone, and all the world go free?" They would start at the first light, before the dew had dried, for dew on the cotton would add to the weight, and all of them were interested in weight, as they were paid at sundown by the pound. Everything was fair in cotton-picking—even rocks in the sack—and you had to watch every bagful of cotton. "There's nothing like a good field stone," Mary once said, "to bring your poundage to two hundred." One time Mary was paid for a stone in her cotton bag; the weigher did not detect it, and that night Mary had that rock on her mind. She worried about it and she worried —what if the rock should slip unnoticed into the cotton gin, would it not ruin the gin? Next morning, she said to my cousin Stephen John that she had dreamed there was a rock in her cotton, she did not know how it got there, but she believed one was there—someone had better go through her cotton bag, for she had dreamed about a stone. Mary had true goodness in her heart, and I have always known why Mary could be so happy with so little to show for her work. Always she has done what our grandparents said all of us should do: she has lived with dignity, she has lived with plainness and honor.

After we had picked the cotton and had sold the bales, we paid for fertilizer, we settled with the stores, we paid for the Bibles and clocks and radios and cars. Then we bought a pair of shoes, a few clothes, we bought a bottle of government liquor, and after that little or nothing was left. All that we had to look forward to was hunting and fishing and the next year's cotton crop.

During laying-by time in August, on the second Monday in the month, we always held a reunion of all the kinfolks, usually at one of the houses over on Chauga Creek. About three hundred would attend, and we would arrive in carriages, in wagons pulled by mules, and on horseback and afoot; we would drive up in automobiles, and once one of our cousins landed in the bottoms in an airplane. During the morning we would sit in the shade of the trees and our cousin Unity and our Great-Aunt Narcissa and our cousin Ella would begin at the beginning of time, long before the Revolution, and trace the kinfolks from then until the moment of that reunion. They would tell us who had married whom, who had gone where, and what had happened. At noon someone would ring the yard bell and the three hundred of us would sit down on benches before long board tables—three hundred of us would eat an old-time dinner. About a hundred chickens would be fried and served on platters, and there would be fried steak, venison, fried fresh pork, whole boiled hams, sugared and spiced, and there would be roasted duck, baked turkey, cold veal, stuffed eggs, and beans, potatoes, roasting ear corn, cheese straws, lemon tarts, and bowls of highly seasoned chow-chow pickles and peach preserves made from the wild clingstone peaches that grew on the cotton terraces, and there would be clingstone peach pickles, and blackberry jelly and apple jelly and pound cake, chocolate layer cake, coconut layer cake, marble cake, banana layer cake, caramel layer cake, sponge cake, angel-food cake, apple pie, peach pie, huckleberry pie, ambrosia, boiled frozen custard, fresh grapes, cold watermelons, cantaloupes, muskmelons, pomegranates. For drink there would be blackberry cordial, cider, hard cider, blackberry wine, sweet and deep purple in color, and there would be a dry scuppernong wine and muscadine wine, a strong elderberry wine and dandelion wine, clover-blossom wine, and pitchers filled with sweet milk, buttermilk, and water from the spring branch. Of course, we considered it outrageous and disgraceful for any of our kinfolks to drink corn liquor, so we did not serve white lightning at the dinner table. Those who drank that did so behind the barn.

Once I remember seeing my Great-Uncle John coming up the garden path smiling and talking to everyone and all the time mopping his fiercely flushed face. At the gate he started to walk toward the far edge of the yard, but at that moment my Great-Aunt Kate yelled to him from the front porch.

"John," she cried, "where did you get that liquor?"

"Why, Kate!" exclaimed my great-uncle, astonished.

"You heard me," continued my great-aunt. "Where did you get it?"

"I hardly touched it," said my great-uncle. "Just took a drop."

"You come on up here and sit down," said my great-aunt. Obediently my great-uncle went up on to the piazza, and from then on until time to go home he sat there in a chair. He sat there in silence—he did not say a word.

When we had eaten dinner at the reunions, somebody would talk about us and olden times, and then we would pack up and start early for our houses. All of our lives we had to start early from places, for we had stock at home to attend to. We had to milk and feed, and my kinfolks were the kind of people who believed that cows should be milked and mules fed at exactly the same hour, day after day. We might inconvenience ourselves, but not our livestock. It was low-down and trifling to inconvenience livestock.

Drayton Mayrant (1890–1969)

Charleston-born Katherine Drayton Mayrant Simons, writing under the pseudonym of Drayton Mayrant, was a prolific poet, novelist, historian, onomatologist, and editor until her death on March 31, 1969. Though she is perhaps best known for her nine historical novels, two of which—*The Running Thread* and *The Red Doe*—have South Carolina settings, her poetry may yet earn for her a more enduring literary niche. Two of her early volumes were *Patteran* and *White Horse Leaping,* in which the following selections appear. Later poems appeared frequently in magazines and in the yearbooks of the South Carolina Poetry Society. As a contributing editor of *Names in South Carolina* she offered numerous historical articles, as well as a linguistic series on Charleston alleys. She was also a charter member of the John Doyle Writing Group in Charleston.

Photograph from a Rocket

The planet's curve against the void of space
Is thin and scarcely more opaque than cloud.
The shades of light and darkness have endowed
The plate with sea and land, but not a trace
Of man. His long achievements, good or base,
Are leveled like an acre cut and plowed.
Perspective such as this has not allowed
For trivia upon creation's face.
If time, like space, reverse the telescope
To show a spinning mote too small for blame
Among the galaxies, there may be hope
That final judgment will acquit the name
Of dwarfish Earth whose little lightnings grope
Like glow-worms lit by sparks of cosmic flame.

Drayton Mayrant, "Photograph from a Rocket," "Sea Island," "Song for a Winter's Night" in *White Horse Leaping* (Columbia, S.C.: University of South Carolina Press, 1950), pp. 2, 20, 7. Copyright 1951 by University of South Carolina Press. Reprinted by permission of the publisher.

Sea Island

Behind its windbreaks of cassena lie
    Its silted fields, suckled with brackish slime
    Fecund as ooze primordial of Time.
Above their corn the slanting sea gulls cry.

Infrequently at dusk across the bay
    The land wind brings the sound of steepled bells,
    Whose slow carillon hesitates and swells
And lacking any answer dies away.

These reddened marshes where the sunset keeps,
    Although the sun has gone, are alien sod.
    This is terrain of night. A jungle god
Is regnant here while all the mainland sleeps.

The drowsy scent of muscadine at noon
    May fill the woods, the harsh cicada hum;
    But I have waked by night to hear a drum
Talking beneath the bladed setting moon.

Song for a Winter's Night

Who looks upon Orion can
No longer love a mortal man.
No other hero gems his blade
With nebulae, where unafraid,
Against the angry Bull he wheels,
With baying Dogs upon his heels.
He whistles laggard Procyon
And Sirius. His stepping stone
Is Rigel's sun. He hunts alone.
He clasps his cloak with Betelguese,
This lover of the Pleiades.
So never look on winter skies,
For fear The Hunter blind your eyes
And you go lonely all your span,
Unseeing any mortal man.

Elizabeth B. Coker (1909–)

Elizabeth Boatwright Coker was born in Darlington on April 21, 1909, received her A.B. from Converse College in 1929, and married James Lide Coker on September 27, 1939. *Daughter of Strangers,* published in 1950, was her first novel. Since then, she has published several other historical novels—*The Day of the Peacock* (1952), *India Allan* (1953), *The Big Drum* (1957), *La Belle* (1959), *Lady Rich* (1963), and *The Bees* (1968).

The Wishing Bone

I found him wrapped in one of Mrs. Suggs' old wore out blankets lying in a manger down to the livery stable on Christmas morning. Of course I knowed right off who he was, seeing as how Beadie's daughter from off with her belly big as a oat barrel, had been in our kitchen whining at her mother ever day the week before.

Anybody could of told he was kin to Beadie anyhow. He had the same big black velvet eyes and the softest, shiningest straight hair of any coon I ever seen. Mrs. Suggs thought as how I found him on Christmas and our boy was off in the Marines we ought to keep him for awhile. Say until he was three or four and big enough to put in a orphanage. Beadie didn't say nothing but her face lit up when I give him to her and said he could sleep in her room back of the kitchen. She wouldn't have looked at him twice if he hadn't been her own grandson; not even if he hada been the poor little Jesus boy himself. Beadie ain't charitable like me and Mrs. Suggs.

He was a cute little fellow from the first. Playful and laughing like crazy all the time. He learnt to sing before he learnt to talk and he could dance up a storm when he couldn't hardly walk two straight steps across the floor.

When he was three he began follering me down to the livery stable and he loved them horses like they was people. Folks used to come jest to set and look at him opening the stall doors and bossing them big old skinny nags. He'd say, "Come on—you!" And them horses would put their heads down and sorta wriggle into the halter like they knowed it pleased Jim, and out he'd come—proud as Lucifer—leading them to get water or sometimes jest to eat a bite o' grass.

By the time he was five there weren't a horse in the barn he couldn't ride anywhere in the town. Nights he'd come and set in my lap while Beadie done the dishes.

"Daddy Suggs, when you gonna get me a pony?"

"Next summer, Jim. A white pony. A high stepping winning white pony."

"Kin I ride it in the horse show up to Windy Rock?"

Reprinted by permission of Mrs. Elizabeth B. Coker.

I take the horses up to the mountains ever summer, me being from them mountains to start with. That was where I made my real living at. Riding in Pine View, North Carolina, in the winter weren't near so profitable as them summer people to the Rock.

"Sure. You can ride in the Six Year Old and Under class."

"What his name go be, Daddy Suggs?"

"His name? Why, Jim's pony's name gonna be Prince Suggs. Yessir; Prince Suggs."

And that fool little fellow would chuckle and curl up in a soft ball in my lap and go off to sleep like a puppy. One night him and me was talking about his pony when Beadie come into the room to put up the dishes. Mrs. Suggs was to the pitcher show and I was laying it on thick about the stylish pony Jim was gonna have up to the Rock.

"Mr. Suggs," Beadie said, "you gonna ruin that boy. Pony! White pony name Prince! You know Jim ain't never gonna have no white pony. Why you tease him so?"

"Shut up," Jim screamed, running and kicking Beadie on her shin. Beadie reached back and knocked him clear across the room.

"Git on to bed," she yelled. They looked like two chickens fighting. I most died laughing. Then Jim run through the kitchen crying and Beadie stuck out her lip. I went to the sideboard and poured her a drink of corn.

"Why you mind my teasing the boy? He got to learn to take teasing."

She drank the oily raw liquor without so much as a drop of water. It woulda frizzled my tonsils but she didn't even squinch her nose.

"It just ain't fair him thinking he can ride in a white folks horse show and have a pony all his own. He's a soft skinned young one. He ain't tough in his heart like them bad Mercer boys what lives next door."

"Aw," I said, "pour you another drink, Beadie. You ought to get on your knees and be grateful how good I been to Jim. He weren't nothing but a bastard thrown out to die and I taken him in from the night. Him and me enjoys our little fooling. And here you come with a dern chip on your shoulder telling me what to say to Jim. I'm a good mind to fire you. Yes, I am." I was getting madder ever minute and Beadie seen I was mad.

"Oh, I didn't mean nothing, Mr. Suggs." She begun to sniffle and edge away. I knowed I had her so I acted hurt.

"We even decided, I and Mrs. Suggs, not to never send the boy to no orphanage but jest let him stay on here. Why, I planned to take him on at the livery stable later and pay him a salary. I had all sorts of plans for Jim. But if you don't like the way I treat him—you just go on and pack your rags and get out. I'll shore miss the little fellow though."

"No, no, Mr. Suggs. Excuse me. Excuse me. Please forgive old Beadie. It's good for Jim to be teased. Anyway he likes it. Please don't pay no attention to old Beadie, Mr. Suggs."

So Jim and me went on talking about his white pony and when Christmas got near Jim said,

"Daddy Suggs, will you write me a letter to Santa Claus?"

Mrs. Suggs was hooking a rug and she put down her big wooden hooker needle and said, "Go over and get me a pencil off the telephone table and I'll write the letter. Daddy Suggs can't write good enough for Santa Claus to read."

He run and brought back the pencil and paper and Mrs. Suggs wrote the letter just like he told her. He looked cute as all get out against the pile of red and blue wool, his great big eyes shining like an animal's in the firelight, and his straight black hair combed up high in the front like I comb mine.

"Dear Santa Claus:
Please bring me a white pony. A winning white pony named Prince Suggs. That's all. Not nothing else. And bring Daddy Suggs a hundred dollars and Mama Suggs a hundred dollars and Beadie a dollar.

Your friend,
Jim."

While he was standing there looking like a little dark angel I got a idea from a old joke what had hung around the horse business since I was a boy.

"What you grinning at?" Mrs. Suggs asked. "You must be thinking up some mischief. Let's don't pay him no attention, Jim. Here, touch the end of the paper to the fire and then send it up the chimney. Turn it aloose quick 'cause if it falls back in the fire Santa won't bring you nothing."

Jim squatted down, touched the paper to the fire and it went flaming up the chimney.

"Beadie! Beadie! I'm gonna get my pony. I'm gonna get my pony!" He run out in the kitchen happy as a bee in a apple tree at blossom time.

I and Mrs. Suggs laughed and pretty soon we went to bed. It was turning cold and looked like snow outside. At first I couldn't sleep good; then after a while I heared Beadie down in her room singing Sweet Little Jesus Boy to Jim. She had a low husky voice that sounded like it was full of cane syrup and it sent me right off to sleep.

Two days later it was Christmas Eve. Pine View was all covered in snow. Them Yankee people up to the hotel had found some sleighs from somewhere and I done a fine business. Jim spent the time fixing up a stall for his pony. He had the manger full of oats and the hay rack stuffed with the best alfalfa that I keep for the board horses.

"That's the same dern manger I found you in," I said when I went to tell him it was time to go home for supper.

"You reckon Santa Claus go bring Prince here or home?"

"Home. Santa Claus never come to no stable."

"He brung me in a stable."

"Santa Claus never brung you. Why, you come from—"

"Beadie says Santa Claus come to this very stable with me when I was just borned."

I seen Jim's lip trembling. He'd been down here in the cold all day and I knowed he was wore out.

"O.K., O.K., Santa Claus brung you, now let's go home. Ain't it time for you to hang up your stocking?"

I picked up the sack I'd fixed and we walked up the frozen street in the falling snow. There was Christmas trees lighted with red and yellow balls in the windows of the houses and wreaths of holly and pine on all the doors.

"Ain't tonight pretty, Daddy Suggs?" Jim said, stretching out his hands and letting the snowflakes whiten them.

We made a great to-do about hanging up Jim's stocking. It was a old one of Mrs. Suggs' and after he'd went to bed Mrs. Suggs filled it full of nuts and candy and fruit and laid a red fire truck she'd bought at the dime store on the floor under it.

"Wonder what Beadie's got for him?" she said.

"Oh, she ain't got nothing for him. You go on upstairs. I'll be to bed when I finish this pipe."

I smoked a long pipe just setting by myself in the dying firelight. Then I took and emptied the fruit and candy from out the stocking and filled it with the stuff I'd brought from the stable in the sack. It sure did look funny and I didn't have no trouble going to sleep that night at all.

It must have been nearly six o'clock when I heared Jim come tip-toeing in my room. His round little face wasn't no higher than my pillow and he said real easy like,

"Daddy Suggs, there ain't no pony downstairs."

"Aw, you joking! Shore there's a pony downstairs. I woke up about a hour ago and heared him neighing and pawing to beat the band. Hand me my wrapper. I'll go down with you."

We crope down and I could hardly keep from busting out laughing. Beadie was standing by the chimney with her lips stuck out a mile.

"What you done now, Mr. Suggs?" she asked, and I knew she'd seen the stocking.

I made out I hadn't seen her. "There's shore a pony been here," I said, wrinkling up my nose. "I can smell there's been a pony here."

"Where? Where, Daddy Suggs? You sure? I don't smell nothing."

"Come here, I'll show you," I said. Jim run over and I took down the stocking and dumped the manure onto the floor. "There," I said, "Santa brung you a pony but you was asleep. The pony had been here. See. You can see for yourself there was a pony here! He musta got away. That's what. He's done runned away. If you'd been up in time you coulda caught him."

The next summer we was lucky. A little rich girl from South Carolina brought her white pony up to the Rock and, what do you know, his name was Prince!

"You see," I told Jim, "Daddy Suggs promised you a white pony named Prince to ride this summer. Too bad you let the one Santa brung get away but this one is prettier."

"Is he a winning pony, Daddy Suggs?" Jim was so excited when we unloaded the pony he jigged and turnt a cartwheel.

"This here is a winner."

"Is he mine, Daddy Suggs?"

"Well—" I didn't dare go too far this time. Not after the way Mrs. Suggs sided with Beadie against me last Christmas and made me go down town and buy a dern second hand bicycle for Jim. But his face was so believing and serious I just had to tease him a little. "Sorta yours. It's thisaway. He rightly belongs to a little girl what won't ride him much and you can ride him whenever you please."

"In the horse show, Daddy Suggs?"

" 'Course."

"You sure he is a winner, Daddy Suggs?"

"You bet. Wanta try him?"

Jim could really ride that pony. I charged the Randolph's a extra ten dollars a month for Jim exercising him so good. The little girl was named Daisy and all she wanted to do was ride Prince in the ring about fifteen minutes a day to keep herself in practice for the horse show. She didn't love riding the pony the way Jim loved riding him. Jim could put Prince in a fast trot and he would pick up his front feet so high he most knocked his chin off ever time. They was something: that little black boy and that snappy white pony, both holding up their heads as proud as governors. I never seen a kid of five ride like Jim. Daisy was ten and she couldn't do nothing with Prince but Jim rode him like a professional.

Mrs. Suggs fixed up some old jodhpurs of Billy's and Beadie took and went over to Boone and bought Jim a couple of nice white shirts and a pair of little cowboy boots and with his pretty hair combed so high and nice he coulda rode Prince in the Garden against the top kids from off.

Mr. Randolph would watch Jim school the pony ever day. After, he'd

give Jim a dime and pat him on the back. Once he took Jim on a picnic
with him and Daisy and come back telling me what a smart boy Jim
was and how he hoped I was planning to send him to school next year.

"School!" I laughed. "What good will school do Jim? Crazy about
the horses as he is I'd better learn him the horse business so he'll have a
trade."

"It won't hurt him to have some education too."

I don't never argue with my paying customers, so I made as if a fly
was in my ear and changed the subject. Things went on like that till
the day before the horse show when Mr. Randolph came up to me and
said, worried like,

"Mr. Suggs, I believe Jim thinks you are going to let him ride Prince
in the show. It's all right with me for him to show the pony in the Six
Year Old and Under class since Daisy rides him in the Eleven and
Under."

"Jim ride? You know these summer folks wouldn't stand for Jim to
ride in their horse show, Mr. Randolph. I wisht he could. But you know
how it is. I'll fix up something to make up to him. Don't you worry.
Your pony is in fine shape. Jim's got him going perfect. Daisy is sure
to win."

I meant to tell Jim that night he couldn't ride, him being a colored
boy, but him and Beadie was fussing over which tie to wear and was
his shirt ironed right, and Mrs. Suggs kept asking me what was I going to do about Jim and it begun to aggravate me, so many people
worrying about Jim and me doing all the work. I answered sharp.

"He's going to ride in the horse show. I promised him, didn't I?"

I put on my hat and went out and cranked up the pickup and drove
to farmer Lydey's up on Peak Gap and borrowed his little stud donkey.
I told Pete, the boy who helped give the kids lessons, what I had in
mind and we had everything ready when the show started.

Jim come to the grounds with Beadie and Mrs. Suggs dressed to kill.
"I'll get Prince," he said.

"Go ahead," I told him, "your class is next. We done moved Prince
into the third stall."

Jim run off and come back in a minute looking like he was going
to cry. "Prince ain't in that stall. A old no good donkey is in that stall."

"Well—" I could hear the announcer calling Six Year Old and Under, "Mr. Randolph says he don't want you to ride Prince. You'll have to ride the donkey or nothing."

"I won't ride nothing," Jim said.

"Oh, yes, I done drove half the night finding you something to ride. It'll give the stands a big laugh and help our business. Go on in there and show your stuff, boy."

"I ain't."

Mrs. Suggs said, "It's better than not riding."

And Beadie said, "It's riding in a white folks' show, honey."

"I ain't," Jim said.

"By golly, you are!" I'd had enough of this nigger kid thinking he was somebody. "Bring out the donkey, Pete!"

Pete brought the donkey and I histed Jim up and before the class begun I'd done led Jim to the ring and shoved him and that donkey in.

"Walk your horses," the judge called and the donkey begun to buck and hee haw. The crowd took a look at Jim on that little jackass and from then on he stole the show. If he'da been on Prince they woulda resented him but being on the donkey they knew he was there to make them laugh. Yet instead of being just a clown for the audience, like I planned, he made the donkey walk, trot, and canter. He musta been mad 'cause fer as I knew nobody had ever set on the stud before. And what do you know? The judge give him the blue ribbon! I was so proud I coulda bust. Little old Jim riding on a ass and winning a blue ribbon in a society horse show with the crowd waving and clapping like a multitude. When he come out of the ring Mr. Randolph was waiting by the end gate.

"Good show, Jim," he said, "but why didn't you ride Prince?"

Jim looked over at me and I guess my face turnt red. Then a old sort of expression almost like he pitied me come in Jim's eyes.

"Daddy Suggs thought this donkey would make people laugh," Jim said.

I give Jim a big hug and a whole quarter when he got off. He's one good kid.

"This Christmas I'll write Santa Claus to turn you white and you can really ride Prince in the show next year."

Even Mr. Randolph laughed at this.

We all thought Jim had took it as a joke too but evidently he hadn't 'cause soon after Thanksgiving he started pestering me about had I really writ Santa Claus to turn him white for Christmas. When Mrs. Suggs or Beadie was in the room I wouldn't say nothing much but down to the stable I'd tease Jim a sight and he'd laugh and sing around the place like a bird. He knowed I was joking. Leastways he shoulda knowed. Him being almost six year old and well growed for his age. All kids get excited when Christmas is in the air. I didn't see nothing strange about that.

But Mrs. Suggs kept nagging at me, "Now, Mr. Suggs," she'd say, "don't you play no tricks on that boy this Christmas. I got him a second hand suit of clothes from a sale and Beadie has bought him some new shoes and I'm going to send him to school in January. Him and that white pony! All he can think about is getting turnt white himself so's he can ride Prince in the horse show. You better leave that boy alone. Maybe school will bring him down to earth."

I agreed. I wasn't actually planning to do nothing this year, leastways not until the package come for Jim on Christmas Eve and the letter to Beadie. Beadie let Jim open the package right away. It was from Mr. Randolph. The prettiest Roy Rogers cowboy outfit you ever see. Big white hat and fine black pants and shirt all covered with white fringe and silver buttons. Jim like to had a fit. He put them fancy clothes on and went strutting down the street like he owned the world. When them Mercer boys next door come out to look at him he hollered, big as all get out—"I'm going to be turnt white tonight and tomorrow I'm coming in your yard and beat you up."

Course they went for him right off but Beadie heared Jim mocking them and got to him first and drug him inside the house before the dirt balls they was making hit him. He didn't seem to care at all. That suit just witched him proper.

"He needs to be learnt a lesson," I told Mrs. Suggs. "He's heading for trouble."

"You're just sour because Mr. Randolph sent him such a grand present. You'd be sourer if you knowed what he wrote to Beadie."

"What did he write to Beadie?"

"Oh, something."

Women is all mean. I never seen one, mare nor person, aught but ornery and full of kicks. So I used guile. "I give up. Tell me."

"He ast Beadie to let Jim come to his plantation and stay along of his cook. Said the pony warn't no good at all without Jim to exercise him. Said his cook was a fine woman with three little boys of her own and wanted Jim to make a even number. Don't look so crabbed. Jim ain't planning to go. He wouldn't leave you for nothing. Though why he loves you so much I can't fathom."

That there was a long speech from Mrs. Suggs, so I poured her a drink and she decided to go to prayer meeting at the Holiness Church. Beadie had went to a party in Hop Town. Jim and me was alone together.

The fire was nice and warm. A big wind was up and the radio said the morning would be freezing with maybe snow or sleet. Jim still had on his pretty suit and he set down on the floor rubbing his soft shiny head against my leg. I put out my hand to pat his hair, him looking so cute, and the rocker of my chair hit the table leg.

"What that?" Jim set up, his big eyes like to pop out he was so excited. "Is them reindeer hoofs I hear?"

I nodded and reached in my pocket and jingled some coppers together what was lying loose. Jim cocked his head on one side like as if he was hearing bells ringing.

"You hear that jingling, Daddy Suggs?"

"Shore do. Are you ready to be turnt white, Jim, or do you think you better stay colored? Say quick because I still got time to tell Santa Claus to let you alone."

Jim stood up straight and stiff, grabbing my hands in his. "Please let him turn me white, Daddy Suggs, so I can ride that winning pony. Please don't send him away, Daddy Suggs."

"Then you better put on your nightdrawers and go to bed."

"Un-unh," he shook his head solemnly, "I'm going to keep on my good clothes so I'll look good all over when I'm turnt."

"Well, seeing as how Beadie ain't here, go in the spare room and sleep on the cot." He did that often when Beadie would decide she needed a night out. Beadie wouldn't miss him. Not tonight nohow. Hop Town was lit up like a circus with celebrating colored people.

Long about five o'clock I woke up hearing them Mercer boys next door shooting off firecrackers and torpedoes. I slipped out of bed so Mrs. Suggs wouldn't wake and went down and got the ham grease I'd hid in the pantry and a sifter full of flour. Jim was still asleep and didn't even feel me when I rubbed the grease over his face and sifted the flour on it. In the half light he sure enough did look white! I was just finished sifting when he woke up.

"Hey, who in here?"

"Me. Daddy Suggs. Jim, you know what?"

"Am I white, Daddy Suggs? Am I white?"

"You shore are white, Jim. Get up and go look in the glass."

Jim hightailed it off that cot and over to the mirror. As I said, in the half light he did look white and being so excited he didn't notice the flour what had fell on his black shirt. He was like a wild colt. Jumping and singing and hollering. Mrs. Suggs called from her room.

"You wake, Jim?"

"Tell her 'yes'," I whispered.

"Yes, Mama Suggs. Can I shoot firecrackers with them Mercer boys?"

"Go on. There's a whole pack of crackers in the top of your stocking and here's some matches," I said.

He run out and I went to the window to see what would happen when he met up with them toughs.

It was a ugly daycome as I ever seen through the window glass. The big bare old sycamore trees with their naked trunks was clutching at each other like they were trying to ram each other's branches down their throats. Everything looked so angry there in the dead greyness that it put a chill all down my back.

I raised the window, quiet as I could. Jim was going down the steps when Beadie come running—still in her party dress.

"Where you going?" Beadie said.

"Get away from me, Beadie. I'm a white boy now. I'm going to throw rocks at them Mercer boys."

"Throw rocks nothing. You fixing to get throwned in jail. What make you think you white? Putting ham grease and flour on your face! White!" She looked up and musta seen me in the window 'cause she said real mean and loud: "Daddy Suggs done played another trick on you."

"He ain't. Not Daddy Suggs. It ain't no trick, Beadie. I seen my face in the mirror and it was white. I seen it white as—"

"White as Jesus," Beadie answered and she took one of Jim's hands and raked it down his face.

When he seen it come off smeared in ham grease and flour he looked up at me a minute, then he sorta give way and let Beadie pick him up, big as he is, and tote him back in the house.

It shoulda been funny but somehow with the wind blowing them trees so ugly and the sleet starting to fall I didn't feel like laughing. I closed the window and snuck back in bed with Mrs. Suggs. It was nice and warm, her being so fat and flabby, and I got to sleep easy, having decided to give Jim a whole silver dollar for his Christmas present.

When eight o'clock struck we went down to breakfast, only there weren't no breakfast. The kitchen was dark and no fire lit in the stove nor nothing.

"Well," said Mrs. Suggs, "of all the ungrateful people. I bet Beadie got drunk and didn't come in at all last night. And it Christmas! Where's Jim? He ain't touched his stocking, nor seen his suit I bought. But the shoes are gone. The shoes Beadie bought are gone." She give me such a fierce look I had to unloose and tell her what I done.

All day she ain't spoke to me. When the telegram come from Mr. Randolph in the afternoon saying Jim had got there safe on the bus, Mrs. Suggs brung her hooker needle and set with me. And later when I heard Beadie singing Poor Little Jesus Boy in the kitchen, fixing to cook the turkey for supper, I felt less lonesome. But the house shore is empty. I miss Jim. Him and me always pulled the wishingbone together.

William Price Fox (1926–   )

Born in Columbia on April 9, 1926, William Price Fox, Jr., studied at the University of South Carolina, graduating in 1950 after spending three years (1943–46) in the U.S. Army Air Force. He held sales jobs for almost a decade before enrolling in writing courses at the New School of Social Research in New York in 1959. In 1964 he began writing fiction, magazine articles, and movie and television scripts full time. Many of his best short stories were published in the *Saturday Evening Post*. His books include *Southern Fried* (1966), *Moonshine Light, Moonshine Bright* (1967), and *Southern Fried Plus Six* (1968). Since 1967 he has taught in the writer's workshop at the University of Iowa.

Have You Ever Rode the Southern?

Cora Lee and I had been writing pretty hot and heavy there while I was in advanced training, so when I got my commission, my wings and the thirty-day furlough that went with it I decided to get home and ask her to marry me before someone beat me to it. The planes were all booked up, so I got me a ticket on the Sante Fe. Now the Sante Fe is a pretty good line and even though it was day coach for sixty-eight hours I got into Dallas feeling pretty good. At Dallas we changed to the Texas and Pacific. It was forty-four more hours from Dallas to Atlanta, and while I didn't get much sleep I made that part all right too.

But at Atlanta we changed over to the Southern.

Brother, have you ever rode the Southern from Atlanta to Columbia?

The first fifteen or so miles went by fast. Then we started stopping. We made three stops out in the dark before we reached Buford, Georgia. There, a tall guitar player with a red bandanna around his neck got on. He looked at the seat next to me.

"Lieutenant, you mind if I join you?"

"Sure thing."

"That's mighty considerate of you."

I sighed to let him know I was too tired to talk and leaned against the window. I closed my eyes, but I was wide awake. I hadn't slept in I don't know how long, and now I was too tired to sleep.

He laid his guitar across his knees. It was an expensive Gibson with a vine of red roses and leaves painted around the edge. On the black frets down the neck he had a list of all the towns he'd been to; Atlanta, Savannah, Mobile, Charleston, Muscle Shoals, Columbia, Macon and Augusta.

I glanced at him out of the corner of my eye and that was all he needed. His Adam's apple rose and sank before he spoke. "This shore ain't much of a car, is it?"

I knew he was waiting for my answer. "Not much." I looked back outside. We were finally leaving Buford.

"Where you heading?"

"Columbia."

"That's a fine town. Fine." He moved his hand off the guitar neck so I could see all the cities listed. Columbia was next to Macon, near the bottom.

"You know, I've been riding the Southern since I could walk, but I 'spect this is the sorriest car I've ever seen. Look up there at those gas spigots. They made this car before they had electricity."

The train hit a bump and bounced. Ash dust from the big Ben Franklin stove in the middle of the aisle shot up in the air and drifted back over us. I didn't brush it off.

He went on, "Well, I reckon them boys overseas are riding in cars a heap worse than this."

I stared outside. The black fields seemed to relax me. I counted the hours since I slept last but I couldn't keep the figures straight. I figured five and a half more wouldn't matter.

"Lieutenant, I'd be obliged if you'd let me pick my guitar a little." He smiled. "My fingers are getting a little itchy."

I spoke at the window, "Go right ahead."

He looped the guitar cord behind his neck. He cocked his head to one side as he played and kept time with his big brogan shoe. He wore no socks. When he sang he looked at the red roses on the guitar. He seemed to be singing to them. "I recommend the Lord to you." He sang in a low voice that carried the length of the car. When he finished the song he continued strumming. "How you like that?"

"Fine."

He looked around the coach and exchanged nods and smiles with the other passengers. The lights were on. No one was sleeping. A man in a glare-blue suit, across the aisle, had some whisky concealed in a brown paper bag. He offered us the bottle. I took a drink, but the guitar player shook his head and continued strumming and tuning up the Gibson.

The man took the whisky back. "Musician, you know any fast music? I don't mean any fast hymns. Something beside hymns."

The guitar player smiled. He picked the E string hard and listened close. He must have figured the guitar was in tune because he suddenly brought his brogan shoe down hard on the floor. "How about this?"

His fingers flew into "Won't You Be My Salty Dog." He played fast and grinned.

The man shouted, "Sing the words! Sing the words, guitar man!"

He played faster and shook his head in time with the music, "Can't do that. Ladies present."

The man said, "That's good! That's mighty good! Let's have some more of that!"

He strummed down to a whisper, "All right. Time for one more. Then I got to get me some sleep."

He nudged me with his elbow and smiled. "This one's for my friend the lieutenant here."

He tuned the G string. His smile faded. He looked white and dead serious. He began "The Air Corps Song." He sang the words in a low nasal tone right at the side of my head. "Off we go into the wild blue yonder. . . ." He sang the entire song. He knew every word, every word for three verses. He softened down toward the middle and then began rising until at the end he shouted, "NOTHING CAN STOP THE ARMY AIR CORPS!"

My head was splitting. The man with the whisky applauded and the guitar player stood up and beamed at the rest of the crowd. He sat back down. "I feel a lot better now. How about a little something to eat?"

I couldn't tell if I was hungry or not. He reached into his zipper bag and handed me a pepper-sausage sandwich.

"These biscuits were fresh-made this morning. I just can't sleep on no empty stomach."

We ate the sandwiches. The biscuits were heavy but the meat was good. He smiled as he wiped his fingers on the red bandanna around his throat and carefully laid the guitar across his lap. The neck brushed against my leg and I moved closer to the window. The minute he closed his eyes he was asleep. He slept sitting straight up with his hands on the steel strings.

The lights were still on in the car. It seemed warmer, and the smell of the ashes made me thirsty. The window began to rattle and I leaned against it to make it stop. I tried to sleep in the position he was in but the window noise was too loud. I shifted away from the guitar and tried crossing my left leg over my right. Then I tried crossing my right leg over my left. The window had to be held tight and my legs kept going to sleep.

The train kept stopping in the small towns and out in the dark between the small towns. I never saw anyone get on or off and I gave up trying to figure out why we made so many stops. I wedged my knees up into the seat in front of me, leaned hard against the window and kind of rooted down onto the bottom of my backbone. Somehow I got to sleep near Toccoa, Georgia. I don't know how, but I did.

We were coming into Greenville, South Carolina, and I had been sleeping for a half an hour or so when the train bounced hard and then stopped hard. We were both awake. It was quiet and I thought we were getting some water or coal or something. All of a sudden the door burst open and this terrible racket came at me.

You know what it was at two-seventeen and fifteen seconds in the morning? It was a band. Must have been seven of them. They were all about ten years old and they had cornets and those little tambourines. They paraded up the aisle and back. You never heard such a racket in your life. They seemed to all be playing different tunes. One of them got up on top of the Ben Franklin stove and did a little dance while the others came around collecting money. They were a nice bunch of kids, and they said they needed the money for uniforms for their baseball team. Everyone was groggy; we all chipped in dimes and quarters.

The train started moving again and the kids jumped off into the dark. I tried the same sleeping position but the small of my back was too sore. The guitar player laid his hands back across the strings, smiled, and went back to sleep. We moved forward about five hundred yards and stopped. While the train stood still I began to doze. I slept sitting straight up with my head back. When the train started I leaned against the window and dozed in little short nervous snatches. The glass felt cool. We stopped at Piedmont, South Carolina, and a new conductor got on. He examined every ticket and every passenger. He got in close and peered into my face. He had a breath like a cat.

Another few miles and we stopped hard. I thought we'd hit another train. Everybody was wide awake and the lights were on full blast. Someone was shouting. A whistle sounded ten feet away. It was the new conductor. He shouted, "Belton, Belton, South Carolina! Everybody out for Belton, South Carolina."

I was delirious. My hands were wet and that whistle screeching had given me palpitations. Outside there were no lights. We were in the middle of a swamp.

I shouted back at him, "What do you mean waking us up for this mudhole?" He looked me in the eye and shouted again. Louder, "Belton, South Carolina! Everybody out for Belton!"

I was mad and began getting up. He was too old to hit but I figured I'd shake him down a little bit. The guitar player touched my sleeve. "It don't do no good. He can't hear. He's deaf. Stone deaf. Don't do a bit of good to holler at him."

I was nervous. The sweat was streaming. The palpitations were stronger but I felt weaker. I knew I'd never get to sleep now.

It was three-forty-seven and I watched the minute hand on my watch heading for four o'clock. We were due in Columbia at seven-fifty.

The passenger in front of us got off and the guitar player swung the seat back. We each had a full seat now.

"You better lie down, Lieutenant. You look like you could use some rest."

Man, I did. I really did. The window was chattering away, but now it didn't bother me. I was desperate for sleep. I stretched out on that cane seat and hooked my legs in behind me. I put one hand under my head and one hand in my pocket. Oh, that is one tough position to sleep in. There's just enough room in that double seat to confuse you. You can't lie down, but still you feel something can be worked out. It can't. There just isn't any way unless you can go to sleep in a hurry. I tried to do that but I got confused again. I lay there a while with my feet and legs asleep and nothing else. I could feel the imprint of that woven cane seat on my hand and face, but now I was too weak to care. Finally I dropped off. I seemed to be sinking in some hot black well.

I wasn't asleep more than twelve minutes when the conductor started shouting we were in Shoals Junction.

It was four-thirty and ten seconds and it was still dark. As the train stopped, two colored kids came running through the aisle selling fried chicken in the box.

I was trembling now. I thought I was going to be sick. A cold draft whipped the ash dust over us, but I was sweating. When I sat up my feet were all puffed up and bulging inside my jodhpur boots. They were prickling, and when I lifted my numb legs over and put my feet on the floor the pain was terrible. The bones in my face ached from the cane pattern and the hand I had held in my pocket was paralyzed there.

Before I knew what I was doing I bought a box of chicken. The train sat there in Shoals Junction for fifty-two minutes and twenty seconds on my new Air Force watch. The conductor shouted several times that a bull was sleeping on the tracks and they were having trouble finding the owner. The guitar player and I ate the chicken and the lettuce and tomatoes and the French fries. There didn't seem to be anything else to do. "Lieutenant, when you lay back down you better turn the other way. That cane stitch has kind of messed up the side of your face."

The train started again and I lay back down. I knew the chicken was a terrible mistake and for some strange reason I began to giggle. The heavy grease stayed on the roof of my mouth and I could taste it all the way down my throat. I lay back with my head on the armrest and my knees toward the window and watched the farms go by. It was peaceful. The moon was still up and I could see the tin roofs shining out in the black fields. I tried to think about Cora Lee, but when I closed my eyes I couldn't make her face stay in focus. I'd wired her from Atlanta and told her to meet the train. I was going to propose at the station. Right there on the platform at South Broad. If she accepted, we would be married in two days and we'd have twenty-two more glorious days and nights together. But I had to have some sleep. The guitarist was sleeping again. His mouth was wide open but he wasn't snoring. His left index finger was on the fret marked "Macon." I began to think. When had I slept last? I didn't want to count up the hours but I did; it was forty-seven. I'd be in Columbia in a couple of hours. It was getting light outside, I began to panic. *I had to have some sleep.* I felt like shouting it. I didn't want Cora Lee to see me like this. *I had to have some sleep.* My hands were soaking wet and I could hear my heart pounding. It sounded weaker. Every fourth beat sounded different, like it was leaking. Maybe I was dying. Everything seemed blurred. The lights looked orange with strange purple halos spreading out around them. The ash smell came back. The chicken grease thickened on the roof of my mouth and the whisky taste belched up. I was in a coma. My legs and left arm were sound asleep. Very skillfully I tried to figure how I could make the sleep come up from my legs to my head. It seemed simple. It was down there, sleep was down there in my legs, all I had to do was pull it up. I opened my belt to let it flow up. I was clean out of my mind.

I shook away the dizzy spell and tried to think. Lord, I was weary. I was so weary. I was so weary and tired and miserable. All I wanted to do was sleep or lay my head down and cry. But second lieutenants in the Air Corps don't cry. I tried to keep my eyes closed.

There was a light in the east and I tried harder to keep my eyes closed. I knew what it was in the east. It was the sun in the east and I didn't want to see it. But I did. It was tipping up beyond the cotton fields and I knew that the night was over. I began to pray. I actually began to pray. *"Lord,"* I said, *"Lord, please. Please let me sleep, Lord. Please, Lord. Please."*

He must have heard me right outside Dyson, for there a calm sweetness passed over me and I slept. Yes, the Lord heard me that morning and only He let me sleep on that Southern day coach. The sun was in my eyes and sparkling on the red and green shellacked roses of my guitar-playing friend, but I slept. My legs were jackknifed up in the air and my head was lolling out in the aisle. The taste of grease and ashes and whisky had miraculously been taken away and a lovely gentle sleep folded over me like freshly carded wool. What a fine, fine sleep. My head was in Cora Lee's lap and she was sitting under the big loblolly pine on Laurel Hill. There were soft clouds in the sky and a soft, sweet smile on her lips. My fingers were on the hem of her blue and white dress and her fingers were gently stroking the soft part over my eyes.

Yes, the Lord got on that day coach right outside Dyson, South Carolina, and he stayed with me all the thirty flat miles to Pomaria. But at Pomaria, that rascal got off. He left me. I woke up jumping. The train had stopped. A vendor was shaking me and shouting in my face.

"COFFEE!" he screamed. "Coming into Columbia! Get your coffee while it's hot!" I shouted back, "What's that?"

"Columbia, next stop! Get your coffee now! Last chance!"

I looked outside. The sun was high and hot. It blinded me and I couldn't see. Every bone and muscle in my body was jumping.

I was too nervous to speak softly. I shouted again, "How far to Columbia?"

"We're right at it."

I looked down at my hands. In my right was a Dixie cup of coffee, in my left a package of Del Monte raisins.

I stared at the guitar player, "How'd I get these?"

"You bought 'em, fifteen cents for the coffee, ten cents for the raisins."

He pointed at the coffee. "You better make haste and drink that. Them cups melt fast and you can't hold 'em too long."

And then I noticed my fingers were burning up. I dropped the coffee on the floor and watched it spread out into the aisle. I wiped my burning fingers on my socks and started to get up.

I looked outside, "Wait a minute. We aren't even close to Columbia. We're in Pomaria. We got another hour yet."

The vendor was leaving the car. I started to tell the guitar player that he had made a mistake, that we weren't in Columbia, we were in Pomaria. And then it dawned on me. I hollered at the vendor. "You told me we were in Columbia! You lied to me! I could have slept another hour."

"Lieutenant, where you going?"

"I'm going to fix his ass, that's where I'm going."

I took a step and had to stop. My feet were asleep and felt like a thousand needles were stabbing them. I stood in the coffee and held onto the back of the seat.

"Give me a second. Wait till I catch my breath. I'll be all right in a minute."

"Lieutenant, you better sit down before you fall down."

"No, leave me alone. I'm going to get that lying bastard. Only take a minute. I'll be all right in a minute."

But I wasn't. I tried again and almost slipped down. I was too weak to walk. My strength had been taken away in the night and there was no fast way of getting it back.

The guitar player took my arm and lowered me to the seat. I put my head between my knees and breathed through my mouth.

I shook my head. I couldn't believe it. I was too weak to get up. Tears were in my eyes, I looked up at the guitar player. "If I had any sleep, you hear, any sleep at all, I'd fix his ass."

I gritted my teeth and clenched my fists, but nothing happened.

The guitar player said, "He knows."

"He knows what?"

"He knows you been on this train from Atlanta and he knows you're pretty weak."

My head was clearing, "You mean he does this all the time?"

"He shore does. Oh, once in a while some young buck like yourself will jump up and raise hell. Usually he just touches them on the shoulder and they sit back down."

I saw the vendor out the window. He was coming down the platform towards our end of the car.

I strained at the window. "Give me a hand here."

We got the window open just as the train began moving.

I stuck my head out and shouted. "Coffee vendor!"

He came back and stopped under the window. The train was moving out now.

"Listen, you bastard, I live in Columbia. You hear that? I live in Columbia and I'm getting me a car and coming back here tomorrow and cut your ass. You hear that?" My strength was coming back now. "Just wait, bastard," I shouted. "Just wait. . . ."

He frowned and placed his coffee bucket and vendor tray on the platform. He then put his right hand on his left arm and raised a long hand and finger to the sky.

I stepped back from the window, wound up, and winged the box of raisins at his head. It missed. As the train picked up speed I watched him pick up the box, wipe the dust off and put it back in his tray. I turned to the guitar player. "And you say he does that all the time? Tells all those people that they're coming into Columbia so he can sell them coffee and raisins?"

"Before God, Lieutenant, I ain't lying. Lots a times he tries to sell the folks Cupid dolls."

He looked at the roses on his guitar and then back at me.

"Lieutenant, I ain't going to sit here in front of you and criticize the Southern Railroad. No, sir, I'd never do a thing like that. I been riding it too long and it's been right good to me. But I'll say one thing."

He traced his finger down the list of cities on the fretwork. He seemed embarrassed.

"I've been on every road on the Southern, the Seaboard and the Atlantic Coast. Every one of them, and I know every spur and roundhouse on the line. And all that time I don't believe I've ever had cause to enter what you might call a formal complaint. But it shore do look like those Southern Railroad folks could make some improvements on this Atlanta-to-Columbia run."

When the train arrived in Columbia, the guitar player helped me off and then got on the Charleston train across the platform. My feet were still asleep and my arms were so weak I dropped my B-4 bag. Cora Lee shouted and came running down the boardwalk. She was directly in the sun. I couldn't focus my eyes and I didn't see her until she stood before me. I knew my eyes were bloodshot; I knew I looked a great deal older than I really was. I looked around for some shade to stand in but there wasn't any. She took my hands in hers and looked at my eyes. She had to look away. Something in my eyes had frightened her. I started to say, "I haven't slept in five days," but I didn't. I waited to see what she would do next, figuring that true love would triumph. She looked at me again. This time something in her eyes frightened me.

"Oh, Billy, your wings look so nice." She looked at the wings and then at the Lieutenant bars and then back at the wings. Never in my eyes.

And then I saw the red Ford parked by the taxi stand. Behind the steering wheel sat a captain. It was Talmadge Kelly, an old flame of Cora Lee's. She talked fast. "Billy, there's something I been wanting to tell you. . . ."

I didn't want to hear it.

"Getting married tomorrow at the Green Street Methodist. And guess what?"

I didn't guess.

The guitar player was watching us from the Charleston train window. He had a drawn and serious look on his face.

"Want you to be our best man. Oh, please say you. . . ."

I had my right hand over her mouth. I didn't know what I was going to do. Just squeeze it shut, maybe. Then a whooshing cloud of steam blew out from under the train. When it cleared I looked down, and there was Cora Lee sitting on my B-4 bag, pulling down her skirt and starting to cry.

The guitar player leaned out the window. "Come on, Lieutenant. Come on down to Charleston with me."

He met me at the train steps and helped me with the bag.

As the train moved out of the station, the signs on the rat-colored houses that lined the tracks all ran together. Grove's Chill Tonic, Tom's Toasted Peanuts, Eat Bit-O-Honey, Chew Brown Mule, Drink Dr. Pepper. The guitar player began tuning up for the long flat stretch to Charleston. My head was clearing. "Play something fast."

He whipped into "Take Me Back to Tulsa, I'm Too Young to Marry," held it still for a minute, then stopped. "You like that?"

"That's fine. Perfect. Play it a couple times."

He smiled and leaned down close to the strings to watch his flying fingers as the train made a wide swinging turn through Colored Town and headed out for Charleston and the sea.

Ellington White (1924–)

John Ellington White was born in Anderson, on June 9, 1924. He studied at Kenyon College (B.A., 1950), at Johns Hopkins University (M.A., 1954), at Washington and Lee (1946–48), and at the University of Iowa (1952–53). He has taught in the departments of English at the University of Richmond (1954–57), University of Southern Mississippi (1960–61), Longwood College, (1961–65), and Hollins College (1965–67), as well as at Kenyon College, where since 1967 he has served as associate editor of the *Kenyon Review*. In 1958 he held a *Sewanee Review* Fellowship in Fiction. His stories and essays have been published in various anthologies and in periodicals such as the *Kenyon Review, Sewanee Review, Georgia Review, New Story Magazine, South Carolina Review*, and *Sports Illustrated*.

The Perils of Flight

Here it was Monday again, three o'clock—doves mooning in the heat, squirrels scuttling along the drain pipes, the slumberous drone of bees attacking the peach orchard. Midway between the house and the river stood a locust tree; beyond that a fish shed going to pieces, all splinters and nails and the bow of a boat piercing the shingled roof. A falling tide drew the river seaward, but drew it at the river's own unhurried pace, moving along as slick and heavy as oil, too far inland to care much about tides: when the river fell it fell only a few feet, displaying two shelves of mud, perhaps fifty yards apart, onto which logs had drifted, hung, and rotted. Carp wallowed in the warm shallows; a cow plodded shoreward across the marshy flats. A heron rose and floated over the river, a long blue gliding flight which Effie Miles, standing before her bedroom window, followed until a yawn momentarily closed her eyes and she lost the heron in a dazzling haze of water and summer sky. But never mind—heron and river would be there again tomorrow; so would the wallowing carp and sun bearing down out of a cloudless sky; so would she, who had lived among these things all her life and at the edge of sixty-five was not likely to leave them overnight.

But here my mother interrupts: "Effie was always the quiet sister."

And Father replies, "Quiet, hell! She was nuts."

Father remembers too well when Effie used to visit us in Philadelphia, bringing slabs of country ham, apples and peaches, and vegetables from the garden because she assumed that these things were inaccessible in Philadelphia, an assumption which Father naturally objected to and so made himself scarce while Effie, seated in the living room after dinner, told us about the home place, as she was the sister who had stayed there to look after Grandmother after Grandfather died—Effie the family martyr, short, plump, nearsighted old maid. How we pitied her and laughed when she told us about the pool of quicksilver in the river woods. "I think you mean quicksand, Effie." Quicksand, yes, that was what she meant. A cow had broken down a fence and wandered into the stuff. "Poor thing, it cried all one night. Mother got terribly

Ellington White, "The Perils of Flight," *The Georgia Review*, XIV (Fall 1960), pp. 259–74. Copyright 1960 by The University of Georgia Press. Reprinted by permission of Ellington White and *The Georgia Review*.

upset." "And how is Mother, Effie?" "The same. I try to make her comfortable. Brother Samuel is having central heat installed. You know he has taken over the mortgage and plans to come back when he retires." Yes, we knew that. "And what about you, Effie? Will you stay on?" "If Samuel wants me I will." Of course Samuel wanted her! The real question was whether she wanted Samuel. Her answer: "We got on very well as children."

"A nutty woman," says Father, who also remembers Samuel.

Grandmother Miles died at the age of eighty-two, and a year later, true to his word, Samuel returned to the Miles Place Overlooking the Seven Mile Reach, so named because here the river yielded to a perverse seven-mile whim and doubled back on itself, as though, having fallen under the ocean's influence, it regretted its course and had swung around sluggishly in search of another. The place belonged to Samuel by then. At first Mother thought how lovely it was, this picture of brother and sister again united in the old homestead, there to live out the golden years among orchards and barns and the sweet noise of rain crossing the river on idle summer afternoons. Father, however, being more realistic, said that Mother was too sentimental and that her picture was lovely only because she had conveniently removed from it all the differences between the two people involved. Effie was like Grandfather Miles, who had failed as a farmer and ended his days selling Rawleigh products: she was mild and submissive. And Samuel, an Atlanta lawyer and industrious dabbler in real estate, a petrified bachelor, had learned to look upon these traits, especially the latter, as signs of weakness, as something one took advantage of, like poor arithmetic. Perhaps too they reminded him of his father. In any case, if they ever dawned, the golden days soon passed over, and into their place moved the winter of Samuel's discontent. Shivering and numb, Effie withdrew into a corner, there to write us lengthy letters about her feeble-minded inadequacies and poor Samuel who had to put up with them. Poor Samuel: People sent him messages by Effie and so anxious was she to remember them that she forgot who sent them. Poor Samuel: Accustomed to efficiency, he now had someone on his hands who couldn't find the monthly phone bill an hour after it arrived. Poor Samuel: He soon gave up relying on her for anything and went days without speaking because what was the use of speaking to someone who when she spoke, seldom though it was, when the silence had grown too heavy to bear, said quicksilver when she meant quicksand and cows when she meant steers, whereupon, looking away, Samuel would groan with such disgust that she wanted to cut out her tongue. "Didn't Father own a set of *Encyclopedia Britannica?*" Effie asked Mother in one of her letters. "I was trying to find them the other day. There is something I want to ask Samuel, but first I have to make sure I'm asking him about the right thing. Otherwise he won't answer me." Another time she wrote that after lengthy deliberation Samuel had decided that "I need someone on the place to help me. Of course he's right. I'm no longer young, you know." This letter was dated January 6, 1952, and by the middle of February the woman had arrived. Her name was Sara Stramp. "A wonderfully stout, healthy person," according to Effie, "who tells me she has been widowed twice. Imagine! She'll do the house work and get breakfast. I'll fix the other meals." Before long, however, it became apparent that Effie had nothing more to do with the kitchen, that she had turned it over to Mrs. Stramp, whose meals pleased Samuel more than her own—Effie said Mrs. Stramp was, after all, used to cooking for men—and still wanting to be helpful, now that the kitchen was gone, Effie picked up Mrs. Stramp's mop, made Mrs. Stramp's bed, and went on pretending to us that nothing unusual had really happened. "It's marvelous," she wrote, "how Mrs. Stramp has managed to take hold in the few short weeks she has been here." But more marvelous still, as far as we were concerned, was another letter we received from her after Samuel had asked for certain closet keys, keys which Effie had inherited from her mother, but which Samuel felt would be safer with Mrs. Stramp. "I had never realized before," she said, "how nice it is to be without responsibilities." We chose to believe she was telling the truth and hoped with all our hearts that Mrs. Stramp would soon grow to like her.

With nothing to do, deprived of her kitchen, keyless and stifling a yawn, Effie stood before the bedroom window one afternoon buried at the fiery center of July and watched the swallows schooling over the barn like scraps of burned paper blown out of a chimney. Except for Mrs. Stramp, whose room was further down the hall, and who was napping, the house was empty. More squirrels ran down the gutter. Fortunate for them Samuel was away or he would shoot them. Samuel hated squirrels because they robbed the pecan tree and built nests under the eaves. He loved to step out in the morning and blast away. Sunlight and gunshots and warm piles of furry bodies: those were Effie's immediate recollections, and she shivered. An electric fan hummed; so, she noticed, did the air hum over the barn, and looking that way she saw why: the swallows had been joined by a solitary lump of silver flashing down the sky, an airplane crackling like fire. Effie watched it roll over the orchard and then disappear behind the house. "How lovely," she said, crossing the room for a final glimpse through the opposite window, but before she could get there, having stupidly paused midway to debate with herself whether or not to wake Mrs. Stramp, which she decided finally not to do, all signs of the lovely thing had vanished. Oh well, there was nothing unusual about airplanes these days, she thought, and returned to her customary view of the river. It saddened her to think that Samuel was going to have the old fish shed torn down. He was afraid of being sued if it fell on someone, as if that was likely to happen. But perhaps he was right. She didn't know. All things seemed to outlive their usefulness. But the fish shed. . . . She tried to imagine the view without it. Very flat, she was afraid, and calculated—all that green green grass falling without a break into the river. Samuel had said nothing so far about the broken-down wharf in front of the shed, but having been warped lopsided by too many winters, it would have to go soon, she felt, and with it the double row of old pilings, each crowned by a thick bushy growth, which still managed to keep their rotten heads a foot or so above the muddy water. Their heads and the head—she looked closer—the head of another. A bird swooped and the thing moved.

Effie cried, "Mrs. Stramp, Mrs. Stramp come here! Hurry!"

Squeaking bed springs, a thump, feet padding down the hall, and Mrs. Stramp was there, fixing a pair of glasses on her large nose—a short shapeless woman standing on thick legs.

"There!" Effie said, pointing towards the river.

Mrs. Stramp peered out of the window.

"I don't see anything."

"Look!"

Again the bird dove, followed by a heavy splash, and stunned, Effie and Mrs. Stramp, who jumped back, watched a pair of white arms emerge from the spray—whiter, they seemed, than the wings of the diving bird. Slapping first the water, then the air, they were bringing a man to shore, bringing him slowly, none too expertly, but bringing him ashore all the same. Effie grabbed Mrs. Stramp's arm. It was a grip which said we are two old ladies in a house by ourselves and here comes a man swimming towards us: what are we going to do?

Among waves of his own making, thrashing and churning, a man washed ashore. He plodded across the muddy flats, still striking at the air, and fell headlong into the fish shed.

"What do you suppose he wants in there?" Effie asked, her voice trembling as thoughts of Samuel entered her mind. "We had better telephone Samuel," she said.

"And tell him a man's in the fish shed? Fat chance he'd believe that."

"He's got to believe it."

"Not him."

"No?"

"No."

"But we can't just stand here."

"I don't know why not."

Effie said, "But the man may be hurt."

"He didn't look hurt to me."

"What can we tell from here."

"All right, then, we'll go down *there*."

"Alone?"

"It was your idea."

Was it? Effie couldn't seem to remember. She said, "Shouldn't we take the first aid kit?"

"Suit yourself," Mrs. Stramp replied.

Some years later, when Mrs. Stramp was dead and Samuel occupied the same bed in which his mother had died, and had the same nurse— in 1957, to be exact, when Effie, on her way north to visit Buddy Stramp, her dear friend's only son, stopped over in Philadelphia to see us, she said that neither she nor Mrs. Stramp, "Sara," found anything to talk about after leaving the house and starting down the hill. "Sara looked calm, but then she always did. I kept thinking there ought to be a storm approaching, some of those monstrous black clouds such as you see in the summer, all swollen with thunder and spouting lightning." But no storm was in sight. A few of Samuel's cows gazed at them from the woods and mild little butterflies fluttered around their ankles.

When they reached the shed, they heard a moan, followed in the same breath by "Survival kit, hell!" and a little package sailed through one of the holes in the wall and dropped at their feet. A boy sat in the shed among rotten fish nets, in which his feet had somehow become entangled, like a fish covered with mud and green slime that had flopped ashore. Wet black hair hung over a face as incapable of inflicting harm as the butterflies through which they had walked to reach him.

"You there," Mrs. Stramp said. "Hello."

The boy looked up, blinking and dazed. He looked first behind him, then at the vacant door.

"Over here," Mrs. Stramp said, rapping sharply over the hole that once upon a time had been a window.

The boy saw her and words rushed out of his mouth. "Stay away from that river, lady! Snakes, birds. . . . Where am I anyway?"

"Mr. Samuel Miles's place," said Mrs. Stramp, to which, Effiie, leaning over her shoulder, added, "He's a lawyer. Who're you?"

The boy shook his head.

"Are you in pain?"

"Pain," he repeated.

"Yes, pain." And Effie held up the first aid kit so that he could see it. He turned away.

"I wrapped myself around a piling out there and looked a snake in the eye bigger around than your head."

"Why don't you come out if your're not hurt," Mrs. Stramp said. "We want to look at you."

He muttered something about birds and ground his heels into the dirt.

"What about birds?"

"One attacked me."

"Well, there aren't any birds out here now."

"You're sure of that."

"Of course I'm sure."

Disentangling himself, the boy stood up, groping for the door, and saying, as he emerged, "Why should a bird have it in for me? I think it was an eagle." He was tall and thin, almost frail, and dressed very oddly in a single-piece brown outfit.

"Can't you find anything to talk about except birds and snakes?" Mrs. Stramp said. "Who are you anyway? How'd you get here?"

"This is posted land," Effie reminded him.

The boy looked out over the river. "And I thought I was safe when I reached those pilings. Ha! I mean it was like a zoo out there."

Mrs. Stramp turned to Effie. "He must be out of his mind."

"House on hill," Effie said. "Big white house. Can you make it?"

She took one of his arms, Mrs. Stramp the other, and slowly they led him away from the river. He came willingly enough, but he came like someone who talked (about birds and snakes) as well as walked in his sleep, and when at one point along the way the shadow of a buzzard slid across the grass in front of them, he stopped dead. "I tell you, that bird's after me."

"Don't be such a fool," Mrs. Stramp said. "Either you keep quiet or we'll all lose our minds."

"I almost lost my head," the boy mumbled. "The way that bird zoomed down. . . ."

"Now listen," Mrs. Stramp said, "do you want us to leave you right here, 'cause if you do just say one more word about birds and snakes?"

Effie touched her on the shoulder—"Don't." How could they expect the boy to defend himself against animals and them too, all in the same day? She placed her hand on his thin shoulders, which a lifetime of mistreatment, she imagined, had broken down, and smiling asked him to take a step forward.

"Now another," she said.

And soon they were walking again. The boy refused absolutely to go near Samuel's cows, which had stepped out of the woods, and this meant they had to go around the house and approach it from the rear. The back door was locked and while Mrs. Stramp went inside to open it, the boy sat down on the steps and looked around him bewildered.

"Where'd you say this was?"

"Samuel Miles' place," Effie told him.

"I mean what state."

"Why, Georgia!" Effie said.

"Hell, I thought I was further along than that."

"Were you swimming someplace?"

"I was swimming to get out of that river, mam."

"But where did you begin?"

"Florida. About an hour ago, I guess."

Effie shook her head. Poor boy, why should insanity have chosen him. Those nice clear eyes and smooth fair skin. . . . No, it didn't seem fair, she thought, standing over him until Mrs. Stramp opened the door, whereupon, helping him to his feet, Effie said, "Let's go inside and rest."

Something resembling a path had been worn through the dying-ground of discarded furniture called the back porch. Rising under the eaves on one side were chairs, numerous broken tables, lamps and ruined suitcases; on the other, holding back a stack of old newspapers and magazines, stood a cushionless sofa. With a heavy groan the boy collapsed onto the bare springs.

"No!" Effie cried, trying to catch him, "upstairs."

But this was the end of the road for him. He opened one eye and looked up hazily.

"You might telephone the police and tell them where the wreckage is."

"Wreckage?" Mrs. Stramp stepped closer. "What's he talking about?"

The boy mumbled something to himself, rolled over and fell asleep.

"Do you know what he means?"

Effie shook her head, smiling. "No," she said, "but neither does he."

"I'm not so sure. All that garble about birds and snakes. It sounds fishy."

Effie wiped a spot of mud away from the boy's face. She couldn't get over how young and honest it was. "Something's after him," she said. "Something"—she wanted to say "like Samuel" but refrained—"something awful I know. The least we can do is to let him rest here a while. He looks hungry to me. No telling when they fed him last."

"They?" Mrs. Stramp inquired.

"Wherever he came from. He had to come from some place. Florida he says, but you can't believe that. An institution maybe." An idea had formed in her mind that after years of confinement the boy had squeezed through a window, slid down the drain, stumbled long dark miles and found himself at the river's edge with tireless dogs baying at his heels.

"The point is where does he go from here," Mrs. Stramp said, walking into the house.

A moment later she was back, spinning through the open kitchen door—"Samuel's home!"

Samuel! To Effie the word meant police, efficiency, wailing sirens, and cruel muscles stuffing the poor defenseless boy into a strait jacket. She cried, "Oh, no!"

"Oh, yes," said Mrs. Stramp. "He must have come back while we were gone."

There followed a moment of panic. Pushing past Effie, Mrs. Stramp lost her balance, and striking out blindly for something to steady herself, she came in contact with the magazines. Down they slid, by the dozens, and the boy who was sleeping in the path vanished from view.

Effie was struck dumb.

Mrs. Stramp, who had come to rest on her face at the top of the pile, turned over, blowing hair out of her mouth. "If Samuel hears him, he's done for!" she gasped, and began shoveling magazines off the boy's head. How quietly he lay there, how still! Now they saw why. His forehead carried a small lump over one brow, left there by the blow that had knocked him insensible.

So began an odd course of events; so began a friendship. Telling us about it, Effie grew excited at this stage of her story. For her it was the climax, the moment of revelation, when the unspoken word issued forth and the word was *yes*—Mrs. Stramp, who had but lately arrived on the Miles scene, Mrs. Stramp stout and worldly, who commanded a male's wisdom, having inherited it from her two husbands, Mrs. Stramp was on her side, on Effie's hitherto defenseless side drawn up around the boy's body, waiting for Samuel to attack. "Oh, Sara, dear Sara," Effie exclaimed, "she was wonderful!" And the boy, what about him, lying among the junk of a generation: wet, muddy, with a lump on his forehead—was he wonderful too? "Oh, yes, everything considered, he was wonderful too. You see, poor thing, he had no way of knowing that what we were doing was being done in his behalf. How could he, not knowing Samuel! After tying his arms and legs and after Sara had put the towel in his mouth. . . ." (Here we sat forward on our chairs— "You mean you gagged him?") "To keep him from crying out when he came to, yes: to keep Samuel from hearing him. It was Sara's idea that when Samuel went to bed we would take him upstairs with us. Wonderful Sara! To think that after all those weeks of being with her I had never glimpsed her kind generous soul!" Enough of Sara. What about the boy? ("After you bound and gagged him. . . .") "Well, he woke up; he began to thrash and kick something awful."

(You see he had no way of knowing that this thing which had happened to him had happened for his own good.)

So he complained.

"Hush, hush," Effie pleaded, "you've got to lie quiet."

Crude animal noises filtered through the towel as he pitched about on the rusty springs, so heedlessly that Effie dropped to her knees beside the sofa—"Please, please"—stroking his face—"please! There's someone here who mustn't hear you, an awful person." Round, rolling, terror-stricken eyes pitifully betrayed by her who now leaned over him, overcome, and kissed his forehead, whereupon he began to thrash with renewed vigor.

"Now look what you've done," Sara hissed.

"Don't," Effie said. "Please don't. It's for your own good, everything." She thought they should take the towel out of his mouth, but Sara shook her head and said, "No."

"He looks so worried."

"He'll look worse than that if Samuel gets hold of him."

The sun had dropped behind a bank of pink clouds, casting over the porch a hot lurid glow. Dinner time was approaching and somewhere within the house sat Samuel eyeing the clock. In time the boy wore himself out and lay still. Effie found a chair which she drew up beside him while Sara took down her apron from a hook near the kitchen door and tied it around her.

"I'll tell Samuel you aren't feeling well," she said, to which Effie replied, "You might blame something on me too; that always makes him feel good."

The boy moaned.

Effie said, "Please don't do that. We're only trying to help you. Won't you believe me?"

Again those coarse animal noises, less strident than before but no less painful to hear. Effie held his bound hands in hers, rubbing them. The air grew cool, rising off the river. The first stars appeared. He tried to say something.

"What?" Effie leaned closer.

There was another attempt then silence, followed by a despairing moan.

"If I remove the towel," Effie said, "will you promise not to make a sound?"

Not a sound, his eyes answered hopefully.

"And you won't tell Sara?"

Never.

When Effie had ungagged him, words rushed forth—"Undo my feet, lady, and let me go! How about it, huh? I haven't done anything to you, honest!"

"Whoever said you had?"

"Then turn me loose. What do you say?"

The boy was wild—round beseeching eyes, trembling voice, a pale wet mouth which trembled when he spoke.

"When Samuel goes to bed, we'll talk about it," Effie said.

"Is he like you are?"

"Like I am?"

"You know. . . ." But that was as far as he got before confusion overcame him. He said, "Just turn me loose, that's all."

"Where would you go?"

"Back to the river, anywhere."

"Birds and snakes," Effie reminded him.

"I'll take my chances. Just untie me. You won't be sorry. I'll send you other things to play with, dolls, games. . . ."

Effie nodded and smiled. "You rest now. We'll play games when Samuel goes to bed."

The boy was silent for a moment; then he eyed her suspiciously and said, "Just what kind of game do you have in mind, lady?"

"Hide and Seek, Red Light, anything you want."

"Why don't we play now? I'll hide, you seek me."

"But Samuel might find you," Effie laughed.

"Oh, no, he wouldn't."

"I don't know. He's awfully clever about finding things."

"He wouldn't find me."

"He will if you don't speak lower."

Fireflies drifted beyond the screening. Effie rolled the towel into a pillow and placed it under his head. She removed his shoes, then his socks, and drew a pan of water to wash his face. His eyes looked swollen and tired. It pained her to touch the lump on his forehead, a small lump, but nevertheless they had inflicted it upon him. The least she could do was make him comfortable. He seemed to have no objections and closed his eyes wearily while she massaged his temples. A light wind had sprung up, rustling the pecan tree beside the porch. Going round and round, her finger tips grew numb and her eyes heavy while herons roosted along the river bank and the boy said dreamily, "There's another game I've always liked. It's called 'Telephone the Police'. Ever hear of it? You pretend there's been an airplane crash and want the police to know where the pilot is."

"That sounds like an interesting game," Effie said. "Are you a pilot?"

"I think I am."

"Isn't that nice. Sleepy, pilot?"

"I'm tired."

"Then sleep. Maybe you'll dream of airplanes, lovely silver airplanes. Maybe one of them will be yours and you'll be zooming across the sky."

"But what if I crash?"

"Oh, you won't crash."

"But what if I do?"

"Whoever finds you will take you in. They'll look after you."

"Tie me up?"

"If it's for your own good they will."

"Will they ever turn me loose?'

"If you want them to."

"I want them to now."

"But you aren't dreaming."

"I think I am. Dreaming that a bird chased me out of the river and two old women tied me up and"—his voice gave out—"here I am."

"Here you are," Effie said, smiling because she did not know when she had felt quite so rested and quiet as she felt now, yes, and happy because through the boy she had found Sara: she had found a friend. No longer would she be alone with Samuel in the Miles Place Overlooking the Seven Mile Reach. Sara would be with her, and together—well, together they could do anything, anything, she thought, looking around for something to lay over the boy's shoulders. Finding nothing on the porch, she walked into the kitchen. Through a crack in the door she caught a glimpse of Samuel sitting at the far end of the dining room table; his white hair, his cast iron chin, his strong hooked nose were poised intently over the mouth of a portable radio while Sara, sitting across from him, looked at her plate and said nothing to interfere with the evening stock market report: such a ghastly scene that Effie shivered and turned away. As she did so a light flashed across the kitchen. A car had driven into the front yard. Drawing close to the window, Effie watched a man get out of the car and walk into the head-lights, displaying the uniform of a policeman. She almost screamed: here came the snake, here came the pursuing bird!

Mumbling in his sleep, the boy said, "Got to get away. . . ."

And so you will, Effie thought, and so you will, as she stuffed the towel in his mouth—"No sudden noises," she whispered—and freed his feet.

"Now stand up," she said with the door bell ringing furiously. "Hurry!" She knew exactly what to do.

Half asleep he responded, as though conditioned by previous bad dreams. Here was another coming up. Why question it? He clubbed along behind her on bare leaden feet.

They crossed the backyard and went through an opening in the fence. Ahead lay the orchard, beyond that another fence and more trees sagging in the pale light of a half moon. Rotten apples breaking open under their feet released a sharp tingling odor. Frogs groaned in the distance. They slithered on. Splintered hips, the peril of old women, flashed across Effie's mind, but nothing, nothing, she felt, could break her bones this night.

"Not much further," she panted, pulling the boy through a gate and into a field where cows were grazing around a small frame shed. Dew lay on the roof, glistening in the moonlight.

"I used to come here when I was a girl," Effie said without any reason for saying it, and swinging back on rusty hinges, the door sounded as though it had not been opened since then. She drew him inside and shut the door. Small feet scampered away in the darkness.

"Mice," Effie assured him. "But we won't be here long. As soon as the policeman leaves we'll go back."

The boy squealed—a glimmer of insanity, Effie thought, showing through his feeble-mindedness—and began to stamp his feet.

"Shake your trousers!" Effie cried, thinking of mice.

He rushed against the door. He kicked it and tried to bite Effie's hand when he found it holding down the latch. Then he turned against the back wall where wood was stacked to the ceiling and assaulted it with all his force. Logs three feet long crashed down on his shoulders.

Effie had to dig him out.

"It's a wonder you don't hurt yourself carrying on like that," she said. "That policeman's not going to harm you."

The boy wouldn't move. He had had enough for one day. Logs on top of snakes, birds, and two old women had altogether subdued him, and he lay there quietly gasping while Effie hovered overhead. When his breathing had grown more regular, she slipped out of the door and locked it behind her.

By the time she reached the house, the policeman had gone and a light burned in Samuel's downstairs bedroom. For once in her life, she thought, she had put something over on him, and this gave her a curious sense of power. She crossed the backyard and ran happily up the steps. Sara was waiting in the kitchen.

"They must have done terrible things to him, Sara," Effie said, recounting her adventure. "I just mentioned the word 'policeman' and he threw a fit."

Sara shook her head. "Sit down, Effie. I've got something to tell you."

There was a frightening note in her voice. Like the tolling of a fire bell, it announced disaster. "What's that, Sara?"

"He's a pilot."

"Who? That boy!" Nonsense.

"Boy nothing! He's a young man. Everybody for miles around is looking for him. His plane crashed further down the river."

"Oh, my goodness." Her voice whistled as she sat down and after a moment or two of stunned silence she said, "Does Samuel know?"

"Know that he's locked up here? Know that we bound and gagged him? Know that we captured him?"

Effie winced and nodded her head.

"Not yet, but by morning he will. All I can think of is how it will look in the papers: 'Women Hold Pilot Hostage'."

"They would say that!"

"Of course they would. That's exactly what we've done."

"But we didn't mean to."

"It doesn't matter whether we meant it or not. The point is we did it and now have got to find some way of undoing it."

"Couldn't we just open the door to the wood shed and run? He doesn't know where he is."

"We told him, didn't we?"

"But how will he remember that? He was out of his head. Besides, if I were a pilot, I'd be ashamed for anyone to know that two old women had captured me."

"His pride might not be as large as yours, Effie."

"Oh, I think it is."

"All we can do is hope it is. Did you untie him?"

"I untied his feet."

"And his hands."

"No."

"We'll have to do that."

Walking back through the orchard, through the odor of rotten peaches and the sound of rustling leaves, they heard wailing whippoor-wills and boards breaking in the distance. "He must be trying to get out," Sara said, to which Effie, who had been thinking of how she had pulled him through here in his bare feet, added, "He must think we're a little bit crazy."

Sara's reply: "If that's all he thinks I'm grateful."

"What else could he think?"

"We're two old women, Effie. He's a young man."

"Sara, he wouldn't dare!"

As they came out of the orchard into a patch of moonlight, a figure suddenly joined them, leaping over a fence. He seemed to turn in space, his bare ankles flashing like blades, and the next thing they knew he had gained the branches of a peach tree and pulled himself among the leaves.

"Stay away!" he snarled. "Both of you. Come one step nearer and I'll kick your heads off!"

"We were bringing you these," Effie said, holding out his shoes.

"Put 'em on the ground. I'm wise to your tricks now." Shrouded in leaves, he swayed to and fro, lean and fierce looking, more monkey than man, more man than boy. "Think you could hold me, did you!"

Sara said, "We were coming to untie you."

"Yes," Effie smiled, "you're free."

"You bet I'm free, lady, and I intend to stay that way. Now clear out!" He kicked at them, shaking the branches.

"Won't you please climb down and get your shoes?" Effie asked him. "There's something I want you to know."

"I'm listening."

"Not in a tree."

"I'd rather be in a tree than anywhere else on this place."

"Put the shoes down, Effie." This from Sara, who pointed to the fence. "We'll go stand over there."

"Further," the boy said. "Further still. Keep moving."

"We can't. There's a fence."

"Climb over it."

"You climb down. We've gone far enough."

The boy hesitated for a moment, then warily dropped to the ground. "All right," he said, pulling on his shoes, "I guess that does it. I'm off."

"Any place in particular?" Sara asked him.

"I'll find a road."

"Would you believe me if I told you where to find it?"

"I might."

"Beyond the orchard," she said, "you'll come to a gravel lane. Follow it through the woods."

The boy walked away. Walking behind him came Effie—"Watch out for quicksilver"; and behind Effie came Sara—"She means quicksand"; and the boy, glancing over his shoulders, began to walk faster.

"We could fix you a box of lunch," Effie called. Then: "Whatever you may think of us, don't think for a moment that we weren't thinking about you too."

The boy began to run.

Sara ran a little ways herself—"What she means is that we weren't thinking about ourselves."

Soon his outline faded among the trees, so quietly, so quickly, that neither of them was quite certain that the departure had really occurred and stood there in the wet grass waiting for something further to happen.

"But it never did," Effie said, looking at her watch. "I'm not going to miss my train, am I?"

"To hell with your train!" This from our Philadelphia-born father, ordinarily calm, who had edged into the living room without our knowing it—"Go on! What happened then?"

Effie smiled. "Oh, nothing," she said.

"You mean. . . ."

"I mean I was right. The boy was too proud, too fine, to tell the authorities about our mistake. He said he had been lost. At least the newspapers said he had been lost."

"And Samuel never found out?"

"Oh, yes, we told him everything. Poor Samuel," she sighed, "he was in much the same fix as the boy. Too proud to admit we had put something over on him. He refused to believe us. He couldn't believe us and still have the last word, and the last word, you know, is something that Samuel can't do without, like some people can't do without drink, regardless of what it costs them. He told us to go to bed, that we were out of our minds. And that, of course, is what the boy thought too. Oh, men," she said, "they're all alike."

Max Steele (1922–)

One of the founding editors of the *Paris Review,* Maxwell Steele was born in Greenville in 1922 and educated at Furman University, Vanderbilt University, the University of North Carolina, and the Sorbonne. His novel *Debby* (1959) won the $10,000 Harper Prize for fiction and the Mayflower Cup, and was reissued under the title *The Goblins Must Go Barefoot* in 1967. A volume of short stories, *Where She Brushed Her Hair and Other Stories,* was published in 1968. Mr. Steele is presently the head of the creative writing program at the University of North Carolina at Chapel Hill.

The Ragged Halo

During the five years that he was in Europe, Richard Gates' mother had written in almost every letter how fast the little Piedmont town was changing, how suddenly it was becoming full of Northerners and other outsiders, and how if he didn't hurry home he would not even recognize Main Street.

But as the "Cotton Queen" braked to a hush in the station he could see no change whatsoever. In the murky dawn, there it stood: the grimy, painted-red, brick station with its steep and sooted tile roof and ginger-bread trimmings. After having admired the magnificent clean lines of the cool post-war railroad stations in Rome and in Florence and in numerous little German villages, built in part or in all with American dollars, he wondered why Leesville had not managed to get itself onto a War Relief list.

The day before, as the *Ile de France* was docking, a cabin steward had handed him a cable. The unsigned cable had simply said: "Phone home immediately." He had written to his mother that he planned to go to Indiana to see Kathryn even though they were no longer engaged and so he could not imagine why she should, after this long, be so impatient; but mainly he wondered how the seventy-year old lady had known in what way to cable a passenger on an in-coming ship. The truth was that by such thinking he was delaying panic until he could get through Customs and to a telephone. He had not been at all surprised, in fact, when Hattie, his oldest sister, answered in a tear-tightened voice: "Richard, can you come on home . . . Right now. Mama's awful sick . . . two days ago . . . No. She won't go to the hospital. Dr. Henry Beetle's afraid she won't live till you get here . . . she doesn't know I cabled, but she keeps asking if you're on your way yet. Deliah got in from California yesterday and we're all just waiting for you now . . . well, it's *real* real good to heah you, heah?" In spite of the sorrow, the voice was pleasant and so Southern he'd almost laughed.

Standing outside the grimy station, the heavy packs in hand, he scanned the asphalt square for one of his brothers or sisters. All the

Max Steele, "The Ragged Halo," *The South Carolina Review,* I (Nov. 1968), pp. 23–37. Copyright 1968 by *The South Carolina Review.* Reprinted by permission of Max Steele and *The South Carolina Review.*

new cars were the same to him: all outlandishly long: pastel: pinks, blues, creams, like the ridiculous shirts which even the workmen were wearing. The whole country looked like a Danny Kaye musical.

"Reechie! Reeeechie Gates!" Across the square a car door opened. A frail little lady, Miss Annie Pickens, was waving a newspaper and making a song of his name: "Ree-e-e-chie! Reee-e-e-chie Gea-a-tes!" Her white hair, cropped short in an Italian cut, framed her face in silver light. With apelike elegance, his knees bent and his arms extended by the luggage, he swung across the square.

"Honey, it's so *good* to see you!" Miss Annie Pickens turned her spinster cheek to be kissed and held him till he'd touched his lips quickly and without pressure to her dry, wrinkle-webbed face. Before he could tell her that she was certainly looking well, she stepped back and cried: "Look at me. I'm sixty-eight. Same age to the very week as your Aunt Mamie. Neeavah felt bettah in mah life!" She did a Suzy-Q in her baby-blue tennis shoes, her fresh pink seer-sucker flaring up and out. "Get in the car. I'm gonna take you to your Mama." She had come expressly to the station to fetch him. He didn't really know her that well, had never really talked to her except once: she had invited him to tea to brief him on his European trip and since then they had exchanged a few picture postcards.

She talked all the way through town as though they were the oldest of friends: "Chicken! I know if there's two there's a dozen fried chickens in that house this minute. Everybody in town. Cantaloupes! And potato salad! I told your sister Hattie, that sweet thing, just to politely shut the door in the face of anyone else who couldn't offer anything better than their old potato salad. In weather like this, I wish you would!" She raved on about the frozen pistachio-pear salad she herself had made and carried: "Cream! Pure cow's cream and a quart of it. But I don't reckon there's anybody what 'preciates your mama like I do. We *know* what she's been through."

As he lifted his bags out of the car and asked her again to come in and have breakfast with him, she said what he'd been waiting for her to say but which out of respect for the gravity of the illness she had refrained from uttering: "But I want to heah all about your trip to Europe." Meaning, of course, that she wanted to tell him in detail about her locally famous (and secretly ridiculed) tour of Europe with her father, after the death of her mother, some fifty years ago.

In the same way a barren woman attaches herself to pregnant women, Miss Annie attached herself to anyone either going to or returning from Europe, and made them share with her the excitement of that eighteen-year old girl who would be forever on a cafe terrace sipping her first wine. "Chianti! Honey, did you drink any Chianti when you were over there?" Now an avid W.C.T.U. leader, Miss Annie, nevertheless, sparkled when she asked in a lowered voice: "Isn't it the *best* thing you ever did taste?" Later he would go sit on her porch and hear again how the yellow-gold, butterfly broach, which had belonged to her mother: "Just kindly dropped off and fluttered to the silver floor of that beautiful Grotto. And I didn't care! Didn't care one teenie bit! That's how foolish I was over that Italian fisherman. Ugliest man in the world! Had a fishhook scar on his left jaw! And I'd never even laid my eyes on him before that very morning. He couldn't speak a wuhd of English. Not a wuhd. But with those eyes he didn't need to!"

He shut the car door and leaned through the window to thank her again for getting up early enough to meet the six o'clock train. "Can't come in. Got to go this minute and put myself in a big tub of cold water . . ." Suddenly she interrupted her social voice with one quite different, intimate, and sober: "You didn't find yourself a wife while you were over there?"

He was tempted to tell her about Kathryn and their plans to be married if they liked each other as much in the States as they had in Paris, but suddenly he saw in his mind the letter from Kathryn breaking the engagement. "You don't," he was uncertain whether to shock her or not, "have to get married in Paris."

For a second she caught her breath. "Don't wait too long." She looked directly at him, then laughed her easy, social, meaningless laugh as the car rolled out and away from the curb. "Tell your mother I love her."

The full milk bottles were still in the basket on the wide, shrub-darkened porch. Richard Gates slid his luggage to rest by the column and sank onto the swing, over which a crape myrtle was shedding burgundy blossoms. Waiting for lights or for footsteps in the house before twisting the brass bell handle, he could hear over and over, as one does after a night without sleep, the last words spoken to him: "Tell your mother I love her."

He could predict and hear his mother's answer: "Wish she and some of her fine friends might have shown it earlier. When you children needed help and before you got out doing things on your own. Think she'd ever have gone to meet you if you'd been coming in without even carfare, like you used to, from the University?"

Ordinarily his mother was not a bitter woman nor a cynical one, but when she suspected slights against her children, she could be both with pride and with fury.

But still, Miss Annie had met him and had, as far back as he could remember, always seemed especially interested, however briefly and distantly, in each of them. And she had said: "Nobody 'preciates your mama more than I do. Cause I *know* . . ."

Many people in the town said the same, but what really did they know, most of them who had never even seen her? That she had borne ten children, two dead, and raised eight? That for 35 years she had had children to send off to school each September? But did they know that for 20 years she had made the dresses and petticoats, coats and scarves for four daughters and the shirts for four sons and a husband? That during the Depression she had handwashed their clothes, and on hands and knees, steamed and pressed their suits on the kitchen floor when she was too tired to stand to iron? And that she had cooked for them and fed them all, sometimes, as in the summer of 1932 on as little as ten cents a meal?

He had been seven years old that summer and the Depression was only a vague word to him. To keep him out of the house, which, with the three sister-in-laws, now held 13 people, his job was to mow the front lawn and side yard, rake the leaves, and trim the crape-myrtle which, otherwise, hung into the porch and over the steps. Each morning he was given a nickel with which to buy the biggest watermelon which the Negroes pushed by in their carts; and he was to send Uncle John McGraw to the door if he had pole beans by the gallon or roastnears by the dozen.

He had been too young then to know what was happening to his mother. She was simply the tall, angry woman who pushed back her sweat-drenched pompadour with a dripping hand, and removing her apron, swooped from time to time into the yard to issue sharp orders to him or to Deliah who sometimes helped with the weeding. From morning till night she had not a moment to listen to him, and when she spoke it was to remind them that without her they would be triflin', goodfornothin', lazy young'uns who would never get anywhere in this world.

Her fury subsided only when she occasionally cried and pleaded forgiveness: "My back is killing me and my feet are like boils." Too proud to wear house slippers, and too poor to buy new shoes, she, for awhile that summer, had made her way from sink to stove to sink in the painful steps of a Chinese bound woman. Finally, Mrs. Carlisle had given her a pair of old satin dance slippers with heels cut low. The black satin was in strings and the thin soles loose at the toe, but they were exactly large enough to remove all pressure and yet give support. Every day after that when the thirteen of them sat down to dinner, his mother with a clean afternoon dress on and her hair newly combed and with a more pleasant face than they had seen that summer, his father would end the blessing, saying: "And bless Mrs. Carlisle for those satin slippers!"

However, the day had finally come, late in July, when even his father could not make them laugh: again that day, as every day, there were only greenbeans, cornbread and cantaloupe to eat. But no one laughed at his new joke about the monotonous menu. Instead, when he expressed his surprise at the lunch, a terrible silence hung over the table, with only the silver tinkle of ice in the tea glasses making fine eddies of sound in the still air. Elizabeth and William, who sat at the far end of the table and gossiped usually about the university and how and if they could manage to go back in the fall, began, in the terrible silence, to speak very quietly in French.

His mother leaned forward, a strange and puzzled look on her face.

"Mama," he had wanted to tell her that for seven cents, only two pennies more, he could have bought a thirty pound watermelon for that afternoon, but her hand closed over his and pressed for silence. She listened to Elizabeth and William speaking French and turned her head in a querulous fashion. Everyone was watching her, alarmed. Elizabeth stopped in the middle of a word and, with arched brows and tilted head, stared down the table at her mother, demanding explanation.

"Elizabeth," his mother said, and a shy, wounded smile distorted her face. "What kind of talk is that?"

"French," Elizabeth said.

"Is *that* what we're sending you to college to learn?" His father would make a joke of it yet. (Even later, on his death bed, he had made jokes to help them.)

"Hush, James!" his mother said. "Go on," she pleaded, suddenly timid before Elizabeth. "Speak some more."

Elizabeth stammered through another sentence and then William answered, fluently but briefly, for the silence closed in over his words.

"Go on!" his mother prompted.

They tried to speak a little more, but abruptly, his mother, smiling oddly, pushed back her chair, and without excusing herself, fled from the room.

He was not allowed to follow. While he and Deliah peeped from the kitchen window and the older ones from the backdoor his father went out to where she was sobbing, huddled over on a small box, under the fig tree, which was in bloom with three dozen drying dinner napkins.

His father had talked awhile, picked a green fig, examined the milk-drop, tossed it aside and returned to the house.

"Leave her alone. Come finish your dinner. She needs to cry awhile."

They had followed him back to the table where he began telling a long story about Mrs. Roosevelt and a Negro which no one, not even Deliah, listened to.

"But what's she crying about," Elizabeth asked. "We weren't talking about her."

"It's her age."

"But my God!" William put down his fork. "It's been her age for ten years now. Any other doctor would have stopped it five years ago."

Richard and Deliah had exchanged glances over the table and at a signal had excused themselves, unnoticed, carried their dishes and glasses to the cooktable and fled to the backyard where their mother sat, still weeping, but softly to herself. They had stood quietly, one on each side of her, and held their fingers to their lips. Even without looking up, she knew they were there. "Children," she said in attempted firmness, "go on back in and finish your dinner."

Deliah fingered the lace at her mother's neck and touched with outstretched fingertips the cameo. "Mama, why are you crying?"

"I don't know, baby."

"Is it because you're getting old?"

"I'm just so tired."

"But you don't cry every day."

"I feel like it. When I look at the way you're being brought up. When I think what Ma would say . . ." She shook her head from side to side. "I don't even have time to teach you proper manners."

She dried her eyes on the hem of the voile afternoon dress and pushed them away. "Don't stand so near. It's too hot." She stood, sighed heavily, and began plucking the stiff napkins from the tree. They had, the older children, argued with her to use paper napkins, but she had answered that they would have linen and silver at every meal even if they didn't have a bit to eat. Often she was washing table cloths at midnight; and he and Deliah, every Sunday after church, had to polish silver.

"They weren't talking about you," he told her.

"Who?" She was gathering the napkins in slow, uncertain gestures.

"William and Elizabeth."

"Why were you crying?" Deliah asked again.

With no warning, as though her knees had lost all strength, she sat down again on the box. "I'm so silly." She tried to dry her eyes. "I just happened to remember something. That was all."

At first she had been reluctant to tell them, but finally when they were sitting on the grass, begging, knowing it was one of those stories that would go back almost to the Civil War, she remembered again, aloud.

"I was no older than Deliah. And Ma, your grandmother, got us up real early one morning on a day as hot as today. 'Children!' She said, 'you must help me this morning. We're going to have company.'"

Richard and Deliah had been told over and over how their grandmother, who was married during the first year of the Civil War, had been brought up never to lift her hand. "She didn't even wash her own

feet," their mother had once told them, "until after she was married."
Meaning that she'd had a servant to bathe her; but they, misunderstanding, had been delighted with their grandmother's apparent unhygenic
condition and had reported it, with great pride, to all of the children at
Park Lawn school.

"She wouldn't tell us," their mother continued, "who was coming,
but we knew it was special cause she made spice cakes and muscadine
punch all morning." She, herself, had swept and cleaned the yard, and
Aunt Mamie had helped in the kitchen. "That was the way she brought
us up: Mamie was the house-hand, I was the yard nigger."

At three on that faraway afternoon the farmyard had been raked
clean, the low, country house swept spotless. And soon afterwards a
horse and buggy drove up the dusty drive and a lady, very like their
grandmother, had stepped lightly out. The two women had embraced
and cried and laughed and cried and acted like young girls. "Her name
was Elizabeth. The only person I ever heard Ma call by first name."
She'd been one of the twelve bridesmaids in their grandmother's wedding. The two women had sat talking on the porch; and the children
(their mother and Aunt Mamie), had sat on the front step, waiting for
the moment when the spice cakes and muscadine punch would be served
on the crystal plates and in the ringing cutglass goblets.

"We were pinching—I remember as well as this morning—the last
crumbs of gingerbread off the plates when Ma and Aunt Elizabeth
started talking in a way we couldn't understand. You've never seen more
puzzled young'uns than Mamie and me. We giggled and acted so silly
Ma had to shake her finger at us. They talked on that way for an hour,
only now and again dropping a word we could catch."

His mother's voice had suddenly stopped and in the shade of the fig
tree, tears had rolled down her face again, and without bothering to
prevent them with the dry napkins which she held in her lap, she
whispered above her weeping: "And I didn't know until this very day
that it was French she was speaking. Like Elizabeth and William." She
wept without sorrow, almost in joy. "I was just a little yard nigger to
her, my own mother, and now to my own children."

Standing quickly, impatient to see her, remembering now with full
understanding the impact of her sorrow, Richard Gates, stepping with-

out caution on the carpet of fallen crape myrtles, arterial red in the morning sun, moved, as in a dream across the porch to the heavy front door.

"Tell me something pretty. Something I know nothing about." It was late afternoon and the house, after being full of visitors all day, was quiet and dark. His mother was lying flat in the bed, so thin as to make scarcely a fold in the cover. Her black hair pressed into the pillow and her dark eyes burned deep in the sockets.

Two days before, she had fallen in the huge, empty house, unable to move her legs. She had lain, calling in her thin voice to Mrs. Carlisle, but without hope, knowing that she could not make herself heard through the tall closed windows of her own house, or across the heavily shrubbed yards to where, perhaps, with luck, Mrs. Carlisle might have been sitting on her side porch.

Pulling herself, face down, on outstretched arms, sleeping a bit from time to time to gain strength, she had, during the next three hours, managed to drag herself the twenty feet to the telephone. Luckily, as she reported later, a band of sunlight had been slanting through the hall window, falling exactly onto the telephone so that she could see to dial. "Elizabeth," she had said into the phone. "Come see about me. I'm sick." Then she had lain and waited.

To Elizabeth and the doctor she had cried: "I've done my best." And in spite of their reassurances she had insisted: "I made them all get out and away from me. Where they could learn something and improve themselves. I made them go."

That morning she had not cried, as Richard had expected her to, when he walked into the room. During the day she had watched her children, all grown now and greying, with the distant and detached interest of a mother cat regarding an old litter.

"I've been waiting so long to hear," she said now that she and Richard were again alone in the almost empty house.

He protested that, after so much company, she must be tired, must need rest, and that there was too much to tell.

"Then just one pretty party or house you went to. Something pretty I can think about in my sleep."

For a long while he thought. "Last spring, a year ago, when the Sorbonne exams were completed, André gave a dinner party for us." (Kathryn, even then had rebelled, had refused to buy an appropriate dress, and had at the last minute put on blue jeans and gone to sit in a cafe while he went off alone to make excuses for her.) He had written his mother about André, a French student with whom he exchanged French-English lessons.

André, himself, was exceedingly poor. His father, when Hitler moved in, had lost both his own and his wife's fortune in a toy factory in Czechoslovakia. Often the only refreshment André could offer when they studied together in his unheated attic room, was a square of sugar, picked up from a table on a cafe terrace.

"No. I know that sort of life," his mother protested.

"I was going to tell you about his friend, la Baronne de Montefair. Actually she was a girlhood friend of André's mother."

"Now a baroness," his mother said. "Is that the same thing as an aristocrat?"

"It doesn't mean much anymore." He explained a bit about the French revolution to her and about the present economic retardation of the country.

"But she still had a nice home?"

"You remember the card I sent you of the little island in the middle of the Seine? The Ile St. Louis? Just back of Notre-Dame."

"Notre-Dame." His mother Americanized the word. "Seems like I've heard of it."

"The cathedral."

"I looked it up in *The World Book* when you wrote home about it. Seems I can't remember anything anymore." His mother read their letters twice, first to see about their health, and then to copy out words and places which in the long evenings she searched for in the encyclopedias which she had, out of the household money, bought for them when the oldest were children.

"Notre-Dame," he said again.

"She lived there then. This aristocrat."

"Yes, m'am. On the Ile St. Louis where the river divides. It's a wonderful, quiet little island in the center of the city. With trees bending over toward the water and bright colored little fishing boats, orange and blue and green, anchored to the cobblestoned quais."

He attempted to describe to her the huge green doors of the 16th century mansion, the magnificent lions' heads, the fine wrought iron balustrade, etched in brass, bordering the worn marble steps which curved graciously upward to the apartments of the baroness. He tried to carry her with him through the double mahogany doors into the elegant rooms, panelled in white, traced in gold, and to let her see the delicate, gilded chairs dancing across the rose and grey carpets, all reflected in a dozen extravagant mirrors that reached from floor to ceiling and to show her the baroque splendor of the heavily candelabraed table, the tense thin goblets, the dusty bottles of deep red wines and the silver buckets of cooling champagnes. He wanted her to taste the potage á la reine Margot, the thon mariné, the fricassé de poulet, the rôti, the salades, the bleues, the coupes des fruits with fine clear kirsch . . .

But in a flat exhausted voice she interrupted: "I don't know enough to know what you're talking about."

"Food," he said.

"Sweet one, are you hungry? Is there anything in the house to eat? I've plumb forgotten you poor children." She seemed for the moment not to realize that she was mortally ill and that they were grown.

He told her what Miss Annie had said about the hams and chickens and what she had instructed Hattie to do with people bearing gifts of potato salad.

"Leave it to Annie Pickens to try to say something."

"I'm not studying that woman." She pressed her lips together and let her eyes shut to hide the truth. "I've nothing against her. She's been nicer to me than I have to her."

"She seemed very pleasant this morning."

"Oh, she's clever enough. I've never known of her saying a word of harm about anyone." His mother waited. "I've never in fact heard of her ever talking about anything except taking a bath and going to Europe."

Richard laughed. "Does she really talk that much about it?"

"You'd think to hear her tell it," his mother sighed, "that she lived in a tub all summer and Europe all winter."

"She couldn't come in this morning because she had to go get in the tub."

"I just plain out told her once when she caught me cleaning out the stove, with my head all done up in a rag . . . and there she sat just as fresh as a daisy talking about going home to get in the tub . . . I just came right out and said, 'Annie, you must be awfully clean or awfully dirty one to take so many baths.'"

"I don't remember her ever coming here."

"Not much, she didn't. But she never failed to when I had a new baby. She'd come and hold it and say: 'You've got so many, you've got to give this one to me!'"

For awhile he sat silently trying to imagine his overworked mother's temptation, which could explain in part her peevish attitude toward Miss Annie. "She probably envied you," he ventured.

"Me!" his mother said, incredulously. "Annie Pickens?"

"You've lived a pretty full life compared to hers." His mother could never appraise herself in such terms and now she lay, trying hopefully to see if there were any truth in his words.

"Wonder," he thought aloud, "why she never married?"

"Too proud. Like most the Pickens."

"I mean the real reason."

"She used to say when she was young and could have married, 'The pickin's are too good.' But everybody understood she meant *Pickens* were too good. Then after she got back from Europe, she had that nervous trouble and had to go away for another year, and when she came home to stay, all changed, everybody was already thinking of her as an old maid. By the time she was twenty-five she was just like she is today."

"That's how old Kathryn is." He'd told his mother earlier about the letter breaking the engagement, mainly to reassure her that her illness was not an inconvenience to him, that she was in no way "holding him back."

He hadn't told her how empty, as a result of the letter, he had been feeling, as though his own life were a play which he was watching, without too much interest, through the wrong end of opera glasses. Somewhere during the last five years he had lost contact with himself and only Kathryn, he felt, could have saved him from complete and perhaps permanent isolation.

"You never said much about her background."

"*Oh bullshit!*" he wanted to shout. "What's background got to do with anything?"

But he remained silent, knowing that he had been guilty of the same sort of thinking and that that was why Kathryn always called him a snob and all Southerners "proud hypocrites." It was precisely why, once back in the States, in the democratic Midwest, away from the strict social order of France and the implicit ones of the South, she had seen their different values more clearly and known that a marriage between them would be foredoomed.

When he glanced back to the bed his mother was studying his clenched jaw and narrowing eyes. With her usual tact she did not press further. Instead she tried to raise her head, but let it fall back. "Over there, under my sewing basket. I got it out when you wrote you were coming."

He leaned over to the drop-leaf table and slid a book out from under the basket. It was an old book, suede and leather, dusty, with gold letters hardly traceable in the worm-eaten leather. A flowerprint rag, evidently as old as the book itself, was tied in string fashion to keep the cover from falling off. "Aunt Elizabeth gave it to Ma. I've had it in her trunk all these years. But I want you to have it." She added, almost with timidity, her voice weakening: "If it's worth having."

He held the spine to the lamplight and tried unsuccessfully to make out the embossed letters.

"See if you can read any of it."

He untied the careful knot, let the unglued binding fall back, and read the small print midway down the brown page: "Resté dans l'angle, derrière la porte, si bien qu'on l'apercevait à peine, le *nouveau* était un gars de la campagne, d'un quinzine d'années environ, et plus haut de taille qu'aucun de nous tous. Il avait les cheveux coupés droit sur le front, comme un chantre de village, l'air raisonnable et fort embarrassé . . ."

When he glanced up, his mother was watching him with the cold eyes of a stranger. She brushed the sheet smooth with her worn hands and asked in a peculiar voice: "And what's that trying to say?"

He told her briefly that it was the description of an awkward country boy, Charles Bovary, entering a new school.

"Couldn't they have said it just as well in English?" It was a note of near-anger which was giving the peculiar quality to her voice.

"Maybe," he laughed, not unkindly. "But it's pretty in French, isn't it?"

"It's pretty enough, I reckon. If you know what the words mean."

"Quoi qu'il ne fut pas large des épaules . . ." He began again, but over the book he could see his mother's impatient hand on the sheet. She sighed deeply and let her head turn away from him. When he stopped reading she spoke.

"I'm just so tired," she said without opening her eyes. "Everything seems so useless. So foolish."

He kissed her on the forehead and, turning off the little lamp, left the room in the growing twilight.

For awhile he stood on the wide porch and watched a hummingbird hanging and darting and hanging again over the crape myrtles. The dread emptiness, which before his nap he had ascribed to lack of sleep, seeped back into him, with the difference now that it seemed permanent, as though it would never leave. In that moment, at least, he was no longer a young man.

"Don't wait too long," Miss Annie had said about his marrying, and she had stared at him in a strangely penetrating way.

"Poor Miss Annie," he thought. Then, in a happy, fleeting moment, he realized that it was not a yellow-gold, butterfly broach Miss Annie had lost at Capri! There had never been a butterfly broach! That was merely her way of declaring to them without revealing. Nor had it been simply her virginity which she had lost there. In the deepening dusk, he knew with certainty and with sadness that lost also, in the ensuing complications, was that part of her being which could have spun out webs of love strong enough to bind her permanently to another human being. Now there were left only broken wisps of feeling, making about her an impractical, ragged halo of affection.

He shivered and felt immediately the need of light and of human voices. He walked compulsively into the dark house, clicking on lamps as he went. At the telephone he looked up the number and dialed rapidly, without knowing what he would say.

"Miss Annie?" he faltered a moment, then fairly shouted into the phone, "this is Richard Gates. I was just wondering if I dropped a gold cuff link in your car this morning."

There was a long pause and then that charming, meaningless, social laugh, cultivated eventually by each isolated person whose only life is public. "Why honey," she said in the teasing voice of the perpetual flirt, "you know you had on shawt sleeves."

James Dickey (1923–   )

Regarded by many as America's greatest living poet, James Dickey was born in Atlanta on February 2, 1923, and served in the U.S. Air Force in World War II and the Korean War. After attending Clemson on an athletic scholarship, he graduated from Vanderbilt University in 1949, obtaining an M.A. degree there in 1950. That same year, he joined the English faculty at Rice Institute, where he returned to teach from 1952 until 1954. He went to Europe from 1954 until 1955 under a *Sewanee Review* Fellowship for poetry. Dickey taught English at the University of Florida in 1955–56, then spent nearly six years with advertising agencies in New York and Atlanta. A Guggenheim Fellowship permitted him to study abroad in 1961–62. He was writer-in-residence at Reed College in 1963–64, at the San Fernando Valley State College in 1965, and at the University of Wisconsin at Madison in 1966. In the latter year he was appointed Consultant in Poetry in English at the Library of Congress, remaining in this position until September 1968, when he became Professor of English and poet-in-residence at the University of South Carolina. He now considers Columbia his permanent home.

Dickey's earlier books of poetry are *Into the Stone and Other Poems* (1960); *Drowning with Others* (1962); *Helmets* (1964); and *Two Poems of the Air* (1964). In 1967 his *Poems 1957–1967* was published, followed in January 1970 by his most recent volume, *The Eye-Beaters, Blood, Victory, Madness, Buckhead and Mercy.* He is also the author of *The Suspect in Poetry* (1964) and *Babel to Byzantium: Poets and Poetry Today* (1968), selections of his critical essays.

Among honors accorded Dickey in recognition of his poetry are an award from the Longview Foundation for a poem in the *Sewanee Review,* two awards from *Poetry* magazine (the Union League Civic and Arts Foundation Prize in 1958 and the Vachel Lindsay Prize in 1959), and the Melville Cane Award from the Poetry Society of America in January 1966. His 1965 volume of poems, *Buckdancer's Choice,* won the National Book Award for poetry in March 1966. Since then his reputation has risen steadily and rapidly, culminating in widespread critical acclaim for his first novel, *Deliverance,* recently published (1970).

May Day Sermon to the Women
of Gilmer County, Georgia,
by a Woman Preacher Leaving the Baptist Church

Each year at this time I shall be telling you of the Lord
—Fog, gamecock, snake and neighbor—giving men all the help they
    need
To drag their daughters into barns. Children, I shall be showing you
The fox hide stretched on the door   like a flying squirrel   fly
Open   to show you the dark where the one pole of light is paid out
In spring by the loft, and in it the croker sacks sprawling and shuttling
Themselves into place as it comes   comes   through spiders dead
Drunk on their threads   the hogs' fat bristling   the milk
Snake in the rafters unbending through gnats to touch the last place
Alive on the sun with his tongue   I shall be flickering from my mouth
Oil   grease cans   lard cans   nubbins   cobs   night
Coming   floating   each May with night coming I cannot help
Telling you how he hauls her to the centerpole   how the tractor moves
Over as he sets his feet and hauls   hauls   ravels her arms and hair
In stump chains: Telling: telling of Jehovah come and gone
Down on His belly   descending   creek-curving   blowing His legs

Like candles, out   putting North Georgia copper on His head
To crawl in under the door in dust red enough to breathe
The breath of Adam into: Children, be brought where she screams
    and begs
To the sacks of corn and coal   to nails   to the swelling ticks
On the near side of mules, for the Lord's own man has found the limp
Rubber that lies in the gulley   the penis-skin like a serpent
Under the weaving willow.
                  Listen: often a girl in the country,
Mostly sweating   mostly in spring, deep enough in the holy Bible
Belt, will feel her hair rise up   arms rise, and this not any wish

Of hers, and clothes like lint shredding off her   abominations

In the sight of the Lord: will hear the Book speak like a father
Gone mad: each year at this time will hear the utmost sound
Of herself, as her lungs cut, one after one, every long track
Spiders have coaxed from their guts   stunned spiders fall
Into Pandemonium   fall   fall   and begin to dance like a girl
On the red clay floor of Hell   she screaming   her father screaming
Scripture   CHAPter and verse   beating it into her with a weeping
Willow branch   the animals stomping   she prancing and climbing
Her hair   beasts shifting from foot to foot about the stormed
Steel of the anvil   the tractor gaslessly straining   believing
It must pull up a stump   pull   pull down the walls of the barn
Like Dagon's temple   set the Ark of the Lord in its place   change all
Things for good, by pain. Each year at this time you will be looking up
Gnats in the air   they boil   recombine   go mad with striving
To form the face of her lover, as when he lay at Nickajack Creek
With her by his motorcycle   looming   face trembling with exhaust
Fumes   humming insanely—each May you hear her father scream
    like God
And King James as he flails   cuds richen   bulls chew themselves
    whitefaced
Deeper into their feed bags, and he cries something the Lord   cries
Words! Words! Ah, when they leap   when they are let out of the
    Bible's
Black box   they whistle   they grab the nearest girl and do her hair up
For her lover in root-breaking chains   and she knows she was born
    to hang
In the middle of Gilmer County   to dance, on May Day, with holy
Words all around her   with beasts with insects   O children NOW
In five bags of chicken-feed the torsoes of prophets form   writhe
Die out as her freckled flesh   as flesh and the Devil twist and turn
Her body to love   cram her mouth with defiance   give her words
To battle with the Bible's in the air: she shrieks sweet Jesus and God
I'm glad   O my God-darling   O lover   O angel-stud   dear heart
Of life put it in me *give*   you're killing   KILLING: each
Night each year at this time I shall be telling you of the snake-
doctor drifting from the loft, a dragon-fly, where she is wringing

Out the tractor's muddy chains   where her cotton socks prance,
Where her shoes as though one ankle were broken, stand with night
Coming   and creatures drawn by the stars, out of their high holes
By moon-hunger driven   part the leaves   crawl out of Grimes Nose
And Brasstown Bald: on this night only I can tell how the weasel pauses
Each year in the middle of the road   looks up at the evening blue
Star   to hear her say again   O again   YOU CAN BEAT ME
    TO DEATH
And I'll still be glad:
                  Sisters, it is time to show you rust
Smashing the lard cans more in   spring after spring   bullbats
Swifts   barn swallows   mule bits clashing on walls   mist turning
Up white out of warm creeks: all over, fog taking the soul from the
    body
Of water   gaining   rising up trees   sifting up through smoking green
Frenzied levels of gamecocks sleeping from the roots   stream-curves
Of mist: wherever on God's land is water, roads rise up the shape of
    rivers
Of no return: O sisters, it is time   you cannot sleep with Jehovah

Searching for what to be, on ground that has called Him from His
    Book:
Shall He be the pain in the willow, or the copperhead's kingly riding
In kudzu, growing with vines toward the cows   or the wild face
    working over
A virgin, swarming like gnats   or the grass of the west field, bending
East, to sweep into bags and turn brown   or shall He rise, white on
    white,
From Nickajack Creek as a road?   The barn creaks like an Ark   beasts
Smell everywhere the streams drawn out by their souls   the flood-
sigh of grass in the spring   they shall be saved   they know as she
    screams
Of sin   as the weasel stares   the hog strains toward the woods
That hold its primeval powers:
                  Often a girl in the country will find
    herself

Dancing with God in a mule's eye, twilight drifting in straws from the
    dark
Overhead of hay   cows working their sprained jaws sideways at the
    hour
Of night all things are called: when gnats in their own midst and fury
Of swarming-time, crowd into the barn   their sixty-year day consumed
In this sunset   die in a great face of light that swarms and screams
Of love.
            Each May you will crouch like a sawhorse to make yourself
More here   you will be cow chips   chickens croaking for her hands
That shook the corn over the ground   bouncing   kicked this way
And that, by the many beaks   and every last one of you will groan
Like nails barely holding   and your hair be full of the gray
Glints of stump chains.   Children, each year at this time you will have
Back-pain, but also heaven   but also   also this lovely other life-
pain between the thighs: woman-child or woman in bed in Gilmer
County   smiling in sleep like blood-beast and Venus together
Dancing the road as I speak, get up   up in your socks and take
The pain you were born for: that rose through her body straight
Up from the earth like a plant, like the process that raised overhead
The limbs of the uninjured willow.
                            Children, it is true
That the kudzu advances, its copperheads drunk and tremendous
With hiding, toward the cows   and wild fences cannot hold the string
Beans as they overshoot their fields: that in May the weasel loves love
As much as blood   that in the dusk bottoms young deer stand half
In existence, munching cornshucks   true that when the wind blows
Right   Nickajack releases its mist   the willow-leaves stiffen once
More   altogether   you can hear   each year at this time you can hear
No   Now, no   Now   Yes   Again   More   O   O my God
I love it   love you   don't leave   don't   don't stop O GLORY
Be:
        More dark   more coming   fox-fire crawls over the okra-
patch   as through it a real fox creeps to claim his father's fur
Flying on doornails   the quartermoon on the outhouse begins to shine
With the quartermoonlight of this night   as she falls and rises,

Chained to a sapling like a tractor   WHIPPED for the wind in the
    willow
Tree   WHIPPED for Bathsheba and David   WHIPPED for the
    woman taken
Anywhere   anytime   WHIPPED for the virgin sighing   bleeding
From her body   for the sap and green of the year   for her own good
And evil:
                Sisters, who is your lover? Has he done nothing but come
And go?   Has your father nailed his cast skin to the wall as evidence
Of sin?   Is it flying like a serpent in the darkness   dripping pure
    radiant venom
Of manhood?
                Yes, but *he* is unreeling in hills between his long legs
The concrete of the highway   his face in the moon beginning
To burn   twitch   dance like an overhead swarm   he feels a nail
Beat through his loins far away   he rises in pain and delight, as spirit
Enters his sex   sways   forms   rises with the forced, choked, red
Blood of her red-headed image, in the red-dust, Adam-colored clay
Whirling and leaping   creating   calling: O on the dim, gray man-
track of cement flowing into his mouth   each year he turns the moon
    back
Around on his handlebars   her image going all over him like the wind
Blasting up his sleeves. He turns off the highway, and
                                        Ah, children,
There is now something élse to hear: there is now this madness of
    engine
Noise in the bushes   past reason   ungodly   squealing   reverting
Like a hog turned loose in the woods   Yes, as he passes the first
Trees of God's land   gamehens overhead   and the farm is ON
Him   everything is more   *more*   MORE as he enters the black
Bible's white swirling ground   O daughters   his heartbeat great
With trees   some blue leaves coming   NOW   and right away fire
In the right eye   Lord   more   MORE   O Glory   land
Of Glory: ground-branches hard to get through   coops where
    fryers huddle
To death, as the star-beast dances and scratches at their home-boards,

His rubber stiffens on its nails: Sisters, understand about men and
    sheaths:

About nakedness: understand how butterflies, amazed, pass out
Of their natal silks   how the tight snake takes a great breath   bursts
Through himself and leaves himself behind   how a man casts finally
Off everything that shields him from another   beholds his loins
Shine with his children forever   burn with the very juice
Of resurrection: such shining is how the spring creek comes
Forth from its sunken rocks   it is how the trout foams and turns on
Himself   heads upstream, breathing mist like water, for the cold
Mountain of his birth   flowing   sliding in and through the ego-
maniacal sleep of gamecocks   shooting past a man with one new blind
Side   who feels his skinned penis rise like a fish through the dark
Woods, in a strange lifted-loving form   a snake about to burst
Through itself on May Day   and leave behind on the ground   still
Still   the shape of a fooled thing's body:
                                        he comes on   comes
Through the laurel, wiped out on his right by an eye-twig   now he
Is crossing the cowtrack   his hat in his hand going on before
His face   then up   slowly over   over like the Carolina moon
Coming into Georgia   feels the farm close its Bible and ground-
fog over him   his dark side blazing   something whipping
By, beyond sight: each year at this time I shall be letting you
Know when she cannot stand   when the chains fall back on
To the tractor   when you should get up   when neither she nor the
    pole
Has any more sap   and her striped arms and red hair must keep her
From falling   when she feels God's willow laid on her, at last,
With no more pressure than hay, and she has finished crying to her
    lover's
Shifting face   and his hand when he gave it   placed it, unconsumed,
In her young burning bush.   Each year by dark she has learned

That home is to hang in   home is where your father cuts the baby
Fat from your flanks for the Lord, as you scream for the viny foreskin

Of the motorcycle rider. Children, by dark   by now, when he drops
The dying branch and lets her down   when the red clay flats
Of her feet hit the earth   all things have heard—fog, gamecock
Snake and lover—and we listen: Listen, children, for the fog to lift
The form of sluggish creeks into the air: each spring, each creek
On the Lord's land flows in two   O sisters, lovers, flows in two
Places: where it was, and in the low branches of pines where chickens
Sleep in mist   and that is where you will find roads floating free
Of the earth   winding   leading unbrokenly out of the farm of God
The father:

                    Each year at this time she is coming from the barn   she
Falls once, hair hurting her back   stumbles walking naked
With dignity   walks with no help to the house   lies face down
In her room, burning   tuning in   hearing in the spun rust-
groan of bedsprings, his engine root and thunder like a pig,
Knowing who it is   must be   knowing that the face of gnats will wake
In the woods, as a man: there is nothing else this time of night
But her dream of having wheels between her legs: tires, man,
Everything she can hold, pulsing together   her father walking
Reading   intoning   calling   his legs blown out by the ground-
fogging creeks of his land: Listen   listen like females each year
In May   O glory   to the sound   the sound of your man gone wild
With love in the woods   let your nipples rise   and leave your feet
To hear: This is when moths flutter in from the open, and Hell
Fire of the oil lamp shrivels them   and it is said
To her: said like the Lord's voice trying to find a way
Outside the Bible   O sisters   O women and children who will be
Women of Gilmer County   you farm girls and Ellijay cotton mill
Girls, get up   each May Day   up in your socks   it is the father
Sound   going on about God   making, a hundred feet down,
The well beat its bucket like a gong: she goes to the kitchen,
Stands with the inside grain of pinewood whirling on her like a cloud
Of wire   picks up a useful object   two   they are not themselves
Tonight   each hones itself as the moon does   new by phases
Of fog   floating unchanged into the house   coming atom
By atom   sheepswool   different smokes   breathed like the Word

Of nothing, round her seated father. Often a girl in the country,
Mostly in spring   mostly bleeding   deep enough in the holy Bible
Belt   will feel her arms rise up   up   and this not any wish
Of hers   will stand, waiting for word.   O daughters, he is rambling
In Obadiah   the pride of thine heart hath deceived thee, thou
That dwelleth in the clefts of the rock, whose habitation is high
That saith in his heart   O daughters   who shall bring me down
To the ground?   And she comes down   putting her back into
The hatchet   often   often   he is brought down   laid out
Lashing   smoking   sucking wind: Children, each year at this time
A girl will tend to take an ice pick in both hands   a lone pine
Needle   will hover   hover: Children, each year at this time
Things happen quickly   and it is easy for a needle to pass
Through the eye of a man bound for Heaven   she leaves it   naked
      goes
Without further sin through the house   floating in and out of all
Four rooms   comes onto the porch on cloud-feet   steps down and out
And around to the barn   pain changing   her old screams hanging
By the hair around her: Children, in May, often a girl in the country
Will find herself lifting wood   her arms like hair rising up
To undo locks   raise latches   set gates aside   turn all things
Loose   shoo them out   shove   kick   and hogs are leaping ten
Million years back through fog   cows walking worriedly passing out
Of the Ark   from stalls where God's voice cursed and mumbled
At milking time   moving   moving   disappearing   drifting
In cloud   cows in the alders already lowing far off   no one
Can find them each year: she comes back to the house and grabs double
Handfuls of clothes
                        and her lover, with his one eye of amazing grace
Of sight, sees her coming as she was born   swirling   developing
Toward him   she hears him grunt   she hears him creaking
His saddle   dead-engined   she conjures one foot whole from the
      ground-
fog to climb him behind   he stands up   stomps   catches   roars
Blasts the leaves from a blinding twig   wheels   they blaze up
Together   she breathing to match him   her hands on his warm belly

His hard blood renewing like a snake   O now   now as he twists
His wrist, and takes off with their bodies:

each May you will hear it
Said that the sun came as always   the sun of next day burned
Them off with the mist: that when the river fell back on its bed
Of water   they fell from life   from limbs   they went with it
To Hell   three-eyed   in love, their legs around an engine, her arms
Around him.   But now, except for each year at this time, their sound
Has died: except when the creek-bed thicks its mist   gives up
The white of its flow to the air   comes off   lifts into the pinepoles
Of May Day   comes back as you come awake in your socks and
    crotchhair
On new-mooned nights of spring   I speak   you listen and the pines
    fill
With motorcycle sound as they rise, stoned out of their minds on the
    white
Lightning of fog   singing   the saddlebags full of her clothes
Flying   snagging   shoes hurling away   stockings grabbed-off
Unwinding and furling on twigs: all we know   all we could follow
Them by was her underwear   was stocking after stocking where it tore
Away, and a long slip stretched on a thorn   all these few gave
Out. Children, you know it: that place was where they took
Off into the air   died   disappeared   entered my mouth   your mind
Each year   each pale, curved breath   each year as she holds him
Closer wherever he hurtles   taking her   taking her   she going
    forever
Where he goes   with the highways of rivers   through one-eyed
Twigs   through clouds of chickens   and grass with them bends
Double   the animals lift their heads   peanuts and beans exchange
Shells in joy   joy like the speed of the body and rock-bottom
Joy: joy by which the creek bed appeared to bear them out of the Bible
's farm   through pine-clouds of gamecocks where no earthly track
Is, but those risen out of warm currents   streams born to hang
In the pines of Nickajack Creek: tonight her hands are under
His crackling jacket   the pain in her back enough to go through
Them both   her buttocks blazing in the sheepskin saddle: tell those

Who look for them   who follow by rayon stockings   who look on human
    human
Highways   on tracks of cement and gravel   black weeping roads
Of tar: tell them that she and her rider have taken no dirt
Nor any paved road   no path for cattle   no county trunk or trail
Or any track upon earth, but have roared like a hog on May Day
Through pines and willows: that when he met the insane vine
Of the scuppernong   he tilted his handlebars back and took
The road that rises in the cold mountain spring from warm creeks:
O women in your rayon from Lindale, I shall be telling you to go
To Hell   by cloud   down where the chicken walk is running
To weeds   and anyone can show you where the tire marks gave out
And her last stocking was cast   and you stand as still as a weasel
Under Venus   before you dance   dance yourself blue with blood-
joy looking into the limbs   looking up into where they rode
Through cocks tightening roots with their sleep-claws. Children,
They are gone: gone as the owl rises, when God takes the stone
Blind sun off its eyes, and it sees   sees hurtle in the utter dark
Gold of its sight, a boy and a girl buried deep in the cloud
Of their speed   drunk, children   drunk with pain and the throttle
Wide open, in love   with a mindless sound   with her red hair
In the wind streaming gladly for them both   more than gladly
As the barn settles under the weight of its pain   the stalls fill once
More with trampling like Exodus   the snake doctor gone the rats
    beginning
On the last beans   and all the chicks she fed, each year at this time
Burst from their eggs as she passes:
                       Children, it is true that mice
No longer bunch on the rafters, but wade the fields like the moon,
Shifting in patches   ravenous   the horse floats, smoking with flies,
To the water-trough   coming back less often   learning to make
Do with the flowing drink of deer   the mountain standing   cold
Flowing into his mouth   grass underfoot   dew   horse or what
ever he is now   moves back into trees where the bull walks
With a male light spread between his horns   some say screams like
    a girl

And her father yelling together:

                                  Ah, this night in the dark laurel
Green of the quartermoon I shall be telling you that the creek's last
Ascension is the same   is made of water and air   heat and cold
This year as before: telling you not to believe every scream you hear
Is the Bible's: it may be you or me   it may be her sinful barn-
howling for the serpent, as her father whips her, using the tried
And true rhythms of the Lord.   Sisters, an old man at times like this
Moon, is always being found   yes found with an ice-pick on his mind,
A willow limb in his hand.   By now, the night-moths have come
Have taken his Bible and read it   have flown, dissolved, having found
Nothing in it for them.   I shall be telling you at each moon   each
Year at this time, Venus rises   the weasel goes mad at the death
In the egg, of the chicks she fed for him by hand: mad in the middle
Of human space he dances   blue-eyed   dances with Venus rising
Like blood-lust over the road   O tell your daughters   tell them
That the creek's ghost can still   O still can carry double
Weight of true lovers   any time   any night as the wild turkeys claw
Into the old pines of gamecocks   and with a cow's tongue, the Bible
       calls
For its own, and is not heard   and even God's unsettled great
       white father-
head with its ear to the ground, cannot hear   know   cannot pick
Up where they are   where her red hair is streaming through the white
Hairs of His centerless breast: with the moon   He cries with the
       cow all
Its life penned up with Noah in the barn   talk of original
Sin as the milk spurts   talk of women   talk of judgment and flood
And the promised land:

                       Telling on May Day, children: telling
That the animals are saved without rain   that they are long gone
From here   gone with the sun   gone with the woman taken
In speed   gone with the one-eyed mechanic   that the barn falls in
Like Jericho at the bull's voice   at the weasel's dance   at the hog's
Primeval squeal   the uncut hay walks when the wind prophesies in
       the west

Pasture   the animals move, with kudzu creating all the earth
East of the hayfield: Listen: each year at this time the county speaks
With its beasts and sinners   with its blood: the county speaks of
     nothing
Else each year at this time: speaks as beasts speak to themselves
Of holiness learned in the barn: Listen O daughters   turn   turn
In your sleep   rise with your backs on fire   in spring   in your socks
Into the arms of your lovers: every last one of you, listen one-eyed
With your man   in hiding   in fog where the animals walk through
The white breast of the Lord   muttering   walk with nothing
To do but be   in the spring laurel in the mist and self-sharpened
Moon   walk through the resurrected creeks   through the Lord
At their own pace   the cow shuts its mouth and the Bible is still
Still open at anything   we are gone   the barn wanders over the earth.

The Sheep Child

Farm boys wild to couple
With anything   with soft-wooded trees
With mounds of earth   mounds
Of pinestraw   will keep themselves off
Animals by legends of their own:
In the hay-tunnel dark
And dung of barns, they will
Say   I have heard tell

That in a museum in Atlanta
Way back in a corner somewhere
There's this thing that's only half
Sheep   like a woolly baby
Pickled in alcohol   because
Those things can't live   his eyes
Are open   but you can't stand to look
I heard from somebody who . . .

But this is now almost all
Gone. The boys have taken
Their own true wives in the city,
The sheep are safe in the west hill
Pasture   but we who were born there
Still are not sure. Are we,
Because we remember, remembered
In the terrible dust of museums?

Merely with his eyes, the sheep-child may

Be saying   saying

I am here, in my father's house.
I who am half of your world, came deeply
To my mother in the long grass
Of the west pasture, where she stood like moonlight
Listening for foxes. It was something like love
From another world that seized her
From behind, and she gave, not lifting her head

Out of dew, without ever looking, her best
Self to that great need. Turned loose, she dipped her face
Farther into the chill of the earth, and in a sound
Of sobbing   of something stumbling
Away, began, as she must do,
To carry me. I woke, dying,

In the summer sun of the hillside, with my eyes
Far more than human. I saw for a blazing moment
The great grassy world from both sides,
Man and beast in the round of their need,
And the hill wind stirred in my wool,
My hoof and my hand clasped each other,
I ate my one meal
Of milk, and died
Staring. From dark grass I came straight

To my father's house, whose dust
Whirls up in the halls for no reason
When no one comes   piling deep in a hellish mild corner,
And, through my immortal waters,
I meet the sun's grains eye
To eye, and they fail at my closet of glass.
Dead, I am most surely living
In the minds of farm boys: I am he who drives
Them like wolves from the hound bitch and calf
And from the chaste ewe in the wind.
They go into woods   into bean fields   they go
Deep into their known right hands. Dreaming of me,
They groan   they wait   they suffer
Themselves, they marry, they raise their kind.

The Firebombing

Denke daran, dass nach den grossen
    Zerstörungen
Jedermann beweisen wird, dass er
    unshuldig war.
        —*Günter Eich*
Or hast thou an arm like God?
        —*The Book of Job*

Homeowners unite.

All families lie together, though some are burned alive.
The others try to feel
For them. Some can, it is often said.

Starve and take off

Twenty years in the suburbs, and the palm trees willingly leap
Into the flashlights,
And there is beneath them also
A booted crackling of snailshells and coral sticks.
There are cowl flaps and the tilt cross of propellers,
The shovel-marked clouds' far sides against the moon,
The enemy filling up the hills
With ceremonial graves. At my somewhere among these,

Snap, a bulb is tricked on in the cockpit

And some technical-minded stranger with my hands
Is sitting in a glass treasure-hole of blue light,
Having potential fire under the undeodorized arms
Of his wings, on thin bomb-shackles,
The "tear-drop-shaped" 300-gallon drop-tanks
Filled with napalm and gasoline.

Thinking forward ten minutes
From that, there is also the burst straight out
Of the overcast into the moon; there is now
The moon-metal-shine of propellers, the quarter-

moonstone, aimed at the waves,
Stopped on the cumulus.

There is then this re-entry
Into cloud, for the engines to ponder their sound.
In white dark the aircraft shrinks; Japan

Dilates around it like a thought.
Coming out, the one who is here is over
Land, passing over the all-night grainfields,
In dark paint over
The woods with one silver side,
Rice-water calm at all levels
Of the terraced hill.
                       Enemy rivers and trees
Sliding off me like snakeskin,
Strips of vapor spooled from the wingtips
Going   invisible   passing   over   on
Over   bridges   roads for nightwalkers
Sunday night in the enemy's country   absolute
Calm   the moon's face   coming   slowly
About
        the inland sea
Slants   is woven with wire thread
Levels out   holds together like a quilt
Off the starboard wing   cloud flickers
At my glassed-off forehead   the moon's now and again
Uninterrupted face going forward
Over the waves in a glide-path
Lost into land.

Going: going with it

Combat booze by my side in a cratered canteen,
Bourbon frighteningly mixed
With GI pineapple juice,
Dogs trembling under me for hundreds of miles, on many
Islands, sleep-smelling that ungodly mixture

Of napalm and high-octane fuel,
Good bourbon and GI juice.

Rivers circling behind me around
Come to the fore, and bring
A town with everyone darkened.
Five thousand people are sleeping off
An all-day American drone.
Twenty years in the suburbs have not shown me
Which ones were hit and which not.

Haul on the wheel   racking slowly
The aircraft blackly around
In a dark dream   that   that is
That is like flying inside someone's head

Think of this   think of this

I did not think of my house
But think of my house now

Where the lawn mower rests on its laurels
Where the diet exists
For my own good   where I try to drop
Twenty years, eating figs in the pantry
Blinded by each and all
Of the eye-catching cans that gladly have caught my wife's eye
Until I cannot say
Where the screwdriver is   where the children
Get off the bus   where the new
Scoutmaster lives   where the fly
Hones his front legs   where the hammock folds
Its erotic daydreams   where the Sunday
School text for the day has been put   where the fire
Wood is   where the payments
For everything under the sun
Pile peacefully up,

But in this half-paid-for pantry
Among the red lids that screw off

With an easy half-twist to the left
And the long drawers crammed with dim spoons,
I still have charge—secret charge—
Of the fire developed to cling
To everything: to golf carts and fingernail
Scissors as yet unborn   tennis shoes
Grocery baskets   toy fire engines
New Buicks stalled by the half-moon
Shining at midnight on crossroads   green paint
Of jolly garden tools   red Christmas ribbons:

Not atoms, these, but glue inspired
By love of country to burn,
The apotheosis of gelatin.

Behind me having risen the Southern Cross
Set up by chaplains in the Ryukyus—
Orion, Scorpio, the immortal silver
Like the myths of king-
insects at swarming time—
One mosquito, dead drunk
On altitude, drones on, far under the engines,
And bites between
The oxygen mask and the eye.
The enemy-colored skin of families
Determines to hold its color
In sleep, as my hand turns whiter
Than ever, clutching the toggle—
The ship shakes   bucks
Fire hangs   not yet fire
In the air above Beppu
For I am fulfilling

An "anti-morale" rapid upon it.
All leashes of dogs
Break under the first bomb, around those
In bed, or late in the public baths: around those

Who inch forward on their hands
Into medicinal waters.
Their heads come up with a roar
Of Chicago fire:
Come up with the carp pond showing
The bathhouse upside down,
Standing stiller to show it more
As I sail artistically over
The resort town followed by farms,
Singing and twisting
All the handles in heaven   kicking
The small cattle off their feet
In a red costly blast
Flinging jelly over the walls
As in a chemical war-
fare field demonstration.
With fire of mine like a cat

Holding onto another man's walls,
My hat should crawl on my head
In streetcars, thinking of it,
The fat on my body should pale.

Gun down
The engines, the eight blades sighing
For the moment when the roofs will connect
Their flames, and make a town burning with all
American fire.
               Reflections of houses catch;
Fire shuttles from pond to pond
In every direction, till hundreds flash with one death.
With this in the dark of the mind,
Death will not be what it should;
Will not, even now, even when
My exhaled face in the mirror
Of bars, dilates in a cloud like Japan.
The death of children is ponds

Shutter-flashing; responding mirrors; it climbs
The terraces of hills
Smaller and smaller, a mote of red dust
At a hundred feet; at a hundred and one it goes out.
That is what should have got in
To my eye
And shown the insides of houses, the low tables
Catch fire from the floor mats,
Blaze up in gas around their heads
Like a dream of suddenly growing
Too intense for war. Ah, under one's dark arms
Something strange-scented falls—when those on earth
Die, there is not even sound;
One is cool and enthralled in the cockpit,
Turned blue by the power of beauty,
In a pale treasure-hole of soft light
Deep in aesthetic contemplation,
Seeing the ponds catch fire
And cast it through ring after ring
Of land: O death in the middle
Of acres of inch-deep water!   Useless

Firing   small arms
Speckles   from the river
Bank   one ninety-millimeter
Misses   far down   wrong petals   gone

It is this detachment,
The honored aesthetic evil,
The greatest sense of power in one's life,
That must be shed in bars, or by whatever
Means, by starvation
Visions in well-stocked pantries:
The moment when the moon sails in between
The tail-booms   the rudders nod   I swing
Over   directly over the heart
The *heart* of the fire. A mosquito burns out on my cheek

With the cold of my face   there are the eyes
In blue light   bar light
All masked but them   the moon
Crossing from left to right   in the streams below
Oriental fish form quickly
In the chemical shine,
In their eyes one tiny seed
Of deranged, Old Testament light.
Letting go   letting go
The plane rises gently   dark forms
Glide off me   long water   pales
In safe zones   a new cry enters
The voice box of chained family dogs

We buck   leap over something
Not there   settle back
Leave it   leave it clinging and crying
It consumes them in a hot
Body-flash, old age or menopause
Of children, clings and burns

                        eating through

And when a reed mat catches fire
From me, it explodes through field after field
Bearing its sleeper   another

Bomb finds a home
And clings to it like a child. And so

Goodbye to the grassy mountains
To cloud streaming from the night engines
Flags   pennons   curved silks
Of air   myself streaming also
My body covered
With flags, the air of flags
Between the engines.
Forever I do sleep in that position,
Forever in a turn
For home that breaks out streaming banners

From my wingtips,
Wholly in position to admire.

O then I knock it off
And turn for home over the black complex thread worked through
The silver night-sea,
Following the huge, moon-washed steppingstones
Of the Ryukyus south,
The nightgrass of mountains billowing softly
In my rising heat.
                    Turn and tread down
The yellow stones of the islands
To where Okinawa burns,
Pure gold, on the radar screen,
Beholding, beneath, the actual island form
In the vast water-silver poured just above solid ground,
An inch of water extending for thousands of miles
Above flat ploughland. Say "down," and it is done.

All this, and I am still hungry,
Still twenty years overweight, still unable
To get down there or see
What really happened.
                     But it may be that I could not,
If I tried, say to any
Who lived there, deep in my flames: say, in cold
Grinning sweat, as to another
As these homeowners who are always curving
Near me down the different-grassed street: say
As though to the neighbor
I borrowed the hedge-clippers from
On the darker-grassed side of the two,
Come in, my house is yours, come in
If you can, if you
Can pass this unfired door. It is that I can imagine
At the threshold nothing
With its ears crackling off

Like powdery leaves,
Nothing with children of ashes, nothing not
Amiable, gentle, well-meaning,
A little nervous for no   .
Reason   a little worried   a little too loud
Or too easygoing   nothing I haven't lived with
For twenty years, still nothing not as
American as I am, and proud of it.

Absolution? Sentence? No matter;
The thing itself is in that.

The Salt Marsh

Once you have let the first blade
Spring back behind you
To the way it has always been,
You no longer know where you are.
All you can see are the tall
Stalks of sawgrass, not sawing,
But each of them holding its tip
Exactly at the level where your hair

Begins to grow from your forehead.
Wherever you come to is
The same as before,
With the same blades of oversized grass,
And wherever you stop, the one
Blade just in front of you leans,
That one only, and touches you
At the place where your hair begins

To grow; at that predestined touch
Your spine tingles crystally, like salt,
And the image of a crane occurs,
Each flap of its wings creating
Its feathers anew, this time whiter,
As the sun destroys all points
Of the compass, refusing to move
From its chosen noon.

Where is the place you have come from
With your buried steps full of new roots?
You cannot leap up to look out,
Yet you do not sink,
But seem to grow, and the sound,
The oldest of sounds, is your breath
Sighing like acres.
If you stand as you are for long,

Green panic may finally give
Way to another sensation,
For when the embodying wind
Rises, the grasses begin to weave
A little, then all together,
Not bending enough for you
To see your way clear of the swaying,
But moving just the same,

And nothing prevents your bending
With them, helping their wave
Upon wave upon wave upon wave
By not opposing,
By willing your supple inclusion
Among fields without promise of harvest,
In their marvelous, spiritual walking
Everywhere, anywhere.

Buckdancer's Choice

So I would hear out those lungs,
The air split into nine levels,
Some gift of tongues of the whistler

In the invalid's bed: my mother,
Warbling all day to herself
The thousand variations of one song;

It is called Buckdancer's Choice.
For years, they have all been dying
Out, the classic buck-and-wing men

Of traveling minstrel shows;
With them also an old woman
Was dying of breathless angina,

Yet still found breath enough
To whistle up in my head
A sight like a one-man band,

Freed black, with cymbals at heel,
An ex-slave who thrivingly danced
To the ring of his own clashing light

Through the thousand variations of one song
All day to my mother's prone music,
The invalid's warbler's note,

While I crept close to the wall
Sock-footed, to hear the sounds alter,
Her tongue like a mockingbird's break

Through stratum after stratum of a tone
Proclaiming what choices there are
For the last dancers of their kind,

For ill women and for all slaves
Of death, and children enchanted at walls
With a brass-beating glow underfoot,

Not dancing but nearly risen
Through barnlike, theatrelike houses
On the wings of the buck and wing.

Gamecock

Fear, jealousy and murder are the same
When they put on their long reddish feathers,
Their shawl neck and moccasin head
In a tree bearing levels of women.
There is yet no thread

Of light, and his scabbed feet tighten,
Holding sleep as though it were lockjaw,
His feathers damp, his eyes crazed
And cracked like the eyes
Of a chicken head cut off or wrung-necked

While he waits for the sun's only cry
All night building up in his throat
To leap out and turn the day red,
To tumble his hens from the pine tree,
And then will go down, his hackles

Up, looking everywhere for the other
Cock who could not be there,
Head ruffed and sullenly stepping
As upon his best human-curved steel:
He is like any fierce

Old man in a terminal ward:
There is the same look of waiting
That the sun prepares itself for;
The enraged, surviving-
another-day blood,

And from him at dawn comes the same
Cry that the world cannot stop.
In all the great building's blue windows
The sun gains strength; on all floors, women
Awaken—wives, nurses, sisters and daughters—

And he lies back, his eyes filmed, unappeased,
As all of them, clucking, pillow-patting,
Come to help his best savagery blaze, doomed, dead-
game, demanding, unreasonably
Battling to the death for what is his.

List of Sources

William Hilton, "A Relation of a Discovery, by William Hilton, 1664" in A. S. Salley, ed., *Narratives of Early Carolina* (New York: Charles Scribner's Sons, 1911), pp. 37–61.

Francis Le Jau, *The Carolina Chronicle of Dr. Francis Le Jau, 1706–1717,* ed. Frank J. Klingberg (Berkeley and Los Angeles: University of California Press, 1956), pp. 16–21.

Charles Woodmason, "C. W. *in* Carolina *to* E.J. *at* Gosport" from Hennig Cohen, "A Colonial Topographical Poem," *Names,* I (Dec. 1953), pp. 253–56.

————, "The Need for Education" from *The Journal,* in Richard J. Hooker, ed., *Carolina Backcountry* (Chapel Hill: University of North Carolina Press, 1953), pp. 118–22.

Anonymous, "Extract of 'a POEM, intitled INDICO'," *South-Carolina Gazette,* Aug. 25, 1757. (See *Agricultural History,* XXX [Jan. 1956], pp. 42–43.)

"Philo Patriae" [pseudonym], "On Liberty-Tree," *South-Carolina Gazette,* Sept. 21, 1769. (See *South Carolina Historical and Genealogical Magazine,* XLI [1940], pp. 119–22.)

Eliza Lucas Pinckney, *Journal and Letters of Eliza Lucas,* ed. Harriott Pinckney Holbrook (Wormsloe, Ga., 1850), pp. 6–7, 9–13, 17–20, 25–30.

Henry Laurens, "A Narrative of the Capture of Henry Laurens" in *Collections of the South Carolina Historical Society,* I, 18–26.

Joseph Brown Ladd, "Ode to Retirement" and "What Is Happiness?" in E. A. Duyckinck, ed., *A Cyclopedia of American Literature* (New York, 1855), pp. 533–34.

John Drayton, *Memoirs of the Revolution in South Carolina,* II (Charleston, 1821), pp. 293–304.

David Ramsay, "Marion's Brigade," in *History of South Carolina,* I (Charleston, 1809), pp. 228–37.

Washington Allston, "America to Great Britain," "Rosalie," "The French Revolution," "Art," "On the Late S. T. Coleridge" in *Library of Southern Literature,* I (Atlanta, 1908), pp. 98–101.

William Crafts, "Love's Benediction," "Love A Prisoner," "The Mermaid," "The Infidel Girl" in *A Selection in Prose and Poetry, from the Miscellaneous Writings of the Late William Crafts* (Charleston: C. C. Sebring & J. S. Bruges, 1828), pp. 360–61, 46, 370–71, 375–76.

William John Grayson, *The Hireling and the Slave* (Charleston: John Russell, 1854), pp. 51–56.

Hugh Swinton Legaré, "Classical Learning" and "Craft's Fugitive Writings" in Mary Legaré Bullen, ed., *Writings of Hugh Swinton Legaré* . . . , II (Charleston, 1845), pp. 43–51, 147–52.

William Elliott, "The Sea-Serpent" in *Carolina Sports by Land and Water* (Charleston: Burges & James, 1846), pp. 105–21.

John C. Calhoun, "Speech on Henry Clay's Compromise Resolutions" and "Disquisition on Government" in John M. Anderson, ed., *Calhoun: Basic Documents* (State College, Pa.: Bald Eagle Press, 1952), pp. 322–24, 86–97.

James Mathewes Legaré, "The Reaper," "To a Lily," "Haw-Blossoms," "On the Death of a Kinsman" in *Orta-Undis, and Other Poems* (Boston: William D. Ticknor & Co., 1848), pp. 1–2, 10–11, 18–21, 63–64.

Augustus Baldwin Longstreet, "The Horse-Swap" in *Georgia Scenes* (New York: Harper & Bros., 1845), pp. 23–31.

———, *Master William Mitten: or, A Youth of Brilliant Talents, Who Was Ruined By Bad Luck* (Macon, Ga.: J. W. Burke & Co., 1889), pp. 99–110.

John B. Irving, "A Day in the Reserve," *Spirit of the Times,* XII (June 25, 1842), pp. 195–96.

William Gilmore Simms, "Mighty Is the Yemassee" in *The Yemassee: A Romance of Carolina,* new and rev. ed. (New York: Redfield, 1854), pp. 189–90.

———, "The Syren of Tselica," "The Lost Pleiad," "The Eutaw Maid," "The Edge of the Swamp," "The Lay of the Carib Damsel" in *Poems Descriptive, Dramatic, Legendary and Contemplative,* 2 vols. (Charleston: John Russell, 1853), I, pp. 324–27; II, pp. 13–15, 151–52, 201–3, 207–8.

———, "Ballad. The Big Belly," in Miriam J. Shillingsburg, "An Edition of William Gilmore Simms's *The Cub of the Panther*" (Ph.D. diss., University of South Carolina, 1969), p. 125.

————, "The Late Henry Timrod" in Jay B. Hubbell, ed., *The Last Years of Henry Timrod, 1864–1867* (Durham, N.C.: Duke University Press, 1941), pp. 153–65.

————, "How Sharp Snaffles Got His Capital and Wife" in *The Centennial Edition of the Writings of William Gilmore Simms,* II (Columbia: University of South Carolina Press [Forthcoming]); originally published in *Harper's Magazine* (Oct. 1870).

Mary Boykin Chesnut, *A Diary from Dixie,* ed. Ben Ames Williams (Boston: Houghton Mifflin Co., 1961), pp. 1–2, 10–11, 163–64, 527–28.

Henry Timrod, "Lines: There Was a Fire Within My Brain" in Guy Cardwell, Jr., ed., *The Uncollected Poems of Henry Timrod* (Athens: University of Georgia Press, 1942), pp. 83–84.

————, "The Cotton Boll," "La Belle Juive," "The Arctic Voyager" in *The Poems of Henry Timrod,* Memorial Edition (Cambridge, Mass.: Riverside Press, 1899), pp. 6–11, 57–59, 103–4, 164–65.

————, "Sonnet: I Know Not Why," "Sonnet: Most Men Know Love," "Ethnogenesis," "Spring," "Carolina," "The Unknown Dead," "Ode" in Edd Winfield Parks and Aileen Wells Parks, *The Collected Poems of Henry Timrod,* A Variorum Edition (Athens: University of Georgia Press, 1965), pp. 79–80, 92–95, 100, 109–11, 122–24, 126–27, 129–30.

Paul Hamilton Hayne, "Vicksburg—A Ballad," "Under the Pine," "The Spirea," "My Mother-Land," "Fire-Pictures," "Beyond the Potomac," "The Voice in the Pines," "The Arctic Visitation," "To Algernon Charles Swinburne," "Midsummer in the South," "Aspects of the Pines," "The Mocking-Bird" in *Poems* (Boston: D. Lothrop & Co., 1882), pp. 80, 103, 236, 65–66, 111–13, 73–74, 188, 209–10, 269, 192–93, 191–92, 239.

————, "Sonnet: Shelley" in *Poems* (Boston: Ticknor & Fields, 1855), p. 45.

————, "Face to Face," *Harper's New Monthly Magazine,* LXXII (May 1886), p. 884.

Julia Peterkin, "The Red Rooster" and "Son" in *Green Thursday* (New York: Alfred A. Knopf, 1924), pp. 103–14, 132–42.

Archibald Rutledge, "The Tomb," *The Yale Review,* XXXVII (1947), pp. 129–37.

————, "God's Highwaymen," "Requiem," "Lee" in *Deep River, The Complete Poems of Archibald Rutledge* (Columbia, S.C.: R. L. Bryan Co., 1960), pp. 600–602, 398, 454.

DuBose Heyward, "The Half Pint Flask," *Bookman*, LXV (1927), pp. 261–72.

Ambrose Gonzales, "The Lion of Lewisburg" in *The Black Border* (Columbia, S.C.: State Co., 1922), pp. 35–44.

Elliott White Springs, *War Birds: Diary of an Unknown Aviator* (New York: Grosset & Dunlap, 1926), pp. 268–77.

John Bennett, "Tales from the Trapman Street Hospital" in *The Doctor to the Dead* (New York: Rinehart & Co., 1946), pp. 123–35.

Josephine Pinckney, "Sea-drinking Cities," "The Misses Poar Drive to Church," "Street Cries" in *Sea-drinking Cities* (New York: Harper & Bros., 1927), pp. 12–13, 73–74, 5–7.

Beatrice Ravenel, "Poe's Mother," "The Alligator," "The Yemassee Lands," "The Humming-Bird" in *The Arrow of Lightning* (New York: Harold Vinal, 1926), pp. 1–7, 25–29, 30–33, 58–59.

E. C. L. Adams, "Jeff's Funeral Sermon," "Fragment of a Negro Sermon," "His Day Is Done" in *Congaree Sketches* (Chapel Hill: University of North Carolina Press, 1927), pp. 41–49.

William Watts Ball, "A Log-Cabin Law Office" in *The State That Forgot* (Indianapolis: Bobbs-Merrill Co., 1932), pp. 13–26.

Herbert Ravenel Sass, "Charleston" in *Look Back to Glory* (Indianapolis: Bobbs-Merrill Co., 1933), pp. 276–90.

Ben Robertson, *Red Hills and Cotton* (Columbia: University of South Carolina Press, 1960), pp. 218–30.

Drayton Mayrant, "Photograph from a Rocket," "Sea Island," "Song for a Winter's Night" in *White Horse Leaping* (Columbia: University of South Carolina Press, 1950), pp. 2, 20, 7.

Elizabeth B. Coker, "The Wishing Bone," *The South Carolina Review*, II (Nov. 1969), pp. 23–35.

William Price Fox, "Have You Ever Rode the Southern?" in *Southern Fried Plus Six* (Philadelphia and New York: J. B. Lippincott Co., 1968), pp. 196–208.

Ellington White, "The Perils of Flight," *The Georgia Review*, XIV (Fall 1960), pp. 259–74.

Max Steele, "The Ragged Halo," *The South Carolina Review,* I (Nov. 1968), pp. 23–37.

James Dickey, "May Day Sermon to the Women of Gilmer County, Georgia, by a Woman Preacher Leaving the Baptist Church," "The Sheep Child," "The Firebombing," "The Salt Marsh," "Buck-dancer's Choice," and "Gamecock" in *Poems: 1957–1967* (Middletown, Conn.: Wesleyan University Press, 1967), pp. 3–13, 252–53, 181–88, 107–8, 189–90, 220–21.